The Philosophy of Husserl

Continental European Philosophy

This series provides accessible and stimulating introductions to the ideas of continental thinkers who have shaped the fundamentals of European philosophical thought. Powerful and radical, the ideas of these philosophers have often been contested, but they remain key to understanding current philosophical thinking as well as the current direction of disciplines such as political science, literary theory, social theory, art history, and cultural studies. Each book seeks to combine clarity with depth, introducing fresh insights and wider perspectives while also providing a comprehensive survey of each thinker's philosophical ideas.

The Philosophy of Agamben
Catherine Mills

The Philosophy of Derrida
Mark Dooley and Liam Kavanagh

The Philosophy of Foucault
Todd May

The Philosophy of Gadamer
Jean Grondin

The Philosophy of Habermas
Andrew Edgar

The Philosophy of Hegel
Allen Speight

The Philosophy of Husserl
Burt C. Hopkins

The Philosophy of Kierkegaard
George Pattison

The Philosophy of Merleau-Ponty
Eric Matthews

The Philosophy of Nietzsche
Rex Welshon

The Philosophy of Schopenhauer
Dale Jacquette

The Philosophy of Husserl

Burt C. Hopkins

McGill-Queen's University Press
Montreal & Kingston • Ithaca

ISBN 978-0-7735-3822-1 (bound)
ISBN 978-0-7735-3823-8 (pbk.)

Legal deposit fourth quarter 2010
Bibliothèque nationale du Québec

Published simultaneously outside North America
by Acumen Publishing Limited

McGill-Queen's University Press acknowledges the financial support of the Government of Canada through the Canada Book Fund for its activities.

Library and Archives Canada Cataloguing in Publication

Hopkins, Burt C.
The philosophy of Husserl / Burt C. Hopkins.

Includes bibliographical references and index.
ISBN 978-0-7735-3822-1 (bound).--ISBN 978-0-7735-3823-8 (pbk.)

1. Husserl, Edmund, 1859-1938. 2. Phenomenology. I. Title.

B3279.H94H66 2010 193 C2010-906330-9

Printed in the UK by MPG Books Group.

I dedicate this book to my parents.

Contents

Acknowledgements

I would like to thank Noesis Press for kind permission to use material from "Jacob Klein and the Phenomenology of History, Part I", *New Yearbook for Phenomenology and Phenomenological Philosophy* I (2001), 67–110.

This work owes a great deal to institutional support provided by Seattle University. I therefore thank the Office of the Provost for a Summer Faculty Fellowship that coincided with this book's inception and my current Dean, David Powers, for the crucial role he played in upholding the standards of the Endowed Chair that supported its completion.

I owe a substantial debt to a number of individuals who have generously read and commented on this book in manuscript: Eva Brann, Joe Sachs, Joshua Kates, Maria Carl and Claudio Majolino.

Finally, I owe special thanks to Steven Gerrard at Acumen, without whose patience and support this book would not have been written, to Kate Williams, for her careful editing and composition of the book, and to Annie Rose Favreau and Maggie Kellogg, for their assistance in the final preparation of the manuscript.

Burt C. Hopkins

Abbreviations

Where two page or section numbers are given, the first refers to the original edition, and the second to the English translation. Where one page number is given, it refers to the original German page number (which is printed in the English translation). Emphasis throughout is from either the original German or the English translation.

CM	*Cartesianische Meditationen und Pariser Vorträge* (1950)/ *Cartesian Meditations: An Introduction to Phenomenology* (1960)
Conversations	Adelgundis Jaegerschmid, "Conversations with Edmund Husserl, 1931–1938" (2001)
Crisis	"Die Krisis der europäischen Wissenschaften und die tranzendentale Phänomenologie: Eine Einleitung in die Phänomenologische Philosophy" (1936)/*The Crisis of European Sciences and Transcendental Phenomenology* (1970)
EJ	*Erfahrung und Urteil* ([1939] 1985)/*Experience and Judgements* (1973)
FTL	*Formale und Transcendentale Logik: Versuch einer Kritik der logischen Vernunft* (1929)/*Formal and Transcendental Logic* (1969)
Ideas I	*Ideen zu einer reinen Phänomenologie und phänomenologischen Philosophie, I Buch: Allgemeine Einführung in die reine Phänomenologie* (1913)/*Ideas Pertaining to a Pure Phenomenology and to a Phenomenological Philosophy. First Book. A General Introduction to Pure Phenomenology* (1982)
ILI	"Entwurf einer 'Vorrede' zu den *Logischen Untersuchungen*" ([1913] 1979)/*Introduction to the Logical Investigations* (1975)

LI *Logische Untersuchungen* (1900, 1901)/*Logical Investigations* (2001)

OG "Die Frage nach dem Ursprung der Geometrie als intentionalhistorisches Problem" (1939)/"The Origin of Geometry" (1970)

PITC *Vorlesungen zur Phänomenologie des innern Zeitbewusstseins* (1928)/*The Phenomenology of Internal Time Consciousness* (1964)

PRS "Philosophie als strenge Wissenschaft" (1910–11)/"Philosophy as Rigorous Science" (2002)

PROLEGOMENON

Husserl's turn to history and pure phenomenology

Introduction

Edmund Husserl (1859–1938) is the indisputable founder of the method of scientific research called phenomenology. Husserl's phenomenology is unarguably the source of one of the two major philosophical orientations of the past century, what today goes by the name of "continental philosophy". Some seventy years after his death and over a hundred years after the publication of his first major work, however, the scientific significance of phenomenological research remains a matter of dispute and its relation to philosophy, let alone continental philosophy, a matter of intense philosophical debate.

The goal of this book is to introduce the beginner to Husserl's phenomenological research by situating its salient discoveries in relation to traditional philosophy. In particular, the relevance of philosophy to the problems that gave rise to the ancient Greek beginning of the Western philosophical tradition and to this tradition's development in the European beginning of philosophy's modern transformation into universal science will be discussed. This goal is dictated by two interrelated considerations. First, Husserl, by his own admission, "never really studied philosophy, but mathematics and natural science",[1] and so is not the best authority to speak on the relation of his thought to traditional philosophy. Second, Husserl's lack of authority in this matter has largely allowed his critics to determine the relation of phenomenology to traditional philosophy. And the most prominent of these critics, Martin Heidegger and Jacques Derrida, have done so by claiming that Husserl's phenomenology is philosophically limited by its uncritical adherence to basic and unjustified presuppositions that are datable to early modern (Heidegger) and ancient Greek (Heidegger and Derrida) philosophy.

Thus there is a commonplace assumption in contemporary continental philosophical discourse that Husserl's phenomenology is both inseparable from a Cartesian starting point (that supposedly equates "being" with "being known") and informed by the metaphysics of presence (traceable to an origin in the putative "logocentricism" characteristic of ancient Greek philosophy). This assumption is symptomatic of Husserl's critics having gained the upper hand in establishing his phenomenology's relation to the beginnings of ancient Greek and modern philosophy. By introducing the beginner to Husserl's phenomenology from a historically informed philosophical perspective that avoids the historical presuppositions of his major critics, a major aim of this book is to disclose the often facile and superficial assumptions that inform and guide their critiques.

Introducing the beginner to the method and significant results of Husserl's phenomenology faces another historically related problem, however, namely, the historical development of Husserl's own conception and interpretation of this science. This development is characterized by Husserl himself, as well as his critics and followers, as having successive stages that are significantly related to one another, in the sense that the intelligibility of each stage is always, at least in part, inseparable from its often critical relation to a previous stage or stages. Compounding this problem is the fact that Husserl left his phenomenology largely unfinished at his death, with literally thousands (45,000) of pages of unpublished manuscripts, in addition to the half dozen or so books he published during his lifetime. Since his death, forty-two volumes of his collective works have been published, including critical editions of the works published during his lifetime.

In order to address these problems, the principle of selection from among Husserl's texts and the measure for counting the stages belonging to their phenomenological content needs to be addressed, because the criteria employed for both undeniably have a significant impact on determining what is presented as the proper method and content of Husserl's phenomenology. From among Husserl's texts, those that were published or prepared for publication during his lifetime will be used as the source for this introduction to his phenomenology. My reasons for selecting these texts are straightforward: they, more than any other of Husserl's texts, have shaped his phenomenology's presentation and critical appraisal, and Husserl himself, judging by the titles he gave to a number of them, clearly intended some to serve as introductions to phenomenology.[2] These texts will also be used as the basis for my account of the stages of Husserl's phenomenology, and I shall employ as my measure for their differentiation and determination Husserl's own self-critical formulations of the phenomenological method presented in them.

Before identifying these stages, however, I want to address a potential pitfall that the attention to phenomenology's development brings: losing sight of the unity of Husserl's philosophical enterprise from beginning to end.

More than any other twentieth-century philosopher, Husserl was concerned with maintaining the integrity of knowledge. Late in life (1935) he characterized philosophy as "the honesty of the intellect", and observed that:

> [m]y whole life I have fought, indeed, wrestled, for this honesty, and where others had been long-since satisfied, I questioned myself ever anew and scrutinized whether there was not indeed some semblance of dishonesty in the background. All my work, even today, is only to scrutinize and inspect again and again .... One must have the courage to admit and say that something one still considered true yesterday, but that one sees to be an error today, is such an error. (*Conversations*, 337)

Husserl's commitment to knowledge's integrity involves something greater than the theory of knowledge that is today defined under the heading of "epistemology". Beyond theory and its pretension to know, Husserl's philosophical thought, from its initial concern with the philosophy of arithmetic to its final concern with the crisis of European humanity, is driven by the following: the felt need to justify all claims to know, even the seemingly most secure, on the basis of something more original than the computational consistency of logical and mathematical formulae and supposed facts supplied by the natural and social sciences. This "something more" is early on formulated by him as the "things themselves", the return to which was to become not just Husserl's motto but the watchword of the entire phenomenological movement spawned by his thought. "We must", Husserl exhorts us in all his major works beginning with the *Logical Investigations*, "return to the things themselves".

Husserl's answers to the questions what, precisely, the things themselves are, and why it is necessary to go back to them, are clearly what is modified if not outright changed in the course of his thought's development; but the basic concern to maintain the integrity of knowledge that is behind these questions is neither modified nor changed throughout it. That knowledge is something whose integrity is in need of being maintained, that doing so requires some kind of return to things in evidence that moves beyond knowledge's status quo, and that neither the existing formal and natural sciences nor any heretofore extant philosophy are up to the task of addressing, let alone securing, the integrity at issue, are what Husserl seeks to establish and legitimize under the heading of phenomenology. Moreover, each stage of phenomenology articulates a method that is patently reflective and whose quarry is a reflected cognitive content that is more fundamental than the concepts employed in the service of the expressions proper to all previous scientific and philosophical cognition.

Phenomenology's first stage is characterized by a descriptive psychological method whose goal is to uncover reflectively the immanent contents of cognitive acts that neither philosophical empiricism nor empirical psychology is capable of reaching. Because of this, these contents are understood by Husserl to be "presupposed" by empiricism, and phenomenology is accordingly maintained by him to be a "presuppositionless" science. Indeed, presuppositionlessness, as both a principle and a goal, informs Husserl's phenomenological method to such an extent that the reflective exposure and public recognition of phenomenology's own, heretofore concealed, presuppositions become defining and distinguishing marks of his thought. This is especially evident when Husserl is compared with other philosophers who, at one time or another in the twentieth century, chose to assume the mantle of phenomenology for their thought.

The second stage of phenomenology is defined by a pure phenomenological method that is driven by the goal of describing in methodical acts of reflection the essences immanent to pure consciousness. These essences are maintained by Husserl to structure not only all cognitive acts (as presupposed in phenomenology's first stage) but also the basic pre-conceptual and pre-philosophical meanings that shape the natural experience of the world. Because the immanence of pure consciousness is not a natural phenomenon, its discovery and phenomenological exploration require a special kind of methodical intervention that Husserl terms the "phenomenological reduction". And because the "phenomenological being" of conscious immanence excludes all transcendent objectivities and is therefore related only to itself, its essence is understood by Husserl to be at once absolute and transcendental.

Phenomenology's third stage is characterized by a deepening of the exploration of phenomenological being beyond the description of the essences that structure pure consciousness to an account of their phenomenological genesis as units of meanings in a subjectivity that is transcendental. As transcendental, subjectivity is described by Husserl as having a broader and deeper scope than the phenomenological being of pure consciousness. As generated, the unity proper to essential meaning possesses references to the history of its development. Husserl's concern with a "genetic" account of the origin proper to the meanings that are phenomenology's concern has given rise to many misunderstandings, among them the prevalent and utterly mistaken belief that there are two independent kinds of phenomenology, "static" and "genetic". According to this scenario, the former's directedness towards invariant essences is somehow supposed to be intrinsically deficient and the latter's directedness towards the generation of phenomena is somehow supposed to be intrinsically superior. Husserl's talk of "static" and "genetic" phenomenological analyses no doubt lends a superficial plausibility to this belief. However, once one realizes that for Husserl genetic analyses are completely dependent on the invariant meanings uncovered by phenomenology's static analyses and that these invariant meanings can be grounded only in phenomena that are inseparable from their generation, the idea that either of these analyses is driven by "methods" possessing an independent methodological status in Husserl's thought loses any possible basis.

The fourth and final stage of Husserl's phenomenology grows out of its third, in the precise but nevertheless controversial sense that the link in the latter between the genesis of meaning and its historical development in consciousness is extended to include events and texts whose essential meaning is datable to an origin in actual history. The reflection that drives the phenomenological method thus comes to assume in its final phase the character of an explicitly historical reflection, albeit one that is qualified phenomenologically by its being concerned with history understood as a chain of meanings proper to transcendental subjectivity and therefore not as empirically relative events. Meanings in this sense are equally responsible for and hidden from the cognizance of the meanings that are taken for granted by contemporary thought as determining the basic principles of philosophy and natural science. Nothing less than the monumental task of reawakening these hidden and therefore "sedimented" meanings, to the end of discovering heretofore unrealized possibilities contained in them that will allow European science to address the most basic concerns of humanity (as the science of its ancient Greek predecessor once did): that is the goal Husserl sets for the final stage of his transcendental phenomenology. And he sets this goal because it is his conviction that the very same phenomenological reflection that awakens these meanings is able to show that European science's turning away from the soul (from the subjective) as an object of knowledge is what is responsible for a scientific "crisis" whose result is nothing less than the breakdown of European culture in the 1930s, as it yet again finds itself marching off to world war.

Rather than reconstruct the stages belonging to phenomenology by following their chronology, the introduction to Husserl's phenomenology that follows will begin with its final stage. On 16 September 1937, a little over seven months before he died, Husserl characterized the works that articulate this stage – his Vienna[3] and Prague lectures and his last writing based on the latter lecture, "The Crisis of the European Sciences and Transcendental Phenomenology" – in terms of the mature awareness of his "task". He says, "I came out of my shell for the first time, completely spontaneously, and made a small beginning" (*Conversations*, 346), and then goes on: "now I have to stop and leave my task incomplete. Just now, when I am finished, I know that I am beginning from the start, for to be finished means to begin from the start." In my judgement it is fitting to begin a book aimed at beginners with this "small beginning" that – according to Husserl's however reliable or unreliable self-understanding – punctuated a lifetime lived in the service of his science. In what follows, then, Husserl's phenomenology will be introduced starting from the articulation of its mature formulation, in the course of which the development that led to this formulation will be systematically treated and laid out in detail.

Pure phenomenology's most basic principles: presuppositionlessness, pure reflection, essential intuition

The mature statement of Husserl's phenomenology (its fourth and final stage) introduces into its reflective method a historical ambition that is not only absent from its first three stages, but that, on the surface of things, would seem to be precluded from being "phenomenological" when measured according to their articulation of the most basic principles of phenomenology.

These principles include, in the order of importance, presuppositionlessness, pure reflection and essential intuition. Phenomenology is presuppositionless in the precise sense that it is directed towards the cognitive goal of avoiding philosophical claims that rely on knowledge claims not based in the direct apprehension of their objects. Both the empirical sciences, with their cognitive appeal to scientific "facts", and empirical epistemologies, with their philosophical claim to establish the origin of all knowledge in sense experience, are shown in the books that articulate the first two phases of Husserl's phenomenology (LI and *Ideas I*) to violate the phenomenological principle of presuppositionlessness. They do so by making knowledge claims whose content exceeds the capacity of the principles and methods that back them to deliver what is claimed.

Phenomenology strives to have its philosophical claims avoid presuppositions by issuing them from a source that involves the direct apprehension of the objects of knowledge. This source, in contrast to the sources of empirical knowledge claims and empiricistic philosophical claims, is characterized as "pure", in the precise sense that all empirical facts and empiricistic theories are methodically excluded from it. And it is also characterized as "reflective", because only when thought "turns back" on to itself and its natural striving for knowledge is it able to separate out the empirical presuppositions from its cognitive striving and apprehend knowledge's proper content.

Husserl uses the Greek word "*eidos*" to name the proper content of phenomenological cognition, and in an act of remarkable philosophical naivety he gives his reason for doing so the fact that the term is "terminologically unspent". Moreover, this naivety is compounded by his treating the German word "*Wesen*" as equivalent to *eidos*, dismissing as "harmless, though at times vexatious" its equivocations as "essence" and "(individual) being" (*Ideas I*, 6). Husserl calls the apprehension of an *eidos* "Wesensschauen", literally "seeing [of] essences", precisely understood as the intuition of essences or, equivalently, essential or eidetic intuition.

Husserl's naivety in this regard is rooted in his conviction that the phenomenological method, properly learned and practised, yields a "pure seeing" that grants cognition that cannot be surpassed. Thus in a letter written in 1919 he writes that "I speak of phenomenology as a mathematician would of mathematics: that it is a *genuine* science, drawn from pure evidence, a sphere of possible true and false propositions – despite all skeptics and unclear philosophers your phenomenologist speaks like this, because he 'sees'!"[4] What is seen phenomenologically is given more originally than any scientific fact or empirical evidence, and because of this it has the "most basic right" (*Urrecht*) to be called knowledge. Husserl therefore does not hesitate to designate this knowledge *a priori* – "prior" (not in temporal order but in cognitive rank) to empirical knowledge – and absolute, because it cannot be surpassed.

The pure phenomenological critique of historicism

History clearly and decisively does not have a place in Husserl's method of pure phenomenology. Whether understood as the factual cognition about what really happened in the past, or as the related belief (historicism) that posits as absolute the factual sphere of the empirical life of humanity, history is incompatible with the phenomenological commitment to *a priori* cognition. Historical facts presuppose the limits that define empirical cognition and historicism, by reducing all the products of culture, including philosophy and science, to their origin in the actual conditions that generate historical facts, leads to an "extreme skeptical subjectivism" (PRS, 325/280). By "subjective skepticism" Husserl means the philosophical position that denies the absolute validity of ideas and the truths they establish. By maintaining that ideas and truth are factual constructs whose meaning cannot be separated from their "historical development", historicism denies the "objective" independence of ideas and truth. History, understood as the factual sequence and combination of events and evidences that could have been otherwise, is therefore contingent, as is all knowledge (owing to its historical construction).

Husserl advances two arguments against historicism that he thinks are sufficiently powerful to establish once and for all its status as "an epistemological aberration" (PRS, 327/283). First, the *unconditional* assertion that because (allegedly) over a few millennia philosophical and scientific truth have proved to be historically relative the conclusion can be drawn that this assertion must hold for a limitless future is not only a bad induction, but also an assertion that refutes the sceptic who expresses it. The latter point being that if truth is relative and therefore conditional (as is maintained by scepticism), then the assertion that scepticism's truth is unconditional (as is maintained by the sceptic) is contrary to what is meant by scepticism. To assert such a "truth" is absurd and contrary to sense, "like", Husserl points out, "2 + 2 = 5" (PRS, 327/282). Second, the meanings of ideas such as "truth", "theory" and "science" are completely independent of the empirical conditions that govern historical humankind. These ideas, like the essences of phenomenology, are *a priori*, and, as such, outside history's cognitive ambit and historicism's cognitive pretensions.

Reconciling Husserl's late turn to history with pure phenomenology

So effectively does Husserl's pure phenomenological critique of historicism separate the historical and the *a priori*, and thus demonstrate the distinction and opposition between history (and historical science) and essences (and essential science), that his turn to history in the *Crisis* texts raises the serious question whether the last phase of his phenomenology is consistent with its previous phases. For instance, in 1936 Husserl writes: "certainly theory of knowledge has never been seen as a peculiarly historical task. But this is precisely what we object to in the past" (OG, 379/370). The reasons Husserl gives for his objection to what he calls "the ruling dogma of the separation in principle between epistemological elucidation and historical, even humanistic-psychological explanation" are as complex as his statement about their connection is simple. "The problem of genuine historical explanation", he goes on to write, "comes together, in the case of the sciences [including mathematics and philosophy], with 'epistemological' grounding or clarification" (OG, 381/373). And not only does this mean that Husserl now sees a connection between the objective validity of knowledge and its historical origin, but also that the differentiation and opposition between any *a priori* and the historical is apparently no longer in effect. How else to explain the phenomenological appeal in the *Crisis* texts to both the "historical *a priori*" and the "*a priori* of historicity"?

The conclusion that Husserl has belatedly, in the last phase of his phenomenology, come to recognize "the socially and historically conditioned character of consciousness"[5] and knowledge (including phenomenological knowledge), and that this recognition, at the very least, creates a tension with his earlier programme for a "pure" phenomenology, has therefore understandably been drawn by many students of his phenomenology. This is because it is not at all easy to reconcile, for instance, the pure phenomenological statement that "[t]he mathematician will not turn to historical science to be instructed about the truth of mathematical theories; it will not occur to him to link the historical development of mathematical presentations and judgments to the question of truth" (PRS, 326/282), with this statement from the *Crisis* texts:

> In respect to geometry one recognizes … that only the consciously set task of [discovering] its historical origin (within the total problem of the a priori of historicity in general) can provide the method for a geometry that is true to its origins and at the same time to be understood in a universal-historical way. (OG, 381/372)

Two things stand out here as difficult to reconcile. First, there are the seemingly different and opposing views on the relation of mathematics and history; in the one case mathematical truth is presented as not having a relation to the historical development of mathematical thought and in the other providing a mathematical method's true origins is related to the quest to discover its historical origin. Second, there is what appears as Husserl's failure to recognize in the *Crisis* texts the *conceptual* opposition between history's contingency and the *a priori*, or, stated slightly differently, between history's particularity and the *a priori's* universality. Husserl's talk of either a "historical *a priori*" or the "*a priori* of historicity" cannot but seem to posit a conceptual unity from elements that are conceptual opposites.

The problem whether the fourth and final stage of Husserl's phenomenology truly represents a radical break from the founding principles of presuppositionlessness, pure reflection and essential intuition that define its previous stages, however, can be resolved phenomenologically neither by conceptual analyses nor by comparing statements he made at different times about the relation between scientific truth and history. Only the consideration of why, precisely, Husserl saw the need to extend the methodical reach of phenomenological reflection to history, and, in concert with this, the consideration of this extension's relation to phenomenology's founding principles, holds the prospect of answering the question of the philosophical significance of Husserl's turn to history and its phenomenological significance for pure phenomenology.

Reflection on the history of philosophy as Husserl's response to the crisis of European sciences

Husserl's phenomenological concern with history grew out of his personal concern with the imperilled meaning of his own philosophical existence. Despite having striven to live his life as an autonomous philosopher, Husserl finds (in the mid-1930s) both his philosophy and philosophizing future in jeopardy. On the one hand, the philosophical star of his phenomenology had been eclipsed by what he perceived as the irrationalism of Heidegger's existence-oriented "phenomenology", which was defined in part by both overt and covert attacks on Husserl's pure phenomenology. On the other hand, the widespread contemporary mood, especially among the younger generation, that European sciences' concern with objective truth (understood exclusively as facts) is unable to address meaningfully humankind's vital needs (all of which are bound up with the questions pertaining to the meaning of human existence), had precipitated the trend to renounce science as a discipline, including Husserl's scientific philosophy. Therefore, both the specific content of Husserl's phenomenology and its general methodical alignment with science were being taken to task from all sides for supposed "existential" shortcomings. Despite his confidence that he knows what he is striving for under the heading of philosophy, Husserl's response to these criticisms was to admit a lack of satisfaction with this "knowledge". Indeed, he even granted that for himself – as for all autonomous thinkers – "philosophy" remains an enigma with an obscure *telos*.

Husserl therefore found himself in what he characterized as an "existential contradiction". He could not let go of his faith in philosophy being, quite literally, *one*, in the sense that for him the very idea of "philosophy as such" is bound up with the possibility of universal knowledge. That is, for Husserl, the method of philosophy, befitting its source in reason, is singular, while the scope of its object, in line with the all-encompassing rationality of this method, is the totality of what is. As a serious philosopher, Husserl knew that he was called to this possibility as a "task". And yet holding on to this belief in an age that permits hope only for philosophies in the plural, but never philosophy in the unity of a single enterprise, is contradictory, because this belief has meaning only in relation to the recognition of a single goal common to all who philosophize. For Husserl, the only possible way out of this existential contradiction was to discontinue his previous philosophizing, with its vocational concern with this or that philosophical problem (worked on in the interest of furthering his own philosophy) and to reflect, historically and critically, on the meaning of philosophy, with the goal of arriving at a radical self-understanding of its meaning. As he put it: "We shall attempt to strike through the crust of the externalized 'historical facts' of philosophical history, interrogating, exhibiting, and testing their inner meaning and hidden teleology" (*Crisis*, 16/18).

Philosophizing in this manner, however, holds no guarantee for Husserl that he will be able to escape the existential contradiction into which he has fallen. Nevertheless, Husserl is also convinced that the very terms of the contradiction point beyond themselves to the path of its resolution, namely, the discovery of a connection between the results of his own philosophizing and the whole of human existence. Such a discovery would lend a common purpose to Husserl's philosophizing, because what would be at stake in it would no longer be merely a private affair. To establish such a connection, the meaning of the results of Husserl's philosophy would have to exceed that of his private and limited cultural goals. Thus Husserl believes that his philosophizing will stand a chance of clarifying universal knowledge (the possibility of which is inseparable for him from philosophy's *telos*) only *if* the personal responsibility of his own vocation as a philosopher "bears within itself at the same time the responsibility for the true being of mankind" (*Crisis*, 15/17).

Husserl's initial reflections on philosophy's history establish precisely such a connection between his philosophizing and the true being of humankind and, therefore, they establish *the* connection between the singularity of the method of philosophy and the universality of the knowledge that is its goal. They do so by challenging the contemporary (to him) perception of the crisis in the sciences. This perception is based on two considerations: first, that neither the natural nor human sciences are able to speak to the vital needs of the human being, needs that concern the whole of human existence and especially questions pertaining to its meaning and meaninglessness; and second, that both science and reason in themselves are intrinsically limited in their ability to provide tuition that speaks to these needs. Hence (according to this perception) the European sciences cannot address humankind's existential concerns because science and reason as principles of cognition are unsuited to providing knowledge about the true being of humankind. Husserl argues that the belief underlying this perception is mistaken. That is, what is mistaken is not the belief that contemporary European sciences are incapable of addressing the vital needs of the human soul but that the proper explanation for their inability to do so is that science and reason are *intrinsically* incapable of addressing such needs.

Positivism's "decapitation" of philosophy

The inability of contemporary European sciences to address the truth of the human being is therefore a complex affair. At one level, it is rooted in their "objectivity". Science's objective truth, whether about the physical world or the specifically human one, is a matter of establishing what each, in fact, is. In order to be rigorous, everything "subjective" must be abstracted from both worlds. The science of mere bodies (physics) does so as a matter of course, while the science of human reality must exclude all value judgements and all judgements about the rationality of its human subjects and their cultures. "Merely fact-minded sciences make merely fact-minded people" (*Crisis*, 4/7), observes Husserl. And these facts can teach us nothing about values, about reason and unreason in human affairs, and about the meaning of human existence. Thus, despite the undeniable rigour, exactness and theoretical accomplishments of contemporary European sciences, their objectivity makes them poor organs for addressing what Husserl calls the "enigma of subjectivity".

At another level, however, the problem does not lie with the "objectivity" *per se* of the sciences, but with their *kind* of objectivity. Husserl pejoratively characterizes the objectivity of contemporary European sciences as "positivism".

The sciences in general are "positive" on Husserl's view, in the sense that, in accordance with their natural functioning, they are directed primarily towards their objects of investigation and only secondarily towards the methods that make their investigations possible. Being positively directed in this sense is both unavoidable and necessary for the sciences to fulfil their cognitive function. By drawing attention to the "positivity" of science or, more precisely, to the positivity of the natural, humanistic and mathematical sciences, Husserl does not understand himself to be making a negative judgement about "positive" science but rather to be simply characterizing an essential feature of its mode of cognition. Husserl does, however, point out an important implication of this feature, namely, that it places an essential limit on the scope of scientific cognition, which he refers to as its "naivety". Scientific cognition is naive in the sense that it is not directly concerned with the methodical presuppositions that are responsible for it; it is "essentially" naive in the sense that its cognition, in principle, is not suited to investigating these presuppositions on their own terms but only with respect to their function as a part of scientific cognition.

When scientific cognition and knowledge are understood by both scientists and philosophers and by scientifically and philosophically "informed" lay people as providing the definitive method and results for investigating the true being of every kind of reality, scientific naivety is transformed into "positivism", according to Husserl. Positivism identifies objectivity with scientific objectivity and therefore rules out, in principle, the possibility of other kinds of objective cognition besides that of the positive sciences. This identification signals for Husserl the triumph of scepticism about the possibility of a universal philosophy that would provide theoretical knowledge based in pure reason (i.e. reason independent of sense experience) about the world and the human. That is, it signals scepticism about metaphysical knowledge and, with this, the collapse in the belief in "reason" having a cognitive status that is independent of positive scientific cognition. Reason in this independent sense would be that which gives meaning to everything that is thought to be (all things, values and ends), in the sense of its being normatively related to the truth itself of what is, that is, to being. By a "normative relation", Husserl has in mind the relation between the experience of something and *the* ideal limit of what it is for what is experienced to *be* what it is. The "rational" task of fixing this limit, as well as the task of articulating the non-empirical relation of the experience of something to the limit of its possible meaning, that is, to its norm, is, on Husserl's view, rejected as meaningless by positivism.

The traditional failures of pure reason: the naivety of the ancient Greek idea of universal knowledge and modern rationalism

Husserl sums up positivism by saying that it, "in a manner of speaking, decapitates philosophy" (*Crisis*, 7/9), in the sense that it does away with philosophy's concern with reason and ideas. The conception of philosophy, from its "original establishment" in ancient Greece to the "primal establishment" of the modern philosophical age, has been inseparable from the taking "as its task the exalted idea of universal knowledge concerning the totality of what is" (*Crisis*, 11/13). Positivism is able to separate philosophy from this concern because neither philosophy's Greek beginning nor its modern renaissance was able to overcome a fundamental naivety. In the case of the Greeks, the naive obviousness of the task of establishing universal knowledge about the totality of what is becomes transformed into unintelligibility because of the opposition of the ancient philosophical systems. With the moderns, naivety is manifest in its "rationalism": in an unclarified faith in pure reason to form anew the true being of humankind. On Husserl's view these naiveties cancel neither the importance for contemporary humanity of "the *telos* which was inborn in European humanity at the birth of Greek philosophy" (*Crisis*, 13/15) nor the repetition and universal transformation of this *telos* that define philosophical modernity. Husserl succinctly implies this importance in the question whether the Greek distinction between *epistēmē* (science) and *doxa* (opinion), together with the *telos* of universal knowledge it gives birth to, and the movement towards this *telos* manifest in an existence governed by reason, are a "historical delusion" or a breakthrough to something "essential to humanity". In the first case, the *telos* of seeking to exist through philosophical reason, such that being human as such would only be possible in the quest for norms in a philosophical existence, would have the status of an accidental acquisition of one among many civilizations and their contingent lines of historical development. It the second case, Greek humanity would represent the "first breakthrough to what is essential to humanity as such, its *entelechy* [realization of its proper being]" (*ibid.*).

Modern philosophy as the struggle for the meaning of humanity

Husserl thinks that only if rationalism's genuine sense is conflated with the naive rationalism of the eighteenth century can one understand this question as already answered. He does not think it has been answered because neither the naivety of modern rationalism nor the "rationality" of the irrationalism of the present has been carefully thought through. Husserl is confident that thinking through the former exposes its absurdity and thinking through the latter shows its basis in "'lazy reason'" (*Crisis*, 14/16); thus he is confident that it is too soon to pass final judgement on the modern impulse given to the idea of philosophy handed down by the ancients. This impulse, begun by Descartes, boldly and even extravagantly elevates the formal meaning of ancient philosophy, as *one* all-encompassing science of the totality of what is, into the idea of One Philosophy as the unity of a theoretical system that encompasses all sciences and therefore "all meaningful questions in a rigorous scientific manner" (*Crisis*, 6/9).

Husserl thinks it is possible to understand the present crisis of the positive sciences and the attendant "breakdown" situation of European culture only from within the movement of modern philosophy because the only significant "spiritual" struggles of our time are between the competing philosophies bequeathed to it by modernity. Thus, on the one hand, there are the sceptical philosophies "which retain the word but not the task" of clarifying the meaning of universal knowledge and, with this, of the "one" philosophy; and, on the other hand, there are the philosophies engaged in the struggle for the true and genuine meaning of philosophy's unity, which are "the actual and still vital philosophies" (*Crisis*, 13/15). Both kinds of philosophies involve the struggle for "the meaning of a genuine humanity" and, in the struggle of the present, represent the "humanity which has already collapsed" (the sceptical philosophies) and the "humanity which still has roots but is struggling to keep them or find new ones" (*ibid.*) (the actual and still vital philosophies).

Precisely the connection between the history of modern philosophy and the struggle for the meaning of humanity establishes for Husserl the existential connection between his own philosophizing and a purpose common to human existence as such. This connection is what is behind his otherwise inflated-sounding claim: "In *our* philosophizing, then – how can we avoid it – we are *functionaries of mankind*" (*Crisis*, 15/17). The answer to the question whether the true being of humankind is inseparable from the possibility of universal knowledge, and thus to the question whether the truth of humanity is found in its being towards a *telos*, can only be answered, "*if at all*, through philosophy". And this means for Husserl that it can only be answered "through *us*, *if* we are philosophers in all seriousness" (*ibid.*).

The modern transformation of the ancient ideal of philosophy's unity into the form of a universal philosophical science that progresses through ordered insight that is cognitively demonstrated and therefore certain, that is, apodictic, and therefore apodictically grounded in an apodictic method that discovers its own rational norms, is thus treated by Husserl in his *Crisis* texts *not* as a philosophical truth, but only as a historical fact. Indeed, Husserl's turn to history in the fourth and final stage of his phenomenology is made in the acute awareness that modern philosophy has *failed* to realize its idea of universal science when it comes to the truth of the human being. Husserl's historical reflections are therefore not conceived in the service of confirming a philosophical thesis – even the conclusion often quoted by others that "phenomenology is, so to speak, the secret longing of all modern philosophy" (*Ideas I*, 118) – but are the source of arriving at a decision about the truth of European humanity. Husserl therefore ask: is its idea of a knowledge that is universal an absolute idea borne within European humanity itself and not "merely an empirical anthropological type like 'China' or 'India'?" (*Crisis*, 14/16). And he unflinchingly elaborates what is at stake in its answer: deciding "whether the spectacle of the Europeanization of all other civilizations bears witness to the rule of an absolute meaning, one which is proper to the sense, rather than to a historical non-sense, of the world" (*ibid.*). In a word, what is at stake for Husserl is whether Europe has a historical rationale.

The "existential" motivation of Husserl's turn to history considered alone does not resolve the question of a possible inconsistency between the final stage of his phenomenology and pure phenomenology. But it does make clear that the sense of "history" that informs its reflection cannot be restricted to the level of finding out and considering the "facts" of philosophical history and their connection. Externalized historical facts (at least in the case of philosophy), on Husserl's telling, have an "inner" meaning and "hidden" teleology that can be exhibited, interrogated and tested, and, in doing precisely this, he (as a philosophical "functionary" of humankind) is following the only course open to him if he is to continue to live only for truth. He is quite clear about what his critically historical reflection is seeking: "the *practical* possibility of a new philosophy", one whose goals and methods are "ultimate, original, and genuine", and that, "once seen, apodictically conquers the will" (*Crisis*, 16–17/18). Notwithstanding all the suspense surrounding Husserl's formulation of the existential contradiction impelling him on the historical path to provide – "*before all decisions*" – a radical self-understanding philosophy's goals and methods, he almost lets the cat out of the bag when he writes about the sought-after new philosophy "that all philosophy of the past, though unbeknown to itself, was inwardly oriented toward this new sense of philosophy" (*Crisis*, 17/18).

The ancient context and insuperable precedent of phenomenology as presuppositionless science: the controversy over *eidē* in Aristotle and Plato

Before, however, addressing the question whether, as some have opined, Husserl's "new way [in the *Crisis*] leads to the old end of transcendental [pure] phenomenology" (Gadamer 1972: 183), the "purity" (and "transcendentality") of the old way must itself be addressed. And it will be addressed initially from within the context of Plato's and Aristotle's controversy over the proper manner of being of the *eidē*, because this controversy provides the insuperable philosophical precedent and therefore context for understanding all subsequent philosophies of purity (including, of course, Husserl's) as well as the touchstone for all the critiques directed at such philosophies.

The theme of purity in philosophy uncontroversially originates with Plato and, despite its different treatment in the hands of different philosophers, a commonality across its different treatments is detectable. On the one hand, purity is always addressed as the character belonging to some of the objects proper to cognition, specifically, those that are known theoretically. On the other hand, purity is used to address certain changes in the soul (and, later, the mind) that are requisite for pure cognitive objects to be apprehended at all. The characteristic responsible for the purity of pure cognitive objects is always calibrated in relation to the sensible qualities of things and their sense perception. This relation is always negative. Pure objects of cognition do not have sensible qualities, and this means that colours, sounds, odours, tastes and tangibility cannot be truthfully said to characterize such objects. And pure objects, unlike sensible things, do not change. The changes in the soul or mind, as the case may be, that are necessary to apprehend pure cognitive objects are always fixed in relation to the human being's immersion in the practical concerns inseparable for most people from life. This relation is again negative. Not only is some leisure-granting respite from life's practical concerns a part of the changes required of the mind for it to grasp pure objects, but, also, a decidedly non-practical, which is to say, theoretical, interest in them must have been somehow awakened in an individual soul or mind.

Pure objects, then, are only apprehensible by thought and because of this they are universally called "intelligible". The exact nature of intelligible objects' negative relation to the sensible, however, is controversial throughout philosophy's history, as is the number, exact nature and relations among the intelligible objects themselves. Moreover, the apprehension of intelligible objects is lacking a universal designation among philosophers, which is indicative of the great problem that confronts the philosophy of purity throughout its history, namely, how it is that thought's movement is able to arrest itself or otherwise become arrested in order to grasp that which, by its very nature, is prescinded from all change and therefore from motion. Finally, the question of the nature of the origin proper to the intelligible objects has dogged philosophy ever since Aristotle demonstrated a greater allegiance to truth than to his teacher and friend Plato.

Aristotle's dispute with Plato and the ancient Platonists over intelligible objects discloses basic terms and problems that remain relevant for understanding all subsequent philosophical appeals to their purity, including, therefore, Husserl's. Contrary to what is written in most philosophy textbooks, this dispute has nothing to do with Plato being an idealist and Aristotle an empiricist. That there are *eidē*, that the very being of a thing is the being of the *eidos*, is not a matter of controversy between Plato and Aristotle. When addressing the question of whether the most readily available examples of intelligible objects, mathematical things, have being or not, Aristotle's answer is unambiguous: "for us the dispute will not be about whether they have being, but about the *manner* of their being" (*Metaph.* Z 1, 1036a36). The question that divides Plato and Aristotle is *what* and *how eidē* are – their "manner" of being – and not whether they *are* at all. By "manner of being", Aristotle, as well as Plato, understands, above all, the origin of something, whether natural or intelligible. And Aristotle will contend that the truth of the *eidos* is such that there is no need to follow Plato's Socrates and abandon the "inquiry into nature" (*Phd.* 96a) in order to account for this origin and thereby to understand the manner of being belonging to the *eidē* as one of "separation" (*chōrismos*) from sensible things.

Before considering more closely Aristotle's critical departure from Plato over *what* and *how* the *eidē* are, I want to stress the importance of situating Husserl's pure phenomenology in relation to Plato's and Aristotle's "actual" thought about this matter and not the standard interpretations of their thought. Service is done neither to Plato's or Aristotle's philosophies nor to the cause of introducing Husserl's phenomenology from the point of view of its relation to their accounts of the *eidē* by repeating old saws about Plato's theory of forms and idealism, and Aristotle's theory of abstraction and empiricism, not to mention the more subtle hermeneutical "readings" that contrast Aristotle's putatively more practical philosophy with Plato's supposedly more theoretical philosophy. Husserl identified phenomenology's "purity" with its presuppositionless method and the non-sensuous "seeing" of the *eidē* (or the terminologically equivalent "essences") from which all cognitive concepts and all possible meanings originate. At various stages of the development of phenomenology, Husserl referred to its "so-called 'Platonism'" and to the "general essence" it makes manifest as "the *eidos*, the *idea* in the Platonic sense, but apprehended in its purity and free from all metaphysical interpretations" (EJ, 411/341). But he also appealed to "abstraction" to account for the origin of universal meaning, all the while expressing the confidence that phenomenology need not be troubled by the "controversy between Platonism and Aristotelianism" (ILI, 131).

Perhaps Husserl is right that the controversy between Platonism and Aristotelianism need not trouble phenomenology, but that between Plato and Aristotle is another story. The *eidē* originate in abstraction for neither Plato nor Aristotle. "Abstraction" is mentioned by Aristotle only in connection with the origin of the unity of mathematical objects, an explicit context of which is his dispute with Plato over the independent (and therefore separate) manner of being belonging to generic unity in mathematical numbers and to the unities that establish the relations among the *eidē*. Aristotle's account of the origin of mathematical objects "from abstraction" (*ex aphairesis*) is therefore directly (and critically) related to Plato's generic account of "beinghood" (*ousia*) while his account of the "being-at-work" (*energeia*[6]) on some natural material (*hulē*) as the proper manner of being of an *eidos* (or the closely related *morphē*) is directly (and also critically) related to Plato's Socrates' turn away from the "investigation of nature". The two most enduringly controversial tenets of Husserl's pure phenomenology – (i) the complete independence of the *content* of ideal meaning from both sensible objects and cognitive awareness and (ii) the "remarkable duality and unity of *sensuous hulē* and *intentive morphē*" (*Ideas I*, 172) – therefore have an undeniable historical context in precisely the controversy between Plato and Aristotle. When Husserl's own modest interest in the technical details of this controversy is combined with the critical mileage his two major critics (Heidegger and Derrida) get out of criticizing Husserl's pure phenomenology's uncritical relation to "traditional" metaphysics, the importance of situating his phenomenology within the precedent and context of precisely the technical details of this controversy becomes compelling.

Four presuppositions common to Plato's turn away from the investigation of nature and Aristotle's critique of the separate being of the *eidē*

To apprehend properly the reasons for Plato's turning away from the "investigation" (*historia*) of nature as well as Aristotle's critique of the thesis that results from this about the separate being proper to the *eidē*, four fundamental presuppositions common to their philosophies need first to be articulated.

The first presupposition is that the fundamental meaning of "*logos*" is speech and that speech and understanding are inseparable. Speech is composed of the successively uttered sounds that become identifiable as words when that which makes speakers and listeners understand (*noein*), "the intelligible" (*to noēton* – "*noēton*" is a verbal adjective of *noein*), is grasped. The units of the intelligible, *noēta*, singly and in combination, are both the source of understanding and what is aimed at in it. *Logos* bespeaks everything humans are involved with (i.e. it is about something), including the *noēta* presented in speech by the speaker. *Logos* therefore moves exclusively in the realm of the understandable, even when it is ambiguous, obscure, because it can be thus only when a part of it contrasts (at least to some listener) with the clarity of its other parts.

Closely related to the presupposition that speech and understanding are inseparable in the fundamental meaning of *logos* is the presupposition that *logos* and thinking (*dianoia*) are the same thing. Speaking (*legein*) to others audibly manifests thinking while the silent discoursing (*dialogos*) of the soul with itself is also called thinking. Spoken words thus manifest rather than interpret the silent thinking in the soul, because that silent thinking is (already) *logos*.

The third presupposition is that all change (*kinēsis*) implies generation (*genesis*). In all change something new (that has not been) comes into being. Generation is both becoming and coming to be, in the sense that that which is becoming is something that comes to be: generated things are things "to come", the futurity of what they are coming to be in their becoming being crucial to the very sense of the process of generation. Humans generate babies, which come to be men and women; tigers generate kittens, which come to be tigers and tigresses; change of place generates something new with respect to the mobile; growth is continuous generation. In all change and all generation there are three interrelated things that must be distinguished: what is responsible for the origin, the way and the end (*telos*).

The fourth presupposition is that among the different answers to the question why something is as it is, no matter what this something is (including, therefore, the whole world), the decisive, because alone satisfactory, answer is its end, its purpose. The end is therefore the true beginning (*archē*) of anything, even if for some things or occurrences the question why remains unanswerable.

ONE

Plato's Socratic theory of *eidē*: the first pillar of the ancient precedent to pure phenomenology

Impossibility of direct knowledge of *eidē*

A precise exposition of Plato's account of the *eidē* requires that its dialogical mode of presentation be respected and therefore its origin in *logos* be acknowledged. Respecting the former yields the extremely important discovery of two discernibly different accounts of the *eidē* in the dialogues, accounts that nevertheless compose a unified whole. Acknowledging the latter reveals a whole that is unified neither theoretically nor practically, but in a manner that then, as now, can only be termed "dialectically", through (*dia*) *logos*.

Plato's first, and most obvious, account of the *eidē* is discernible in the Socratic elenchi (refutations) of interlocutors who claim to know some commonly acknowledged standard of virtue (*aretē*), such as piety, justice, wisdom, courage, or even virtue itself, or the criteria responsible for something they claim to know about, such as education, love, the soul's nature, or even knowledge itself. In this account the ignorance of the non-philosopher, such as Euthyphro, Meno and Meletus, is manifest in his claim to know what he in truth does not know, and the wisdom of the philosopher Socrates is manifest in his refusal to claim that he knows what he in truth does not. Likewise made manifest is the irony of the philosopher Socrates' wisdom, because what he claims not to know are the *eidē* that no mortal is capable of knowing directly: that is, through perception or thought (*dianoia*). Thus, despite the fact that the *logos* of all mortals cannot help but appeal to the *eidē* when it recognizes the intelligibility of that which is and when it distinguishes that which truly is (such as piety, justice, beauty, knowledge) from its opposite, that which is not (such as impiety, injustice, ugliness, ignorance), Plato's Socratic dialogues make manifest the impossibility of the direct apprehension of the *eidē* by exhibiting the folly of those who claim to be able to do so. Thus, for instance, in the case of a specific virtue, piety, it is Euthyphro, not Socrates, who claims to have knowledge of the "invisible looks" (*eidos*) that all pious actions have in common. And in the case of "virtue itself", it is not Socrates but Meno who claims to know the one *eidos* that is common to anything at all that is recognized as virtuous.

The impossibility of direct knowledge of the *eidē* is shown to result from the following: each *eidos* is presupposed as one, in the sense that it is spoken of as an intelligible unity that excludes its opposite, whereas the things that are rendered intelligible through *logos*'s appeal to the *eidē* are not one but many; and they do not exclude but are rather always perceived (or thought) together with their opposites. This holds for sensible things (e.g. a finger is both big and small, hard and soft), mathematical things (e.g. number is both one and many) and virtues (e.g. justice, which is many because who or what is just is always in dispute among mortals).

The response of Plato's Socrates to the impossibility of direct knowledge of the *eidē* contains the key to the dialogues' first account of them. The response has two interrelated parts. The first is the methodical necessity of abandoning the "investigation of nature" and "taking refuge in *speaking* to investigate the truth of the things that are in *spoken words*". Socrates explicitly situates this necessity within the context of his "next best try" to find the answer why "each thing comes to be, why it ceases to be, and why it is" (*Phd.* 99e, emphasis added). He articulates the reason for this necessity in his failure to grasp these answers by looking at things directly with his eyes and trying to touch them with one of his senses. The attempt to answer in this way the question why about the generation and being of things, and to name as their "cause" (*aitia*) sensible qualities (such as air, water, muscles, bones), threatens to blind his soul, like those who look directly at the sun during an eclipse instead of at its image in some reflective medium.

Logos as image of *eidos*

By giving the name "cause" to what is seen through the eyes or touched with the senses, the soul is exposed to the danger of losing sight of that which it "sees" and gets in "touch" with through *logos* when, in speaking, it communicates what it understands. What the soul *sees* when it understands why something comes to be or why it is are not the sensible qualities of things, with which it is undeniably in touch when these things are perceived, but the *eidē* that are responsible for these things being seen in the first place. Socrates is therefore quick to qualify his reference to "image" when he compares his taking refuge in *logos* with the safe way to perceive the sun during an eclipse, by stressing that he does "not admit at all that he who looks at the things that are *in discourse* sees them as images to a greater degree than he who sees those existing things actually" (*Phd.* 100a, emphasis added). Seeing the things that are in *logos* therefore sees them no more as images than seeing sensible things through the eyes. This can only mean that for Plato the soul's seeing the things that are through their "reflection" in the "medium" of *logos* is unlike seeing them through their reflection in some natural medium. The clear difference between directly and indirectly seeing the things that are through the eyes thus does not hold in the case of seeing them through *logos*. If the "next best try's" seeing of things by looking at them in *logos* were exactly like looking at the sun in its reflected image, seeing the things that *are* through *logos* would be just as indirect as seeing the sun's image. But in the case of *logos* Socrates refuses to admit just this: that the one who looks at the things that *are* in discourse *sees* them as images (and not, therefore, as they are originally *are*) to the same extent that one who sees the sun through its image does not *see* the sun as it is originally.

Unlike the natural image, then, which presents an image of something that is capable of being seen independently of, and more originally than, its reflection by an image, *logos* functions to present things that *are* – the *eidē* – that cannot be seen any more originally than by the soul's looking at them as they are "reflected" through it (*logos*). Thus it is not as if *logos* functions to mediate what otherwise is capable of being seen directly. Rather, there can be no seeing and therefore there can be no apprehension of an *eidos* without its "reflection" in *logos*. In precisely this sense, then, *logos* and *eidos* are the same, without, however, being identical. They are the "same" in so far as the *eidos* is that which is responsible for *logos* being what it is, that is, speech that is understandable. Notwithstanding their sameness in this respect, they are not "identical", because the *appearance* of the *eidos* functions as both the origin and the goal of *logos*. The *eidos*'s appearance is the origin of *logos* in so far as it is that which is referred to when *logos* makes sense and is therefore understandable. And this appearance is the goal of *logos* in so far as rendering it more apparent and thus *clarifying* the *eidos* is the aim of all *logos*. The *eidos* is thus something "seen". Its original Greek meaning is derived from the root (*ido*) that yields both "to see" and "to know". Its Latin translation as *species* is derived from *specio*, to look at, and thus means originally "look" or "looks". "Looks" is therefore the best English translation of *eidos*, followed by "shape" (since the look of something overlaps its shape), then "form" (from the Latin word for shape, *forma*), and, finally, species (defined as kind or class). Because, however, for Plato the *eidos* that is seen through *logos* is not something visible to the eyes, "invisible looks" is the best translation of its original Platonic meaning.

Socratic dialectic

The second interrelated part of Plato's Socrates' response to the impossibility of directly knowing an *eidos* through perception or thought concerns the way Socrates investigates the answer to the questions why the things that come to be come to be and why the things that are have being. Rather than try to find these answers in the thing's direct perception, Socrates relates that he assumes some statement as the "presupposition" (*hypothesis*) that seems to him the most reliable and therefore safest way to understand the answer to the question why in "each case" (*hekastote*). His most basic and therefore safest presupposition is the statement that each of the intelligible objects (*noēta*/*eidē*) "imaged" by the silent and audible words that compose the elements of *logos* has being. Two additional presuppositions follow from this: (i) that all other things derive their names by sharing or participating (*methexis*) in the *eidē*; (ii) that the sharing in the *eidē* by things is the cause (*aitia*) of their being as they are. To these presuppositions Socrates adds two methodical stipulations. The first is that the compatibility or incompatibility of the consequences that (case by case) follow from any one of the safe presuppositions about the cause of something's being must be examined. The second is that the safe presupposition itself must be examined on the basis of the appeal to "higher" presuppositions, each one chosen as the "best", until something "adequate" (*ti hikanon*) is arrived at.

Both the downwards movement of thought (*dianoia*) towards the consequences of presuppositions and its upwards movement towards their origin articulated in Socrates' "second best try" have their source in the "power of dialectic". But it is the upwards movement, which comprises the "mode of passage" (*Resp.* 532b) most properly called "dialectic", that has the greatest significance for clarifying Plato's original institution of "pure" philosophy in the Western tradition. It is characterized as the undertaking, by means of dialectic, without any of the senses and without any visible images, to push on through *logos* to each thing itself that *is*, in a manner that goes from presupposition to (better) presuppositions to an origin free of presuppositions. Arriving at the presuppositionless origin, it then makes its investigation into the *eidē* themselves by means of them, until it arrives at the end of the intelligible realm, the good itself "taken in as a whole" (*noēsis*[1]) (510b, 532ab).

The divided line as image of presuppositionless eidetic originals

Socrates' account of the dialectical "push" to being and its end, while eschewing the senses and therefore the visible images cast by sensible things, is not entirely imageless, as is commonly thought. He employs something visible to the senses (a divided line drawn in a sensible medium) as an image by relating it to a source that is invisible to the senses (the mathematical presupposition of a dimensionless line), in order to "reflect" the "two *eidē*, visible and intelligible" (*Resp.* 509d). In other words, the visible image of an intelligible object is employed in a manner that reflects *not* the proximate source of its origin as an image (the geometrical presupposition of an intelligible line) but that which is *presupposed* when mathematicians employ sensible things as images to investigate mathematical "objects", namely, that sensible things are related to intelligible things.

Three unavoidable conclusions follow from Socrates' manner of employing images here. First, the visible realm (and, therefore, the things in this realm) is in some sense an image of the intelligible realm (and, therefore, the things in this realm). Second, the ultimate source of the things in the visible realm (visible images and their sensible originals) are the *originals* in the intelligible realm – the *eidē*. Third, the *eidē* and not the other denizens of the intelligible realm, the so-called "mathematical objects", are the true originals of the things in the visible realm. The last is the case because the "seeing" of a visible divided line as an image of an intelligible geometrical line is understandable only on the basis of a presupposition that is capable of relating what is seen through the senses to what is "seen" through the understanding (*dia-noia*). The presupposition of mathematical objects is not capable of establishing this relation, because it implies that the relation between the visible (things) and the intelligible (things) is already in place. That is, the mathematical presupposition does not establish but presupposes that what is *seen* through the senses is something that can reflect something that is only truly "seen" through the understanding. Only the presupposition that the manner of being of intelligible things is separate from what can be seen through the senses is able to allow the soul to *see* what is visible to the eyes of the body as a thing with an invisible source in what is "visible" only to thought.

In addition to employing a geometrical object as an image in his account of the power and passage of dialectic, Socrates also uses mathematical proportion (*analogia*) as an image. Proportion is employed to reflect the image–original relation that holds between (i) sensible images and their sensible originals in the visible realm and (ii) presuppositions (*hypotheses*) and their intelligible originals in the intelligible realm. Within the context of ancient Greek mathematics, a proportion is composed of two ratios that are the same, where a ratio is a sort of relation of size between two magnitudes or multitudes. By stipulating that the two segments of the divided line be cut using the same but unspecified ratio, Socrates' parameters for its cutting stipulate the proportional relation between the two segments. This means that the two segments of the lower half of the divided line are related proportionally to the two segments of its upper half. It is also means that the *eidos* of the visible realm is related *analogically* to the *eidos* of the intelligible realm. Thus the relation between *visible* images and their *visible* originals that composes the *eidos* of the *visible* region is *analogous* to the relation between presuppositions and *eidē* that composes the *eidos* of the intelligible region. The analogical relation of the *eidē* of the visible and intelligible regions is therefore what is reflected in Socrates' employing as an image the proportional relation belonging to the ratios of the segments of the divided line. That is, the proportion characteristic of Socrates' divided line is an image of the relation between the visible and invisible regions, which means that this relation is the original that is reflected by the identical mathematical ratios that compose Socrates' image of the divided line. Hence the analogical relation between visible and intelligible *eidē* looks like this: visible images are related to sensible originals in the visible realm as mathematical and eidetic presuppositions are related to *eidē* in the intelligible realm. Thus, while the spatial, that is, geometrical, image of the divided line points to the image–original relation between things in the sensible realm and things in the intelligible realm, the non-spatial image, that is, the same general ratio or proportional relations between its segments, points to an image–original relation between the things in the intelligible realm itself (mathematical and eidetic presuppositions and the *eidē* themselves).

Contemplation of the opposition intrinsic to number and the one draws and redirects the soul towards being

Plato's Socrates steadfastly refuses to relate to his interlocutors "what manner of power dialectic has, and exactly what *eidē* it's divided into, and what paths they take" (*Resp.* 532de), because to do so requires going beyond any image of the intelligible, and thus beyond *logos*, to the truth itself as it is apparent to him. Socrates does not quibble over whether this truth appears to him in its very being or not, since this is undeserving of confident assertion, but he does maintain "that there is some such thing to see is something one can be sure of" (533a). Rather than endeavour at this point to leave the realm of images entirely behind (which, it should be stressed, there is no lack of willingness in principle on Socrates' part to do), the first ("Socratic") account of the *eidē* in the dialogues limits itself to the "prelude to the song" (of the "mode of passage" most proper to dialectic). The Socratic prelude focuses on the "know-how" (*technē*) requisite for "turning around" (*metastrophē*) and "redirecting" (*periogōgē*) (518d) the whole soul from the things that are becoming to what truly is. Plato's Socrates identifies this know-how with the lowly *technē* of counting and calculation used by all who count things and reckon with the resulting sums to solve problems (whether practical or theoretical) of multiplication and division. Socrates stresses, however, that "no one uses it rightly, as something suited in every way to draw someone toward being" (523a).

Counting and calculation, used "rightly", "draw" and "redirect" the soul towards being and the truth itself by forcing it to exercise its highest power of thinking, *nous*, first to clarify opposite sensations that strike the senses and then to contemplate and study the nature of the "pure" numbers employed by those who are formidable in arithmetic (mathematicians).

Opposing sensations (for instance, large and small) reported by the same sense (sight in this case) in the same thing (for instance, in the perception of the ring finger in comparison with the fingers on either side of it) awaken in the soul the "activity of *nous*" (*noēsis*) and counting, in order "to examine whether each of the things passed on to it [large and small] is one or two"; and, if "they appear to be two", to grasp that each "appear[s] as something distinct and one". In the case at hand, *nous* will grasp that "each is one and both together are two", and thus "be grasping the two as separate, because it wouldn't grasp inseparable things as two but as one" (524bc). Sight sees large and small mixed together while *nous* achieves clarity about this by grasping each as one and both as two, and what sight sees is called "visible" and what *nous* grasps is called "intelligible".

All number and its source (*archē*), the one,[2] also appear to sight with something opposite to them, and therefore they, too, lead to the contemplation of what is and redirect the soul to that. Not only does sight see the same thing at the same time as one and unlimitedly many, but even more so does this happen with number. For instance, in the case of number, a line is both one and infinitely divisible; in the case of the one, not only is each number both *one* number and a *multitude* of units, but also there are unlimitedly many instances of each single number (for example, the number six is one number, but the amount of sixes has no limit). Indeed, the contemplation of the nature of numbers is touted by Socrates for its "ease of redirecting the soul itself from becoming to truth and being" (525c), especially when the numbers studied are not those "that have visible or tangible bodies" (525d), but the sort that are made of parts in which "each and every one is equal to every one without even a tiny difference, and with none having any part within itself" (526a).[3] The study of these numbers "obviously forces the soul to use *nous* itself directed at the truth itself" (526ab), because they are "things that only admit of being thought".

Plato's first, "Socratic" account of the *eidē* in the dialogues stops here, at the "prelude" to the song of dialectic and its mode of passage to and beyond the *eidē*. The Socratic endeavour to use dialectic's "power" to redirect the soul towards being and the truth itself therefore remains shrouded in a darkness that is ultimately mythical. Regarding the answer to the question why the sharing in an *eidos* of things is the cause for the being of each one of them, Socrates is not ready, "as yet" (*Phd.* 100d) to state with confidence whether this occurs on account of an *eidos*'s "presence" (*parousia*) in them or on account of its bringing about a "community" (*koinōnia*) among them. His identification of sharing or participating (*methexis*) with "imitation" (*mimēsis*) does not clarify this matter either, because Socrates' account of the image–original relation makes it clear that the *eidē* that function as the originals cannot (like sensible originals) be perceived independently of the images in the *logos* that reflect them. Thus, at the very least, the Socratic account of the image–original relation in "imitation" is paradoxical because both the image's likeness to its original and the original's greater degree of "beinghood" (*ousia*) cannot be established by perception and, therefore, by the "investigation of nature". And, at the very most, the account is (as Aristotle will argue) "without content" (*Metaph.* A, 991a22), as it speaks in "poetic metaphors" (991a 23).

Plato's Socrates therefore does not follow the "push" of his own *logos* to pursue the dialectical mode of passage to its end beyond images in accordance with his own stipulations regarding the "right use" of the study of numbers' nature to lead the soul to being itself and truth. Nowhere is this more apparent than in the myth of recollection's account of the origin of learning and, therefore, of the origin of the soul's *logos* about the *eidē*.

Socratic recollection and dialectical presuppositionlessness

The problem that occasions Socrates' most extensive account of the myth of recollection is the articulation of Meno's paradox. The paradox issues from the presupposition of the rule in technical mathematical thinking that prohibits "unknown" terms from being used in a cognitive investigation, which stipulates that the use of all words in a cognitive enquiry must be "agreed upon [*homologia*]" (*Meno* 75c) in advance by its enquirers. A straight line runs from the presupposition of this rule to the eristic paradox that Meno recites, to the effect that the movement of the soul from ignorance to knowledge is impossible (80d). Such movement is impossible because ignorance, as the condition of not knowing, *precludes* any relation to what is unknown. Ignorance, therefore, rules out a relation to what must presumably (and impossibly) already be "known" in the ignorant soul in order for it to learn: knowing where to seek and what to look for in order to secure the unknown's acquisition. In Socrates' restatement of this paradox, the impossibility of enquiry into the known is added to Meno's statement of the impossibility of enquiring into the unknown (the former because it is already known and the latter because it is unknown) (80e). The myth of learning that Socrates tells in response to both Meno's statement of this paradox and his own restatement of it, however, never addresses the main point raised by Meno's formulation of the paradox: how knowledge that is not currently in the soul was able to get there in the first place. Thus the myth's three major images – (i) the soul's deathless nature responsible for its seeing and having learned all things in both this and the netherworld, (ii) the kinship of all generated things, and (iii) the "recollection" in time of the knowledge of a single thing being able to lead, because of this kinship, to recollecting (learning) them all (81cd) – not only do not address this point but also presuppose that the learning has already occurred. Moreover, the obvious comparison, and indeed confusion, of mythical recollection with psychological recollection invited by Socrates' telling of the myth raises the apparently insuperable problem of how to reconcile the orientation to the future of learning, as the acquisition of knowledge, with recollection's relation to the past, that is, to knowledge already in the soul, but forgotten. In other words, the absence of an account of the soul's original acquisition of the knowledge already in it in Socrates' tale of mythical recollection leaves unresolved the conflict between the directedness to the future of non-mythological learning and the directedness to the past of mythological learning.

The myth of recollection's tale about learning, which relates the soul's acquisition of knowledge in time to its remembrance of pieces of knowledge (*epistēmas*) somehow already in it before this time, together with the only possible conclusion that can be drawn from this – that ignorance is tantamount to the loss of knowledge and therefore to forgetting – represent mythic images whose originals are not mythical. The original of the image of mythical remembrance is the mysterious awareness of having forgotten something, not being able to remember what it is, and searching for and then finding it that characterizes psychological (non-mythical) recollection. This awareness is what distinguishes recollection from memory, because in memory the remembered is precisely not forgotten. And the original of the image of mythical knowledge is the "unknown knowledge" that is appealed to by thinking when it enquires into the difference between true opinion and knowledge. The very point of departure of this enquiry, the ignorance of the difference between true opinion and knowledge, must nevertheless presuppose that knowledge *is* something different from true opinion in order for its enquiry into their difference even to begin. Therefore, pending the acquisition of the knowledge of the difference between true opinion and knowledge, the "knowledge" that the enquiry posits as different from opinion is necessarily something that is and must remain "unknown".

Plato's Socrates' unprecedented connection of learning to the mysterious psychological awareness of having forgotten something that was previously in memory is the presupposition that transports Platonic recollection into the domain of myth. In psychological recollection, it is the soul's awareness of having forgotten something that was previously in memory that initiates its searching forth from this awareness towards its memorial images, in order to test them – somehow – against a "standard" of recognition that remains forgotten until the recollection is successful. The standard must be something less than memory but more than complete forgetfulness, and therefore uncannily in between these two psychological extremes. The movement of the soul that is inseparable from psychological recollection is the original that is reflected and mythically amplified by the image of recollection as that recovery of pieces of knowledge called learning. The mysterious standard of recognition that is a crucial aspect of psychological recollection is the original that is reflected and amplified in the mythical image of knowledge as that which guides its own recovery in the lifetime of the soul from its mythical place in the nowhere "outside" heaven (*Phdr.* 247c). Thus what makes the standard of recognition in psychological recollection "mysterious", its seeming directing of the soul to the sought-after but forgotten memorial image while remaining itself unknown until recollection has occurred, is precisely what is transposed into the realm of myth in Socrates' claim that "learning is nothing but recollection". And no doubt because the original of this mythic image is psychological, Socrates' "demonstration" of the truth of this claim with Meno's slave lends itself to the mixing of image and original, as when, for instance, the uneducated slave's ability to answer correctly questions about the line of a square is explained by Socrates in terms of his soul being for all time in a condition of having learned.

The mythical image of knowledge invites comparison with the power of dialectic, which can be awakened only with the violation of enquiry's technical rule of *homologia*. The *recognition* of opinion's power to cloak the unknown in the guise of the known that initiates dialectical enquiry must therefore posit as known something other than opinion, namely, knowledge. That is, dialectic's investigation of the knowledge sought by the soul but currently not in its possession employs presuppositions that treat opinions about what is unknown as if they were knowledge and, therefore, treats the unknown itself as if it were something known. The soul's acquisition of knowledge in Plato's Socrates' dialectical account of knowledge is therefore accessible only through a kind of opinion, true or right opinion (*Meno* 97e–98b). Hence the knowledge sought by dialectic must remain inaccessible to such opinion, and thus forever beyond the scope of the power of opinion's truth, although the dialectical mode of passage posits knowledge as something other than opinion at every step of its ascension. In other words, the dialectical power to recognize the difference between true opinion and knowledge does not have its source in the soul's acquisition and therefore possession of the knowledge that is posited by dialectic as being different from true opinion. The recognition of this difference stems rather from the soul's mysterious awareness that the knowledge that it does not possess must be something other than that of the true opinion that it alone is capable of possessing.

Nor does Socrates' conviction that there is a difference between true opinion and knowledge (*epistēmē*) have its basis in the criterion of the superior reliability of knowledge, as is commonly thought. Socrates says that he does not know the difference between true or right opinion and knowledge, that he therefore just gropes for the truth about this difference using images even though he is convinced that their difference is not a matter of imagery, and he then adds that this conviction is among the few things he would claim to know (*eidenai*) (*Meno* 98b). Socrates' attempt, nevertheless, to convince Meno that it is precisely the criterion of reliability that distinguishes right opinion from knowledge (97e–98a) does not contradict his claim not to know their difference, but rather illustrates it. "Knowledge", no less than right or true opinion, is unreliable, in the sense that our memory, as the repository of knowledge, is prone to "outgoing of knowledge [*epistēmes exodos*]" (*Symp.* 208a), that is, to forgetting. Thus to "know" the difference between opinion and knowledge (and not just that they are different) would entail having an unforgettable piece of knowledge. Socrates does not know the difference in question because neither he nor any other mortal is in possession of the unforgettable criterion that would permit thought to "calculate" (*logismos*), in the case of *logos*'s imagery of its *eidetic* originals, the difference between image and original. Acquisition of knowledge of this difference, that is, learning it, would have to take place in a learning whose object is capable of being "stored" in memory beyond all forgetting and therefore beyond recollecting, and, thus, beyond the play of image and original. In other words, the difference between the object of opinion (*doxa*) and being (*on*), between the unknown treated as known that characterizes opinion and the true being of that unknown, unmediated by opinion and therefore untouched by images, remains unaccounted for in the Socratic account of the *eidē*. The enquiry into the unknowable "nature" of this difference is what the myth of recollection is intended to initiate, and it is for this reason that it is the prototype for all the other Platonic–Socratic myths.

The Socratic account of the *eidē* nonetheless understands them to be the "invisible looks" that render both sensible and thought things understandable in *logos*'s spoken and silent speech. The proper answer to the question "what is it?" addressed to any thing is precisely what it looks *like*. Because, however, the looks that it looks like are not seen through the eyes but through *logos*'s understanding, which "reflects" them through its invisible word images, the soul's access to the invisible looks of any thing must be "pure", in the precise sense that it must turn away from sensible things and their qualities in order to "behold" them. The disanalogy between the invisible images that reflect the *eidē* in *logos* and the visible images that reflect sensible things in some sensible medium, however, renders paradoxical the purity of the soul's initial beholding of the *eidē*. On the one hand, it uses the same name to refer to both the singular *eidos* and the many things that derive their name and being from it. Both *what* these many things are and their denomination is based on their "looks". On the other hand, unlike a visible original, which can be perceived directly by the soul without the mediation of any image that it casts, the *eidetic* original reflected in *logos*'s imagery cannot be directly perceived by the soul.

These two paradoxical aspects of the soul's sensibly "pure" beholding of the *eidē* are behind the Socratic account of the need for further methodical "purification" of the soul in order for it to investigate them more originally. To do so, the soul must (i) turn away from the many things that somehow share in an *eidos* in order to investigate unambiguously what is originally named by *logos* when it denominates many things with the same name and (ii) dialectically examine the presuppositions proper to *logos* that reflect and thus "image" the *eidetic* originals. The first presupposition examined in the Socratic account of the dialectically more original investigation of the *eidē* is that what is originally named in answer to the question "what is it?" of any thing is *not* the thing but its *eidos*. Socrates articulates the need for the dialectical examination of this presupposition by still "better" presuppositions, in order to serve the end of arriving at the most original investigation of the *eidē*, one that is presuppositionless. As presuppositionless, the original investigation of the *eidē* is imageless and for this reason it is outside the proper ambit of *logos*. And, as thus outside *logos*'s play of "image and original", it leads to that which is "beyond being" (*Resp.* 509b), in the precise sense that dialectic's investigation of the *eidē* (themselves by means of themselves) leads to *nous*'s taking in as a whole – without the mediation of any kind of image – the end (*telos*) that is the source (*archē*) of their being, that is, the idea of the Good.

The employment of images to investigate *eidē* defines the limit of Plato's Socratic account of *eidē*

The employment of images to account for the "imageless" dialectical investigation of the *eidē* and the source of their being in the idea of the Good defines the limit of the most apparent, "Socratic", account of the *eidē* in Plato's dialogues. The crowning image of this account, the myth of recollection, does the double duty of awakening the non-philosopher's soul to the dialectical power that lies slumbering in it and of attuning the philosopher's soul to the defining question and hence to the problem of its very existence: whence the *telos* of the "unknown" knowledge that also provides the presupposition indispensable to the *archē* of the philosophical life, namely that opinion and knowledge are different things?

TWO

Plato's arithmological theory of *eidē*: the second pillar of the ancient precedent to pure phenomenology

Dialectically imageless investigation of *eidē*: Plato's "unwritten teachings"

The dialogues' second account of the *eidē* is neither readily apparent nor Socratic. In place of the dramatic figures of the philosopher Socrates and various non-philosophers, the figure of the unnamed philosopher from Elea (the "Stranger") and the accomplished mathematician Theaetetus pursue to its end – to be sure in the presence of and at the initiative of Socrates – the "right use" of the *technē* proper to counting and calculation for redirecting the whole soul to the source of being and truth. In other words, they complete in deed what is merely prescriptive in the Socratic account of the *eidē*. Their dialectically imageless investigation of the *eidē*, and, more precisely, of the "greatest" (most original) "kinds" (*genē*[1]), is presented in a manner in which the inexactness of the images belonging to Socratic myth is superseded by the exactness of number and the one. (In the *Cratylus*, Socrates calls attention to the crucial difference in exactness between an image and a number by pointing out that an image necessarily lacks attributes of its original, because otherwise it would not be an image but another original, while a number necessarily cannot be missing any part and remain what it is.) Because of their greatest originality, each of these five *genē*, "itself by itself" (*auto kath' auto*), is shown as the necessary presuppositions for the "intelligibility" of any *eidos*. Their investigation is guided by the "nature" of the pure numbers employed by those who are proficient in counting and calculation. However, even with this added exactness, the true manner of being of the *eidē* is proved to exceed *logos*'s ambit, for the simple but profound reason that the intelligible units presupposed by the "know-how" of arithmetical counting to compose the numbers it counts are naturally unsuited to counting the intelligible units that dialectic must presuppose in its imageless investigation of the most original *eidē*. Because Husserl's pure phenomenology grew out of his own investigation of number and its source, Plato's second account of the *eidē* is crucial for understanding phenomenology's relation to traditional philosophy (and especially so because Aristotle's account of mathematical "abstraction" can only be properly apprehended through its critical relation to this second account). Moreover, because this second account demonstrates that the manner of being of the *eidē* is "numerical" without, however, being identical to mathematical numbers, the contents of this demonstration are extremely relevant to both Husserl's pure phenomenological account of the *eidē* and to the major (Heidegger's and Derrida's) criticisms of it. A proper introduction to Husserl's thought must therefore come to grips with these matters themselves, even as they go beyond – as we have already had occasion to notice – the explicit content and competency of his thinking. But that they do not go beyond the ultimate source of the *meaning* of Husserl's thinking is something we shall have occasion to show in the conclusion of our discussion, where we provide the answer to our question of whether the turn to history in the last phase of this thinking remains consistent with the avowed "a-historicality" of its first three stages.

Aristotle's report about Plato's "unwritten teachings" (*agrapha dogmata*), which includes a polemic against Plato's apparent teaching that "the *eidē* are numbers" (*Metaph.* M, 1086a12–13), provides an indispensable context for finding in some of the dialogues themselves veiled references to a genuinely Platonic teaching about "eidetic numbers". This is especially the case in the *Sophist*, where a philosopher and mathematician investigate dialectically the "five" most original *noēta* presupposed by thought whenever speech understands something, namely, the *genē* Motion, Rest, Being, the Other and the Same.

The community (*koinōnia*) of *eidē*

The *Sophist's* discussion of the five greatest kinds is informed by the strange status of the "common thing" (*koinon*) exhibited by the mathematical numbers that are among intelligible objects in comparison with the "common thing" exhibited by non-mathematical intelligible objects. The manner in which the *eidē* of justice and health are shared by more than one thing and are thus common to each of the things that share in them contrasts sharply with the way the things that share in the common thing of a mathematical number are related to what (number) they have in common. Whereas justice and health characterize the many things that share in the *eidos* of each, the many things that have a mathematical number in common are not characterized by the number they have in common. Thus while Socrates and Hippias both share in the *eidos* health and are each healthy, taken together they also have being two in common, although each of them is not two but only one. Hence when it comes to sharing intelligible objects such as the *eidos* health, what each of its "participants" is, both are together as well, whereas when it comes to sharing intelligible objects such as number, what both of them together are, namely two, each of them is not, for it is one (*Hp. mai.* 300a–302b).

The strange *koinon* character of number therefore exhibits a structure that presents an obstacle for any thinking that presupposes that all things that share in intelligible objects must also possess them individually. The obstacle is the "impasse" (*aporia*) that follows the recognition by thought that numbers are intelligible objects for which this presupposition does not hold. Each of the items united by a number is different from the common thing that composes the number, and conversely, the number is different from each of the items that it unites. This *aporia* provides the mathematical key to the Stranger's and Theaetetus' investigation and account of the five greatest *genē*, because their investigation shows that the presupposition that things must possess what it is they have in common does not hold for these most original intelligible objects either.

Beginning with the first three of these objects – Motion, Rest and Being – they investigate what philosophers who presuppose that the whole of Being is composed of two elements (Motion and Rest) address when they say that both and also each of them *is* (*Soph.* 250a–d). In saying that Motion and Rest *are*, they cannot be saying that Motion is identical with Being, because this would presuppose that Rest is not something that is. Likewise, they cannot be saying that Rest is identical with Being, because then Motion would be presupposed not to be. Is Being then addressed as a third thing beside or outside both of them? This is impossible, as it would presuppose that neither Rest nor Motion *is* and that Being, according to its nature, is outside both Rest and Motion (250d). Something at rest or in motion is understandable as something that *is*, whereas something neither moving nor resting is not understandable at all as something that *is*. Thus, if it is presupposed that something that has something in common with another thing must also be characterized as that thing they have in common, it would follow that Motion (itself by itself), by having Being (itself by itself) in common with Rest (itself by itself), would be *identified* as Being (itself by itself), and, in turn, that Rest (itself by itself), by having Being (itself by itself) in common with Motion (itself by itself), would be *identified* as Being (itself by itself): both would be identical with Being and thus with each other. But this is precisely what cannot be presupposed when it comes to understanding what is: that either one of two things that are most opposite to one another *is* what the other one is. If this were presupposed, then what is moving would be resting when it *is* and, conversely, what is resting would be moving in so far as it *is*.

Rather than attempt to resolve this *aporia* of Being, however, the Stranger proposes to Theaetetus that they let the matter rest there and investigate the ways of being together – the "community" (*koinōnia*) – of the *genē* Motion, Rest and Being (251d–253c). The Stranger articulates three: no relation whatsoever between them; all being mutually related; or some being related and some not. The results of the discussion so far rule out both the complete lack of relation between these *genē* as well as all of them being mutually related. They are related in so far as both Motion and Rest *are*; they are not all mutually related in so far as Motion and Rest, being opposites, are not related precisely because something at rest cannot remain what it was – at rest – and be in motion and, conversely, something in motion cannot remain what it was – in motion – and be at rest. Thus the relations between the *genē* Motion, Rest and Being are partial: Motion and Rest, as opposites, do not have a *genos* in common and are thus unrelated, except that, because each *is*, they are in relation to the *genos* Being. Being, as the common thing that unites Motion and Rest, does so in a manner that permits their conjunction as opposites in kind without the terms of this conjunction being based in something that is common to each such that either would encompass completely and therefore be identical with what it is they have in common. Motion and Rest therefore both *are* without either encompassing Being: what they have in common, Being, is not something they share in so far as they are Motion or Rest, but something that they share in so far as Motion and Rest *are*.

The partial community between Motion, Rest and Being exhibited by the Stranger and Theaetetus' investigation brings to light a decisive difference between Being's "common thing" character and that of number, despite the similarity that neither the units that are in community in a number nor the *genē* that are in community in Being can be characterized in terms of the common thing that brings them together. The intelligible objects brought together by the number two are not two, since each is exactly one; and the intelligible objects (*genē*) brought together by the *genos* Being are not Being, but precisely Motion and Rest. In this regard they are similar. But while the units that share in the common thing of a number do not differ from one another and are therefore equal, the *genē* that share in the common thing of the *genos* Being are not only different but most different, opposite.

Eidetic numbers

Aristotle's account of what Plato said in his "unwritten teachings" about eidetic numbers addresses precisely the difference noted here between the community that number brings about and that which the *genos* Being effects. Aristotle reports that Plato distinguished eidetic from mathematical numbers on the basis of their units. Each mathematical number is the unity of a multitude of unchanging units that are alike, while each eidetic number is the unity of unchanging units that are unique (*Metaph.* A, 987b19). The units of mathematical numbers are therefore comparable and capable of combining indiscriminately into any community with one another, while those of an eidetic number are incomparable (*asumblētoi*) (M, ch. 7) and therefore incapable of combining into just any community with each other. Thus the common thing of the *genos* Being (as a whole) that unites a plurality of *genē* (Motion and Rest) exhibits an analogy with the common thing of mathematical number (as a whole) that unites a plurality of *units* (*monads*). In both cases, the unity of a multitude is provided by the common thing of the whole without that whole being partitioned by the multitude: for example, the number two unites units without being partitioned in these units, as each unit is exactly one, not two; so, too, the *genos* Being unites *genē* without being partitioned in these *genē*, as each *genos* (Motion and Rest) is (by itself) precisely not *Being*. However, the analogy between the community of the units united in a mathematical number and that of the elemental *genē* united by the *genos* Being breaks down on the following point. The whole that composes the unity of a mathematical number is not attributable to the units in the multitude that it unites; "two", for instance, is an attribute of neither of the units that are united by the number two, because each is precisely one, not two. The whole that composes the unity of the *genos* Being, however, is attributable to the *genē* in the multitude that is united by this whole, because Being is understandable only if Motion and Rest are presupposed to *be* – without, of course, either being identified as Being itself.

If it is presupposed that the *genē* Motion, Rest and Being, as intelligible objects, are "units" with the same manner of being as the units in mathematical numbers, their number (*arithmos*) would be "three". Motion would be one, Rest another one, and Being a third and final one. But precisely this presupposition was ruled out when the presupposition that the *genos* Being is a third *genos*, and therefore completely separate from the *genē* Motion and Rest, was rejected, because it would follow from this that neither Motion nor Rest would *be* (and therefore share in Being). When it comes to Being, the Stranger and Theaetetus' dialectical enquiry makes its common thing manifest as precisely both Motion and Rest together. The multitude of *genē* that compose Being, therefore, cannot be accounted for on the basis of the presupposition that these *genē* are intelligible objects, like the multitude of ones that compose a number. On this presupposition there are, once more, "three" kinds, Motion, Rest, and Being, whereas the (Stranger and Theaetetus') dialectical examination of this presupposition leads to the better presupposition that Being is not a third kind, but precisely both Motion and Rest together. The presupposition that Being can be made intelligible by employing mathematical numbers therefore cannot withstand dialectical scrutiny, even though Being has a partially "arithmetical" structure, because, like the whole of number, the whole of Being retains its integrity and is not divided among its parts. Yet the non-mathematical but nevertheless "arithmetical" unity that Being is shown to possess in the *Sophist* exhibits the structure of an "*arithmos*" of intelligible objects whose units are *eidē*, which confirms Aristotle's report that Plato distinguished mathematical numbers and *eidē* composed as numbers (*Metaph.* A, 987b15–19; M, 1086a12–13).

The original participation problem and the so-called "separation" (*chōrismos*) thesis

Plato's second account of the *eidē* provides an answer to the question that remains unanswered in his "Socratic" account, about whether the single things in the multitude that "participates" in an *eidos* do so because of the *eidos*'s "presence" in them or because the *eidos* brings about a "community" among them. Participation in the "itself by itself" status of a *genos* is the result of the single things that participate in it being brought together in a manner that establishes their "community" with the "common thing" that characterizes the *genos*. Because this "common thing" is not partitioned in the single things that it establishes as belonging together, the presupposition that it brings them together by being "in" them has to be rejected. The better presupposition is that a *genos* (as a whole) composes the parts that belong together with it (as *its* parts) in a manner that is analogous to the way a number (as a whole) composes its parts together.

Plato's second account of the *eidē* is best characterized as "arithmological" rather than "arithmetical", in recognition of the non-mathematical nature of the units that are united as an "*arithmos*" in an eidetic number (*arithmos eidetikos*). Plato's arithmological account of the *eidē* therefore replaces the Socratic account's metaphorical *logos* of participation with the Stranger and Theaetetus' account's arithmological *logos*. In place of the vague talk of the single things in a multitude "sharing" or "imitating" the *eidos* that is responsible for their name and being, the talk about participation acquires the kind of precision that only the exactness of mathematical number and the (mathematical) one can bring about. This precision, however, is bought at a steep price. On the one hand, it concerns the participation of intelligible objects in one another, both of the *eidē* presupposed in the dialectical passage and of the most original *genē* presupposed by the being of every *eidos*. Thus it leaves unaddressed what is sometimes called the "lower participation problem": that of the participation of the non-eidetic things in the *eidē* that are responsible for their being. On the other hand, it focuses on the inability of *logos* to account for the manner of being of the *eidē* by counting them. (Again, this inability is based in *logos* wanting to count the *genē* of Being, Motion and Rest as three, when in fact there are only two: Motion and Rest.) Not being countable places the manner of being proper to intelligible objects beyond the power of *logos* to provide a complete and a completely clear account of the "beinghood" (*ousia*) of the things in the intelligible realm. Moreover, because these things (*eidē*) are responsible for the being of the things in the visible realm, *logos*'s limit in this regard extends beyond the things in the intelligible realm to those visible things made intelligible by *eidē*.

The greater precision of Plato's second account of the *eidē* over his first thus does not afford it any ultimate advantage in articulating the truth of the "end" (*telos*) of the intelligible realm that (as beyond Being) is the "source" of everything that is. But by "resolving" in the intelligible realm the "participation" problem first encountered in the visible realm, it does permit the relation between the *eidē* of the visible and intelligible realms themselves to be discerned with greater clarity. Just as the *genos* Being (itself by itself) is "separate" (*chōriston*) from the *genē* (Motion and Rest), so, too, is the intelligible realm (as a whole) "separate" from the multitude of things in the visible realm. Therefore, what Plato's so-called "separation" (*chōrismos*) thesis addresses most originally is the "arithmos-structure" proper to the *genos*'s manner of being, which is responsible for composing elements that are fundamentally opposed into parts of a more comprehensive whole. Because participation in this sense is undeniably closer to the "source" of what is than participation in the sense of a multitude of things sharing in the unity of an intelligible thing, the latter sense of participation, that of becoming, with its opposite, Being, may be said to manifest an image of the original participation. In this, and only this sense, is it legitimate in the end to speak (Platonically) of participation as a form of "imitation" – the lower participation imitating the higher.

The common understanding of participation, which identifies it with things in the realm of becoming "imitating" things in the realm of being, is therefore very wide of the mark of how "Platonic" participation looks when the Socratic account of it is dialectically "united" with the arithmological one. Rather than a "two-world theory" of separate realms of becoming and Being that are related as an image to its original, precisely the whole of the image–original relation between becoming and Being is itself seen as an image and therefore an imitation of the whole of the original "participation" proper to the "community of *eidē* (or *genē*)" (*koinōnia ton eidon*). As an image of the original participation relation, the participation of the things that *become* in the things that *are* is a distortion of this original relation. Both the name and the being of the thing that becomes has its source in an *eidos*, which lends itself to the belief that the *noēta* (*eidē*, *genē*) are countable and otherwise related in the same way as the names of the things in the realm of becoming that "share" in them are related to those things. But precisely this presupposition must give way, at the pinnacle of dialectical investigation, to the *nous*'s seeing of the uncountable but nevertheless "arithmological" manner of being proper to the "greatest kinds". At this, the final, level of dialectical insight, the *noēta* presupposed by *logos* (*eidē* and *genē*) are not numerically related as the silent or audible words (*onomata*) that correspond to them are. *Logos*'s counting of the latter (*onomata*) in order to comprehend the former (*eidē* and *genē*) is therefore misleading.

What *nous* sees in the realm of Being cannot be spoken of with complete clarity, because the three most basic presuppositions "natural" to *logos*'s understanding of the things that become do not hold for understanding the community of *eidē*. These are: (i) a number is composed of a multitude of discrete things that can be counted and any one of these things can be added to any other to produce their number; (ii) the *eidē* that things have in common also characterize each of the things that have them in common (horse and dog have animal in common, and both a horse *is* an animal and a dog *is* an animal); (iii) opposites do not have anything in common and therefore cannot be combined or otherwise "harmonized".

The "clarity" that these presuppositions lend to *logos* when speaking of "what is" is sacrificed in Plato's account of the "community of *eidē*" for the sake of addressing what it is *logos* speaks of when it says of "what is" *that* it is, and thus addresses the "beinghood" (*ousia*) of what is. Plato's answer seems to be that what is addressed is a comprehensive *genos* that, itself by itself, composes opposite elements as parts of its greater whole. The pair of *genē* that compose Being, Motion and Rest, when interrogated about what, in turn, is responsible for them, apparently have their cause in another pair of *genē*, the Same and the Other (*Soph.* 255b–d). The Same is responsible for each *genos* maintaining its identity (itself by itself) as what it is with the other *genē* with which it is in community; and the Other is responsible for relating the diverse members of this community, since each *genos*, precisely in so far as it is self-same, is the others' other. The Same and the Other, as the causes of Being, are therefore more comprehensive *genē* than Being, Motion and Rest, because they are in community with all of them (which is why they are their causes), whereas Motion and Rest are not in community with each other but only with Being.

Not-Being and the problems of deception and falsehood

The *genos* of the Other, as that which is responsible for the diversity of *genē*, that is, for each one *not* being the other (the other *genē*, not the *genos* of the Other), is therefore responsible for "Not-Being" having the status of something that necessarily *is*. Motion and Rest (each taken by itself) are *not* Being, just as the Same and the Other are *not* Being. But because all of these *genē* are in community with the *genos* Being, they nevertheless also "partake of Being" (*Soph.* 256e). Hence "it's necessarily the case that Not-Being *is*, both in the case of Motion and with respect to all the *genē*" (256d), although not in a sense that maintains that Not-Being is the opposite of Being. Rather, Not-Being *is* in the sense that each of the *genē* is *not* any of the other *genē* and also *not* any of the things that are sensible. Thus "we will correctly say" (256e) of the *genē*, and "for the same reasons", that they are *not* and that they *are*, that they are beings. The reason they are *not* is because each is other than the others and the reason they *are* is because each nevertheless partakes in Being and therefore is something that is, namely, a being.

Plato draws three interrelated conclusions from the account of the "five" greatest kinds: (i) that with regard to each of the *eidē*, Being is many and Not-Being is unlimited in multitude; (ii) Not-Being is to be "counted as one *eidos* among the many beings that are" (258c); and (iii) that opining and saying what is *not*, namely false opinions and false speech, involves the mixing of Not-Being with both opinion and speech. This mixing is directly tied to the problem of image (*eidolon*) and original, that is, to the image's Not-Being in relation to something that *is*.

The most fundamental falsehood (*pseudos*) for Plato is a false "appearance" or "apparition" (*phantasma*), namely, what *seems* to be like something but is not like it. The appearing (*phantasia*) responsible for an appearance is most often treated by Plato as false, because its *seeming* distorts and therefore appears unlike what it is supposed to look like (236b). Nevertheless, some appearances are sometimes true (264b), which signals that the source of falsehood is beyond the contrariety of Not-Being and Being and, therefore (like the source of truth), beyond Being itself. This is the case because in order for something to be opined about something, said about something, or to appear (*phainetai*) in relation to something in such a way that things that are *not* are taken to *be*, things that are *other* have to be taken in a way that takes them for the *same*. That it is this *mistaken* exchange of the two causes of Being, namely, the Other and the Same, that is responsible for falsehood (an exchange that cuts across *logos*, *doxa* and *phainomena*), and not solely the speech that asserts or denies that something is or is not true, comes into view with Plato's consideration of how "deception" (*apatē*) arises.

Deception comes about once it is established that "the false *is*" (260c); that is, the false has *being*. Because of this, "it's necessary that everything is full of both images (*eidola*) [what *looks* like something] and likenesses (*eikones*) [what *is* like something] and appearance (*phantasia*) [what makes something *seem* to be]" (*ibid.*). The false has being because *logos*, as "one of the kinds [*genē*] that *are*" (260a), comes about "through the interweaving of the *eidē*" (259e), including the *eidos* of Not-Being. This *eidos* comes into view when the way that the unlimited multitude of Not-Being comes about is considered. While Being is many with respect to the other *eidē*, it "itself is other than the others [i.e. the other *eidē* and all the things that are sensible]" (257a), such that "however many the others are, in relation to so many, Being is *not*" (*ibid.*). Being is *not* these others, in so far as, not being them, "it is itself one" (*ibid.*),[2] whereas they "are unlimited in multitude". Thus, when "Not-Being" is said, what is said is not something that is opposite to "Being" but only something that is "other". The "not" placed before a name, for example, before "great" or "beautiful", proclaims "something other than those names, or rather proclaims something other than the things to which the names uttered after the negative are given" (257bc). What the negative "signifies (*semainein*) is not the opposite" (257b) of what is meant by the name that comes after it, but something different, in the cases at hand, something small or equal, or something not-beautiful.

The *eidos* of Not-Being is therefore of the nature of the Other, in the precise sense that "even though this nature is one" (257d), it is composed of separate parts, each one of which concerns something that has its own name. Thus, like knowledge, which is one although there are many "arts" (*technai*) and many kinds of knowledge, the nature of the Other is one although it "appears (*phainetai*) all cut up into pieces" (257c). In the case of the beautiful, there is some part of the Other that is opposed to it, called "not-beautiful", which "is the other of the nature of the beautiful and nothing else" (257d). The not-beautiful is therefore "a certain separate part within one *genos* of beings and opposed to something among beings" (257e). Among a multitude of beings having a "common look" there is then an aspect of that "common look" that is other than the "beautiful" aspect of the "common look" characteristic of some other multitude of beings. The not-beautiful is therefore a being that is opposed to another being, which means that the beautiful, no more than the not-beautiful, belongs to what *is*. Likewise the not-great, the not-just and so on so belong, because the nature of the Other has appeared among the things that *are*. A part of the Other may therefore be opposed to a part of Being, and this opposition "has beinghood [*ousia*] to no less degree" (258b) than "Being itself, for it signifies (*semainousa*) not something contrary to Being but only this much: its other" (*ibid.*). The Other can be said to *be* because it partakes of Being, although, being its "other", it is of necessity Not-Being. Being, likewise, partakes of the Other, and is other than all the other *eidē* and *genē* and therefore none of them but only itself. Being, then, is "indisputably *not* thousands upon thousands of things; and each one of those things and all together in many ways *are* and in many ways are *not*" (259b).

Precisely this, the recognition of multiple ways of being and not-being proper to each and all of those innumerable things that are Not-Being is the key to Plato's account of how "speech that is truly and in its being false" (263d) comes into being. Speech is necessarily "about something [*tinos*]" (262e) and it is impossible for it to be otherwise, namely, for it not to be about something. Not-Being, understood as the opposite of Being, is, of course, not something, and therefore it can be applied neither to Being nor to "something [*ti*]" (237c). However, because each and all the things that are Not-Being both *are* and *are not* in many ways, things that are *not* may be said to *be* about something. About Theaetetus, who is sitting and not flying, it may be said that he flies. Independently of whether false speech like this arises deliberately (for instance, as in the *Sophist*, when the philosopher is making a point) or unintentionally (anytime anyone speaks about what they are unwittingly mistaken about), Plato seems to indicate that the source of the falsehood lies deeper than *logos*'s assertion or denial that something is or is not qualified in some way. For in order to assert (about something) things that *are not* as if they *are*, things that are *other* (than something) must be said as the *same* (as it). Moreover, as long as things that are *other* than something are recognized as such and therefore kept separate from things that are the *same* as it (and likewise recognized as such), it is impossible to assert just this: that things that are *other* are the *same* (*Tht.* 190c–e).

Falsehood therefore must come about when things that are *other* are taken for things that are the *same*. When this exchange is deliberate, the false speech that follows it is dissembling. When it is unintentional, the false speech that follows it is mistaken. In either case, the ultimate source of the saying of things that *are not* as if they *are* is the exchange of the two sources of the *genos* Being, and not the assertion or denial that says erroneous things, for that follows their knowing or unknowing exchange. This exchange therefore has "genealogical" priority over the *eidos* of Not-Being's dissembling or non-dissembling mixing with *logos*. Because of this, the Stranger in the *Sophist* can ask: "Isn't it already manifest that these *genē* – *dianoia* and *doxa* and also *phantasia* – all arise in our souls as false as well as true?" (*Soph.* 263d). This is already manifest, because the intermingling of Not-Being with each of these *genē*, albeit in different ways, follows – as in the case of speech – the exchange of the Other and the Same.

The *genē* of thinking, speech, opinion and appearance (*phantasia*)

In order to understand this priority, what the *genos* is for each and how they differ from one another must first be grasped. In the case of the *genos* thinking (*dianoia*), it turns out that it is the "same" as speech's *genos* (*Soph.* 263e), with one exception: thinking occurs without voice, as the "soul's inner conversation (*dialogos*) with itself" (*ibid.*), while speech (*logos*) flows through the mouth as a vocal stream. In the words (*logoi*) of both voiceless and spoken speech there is assertion and denial, either of which, when mistaken or dissembling, is responsible for falsehood and therefore deception. Assertion and denial that arise in the soul's silent conversation by itself have the common look of the *genos* opinion (*doxa*) and are called only by that name. When the things that belong to the *genos* opinion do not arise in the soul by itself (in silent thinking) but through sensing, they have the common look of the *genos* appearance (*phantasia*) and therefore make something *appear*. When one says, "'it appears' [*phainetai*]" (264b), precisely "the mixture [*symmeixis*] of sensing and opinion" is meant, a mixture that yields sense perception. Hence, when opinion "is present to someone not by itself (*kath' auto*) but through sensing (*di aisthēseōs*)" (264a), it cannot "correctly be called anything other than *phantasia*" (*ibid.*).

Each of these *genē* is most obviously "akin [*suggenōn*]" (264b) to speech in the sense that like it, they too share in the things (assertion and denial) that belong to the *genos* of opinion, and thus can sometimes be false. Moreover, because the assertion and denial proper to opinion is the "final result of thinking [*apoteleutēsis dianoias*]" (264a), they also share in thinking's *genos*. In the case of the *genos* of *phantasia*, then, it is important to emphasize that its very composition as a *genos* involves another *genos*, opinion, as it comes about when opinion's characteristic assertion or denial is mixed with sensing. Because opinion is therefore a part of *phantasia* but distinct from sensing, it follows that for Plato "sensing" and "sense perception" are different. Plato's account of their difference establishes at once *doxa*'s autonomy from bodily sensing and its locus as the source of the exchange of the *same* and the *other* that is responsible for falsehood.

Sensing involves "something of ourselves that's the same" (*Tht.* 184d) and that belongs to our body as it reaches white and black things, high and low tones, hot things, hard things, light things, sweet things and so on. Some of these things are sensed through different "senses [*aisthēseis*]" (*ibid.*), which are "powers [*dunameōs*]" (185a) of the body that enable it, for instance, to see and hear "through [*dia*]" (184c) the eyes and ears "as though they're implements [*organiōn*]" (184d). Things sensed through different senses, in the case at hand those through hearing and sight, "are incapable (*adunaton*) of being sensed through another one" (185a), which means that hearing cannot sense those things sensed through sight, and sight those things sensed through hearing. To think both together therefore does not involve sensing them together through one or the other organ or, indeed, through any sense organ, because each is only capable of reaching those things in its power. Sound *and* colour, therefore, cannot both be sensed together. That "the pair of them *is*", that "each is other than the other and the same as itself", and, finally, that "both together are two, but each is one" (185b), is something likewise incapable of being sensed through any of the bodily powers. However, rather than the many senses "sitting in us as in wooden horses" (184d) – that is, as separate powers in discrete bodily organs – they "all converge into some one look (*idea*) ... with which we *perceive* whatever is sensed" (*ibid.*) through these organs.

This "one look" is the "soul itself, through itself" (185e), whose "power through the tongue [i.e. *logos*]" (185c) reveals "what's common (*koinon*) to all things" (*ibid.*), and, first of all, to the things sensed through each "special organ [*organon idion*]" (185d). To these and other things "the names 'is' and 'is not'" (*ibid.*) are attached by the soul, as well as "likeness and unlikeness, and what's the same and other, and also about one and the rest of number [beginning with two] having to do with them" (*ibid.*). When the soul "looks [*episkopein*]" at things "through the powers that belong to the body" (185e), that is, through the senses, and senses, for instance, "the hardness of what's hard, and likewise the softness of what's soft" (186b), it is called "sensing". When the soul "attempts [*peiratai*] to judge [*krinein*]" (*ibid.*) the "beinghood [*ousia*]" of what is sensed "by going back over" what is sensed "and comparing [*symballousa*] them to one another", it is "called having an opinion" (187a). In this way, the soul tries to make, in the present example, a judgement about the both of them, "what the pair of them are", their oppositeness, and in turn the "beinghood" of this oppositeness. Moreover, it is precisely when the soul "occupies itself, by itself, with the things that are [*ta onta*]" (187a) in this way that the "mixing of sensing and opinion" (*Soph.* 264b) that is *phantasia* comes about and therewith the appearance of what appears in sense *perception*.

The origin of false opinion, false speech and false appearance in the confusion of the same and the other

According to Plato, because "forming an opinion is speaking to oneself, no one in speaking or forming an opinion about both of two things, and touching on both of them with his soul, could say and have the opinion that one thing is another" (*Tht.* 190c). Moreover, the same thing is true when the soul is "having an opinion that is about only one of them, and not at all about the other one" (190d), namely, "one will never have the opinion that one thing is another" (*ibid.*). Thus, so long as the soul's forming of an opinion both distinguishes what is the same from what is other and either compares any two things or opines about only one of them in a manner that its judgement "touches" on them, "it's out of one's power to have the opinion that one thing is another" (*ibid.*). There can therefore be no falsehood in what the soul opines about so long as it neither identifies what has the look of the Same with what has the look of the Other,[3] nor distinguishes them and does not take what has the look of the Other for what has the look of the Same,[4] nor, finally, again in distinguishing them it does not take what has the look of the Same to have the look of the Other.[5]

False opinion can therefore come about only when the soul forms an opinion that either identifies a thing that has the look of the Same with a thing that has the look of the Other, or, despite distinguishing what has these looks, still exchanges them in a manner that confuses either one with the other. It is not in the soul's power to do this when it is "touching" (190c–d) the things it opines about and forms an opinion that judges about both of two things or about only one of them. Therefore a false opinion that is not the result of dissembling must arise through an exchange of things that are the same with things that are other, an exchange that is beyond the power of the soul to recognize at the time it is forming the opinion. Two conditions have the capacity of bringing about such a failure of recognition: (i) the soul forgets what it knows long enough to confuse (in its having an opinion) things that it knew previously to have the look of the Same for things that it knew previously to have the look of the Other, either by taking what is other as what is the same or taking what is the same as what is other; (ii) the soul, not "touching" the thing or things about which it tries to make a judgement by having an opinion, exchanges the looks of the Same and the Other and has an opinion that makes what appears (*phainetai*) *seem* to be like something. When this opinion arises in the soul through sensing, the *phantasia* (sense perception) that brings it about is false and what appears is therefore an "apparition" (*phantasma*).

Either of these two conditions responsible for false opinion brings about deception in the soul, because not only does the soul think it knows what it does not know, but also it is not in the soul's power to recognize this. That is, were it in the soul's power to recognize that it is exchanging what it knows to be different – the Same and Other – and therefore mistaking something that has the look of the one for something that has the look of the other, it would not be in its power to make the exchange. But having made the exchange, things that are *not* are said to *be* (by either asserting what is *not* or denying what *is*) and, with this, non-dissembling falsehood (*pseudos*) in thought, opinion and sense perception comes into being. Deception (*apatē*) therefore arises precisely with the soul's unwitting thinking, opining or perceiving that something *is* what it is *not*. Plato draws two conclusions from the *recognition* that something like deception *is*: that "all things" are full of "what looks like something" and that some of these looks "are what is like something" while others only "seem to be".

Deception and the problem of distinguishing true from false appearances

The recognition that deception *is* brings with it the philosophical task of attempting to distinguish from among the "images" (*eidolon*) that fill everything those whose "looks" are likenesses (*eikones*) of something from those whose "looks" only *seem* like something and are therefore apparitions (*phantasma*). This task is called for by the very nature of deception itself, the power of which makes untrustworthy the conclusion that the appearances of things always coincide with their true being. When a soul is deceived, appearances whose "looks" only *seem* to be likenesses of that which appears are indistinguishable to *that* soul from appearances whose "looks" are likenesses of that which appears. This is why the Stranger says that from the *being* of falsehood it follows that everything is full of both kinds of images, likenesses and apparitions; absent a reliable criterion for distinguishing between the two kinds of images of things, the soul has no way of knowing whether what it takes to be the appearance of something is a true *likeness* or only a distorting *seeming*. The task, then, of searching for such a criterion is accomplished through (*dia*) *logos* – literally, in dialogue – although not all dialogue for Plato is philosophical. Only dialogue that presupposes the following in its investigation of the truth of what *is* is philosophical: (i) that sensing is different from knowledge and therefore that opinion is different from sense perception; (ii) that true opinion is also different from knowledge and that knowledge is therefore inaccessible to opinion; and, finally, (iii) that knowledge is different from an "account" (*logos*) added to a true opinion and therefore that knowledge is something other the being (*on*) of *logos*.

That (i) must be presupposed for a dialogue to be philosophical is established by the Socratic account of the *eidē*, which shows that a *logos* that asserts that "sensing" is knowledge commits the error of failing to distinguish the same and the other and is therefore contradictory.[6] That is, something other than sensing, namely, the intelligible beings presupposed by knowledge, is not distinguished from what is the same as sensing. The dialogue of a soul that fails to make this distinction is therefore blind to the invisible looks of the *eidē* because it fails to distinguish these looks not only from what its soul is "touching" in its sensing (e.g. colour, sound, etc.), but it also fails to distinguish them from the appearance of what appears in sense perception. The intelligible being (*noēton*) of the *eidos* is therefore not distinguished from the sense perception of what appears and is as a result identified with it, with the consequence that what appears only *seems* to be and is therefore an "apparition" (*phantasma*). In order to "see through" the apparition the soul must arrive at the recognition that "common things" such as likeness and unlikeness, one and number, Being and Not-Being, are incapable of appearing to sensing and that therefore another power of the soul must be involved in their being attributed by the soul to beings. Opinion, as the soul's power to compare the beings that it is in touch with through the body's senses and to attempt to make judgements about what is common to them, must therefore be recognized as being different from the sense perception brought about by its attempted judgements. Precisely this recognition is *not* made by a soul that fails to distinguish the intelligible being of the *eidos* from what it is touching in its sensing. And the failure to make this distinction is the sign that this soul is deceived and therefore thinks that it knows what it does not know; in this case, it thinks that the being of what appears is the same as what it senses.

That (ii) must be presupposed is also established by the Socratic account of the *eidē*, when it shows that the power of opinion's attempt to make judgements about the "common things" that are incapable of appearing to sense perception is limited. Because these "common things" cannot be known through sense perception, opinion must investigate them by employing dialectic, which posits them, hypothetically, as already known. Opinion's power to cloak the "unknown" in the guise of the "known" at work in dialectic is therefore inseparable from its positing of knowledge as something that – besides opinion – is known. Because, however, the unknown that is opined as known can be investigated only by attempting to make judgements that cannot have a source in anything other than still more opinions, the knowledge sought by Socratic dialectic necessarily remains beyond the reach of the opinion-making that initiates each step of its enquiry. That is, so long as the soul's search for *knowledge* of the unknown is mediated by its *opinion* that knowledge is something different from opinion, its search will be characterized definitively by its *lack* of knowledge of the *knowledge* it posits as being different from its *opinion*. The claim that true opinion is knowledge therefore takes something that appears through opinion – the *unknown* knowledge that is posited as different from the opinion that posits it – to be that through which it appears, namely the opinion positing it. That through which this unknown knowledge appears is therefore taken to *be* that which appears and thus the appearing inseparable from opinion *seems* to be what it is *not*. This claim mistakes something that is other than opinion – knowledge – for something that is the same as opinion and hence makes a false opinion. False opinion therefore appears to the soul as an "apparition" (*phantasma*), that is, as an image whose looks *seem* to be – but, in truth, are not – a likeness to what appears (*phainetai*).

The Socratic recognition of this "seeming" and the claim that follows it, that knowledge is different from true opinion, is limited, however, by its reliance on images to mark the very distinction between images whose appearances *are* like something and images whose appearances only *seem* to be what appears. The nature of the difference between true opinion and knowledge therefore necessarily remains obscure in the Socratic account of the *eidē*. It remains for Plato's second account of the *eidē* to show that the Socratic distinction between true opinion and knowledge has its source in something whose appearance must be sought elsewhere than in any image, and, most pointedly, elsewhere than in the "spoken images (*eidōla*) of all things" (*Soph.* 234c).

The community of speech (*logos*) with Being and Not-Being

That for a dialogue to be philosophical it must be presupposed that knowledge is something different from an account added to true opinion (point [iii] above) and that, therefore, knowledge is something other than what can be established directly by the being of *logos*, is something that only the philosopher and mathematician together can establish.

Thus the Stranger and Theaetetus investigate the words (*onomata*) that compose a *logos* and its means of "making manifest [*deloun*]" (*Soph.* 261e) the beinghood (*ousia*) of something by signifying it through voice. Two *genē* of words are identified, verb (*rhēma*) and names (*onomata*), the former characterized by its "manifestation [*delōma*]" (262a) of the action (*praxis*) pertaining to this beinghood, the latter by its "vocal mark (*sēmeion*)" (*ibid.*) applied to those who do (or what does) the action (*pragma*). Speech proper is composed of the commingling of at least one verb and one name to say something about something done by something or somebody, and to do so in a manner that what it "tells [*perainei*]" (262d) about the thing done and the doing has to be "qualified" in one of two ways. Speech therefore either (i) states things about the thing done and the doing as they *are* or (ii) states things about them that are *not* as they *are*. In either case, speech accomplishes this by "putting together [*synthesis*]" (263a) the thing done and the doing by means of a name and a verb to manifest thereby its beinghood, albeit in the first case a speech that is true arises and in the second "there arises a speech that is truly and in its very being *false*" (263d).

Plato's investigation of *logos* as one of the *genē* that *are* is situated between the fear that "no limit will ever appear" (261b) in the attempt to show that speech and opinion appear in community with Not-Being and the "observation (*katanoein*)" (264b) that false opinion and false speech "were found sooner" (*ibid.*) than anticipated. This signals both that the dialectical investigation of *logos* is capable of yielding the "appearance" of a being (*logos*) that is not dissembling and that the limit that has appeared to the enquiry into this being's community with Not-Being, while sufficient for the purpose at hand,[7] may not be the final one when it comes to the deeper dimensions of the problem of Not-Being and Being.

The sought-after limit to the enquiry is brought "to appear [*phainetai*]" (261d) in the same manner that the community of *eidē* was investigated, thereby forestalling the feared "altogether endless task" (264d) of searching for false opinion and speech. Specifically, Plato shows the community of speech with Not-Being by exhibiting the conversation of a philosopher (Stranger) and mathematician (Theaetetus) as it brings to appearance speech's most basic unit, most basic necessity, most basic function, and most basic ways of being qualified.

The being of speech (*logos*)

The most basic unit of speech is the fitting combination of a name with a verb, the criterion for which is their interweaving in someone's utterance in a manner that manifests any action or inaction of something and that it is or is not. As was said, the most basic necessity of speech is that it be "about something [*tinos*]" (262e), such that it is "impossible for it not to be about anything" (*ibid.*). Speech's most basic function is to speak about "the things that are or come to be or have come to be or will come to be" (262d) by telling things about what or who is (was or will be) doing what is (was or will be) being done. And finally, speech's combination of the thing done (*pragma*) with the doing (*praxis*) must be qualified as either stating about something the things that are as they are – true speech – or stating things other than they are – false speech.

The "shortest and first speech" (262c) is identified as "when someone says 'man learns'". This speech is the shortest when measured by both the standard of the most basic unit of speech – a name and a verb – and by the standard of speech's most basic necessity – to be about something. Because that "about which [*peri ou*]" (263a) this speech is, is the *genos* "man" and not this or that man, according to Plato it is a shorter speech than another speech whose length would be the same if measured solely by the standard of speech's most basic unit. Thus the length of the speech "Theaetetus sits", which (within the context of the Stranger's and Theaetetus' interlocution) is about the man with whom the one who utters it is speaking, is not characterized as the shortest but as "moderate [*metrios*]" (*ibid.*). Despite both speeches having the same length when measured by the standard proper to the most basic unit of speech, the second speech is nevertheless maintained by Plato to be longer when measured by the standard proper to speech's most basic necessity (having to be about something), apparently because that which it is about specifies within the *genos* man the man (Theaetetus) with whom the one who utters it (the Stranger) is speaking.

That the "about which" characteristic of speech's most basic necessity is a more decisive standard for determining the length of a speech than its most basic unit (a name and verb) is highlighted by the fact that the Stranger's speech, "Theaetetus, with whom I am now conversing, flies" (*ibid.*), is presented by Plato as being "with the utmost necessity one of the shortest" (263c) speeches that could be made. Even though this speech is longer than the speech "Theaetetus sits" when measured by the standard of speech's most basic unit,[8] it is shorter when measured by the standard of speech's most basic necessity, its "about which" characteristic. This is the case because the first speech is about a thing done and its doing that has being, while the second speech is about a thing done and doing that does not have being. Speech about Not-Being is therefore emphatically shorter than speech about Being. From this it follows that the combination and telling of a thing done and its doing that has the look of Not-Being – which must be qualified as false – is of necessity shorter than the combination and telling of a thing done and its doing that has the look of Being – which must be qualified as true. Speech about Not-Being is not shorter than the first and shortest speech "man learns", however, presumably because even though this speech is about something that has Being, what it tells about that which it is about is presupposed by any speech, including, therefore, a speech that is about (and therefore in community with) Not-Being. That is, false speech no less than true speech presupposes that the one uttering it has learned, which is why that "about which" the speech "man learns" tells is necessarily the first and shortest, as it is the indispensable condition for any speech and therefore for speech itself. Being the indispensable condition for speech itself, it therefore has priority over any given speech and is therefore in this sense "first". And it is the "shortest" because the content of the learning is not specified.

Plato's portrayal of the spoken original word images composing the Stranger and Theaetetus' interlocution about speech in written word images makes manifest, as a non-dissembling appearance, not only the community of Not-Being with speech but also its community with Being. Plato's written words do so by manifesting and therefore making appear the beinghood of speech itself in the two speeches uttered by the Stranger to Theaetetus and in Theaetetus' speeches in response to the Stranger's invitation to tell what each of his speeches is about. Speech's beinghood is therefore made manifest in the interlocution between the Stranger and Theaetetus in which Theaetetus tells the Stranger what or who is doing what is done in the Stranger's two speeches, each of which combines (by means of a name and verb) the thing done and the doing itself. What is made manifest and therefore appears in this interlocution is speech's power to make the beinghood of the something it is about manifest and therefore appear, a power that originates in its *being about something*.

Each of the Stranger's speeches weaves together a name (Theaetetus) and verb (sits/flies) to combine a thing done (*pragma*) and the doing itself (*praxis*) and thereby to tell things about someone (Theaetetus). When the things told by the speech about the doing of the thing done by Theaetetus are told as they *are*, that which the speech is about appears as it *is*. When the things told by the speech about the doing of the thing done by Theaetetus are other than they *are*, that about which the speech is about appears as it is *not*. Even in the latter case, however, the speech is about something (Theaetetus). Indeed, speech in which nothing is spoken of is "impossible [*adunatōn*]" (*Soph*. 263c): only when an utterance's fitting combination of words is directed to someone or something does speech arise and it arises in precisely the appearance (either as it is or as it is not) of that to which the utterance is directed.

The community of speech (*logos*) with Being and Not-Being: the appearing of likeness and apparition (*phantasma*)

The being of Not-Being, the *eidos* of which has already appeared in the investigation of the *genos* of the Other, is what is responsible for the things that *are not* as they *are* about Theaetetus (or about anyone or anything else) nevertheless being things that *appear*. The Stranger's speech about Theaetetus that says things about him that *are not* as if they *were* nevertheless says things about him that *are* done, although they are *other* than the things that *are* done by him. Their Not-Being in relation to Theaetetus therefore does not preclude their being in relation to other things, because with regard to Theaetetus or anything else, it has already been established that many things *are* and many things *are not*. Speech's telling of the things done as they *are* and also its telling of them as they *are not*, however, is not what is responsible in either case for the appearing of their appearance as they are or are not. Plato makes this explicit when he has Theaetetus reply "just about [*schedon*]" (*Soph.* 263b) to the Stranger's claim that false speech "says things that *are not* as if they *were*" (*ibid.*) but "exactly [*komidē*]" (*ibid.*) when the Stranger characterizes such speech as "saying things that *are*, which are *other* than the things that *are*" (*ibid.*). For what allows speech to be able to say things that are *not* as if they *were* is the confusion of what is other and what is the same, as the Stranger's account of such speech "truly and in its very being" (263d) makes clear. This account characterizes false speech as the saying of things about someone or something in such a way that "things that are *other* are said as the *same* and therefore things that are *not* are said to *be*" (*ibid.*), and Theaetetus' response to it – "very true" (*ibid.*) – contains no hint of the qualification contained in his response to the account of false speech in which the confusion of the other and the same is unmentioned.

Speech, therefore, notwithstanding its power to manifest and therefore make appear the appearance belonging to the beinghood of something, is no more responsible for the appearance being as it *is* than it is for its being as it is *not*. Rather, it is responsible for the *manifestation* of these appearances when, in conjunction with opinion, things about something or someone are asserted or denied. Likewise, it is neither responsible for the judgement that affirms as true the asserted or denied (as the case may be) appearance of the beinghood of something made manifest by its speaking nor the judgement that affirms as false its apparition. For Plato, that the doing told about in speech is as it is in the thing done, or, in other words, that the community (*koinōnia*) that arises from the proper fitting together of a multitude of names and verbs uttered by someone makes manifest the thing done (*pragma*) itself of the something (*tinos*) spoken about (and therefore in community with speech) is therefore not a matter of speech but of opinion. What appears in the Stranger and Theaetetus' interlocution about speech is its manner of being as a "community", first of the properly fitting verbs and names that manifest the doings of actions (*praxei*) and things done (*pragmata*), then of speech itself together with the Being and Not-Being of that which it is about, and, finally, of the "qualified" telling (via assertion and denial) of the doing with the thing done itself of that which it is about. The "common thing" (*koinon*) brought about by each of these communities is speech in its wholeness, which encompasses and therefore exceeds the elements that in "community" compose its parts. Hence the community of properly fitting verbs and names brings about the common thing of speech proper, namely the *making manifest* of the beinghood of something. This "making manifest" cannot be reduced to what is made manifest by either the names or verbs taken singly, and it is therefore a whole whose wholeness exceeds that of these, its parts. The community of the common thing characteristic of speech with Being and Not-Being brings about, respectively, the common things of the appearances of that which *is* and that which *is not*. Either appearance, as the "common thing" that emerges from the respective communities of speech and Being and Not-Being, cannot be reduced to the "elements" belonging to these communities, namely speech and Being and speech and Not-Being. And, finally, the common thing that emerges from the community of speech's qualified telling of the doing with the thing done itself of that which it is about, namely its assertion or denial, likewise cannot be reduced to either this telling or the doing of the thing done.

Determining the quality of this last common thing – that is, of what is asserted or denied of the thing done in the telling of the doing – as either true or false is also a matter of speech being in community with opinion. Its judgement discerns whether the combination of the doing and the thing done that arises in speech manifests the thing done's beinghood as it appears from *itself* or as an apparition that only *seems* to manifest its beinghood. Plato's most developed account of true and false speech, however, addresses it only as it appears in the Stranger and Theaetetus' interlocutionary observation (*katanoēsis*) of the appearance that appears in *phantasia*'s mixture of sensing with opinion; namely, in sense perception. Plato therefore limits the discussion of true and false speech to speech's power to manifest the beinghood of what appears through the senses, a power that is in community with the opinion that *attempts* to make a judgement about what is "common" to beinghood's appearance, for example likeness and unlikeness, what's the same and other, what is and what is not, and also one and the number two having to do with them. The reason that opinion's judgement through the senses comes up short in its attempt to make a judgement about what is common to the beinghood of the appearance has already been shown in the Socratic account of the *eidē*. The "looks" that characterize the *eidē* are not seen through the eyes but through speech's understanding, which reflects them through its invisible word images. The opinion that attempts to make a judgement about the *eidē* that is confined to sense perception therefore does not distinguish the intelligible being (*noēton*) of the *eidos* from what appears through the senses. The result of this is that the sensible appearance only *seems* to be what is truly responsible (the *eidos*) for its appearing, and therefore this appearance is an apparition (*phantasma*), not a likeness, of the looks that are truly responsible for it.

The Stranger and Theaetetus' interlocution manifests precisely how speech's understanding "reflects" and therefore has the power to make appear that which it is about, albeit only in the case of a thing done that appears through the senses (Theaetetus sitting; Theaetetus flying). That which is responsible for the appearing of the sensible appearance, and, more precisely, that which is responsible for its beinghood, therefore does not appear through their interlocution about what speech is and its community with Being and Not-Being. The *genos* of Being (the community of the *genē* of Rest and Motion), along with that which is responsible for the *eidos* of Not-Being (the *genos* Other) and that of Being (the *genos* Same) – in short, the five greatest kinds – therefore do not appear in Plato's most focused and advanced account of *logos* as a being.

The limit of *logos*'s power of manifestation: appearances of the greatest kinds as likenesses

This is no accident. The greatest kinds have already appeared through the Stranger and Theaetetus' interlocutionary investigation of Not-Being and Being, and their manner of appearing emerged at the exact moment it became apparent that the source of the mathematician's speech about numbers, the "one", was no match for the philosopher's speech about Being and Not-Being. It appeared as no match for the former, because the "units" of Being – Rest and Motion – do not lend themselves to being counted as homogeneous mathematical ones. And it appeared as no match for the latter, because whenever anyone says "something [*ti*]" they "must say some one thing" (*Soph.* 237d). The word "something" "is in fact a mark [*semeion*] of one" (*ibid.*) and, because one and number are among the things that *are*, it appeared impossible "to utter or think Not-Being all by itself" (238c): that is, without Being. Thus, once it appears through their dialogue about speech's being that speech's most basic necessity is that it be "about something", it becomes apparent why the "doing" of the "thing done" that is combined by and told in speech cannot speak with complete clarity about the beinghood of the greatest kinds: by necessarily being about something, that "which is spoken about in speech" (*legomenon*) is marked as "one", and the manner of being of each of the greatest kinds has appeared to be precisely that which – according to the greatest necessity – cannot be apprehended as "one".

Plato's criterion for making the distinction between "likeness" and "apparition" therefore appears when the *logoi* of the philosopher and mathematician's interlocutions about (i) the greatest kinds and (ii) the being of *logos* are brought together. The criterion appears, on the one hand, with respect to *phantasia* (sense perception). That which appears through the community proper to speech's spoken images (names and verbs) is a likeness when what is the *same* as the appearance through the senses of what is spoken about (the doing of the thing done) is made manifest by a speaking that tells things about this appearance that are the *same* as it *is*. That which appears through speech is an apparition when what is the *same* as the appearance through the senses of what is spoken about is made manifest by a speaking that – unwittingly – tells about it things that are other, and therefore are *not* the same as it *is*. Apparition (*phantasma*) is therefore a falsehood (*pseudos*) that appears as a deception (*apatē*): the soul to which it appears does not observe (*katanoein*) that the appearance of the beinghood that it judges to *be* is not as it judges it to *be* and therefore only *seems* to *be*. Because the soul that is in the condition of being deceived does not know it is in this condition, its acquisition of the knowledge that the appearance determinative of this condition is an apparition and therefore a falsehood is something that presupposes *this* soul's dialectical movement *beyond* its deception.

On the other hand, the criterion for the distinction between "likeness" and "apparition" also appears with respect to the *eidē*. That which appears through speech's spoken images is an apparition when the common things that appear through sense perception – the *eidē* – are spoken about as the *same* as the appearance of what appears through the senses. Seeing through this apparition, by speaking about the appearances of the *eidē* as *other* than the *same* as what appears through the senses, yields spoken images that are likenesses of the *appearing* proper to the *eidē* but not of their appearances themselves, that is, of their "looks". That is, *logoi* that combine the doing of the thing done in the case of the appearances of the *eidē*, and that do so by distinguishing these appearances from what appears through the senses, do not disclose the eidetic appearances themselves, but only that their appearing is different from that of sensible appearances. Because what speech must be about in order to speak is something and therefore one (in the sense of the homogeneous unit presupposed in counting and therefore by number), speech's power to manifest the "looks" proper to the *eidē* is limited by its presupposition that these "looks" must be "one" in order to be spoken about. That is, speech in its beinghood is inseparable from the presupposition that the "about which" that it names in order to make it manifest is something that appears as *one*, while the beinghood of the *eidē* can appear only when it is presupposed that they do *not* appear as one but as a multitude of uncountable but nevertheless limited beings.

The "name" and the "about which" of speech therefore do not correspond when the beinghood of the *eidē* is spoken about and for this reason there is an insuperable limit to speech's power to manifest spoken images that are likenesses proper to the appearances of the *eidē*. In other words, in order for the beinghood of the *eidē* to appear through speech, speaking must presuppose that the something that it is necessarily about is not some one thing at all but many things. And it must presuppose that their beinghood as "things" is both "one" and "many" at *once* – and, therefore, that they are at *once* the *same* and *other*. Moreover, it must presuppose that the "units" that compose the multitude of the many *eidē* are incomparable and therefore uncountable. Speech that attempts to tell the doing of this thing done, namely, of an appearance that is one and many, the same and other, and uncountable, however, will necessarily appear to speak against itself and therefore be contradictory. It is for this reason that the "likeness" not only of the appearing of the *eidē*, but of their appearances themselves, can become manifest only in a speech that has employed the power of dialectic to push through both the philosopher's presupposition that speech is necessarily about something (and, therefore, about "one" thing) and the mathematician's presupposition that the units that compose a multitude are identical. The "likeness" of the *eidē* that appears through a *logos* that no longer employs these presuppositions manifests *appearances* that are therefore manifestly *not* images of originals, but rather the originals' appearances themselves. What appears, then, are the invisible looks that, originally, are responsible for the appearance of any sensible or intelligible thing that appears. Hence philosophical *dialogue* makes manifest that the *appearing* of words as invisible spoken images necessarily presupposes the original "looks" of the *eidē* without the words' appearances as images being their *likenesses*. That is, the precise manner of being of an image, which is *not-to be* what it appears like, precludes its being a *complete* "likeness" of the appearance proper to the Being of what it is like, for otherwise it would cease to be what it is – an image of this original – and be the original itself. The difference between the Not-Being of the image and the Being of the original therefore remains beyond the power of any image's appearance to make manifest, and, therefore, beyond the power of speech to do so.

By making apparent speech's weakness in the face of the appearing of the appearances proper to Being and Not-Being, Plato's written word images of spoken dialectical speech make *partially* manifest the sources that are responsible for the beinghood of what speech – according to its own beinghood – is shown to make manifest (the doing of the thing done that it is necessarily about). That which dialectic makes partially manifest is "beyond opinion" in the precise sense that "knowledge (*epistēmē*)" of it cannot be defined as an "account" (*logos*) added to a true opinion. Because opinion is already in community with *logos*, this definition of knowledge takes what is the *same* – (i) true opinion and (ii) true opinion plus *logos* – for what is *other*, namely knowledge, and is therefore rooted in a tautology. And because the original appearances of the *eidē* that are made partially manifest by dialectic are beyond the scope of what speech's word images are able to manifest as likenesses, the original appearances of *eidē* are beyond opinion's power of assertion and denial: its power to qualify as true or false the things that speech tells about what it is about.

Finally, Plato's answer to the question about the sources that are responsible for the most comprehensive sources responsible, in turn, for beinghood, the Same and the Other, seems to be that the source of the Same is the Independent One (also referred to as the Idea of the Good) and the source of the Other is the Indeterminate Dyad (also referred to as the source of motion [*Metaph.* M, 8 1084a34–5] and what is bad [A 6, 988a14]). Plato's reasoning for assigning ultimate sources to the Same and the Other seems to be the following. The "itself by itself" (*auto kath' auto*) unity (as the Same) that composes the "beinghood" of each *eidos* cannot appear as what it is and also appear as mixed with its opposite, that is, mixed with something that in its being is related to what is other than itself. The unity of each *eidos*, therefore, must have its source in the unity of something that appears as a unity or as one completely "itself by itself", and, thus, independent of any mixture with such a one's opposite, namely, with not being one – which is to say – with a multitude. The "being an other of an other" (as the Other) that composes the difference of each *eidos* in the community of *eidē* likewise cannot appear as what it is and also be mixed with its opposite, that is, mixed with the unity proper to what is "itself by itself" (*Soph.* 255c–d). The otherness that relates the *eidē*, therefore, must have its source in something that is completely other than the one: that is, in a multitude that, because the one is not present in it, is unlimited and therefore "indeterminately" other than what is one.

THREE

Aristotle's criticism of Plato's theory of *eidē*: the third (and final) pillar of the ancient precedent to pure phenomenology

Aristotle's dispute with Plato over the manner of being proper to the *eidē*

Aristotle's dispute with the Platonic account of the *eidē* takes issue with its "separation" of the "beinghood" (*ousia*) belonging to a *genos* from the multitude of single things that are encompassed by it. For Aristotle, the answer to the question "Why do things look the same?" is not because there is an *eidos* of a highest rank, the *genos*, that encompasses everything that is, but because each one of the things that are is generated in some material (*hulē*) by an *eidos* whose proper mode of being is "being-at-work (*energeia*)"[1] on it. The "beinghood" of things caused by the perpetual "being-at-work" of the *eidos* (without it ever undergoing change) is perceived and understood by the soul because the very "being-at-work" of an *eidos* responsible for generation also shapes the soul's perception and informs its understanding. The "beinghood" or, more properly within the context of Aristotle's metaphysics, "thinghood",[2] of things has its source in "nature" (*phusis*). Because of this, thinghood, together with *eidos*, *hulē* and *phusis*, are *one* in the generation (*genesis*) that perpetuates life (*zōē*) forever. The perpetuation of life through generation is therefore directed by the unchanging *eidos* whose manner of being is responsible at once for the generated thinghood of that which is and for the generations of generated things being informed by their *eidē*. As the intelligible objects responsible for the soul's understanding of what things *are*, the *eidē* are nevertheless still "of nature". Aristotle's account of the *eidē*, then, remains tied to the "first journey" (the investigation of nature) given up by Plato's Socrates. This is even the case when the *eidē* involved are mathematical objects, because their "abstracted" manner of being is no more capable of existing in separation from the multitude of sensible (natural) things than the *eidē* of chickens or humans or any other natural being.

Aristotle's account of the *eidē* thus takes issue with the two key tenets of Plato's Socratic account of them and the major tenet of the arithmological account, all of which presuppose that an *eidos*'s proper manner of being is accessible through a multitude. In the case of the Socratic account, the claim that the *eidē* are "patterns [*paradeigmata*]" (*Metaph.* A 9, 991a21) of the things that participate in them is rejected by Aristotle because (i) it does not address "what is the thing that is at work [*ergazomenon*], looking off toward the *eidē*" (991a23) and (ii) it presupposes that something can only become like something else by "being an image of it" (991a25). In the case of the arithmological account, Aristotle rejects the view that in the relation between the two causes of things (the independent One and the Indeterminate Dyad) the "*eidos* generates only once" while making "many things out of this material [the dyad]" (988a3–4). Generation "surely" (988a1) happens in the "opposite way" (*ibid.*), with the *eidos* being the cause of the generation of many things, and the material generating only once. And, in both cases, the view that an *eidos* is capable of *existing* in separation from the multitude of things is rejected, albeit for different reasons. For the Socratic account, it is because the cause of each thing's motion remains unaddressed when its thinghood is posited as *existing* apart from it. For the arithmological account, it is because the source of the one is a measure that originates in sensible things, which rules out Plato's account of the source of a mathematical (and, by extension, an eidetic) number being one because of the separate existence of a number's generic unity.

Aristotle's critique of Plato's Socratic account of the *eidē*

Aristotle's critique of Plato's Socratic account of the *eidē* does not reject outright the claim that the *eidē* are "shared in [*metexein*] (*Metaph.* A 9, 990b32) but only that the things that "signify" (*semainei*) (991a) "thinghood" are different in the case of *eidē* and the many things that share in an *eidos* (*ibid.*). There is nothing "apart [*para*]" (991a2) from these things, no "one-over-many [*hen epi pollōn*]" (*ibid.*), but rather there is something "common [*koinon*]" (991a4) between them and their *eidos*. The *eidē* are the thinghood of things in the sense that the pairs that partake of the "Two itself" (990b33) are the same thing (i.e. dual), no matter whether they are destructible or everlasting. Being "dual" is common to both the intelligible object and the things that share in it, which means that the "*eidos* [of the Two itself]" is the "same" (991a7) as the pair, the two things, to which it is applied. Sharing in an *eidos* therefore does not duplicate the world, because the things that share in it do so by virtue of that by which they have being, and this being is the "same" (*tautōn*) (991a6) in the thing as in the *eidos*. The "Two itself" is no more dual than the pair of things that share in them, because it is no more dual "as applied both to itself and to something" (991a4–5).

An *eidos* itself, however, only has thinghood, and therefore each thing only has thinghood, as the manifestation of being-at-work. This is markedly different from the "being" of mathematical things, which are not so composed as to be at work on some material. The manner of being of the thinghood of an *eidos* is therefore "being-at-work" on some underlying material (*hulē*) that has the capacity to be worked on. Material is only material in so far as it is being worked on, and it can only be worked on in so far as it has the "potency" (*dunamis*): the intrinsic tendency to be worked on in a manner that accords with the kind of thing it underlies. The "being-at-work" of an *eidos* on some material that is responsible for the generation of the thinghood of all animals (including humans) is also responsible for perception in all animals, for understanding in the human soul, and, finally, for the "intrinsic order" (*taxis*) that composes the sum total of the things that are into one whole, that is, into the universe or *kosmos*.

Energeia (being-at-work) as the mode of being proper to the *eidos* governing generation

Aristotle's answer to the perennial question, "what is being [*to on*]?" (*Metaph.* Z, 1028b5), which for him is the question "what is thinghood?" (*ibid.*), is therefore that being-at-work is "being as such" (*on haplōs* or *on hē on*). All other manners of being, including potency and the various attributes (*katēgoriai*) that things "share in" and that are accordingly said of them, only *are* in a proportional relation (*kath' analogian*) to being-at-work (V, 1016b31–1017a3). In the doing (*praxis*) of generation, Aristotle finds the fundamental guiding clue for the answer to the question left unaddressed in both of Plato's accounts of the *eidē*; namely, what is it that is at work in an *eidos*, in the sense of its proper manner of being? Aristotle's answer is that the manner of being proper to the *eidos* is its "being-at-work" on some material in order to *bring to be* one of the things that *comes to be*. The fundamental assumption that the account of what is responsible for (and therefore causes) the human "know-how" or art (*technē*) of making (*poiēsis*) is applicable to the account of what causes the doing of generation guides Aristotle's articulation of the *eidos*'s proper manner of being. Moreover, generation provides the most conspicuous phenomenon of an *eidos*'s being-at-work on some material, and all the factors enumerated and articulated in the account of generation as causes of becoming are at work in perception, in understanding as causes of intelligibility, and in the intrinsic order of the *kosmos* as causes of finality.

Aristotle's account of how humans artfully make things provides the answer to the question: why is the thing that *is* made the way that it is? Something not there before has come into being and something and someone must be held responsible. Aristotle's answer is that there are four different kinds of cause (*aitia*) – not four causes – and, thus, four different ways to answer the question why something is such as it is. There is the material (*hulē*) it is made of, there is the maker who is the source of the motion brought to bear on the material to make the thing, there is the shape or looks (*eidos*) – known in advance – of the thing to be made, and, finally, there is the purpose, the end (*telos*) for the sake of which the material was chosen and the looks fashioned into this material. Because the first three kinds of causes all depend on the purpose of the thing, the end that it is made to serve is the thing's true beginning (*archē*). Causation of any kind is therefore the result of what humans call "end". In itself "end" is therefore the intrinsic character of causation, such that without "ends" nothing would be made.

Aristotle's application of the four kinds of cause that are apparent in making to his account of the generation of animals brings into view the workings of the *eidos* and its character as "being-at-work" on some material. In the ever-changing bodies of living beings as well as in all motion (*kinēsis*), the being-at-work that is definitive of the manner of being of the *eidos* is most conspicuous. In the case of generation, the female's embryo corresponds to the material (*hulē*), the male's motion (in coitus and in its semen) corresponds to the source of motion, and nature (*phusis*) corresponds to both the *eidos* that directs the male's motion and to the purpose that determines its characteristics. Nature accomplishes this by overpowering the male animal with the desire to generate by uniting with its object of desire, therewith perpetuating everlasting life (*zōē*). Nature (*phusis*, which is derived from *phuō*, which means to beget, engender, generate), then, is *eidos* and material, and it therefore shares in both being-at-work and material. However, and this is crucial for Aristotle, being-at-work (and therefore *eidos*) has priority in dignity, efficacy and, therefore, in the rank and order of being over potency (and therefore material).

Aristotle's use of his account of making's causality as the guide for his account of generation, together with his emphasis on generation, brings with it his answer to the question of the *eidos*'s proper manner of being that (on his view) remains unanswered in Plato's philosophy. While the *eidos* (as for Plato) is everlasting, it is everlasting in the sense that it is everlastingly "being-at-work" on some material, in that it requires material to be what it is: being-at-work and material are therefore not *two* but *one* in thinghood. Material does not have any being of its own except as that which, as the medium of motion, is worked on in order to become (through its motion) what it is to be when the *eidos*'s "being-at-work" on it reaches its end. Material is therefore the *sine qua non* of any motion, that because of which motion implies generation (the coming to be of what comes to be). The predominance of that which is at work over what it works on establishes for Aristotle the priority of being-at-work over potency, such that the *eidos* is understood to be efficacious *in* the material without itself ever suffering change. The motion in a generation that has "not reached its end" (*energeia atelēs*) is distinguished from the motion in a generation that is complete, fully grown, and thus "being-at-work-staying-itself" (*entelecheia*).

Aristotle therefore sees no need to follow Plato and posit the manner of being of the *eidē* in separation (*chōrismos*) from the multitude of the things that *are*: each one of these things not only has thinghood, in so far as it and its *eidos* signify thinghood, but each is a thinghood, in so far as the "being-at-work" of its *eidos* manifests it as what it is. Nature, as that which both directs the "being-at-work" of the *eidos* on some material and provides this material, is therefore something definite: it is what composes the thinghood of a being and therefore is inseparable from it. This means that what the animal desires in the doing of generation is its own natural being, which is not something distinct from this doing, and therefore something that would be natural in a general sense; it is rather something determinate in the sense that the thing done in its doing *is* this doing itself. Although Aristotle uses the account of causality characteristic of making (*poiēsis*) as his guide for investigating generation, a fundamental difference between it and the doing of generation emerges in Aristotle's account: in making the thing made (the product) is not the producing, whereas in doing the "product" is the doing. Human making turns out to be a poor imitation of the doing proper to nature (generation), and generation, on Aristotle's understanding, is one of the two most perfect manners of doing.

The *energeia* of *eidē* acts on the soul in virtue of something common (*koinon*)

The *eidos* that has priority over material in nature is precisely the *eidos* revealed to the understanding in human *logos*. The "being-at-work" of the *eidos* that directs the generation of living beings is also responsible for the human soul's perception and understanding of this generation. The proper work (*ergon*) of the soul (*psuchē*) is to sustain life in the body and to enable it to sense and understand things. Sense perception (*aisthēsis*) is the result of the soul's power to sense (*to aisthētikon*) being affected by the "sensible *eidē*" (*eidē aisthēta*) (*De an.* 432a3–5) that compose the bodies outside of it. Thinking (*noēsis*) is the result of the soul's power to understand (*noēin* or *nous*) being affected by some one among the intelligible *eidē* (*eidē noēta*) that, because it – as are all the intelligible *eidē* – is comprehended by the divine *nous*, is efficacious as an "intelligible object at work" (*noēton energeia*). For Aristotle, the human soul's powers of perceiving and thinking are therefore like the manner of being of the material of a thing with respect to its *eidos*: these powers are only what they are in relation to the "being-at-work" of the *eidē* that as sensible *eidē* shape the senses in sense perception and the *eidē* that as intelligible inform the *nous* when it has understood. The "being-at-work" of the *eidos* in generation is therefore mirrored in perceiving and understanding.

Aristotle's account of understanding therefore embraces the "first journey" (*prōtos plous*) that Plato's Socrates rejected in the *Phaedo*. Sensing not only makes the human soul the material worked on by the sensible *eidos*, but, also, because "the intelligible things are in the sensible *eidē*" (432a5), the soul's highest cognitive activity, *noēsis* (or, equivalently, *nous*[3]), somehow remains tied to the sensible forms of things (*pragmata*). Despite the fact that the answer to the questions of exactly how the intelligible *eidē* are "in" the *eidē* of sensible things, and, therefore, how thinking is able to comprehend its proper intelligible objects, composes one of the darker chapters in Aristotle's thought, the main lines of his thinking on this matter become clear enough when situated within the context of Plato's thought. Two critical points of departure are then discerned. The first has to do with the Socratic account of the relation between many things and the one *eidos* that they have in common (*koinon*), which on this account characterizes the beinghood of the *eidos* with respect to the *multitude* of single things. The second critical point of departure concerns the nature and role of *phantasia* in the generation of the *phantasm*, and, consequently, the precise nature of the latter in relation both to itself (*kath' auto*) and to the *eidē*.

For Aristotle, there is "something common [*koinon*]" (429b24; b30) between (i) sensible and intelligible beings (*onta*) and (ii) the potency (*dunamis*) of the sensing and knowing capacities of the soul, in the precise sense that it is by virtue of this common thing that "one thing acts and another is acted upon" (429b26–7). That is, the "being-at-work" of the sensible and intelligible beings on the potencies of sensing and knowing requires that the soul is – "in a certain way" (431b22) – both the sensible and intelligible beings that act on it. The way in which this is so is that "what the perceiving and knowing capacities of the soul are in potency are the same things that are either known or perceived" (431b28–30), where the sense of the "same" is here understood not as these beings themselves but as their *eidē*. Sense perception is therefore "an *eidos* of sensible beings" (432a4) and "*nous* is an *eidos* of *eidē* [*nous eidos eidōn*]" (432a3). Because, however,

> there can be no thing done (*pragma*) apart from the determinate magnitudes (*megethē*) that are the separate perceptible things, the intelligible things (*noēta*) are in the sensible *eidē*, not only the so-called abstractions [i.e. mathematical things] but all the active conditions and passive attributes of sensible things. (432b3–7)

Aristotle's account of the *eidē* therefore critically departs from Plato's Socratic account in four crucial regards. First, their status as "something common" does not arise from the soul's relation to a multitude of things but from a single sensible thing's "being-at-work" on the soul's sensible potency. Second, the *eidē* themselves are bifurcated into the sensible *eidē* proper to determinate sensible things and the "one in kind [*eidei*]" (429b28) *eidē* proper to intelligible things. Third, because the intelligible things are in the sensible *eidē*, the thinking (*theorein*) that beholds intelligible things must "behold at the same time some *phantasma*" (432a9) of a sensible *eidos*, for "it is not possible even to think (*noein*) without a *phantasma*" (*Mem.* 449b33). And fourth, *nous* becomes the *eidos* of *eidē* only when it is *one* with all the *noēta* and therefore its potency to become *noēta* has become completely realized, that is, when it is being-at-work *nous* and therefore, since *energeia* requires *hulē*, when it is the material for itself (*noēseōs noēsis*).

These four critical departures from Plato are interrelated and culminate in the crucial roles that Aristotle assigns to *phantasia* in the soul's knowledge (*epistēme*) of the *eidē* and to the "active" *nous* required for anything to be thought. Because the intelligible *eidē* are in the sensible *eidē* and because it is clear that sense perception is different from both "understanding [*phronein*]" (*De an.* 427b11) and "thinking [*dianoeisthai*]" (427b13), the potency of thinking cannot be *directly* informed in sense perception by the "being-at-work" of the intelligible *eidē*. Otherwise, thinking would be perception. The "thinking (*noētikē*) soul" (429a28) is therefore only properly characterized as "a place of *eidē*" (429a27) when "it [the thinking soul] is not [characterized as] the *eidē* in its being-at-work-staying-itself (*entelechia*), but in potency" (429a28). Were it otherwise, that is, if the thinking soul were characterized as the place of the *eidē qua* their being-at-work, intelligible things would always inform thinking directly, which is clearly not the case for Aristotle. On the one hand, this presents Aristotle with the problem of accounting for how *nous*'s potency for understanding the intelligible things in the sensible *eidē* becomes "actual [*entelechia*]"

(429b32), while maintaining the difference between sense perception and understanding. On the other hand, he is presented with the problem of maintaining the priority of being-at-work over potency in the soul as "in all nature" (430a). The mediating role between perception and thinking that Aristotle assigns to *phantasia* as the source of the *phantasma* that is necessary for thinking represents his attempt to address the first problem. And his response to the second problem is the notion of *nous* that in its thinghood is "being-at-work" and therefore "separate" (*chōristos*) (430a18) from *nous* whose thinghood contains potency.

Phantasia and *phantasma*

Aristotle's account of *phantasia* is informed by the view that "[it] is clear ... that *phantasia* could not be opinion along with sensing, nor by way of sensing, nor an interweaving of opinion with sensing" (*De an*., 428a25–7), that is, by an explicit critique of Plato's account of *phantasia* as the "mixing of sensing and opinion" (*Soph.* 264b). Aristotle's main stated reason for rejecting Plato's account is that it is possible for something to appear (*phainetai*) and be false while, at the same time, there is a true opinion about it. Aristotle's example: "the sun appears to be a foot wide, but one believes it to be bigger than the inhabited world" (*De an.* 428b5–6). And *phantasia* by itself is not opinion either, because for Aristotle belief (*pistis*) always accompanies opinion, and being persuaded accompanies belief, but *phantasia* involves neither the conviction that characterizes belief nor the speech necessary for persuasion (428b20–26).

What exactly *phantasia* is for Aristotle, however, is another matter. In addition to distinguishing it from opinion, he distinguishes it from sensing, knowledge and *nous*. In this way, *phantasia* is distinguished from "those potencies or active states by which we discriminate [*krinomen*] something and are either right or wrong" (428a4–5). *Phantasia*, "as that by which we speak of some *phantasma* becoming present to us" (428a2), "seems to be some sort of motion and not to occur without sense perception" (428b12–13). More precisely, "*phantasia* would be a motion coming about as a result of the being-at-work of sense perception, and corresponding to it" (429a2–3). As a motion *phantasia* is therefore derivative of both the motion in sense perception and the being-at-work proper to the sensible beings that bring about sense perception's active state. The *phantasmata* that both "appear to [*phainetai*]" (*Mem.* 450b28) the soul and "remain" (*De an.* 429a5) there (as the result of *phantasia*) are therefore "just like the things perceived, except without the material" (432a10–11).

Aristotle makes a similar claim with respect to each of the separate or proper senses (sight, hearing, touch, taste and smell); namely, that for sense perception in general, "it is necessary to grasp that the sense is receptive of the *eidē* of sensible things without their material, as wax is receptive of the design of a ring without the iron or gold, and takes up the golden or bronze design, but not as gold or bronze" (424a17–21). The difference, however, between a sense's immaterial reception of an *eidos* and a *phantasma*'s immaterial likeness to a thing perceived, seems to be that the former requires the being-at-work of a sensible thing on the soul, while the latter can appear when this condition is not present (428a5–8). The *phantasma* is thus "something like a tracing [*tupos*] or a drawing [*graphē*] in us" (*Mem.* 450b17), which appears to the soul even when the thing that is responsible for the sense perception (whose motion, in turn, is responsible for the *phantasia* that brings about the *phantasma*) is "not present" (450b19) to the soul. The "power of *phantasia* [*to phantastikon*] is therefore the same [*to auto*] as the power of sensing [*to aisthētikō*], but their being [*to einai*] is different" (*Insomn.* 459a16–18). Aristotle goes so far as to link *phantasia* with the soul's power to see, maintaining that, "since sight is the primary sense, *phantasia* has even taken its name from light [*phaos*], because without light it is impossible to see" (*De an.* 429a3–5).

Phantasia and sensing are therefore apparently the same for Aristotle in their common power of sensing inasmuch as the former is derivative from the motions of the latter, which is to say that *phantasia* is derivative from the motions that compose an active state of sensing in the soul. Moreover, as light is the condition for the primary sense's power to see, so, too, it seems, is *phantasia* the condition for the soul's power to see, which indicates that what ultimately makes them the same is their common power's connection to "seeing".

The difference in the being of their powers of sensing involves their respective manners of "seeing". On the one hand, the "seeing" in sensing involves something more than the sensing of the visible object (colour) proper to sight: it involves the sensing that the soul is sensing (*De an.* 425b12–427a17). The sensing of sensing is not the work of the senses proper, because what they sense are their proper sensible objects (colours, sounds, smells, tastes, tangibles), but the "common perceiving power" or "common sense". The common perceiving power or common sense is the sensitive power of the soul that discriminates among the various proper sensible objects (colours, sounds, smells, tastes, tangibles) of sensing (426b12–21), and especially when discriminating among the proper sensible objects, that senses that the soul is sensing (426b22). It is also responsible for the "common perception" (425a28) of the "common sensibles" (425a27) (motion, rest, number, shape, magnitude and unity).

On the other hand, *phantasia*'s making possible the seeing of a *phantasma*, in the sense of its motion bringing about the *phantasma*'s appearing (*phainetai*), involves something more than the power of sensing it has in common with sensing: it involves the potency of the soul that understands, *nous*. *Nous* either "perceives" (*Mem.* 450b28) the *phantasma* as something in its "own right [*kath' auto*]" (*ibid.*) or "beholds (*theōrei*) it in the same way that one beholds what is in a drawing as a likeness (*eikona*)" (450b30). The being of the *phantasma* is therefore dual, like that of "what is drawn on a tablet" (450b21), which "is both a figure [*zōon*] and a likeness, although what it is to be these two things is not the same, and it is possible to behold it both as a figure and as a likeness" (450b21–3). Therefore, "so, too, one ought to conceive of the *phantasma* that is in us being something in its own right, and a being *of* something" (450b24–5). When it is something in its own right, it is "a thing beheld [*theorēma*] or *phantasma*" (450b26) and therefore a "certain thought [*noēma*]" (450b29) comes before the soul, and when "it is of something else" (450b27), the soul beholds it as "a certain kind of likeness or reminder [of things that are absent]" (*ibid.*).

The dual being of the *phantasma* points to the duality belonging to the ways of its being seen and therefore to the duality of the "seeing" that *phantasia* brings about. *Phantasia* illuminates the *phantasma* such that the soul's seeing grasps it as either something that is *itself* in its own right, and therefore something that is seen without relation to anything else, or as something that is seen in a relation of likeness to something else. The dual being of the seeing and being seen of the *phantasma*, in turn, points to *phantasia*'s common origin with the power of sensing, which is responsible for both *phantasia*'s and the *phantasma*'s correspondence with this source. The power of sensing gives rise to "three ways of perceiving" (*De an.* 428b28), the sensing of objects proper to perception (colours, sounds, etc.), the perception of things that are "incidental" to sensed proper objects (the son of Diares is sensed incidentally through the white proper sensible that happens to belong to him), and "in the third place there is perception of the common attributes that accompany the things incidentally perceived, to which the things properly perceived belong" (428b23–6). The common attributes of things are therefore perceived in the company of incidentally perceived things and hence together with the properly perceived things that belong to those that are incidentally perceived. Thus, together with the incidental perception of the son of Diares through the sensing of white, there is the perception of the sensibles whose attributes do not just characterize what is perceived (i.e. Diares) incidentally through the sensing of white (or any other proper sensible), but that characterize all perceptible things, namely, motion, rest, number, shape, magnitude and unity.

According to Aristotle, each of these three ways of perceiving has a different motion, "the first sort being truthful while the perception is present, while the others could be false whether it is present or absent, and especially when the thing perceived is far away" (428b28–30). As a motion that comes about from the being-at-work of sense perception, *phantasia* must itself be at work simultaneously with these three ways of perceiving. The results of this work seem to be the composition of the *phantasma* as both a "trace" of the passively received *eidē* of the proper objects of sensing and a "drawing" of the common attributes of the *eidos* or *morphē* proper to the sensible thing to which these proper objects belong. Aristotle confirms this when he characterizes the *phantasma* as "an attribute [*pathos*] of the common perceiving power" (*Mem.* 450a14). Thus, as has been mentioned, when the traces and the drawn figure that compose the *phantasma* are seen "by itself [*kath' auto*]", and therefore *not* in relation to its origin in the sensing of the objects of the proper senses and the perception of the common sensibles, the *phantasma* comes about in the soul "only as a thought (*noēma*)" (450a2). And when the traces and figure that belong to the *phantasma* are seen as something else, the *phantasma* comes about as a likeness "of that of which it is a *phantasma*" (451a16), the "active holding (*hexis*)" (451a17) of which is memory.

Phantasmata and thinking (*noēsis*)

Because *phantasia* is different from affirmation and denial and therefore from what is true and false, the *phantasma* that it brings about in the soul is properly speaking neither right nor wrong. On Aristotle's view, "where there is falsehood as well as truth there is already some kind of compounding [*sunthesis*] of intelligible things as though they were one" (*De an.* 430a27–9). Compounding arises in acts "of saying something about something, and also of denying" (430b26–7), acts that may also be characterized as "dividing [*diairesin*]" (430b3). The intelligible *eidē* that are "in" the perceptible *eidē* are so in the manner of their thinghood as being-at-work, and this means (among other things) that the *eidos* that organizes the sensible being into a perceptible whole is also the *eidos* that works on the perceiving and thinking soul. The compounding of intelligible things in saying things about the perceptible whole is therefore also a dividing because these things are perceived – albeit "incidentally" perceived – as parts of the perceptible thing in its wholeness. (The incidental perception of intelligible things in the perceptible thing is a consequence of perception and thinking being different potencies. Because of this, the intelligible things act incidentally on the senses, in so far as they are in the sensible *eidē* that work directly on the senses.) Common sensibles belong to this perceptible whole and it is for this reason that, for Aristotle, the common sense does not need to collect together the attributes of the proper sensible objects in order to compose the perceptible thing into a unity. The perceptible thing is already a unity. Thus Aristotle says of "what something is, in the sense of what it keeps on being in order to be at all" (430b27–9), that it "is not one thing attached to another" (430b29). Moreover, thinking what something is, or thinking any of the other intelligible things, "is true" (430b29) for Aristotle "in the same way that the seeing of something proper to sight is true" (430b30). Just as the sensing of colour is truthful when the thing sensed is present, so, too, is the thinking of an intelligible thing truthful when the intelligible thing that is thought is present.

The question, remains, however, how the being of what something is or any other intelligible thing is thought, given both that thinking and perception are different powers of the soul and that "one who perceived nothing would not be able to learn or be acquainted with anything [intelligible] either" (432a7–8). Aristotle's cryptic question and remark in this regard sums up the problem: "So how do the uncombined intelligible things [*noēmata*] differ from being *phantasmata*? But in fact these are not *phantasmata* either, but are not present without *phantasmata*" (432a14–15). The *phantasmata* Aristotle has in mind here are those that are immaterial likenesses of the perceived things, and thus of something. They are therefore not likenesses of intelligible things but of the sensible *eidē* in which the intelligible *eidē* are. Nevertheless, "the thinking potency grasps in thought the *eidē* that are present in the likenesses of things [*phantasmasi*]" (431b3–4). The key to Aristotle's understanding of this seems to be his account of the impossibility of thinking without a *phantasma* that compares it to drawing a diagram in order to think a mathematical object. He writes:

> For the same condition [*pathos*] goes along with thinking which goes along with drawing a diagram, since there, while making no use of the triangle's being of a definite size, still we draw it definite in size; and in the same way, one who is thinking, even if one is thinking of something that is not a quantity, sets a quantity before one's eyes, though one does not think it *as* a quantity, but if the nature of it is among things that have a quantity, but an indefinite one, one sets out a definite quantity, but thinks it just as a quantity. (*Mem.* 450a1–6)

The condition that Aristotle's comparison here sets as the same seems to be this: just as the thinking of a dimensionless mathematical triangle is facilitated by the drawn figure of a triangle with definite dimensions, or the thinking of an intelligible thing that is not a quantity employs the seeing of a quantity, or, finally, the thinking of something that has an indefinite quantity employs a definite quantity, so, too the thinking of an intelligible thing must employ the *phantasma*. Thus the thinking of a thing without the qualities of a sensible thing, that is, the thinking of an intelligible thing, requires the presence to thought of something that manifests the likeness of those sensible qualities, that is, the presence of the *phantasma*. *Nous*'s receptivity to an intelligible *eidos* is therefore mediated by the *phantasma*, even as what is "seen" by its "sight" is not the *phantasma*'s likeness to the sensible *eidos* but the intelligible *eidos* that is in the sensible *eidos* and that is somehow "illuminated" by the *phantasma*'s light-like being.

"Passive" and "active" (*nous*) and the *phantasma*'s dual origin

Why it is the case that "it is impossible to think anything apart from something continuously extended, or to think beings that are not in time apart from time, is another story" (*Mem.* 450a6–9). The thinghood proper to the intelligible *eidē* is responsible for the being of all that is and for all motion and genesis in the world. From this it follows that the intelligible being (*noēton*) must not only be something understandable, that is, a *noēton* with the potency (*dunamis*) to inform *nous*, but that it must "actually be something understood" (*noēton energeiai*). Related to this, the presence of a material thing and a causal and productive thing, and the priority of the latter over the former, "in all nature [*phusei*]" (*De an.* 430a10), and, therefore, the priority of being-at-work over potency, means that "it is necessary in the soul too that these distinct aspects be present" (430a13–14). The material aspect is "*nous* by becoming all things" (430a14–15) and the causal and productive aspect is *nous* "by forming (*poiein*) all things" (430a15). Because the intelligible *eidē* can perform their generating work only when they are being-at-work on some material and therefore "one" with nature, they can only be thought and therefore understood through their "product", that is, through the determinate magnitudes that are the separate perceptible things. And it is precisely the sensible *eidē* of these things that the soul becomes "acquainted with" (*Mem.* 450a9–10) "by means of the primary power of perception" (450a12), that is, by the common sense.

The material or "passive" *nous* that is by "becoming all things" manifests the passivity inseparable from its becoming all things in knowledge (*epistēmē*), which, "in its being-at-work, is the same as the thing it knows" (*De an.* 430a19–21). Because what knowledge knows are the intelligible *eidē*, and because these, in their potency, are in sensible *eidē*, it is impossible for the soul to think the former apart from the determinate magnitudes proper to the sensible beings that cause the soul to receive the latter. But is also impossible for the thinking of "passive" *nous* to think an intelligible being while this being is at work in the perceptible thing that, in turn, is at work on the soul in sense perception. Otherwise, thinking would be perception. This, apparently, is why for Aristotle *phantasia*'s generation of the *phantasma* is necessary in order to make possible *nous*'s being informed by intelligible things. By causing the *phantasma* to remain in the soul in the absence of the being-at-work proper to the perception that is receptive of the sensible thing's sensible *eidos*, *phantasia*'s light-like nature becomes manifest in the *phantasma*'s potency – as *the* likeness of sensible *eidē* – to illuminate the intelligible *eidē*. Thus it is through the *phantasma* that the being-at-work that originates the being-at-work proper to sensible beings, that is, the being-at-work of the intelligible *eidē*, is itself illuminated.

Aristotle also relates to light *nous* that is causal and productive by forming all things ("active" *nous*), albeit differently from how he connects *phantasia* to light. While the latter is light-like, that is illuminating, as a result of its common source in general with sensing and its kinship with the first sense (sight), the former is light-like, that is potentiating, as a result of being like the way light "makes the colours that are in potency be at work as colours" (430a16–17). Aristotle's characterization of the light-like character of *phantasia*, by linking it to its source in the sense of sight, therefore connects it to the necessity of light for this sense to see. As light is necessary for the sense of sight to be able to see when it is perceiving, so, too, is *phantasia* necessary for the soul's ability "to see" when it is *not* perceiving. The light-like character of *nous* is connected to its being "like" the way light "makes" actual colours that are in potency, that is, by making the colours be seen. These two characterizations of being "light-like" are therefore different. In the case of *phantasia*, it is related to allowing that which has the power of seeing to see, whereas in the case of *nous*, being "light-like" is related to making that which is seen be seen. *Nous* in this sense "is by its thinghood a being-at-work, for what acts is always distinguished in stature above what is acted upon, as a governing source is above the material it works on" (430a17–18). And, conversely, being-at-work is *nous*. Thus, "while knowledge in potency comes first in time in any one knower" (430a21), and, so, too, the knower's "passive" *nous*, "in the whole of things it [the potency of knowledge] does not take precedence even in time" (430a21–2). What has precedence is "*nous* that is always being-at-work" (*energeiai nous*), *nous* that is "being-at-work-staying-itself" (*entelecheia*) and therefore *nous* that, unlike "passive" *nous* – which at one time thinks and at another time does not think – is always being-at-work and therefore "not acted upon [*apathes*]" (430a24). As such, it is "separated [*choristheis*]", "just exactly what it is", and "this alone is deathless and everlasting ... and without this nothing thinks" (430a22–5). Eternally at work, "active" *nous* is its own eternal life (*zōē*) and delight (*hēdonē*) and, therefore, it is deity (*theos*). Because it is not acted on, "we have no memory" (430a23–4) of its being-at-work, on whose "ruling beginning [*archē*]" the entire heaven (*ouranos*) and nature hinge (*Metaph.* L 7, 1072b13).

Phantasia's function for Aristotle as the bond within the soul between the perception of the sensible and the knowledge of the intelligible, however, encounters a limit when it comes to *nous* that is separated. Crucial in this regard is the origin proper to the *phantasma* to which *phantasia* gives rise. When seen in its likeness to the sensible *eidē* from which it originates, the *phantasma* serves to illuminate these *eidē* in a manner that allows "thinking [*noein*] to be acted upon [*paschein*]" (*De an.* 429b25) by the intelligible *eidē*. The latter is a necessary consequence of the duality of the "seeing" made possible by *phantasia*, which is rooted in the duality of the "being seen" of the *phantasma*: when seen *according to itself*, the *phantasma* illuminates the results of the soul's capacity for generating appearances, but nothing more. That is, it illuminates the traces of the proper sensibles together with the drawn figure of the common sensibles generated by the motion proper to *phantasia*. However, when seen *as a likeness* that is related to the soul's reception of the sensible *eidos*'s immaterial impression, the *phantasma*'s likeness to this impression becomes the medium through which its origin in what is responsible for this impression is thought; and it is thought in the manner of its intermittent reception by *nous*'s potency. This potency, Aristotle writes, "is in potency in the same way a tablet is, when nothing written is present in it actively" (429b33–430a2), and therefore "what thinks and what is known are the same thing" (430a4–5), although "this sort of thinking is not always happening" (430a6–7).

The origin of the *phantasma* in question, however, ultimately is not simply an intelligible *eidos* that acts periodically on the "sort of *nous* that is acted upon (*pathētikos*)" (430a24), but the "immaterial" (*aneu hulēs*) (430a4) *nous* that is always thinking. *Nous* in this sense, the divine *nous* described above, "separated [*choristos*]" (429b6) from everything else in the world and therefore outside time, "uncontaminated" (*amigēs*) (430a17), "pure [*katharos*]" (*Metaph.* A 8, 989b15–16), without which nothing thinks, is therefore the *sine qua non* for the thinking (*noēsis*) proper to "passive" *nous*. The latter *nous*'s thinking, and therefore its reception of the intelligible *eidos*, is mediated by the *phantasma* without which the thought (*noēma*) of the intelligible thing (*noēton*) cannot be present. In this capacity the *phantasma* must function as the material for the potency proper to the "passive" *nous*'s receptivity to the being-at-work of the intelligible *eidē*. The being-at-work proper to the intelligible *eidē*, however, originates in their uninterrupted and eternally present comprehension by "*nous* that is always being-at-work". Because, however, the being-at-work of the latter is inaccessible to the memory of the "destructible" (*De an.* 430a25) *nous* that nevertheless somehow – according to Aristotle – intermittently shares in its being-at-work, the question emerges: how is it that this *nous* has the potency to think the forever absent being-at-work – absent because inaccessible to memory – of what Aristotle's commentators refer to as "active *nous*" (*nous poiētikos*)?

Phantasma and *eidē* in Plato's Socrates and Aristotle

By separating *phantasia* from opinion and "*nous* always being-at-work" (*energeiai nous*) from "*nous* in potency" (*dunamei nous*), Aristotle's account of the thinghood proper to the *eidos* bypasses Plato's Socratic account of the *eidos* as something that both appears to the soul and that does so through a multitude of images that are constitutionally alienated from their eidetic original. The soul, according to Aristotle, is able to apprehend directly both sensible and intelligible *eidē*, notwithstanding the impossibility of thinking and therefore apprehending them without an appearance (*phantasma*). Precisely the soul's direct apprehension of *eidē* is ruled out by Plato's Socratic account of the insuperable duality of image and eidetic original that is involved in the *eidos*'s appearance. Image for Socrates is something that appears with a manner of being that is numerically distinct from the eidetic original to which it is nevertheless linked as its "likeness". The *eidos* for Socrates is "one" and the images through which it appears are "many".

Aristotle's account of the soul's knowledge of an *eidos* – both sensible and intelligible – establishes the *eidos*'s "numerical" identity with the soul's reception of it. For either kind of *eidos*, the *eidos* that acts on the soul is numerically the same as its reception *in* the soul, such that knowledge of an *eidos* is "one" with the *eidos* itself. Aristotle establishes this identity by distinguishing the soul's affirmation or denial of its truth from the appearance itself, that is, from opinion, which separation results in the appearance's incorrigibility. Thus, unlike Plato's account of *phantasma*, which not only connects it with opinion but connects it with false opinion, Aristotle's account of its independence from opinion results in the appearance having the status of something that, strictly speaking, is neither right nor wrong. Appearance is incorrigibly what appears. As the "same" as what appears, the appearance is "one" with it and therefore cannot distort what appears.

At worst, when what appears is false, its appearance will be also. In the case of the appearance of the proper sensibles, however, even falsehood is ruled out, as the soul's reception of the sensible *eidos* of a proper sensible is always true and therefore, so, too, is its appearance to the soul.

The sensible appearances (*phantasmata*) that mediate the soul's apprehension of intelligible *eidē* are therefore not, as they are for Plato, apparitions for Aristotle. The appearance and what appears are the same, and the truth or falsity of the appearance, except in the case of the appearance of proper sensibles, is not a factor in the *phantasia* responsible for the *phantasma* but is determined by the judgement proper to opinion. Because the intelligible *eidē* are "in" the sensible *eidē*, and because the appearances of the latter are incorrigible, the *phantasia* responsible for the "being seen" of appearances is able to illuminate these appearances in a manner that allows the intelligible *eidē* in them to be apprehended by *nous*. Each of the *eidē noēta* is therefore knowable in its "own right [*kath' auto*]" by the soul in a cognitive relation that is also numerically "one". An intelligible *eidos* is known when its being-at-work informs a passive *nous*. Such a *nous* becomes "one" with what is understood and thereby most truthfully what it is, being-itself-staying-itself (*entelechiai nous*). And so long as the intelligible *eidos* apprehended by passive *nous* is not compounded by *logos* in acts of saying or denying something about something, it is apprehended directly as it is, its falsehood being ruled out by *nous*'s unity with it.

The intelligible *eidos* that is known, as "the thing in common" that allows something to act and something to be acted on in the case of the relation between sensible and intelligible beings that determines all thinking (*noēsis*), however, originates in an intelligible being more primary and with a more encompassing unity than any "one" from among the intelligible *eidē* apprehended by passive *nous*. *Nous* that is always being-at-work, as the divine *nous* that comprehends the sum total of all *eidē*, "separated" from everything else in the world and therefore outside time, is thus the source of being's primary aspect, being-at-work. As such, it is responsible for the *ousia* of the totality of *eidē* that are in its comprehension. Aristotle's answer to the question about what is responsible for so many things looking alike – that it is the *eidos* that acts on some material and thus causes the perpetual chain of generation – therefore presupposes a mode of being-at-work more perfect than that which is the cause of the nearly perfect doing (*praxis*) that is done in generation, and whose change is its own end. Presupposed by this is *nous* that is always being-at-work, which, in its comprehension of the sum of *eidē*, is responsible for the "*kosmos*": the "universe" as the "one whole" of all that is and the "intrinsic order" (*taxis*) that makes this whole a whole.

Aristotle's critique of Plato's thesis of the separate being of the unity belonging to the *genos*

That the unity of the wholeness of the whole that composes the universe, together with the unity of *nous* that is always being-at-work that comprehends it, cannot be "one" in the sense of a *genos* that is separate or has being alongside them, can be seen from Aristotle's account of the origin of the unity proper to a mathematical multitude (mathematical numbers). Aristotle's account of the origin of mathematical numbers presents a fundamental critique of Plato's arithmological account of the unity of number having a source in a *genos* that is separate from the multitude of units composing each number. Aristotle's account is therefore only comprehensible within the context of Plato's arithmological account of the source of the unity of mathematical and eidetic numbers, since it explicitly takes issue with the *chorismos* thesis: the attribution of a *generic* unity to either kind of numbers and the necessity of the supposition of a non-mathematical one (*hen*) in order to ground arithmetically mathematical unity. Aristotle's "dispute" (*Metaph.* M 1, 1076a36–7) with those who speak of mathematical things "as separate from sensible things" (1076a34–5), however, is *not* whether they have being, but, rather, "the manner of their being" (1076a37–8). Number, characterized as the discrete delimitation of a field of units into definite amounts, the source (*archē*) of which is one (cf. *Top.* Z 4, 141b5–7; *Metaph.* I 6, 1056b23), is therefore not in contention in Aristotle's critique of Plato's account of the unity of number.

For Aristotle, then, it is Plato's determination of the manner of being of "pure" numbers as independent of sensible beings that is in dispute, because it misses precisely the dependence on sensible things that is characteristic of each number. From the fact that it is possible to articulate the parts of something in declarative speech (*toi logōi*) before denominating the whole, it does not follow that the "being [*ousia*]" of these parts has priority over the being of the whole (*Metaph.* M, 1077b1–2). Likewise, it does not follow from saying that there is a number of something that this number exists outside that which it delimits with respect to its definite amount. For example, in calling a human being "white", no other being is meant than precisely this white human being (Z 4, 1029b13–14). Likewise, in saying "three trees", "three" has the same status as the "white"; the definite amount of trees, namely, "three", therefore has no proper "nature [*phusis*]" (M 6, 1080a15, 1082a16; 8, 1083b22). The being so many of trees, like their being green, is dependent on there being *trees*. The "being three" of three trees therefore cannot be independent of the trees whose amount is "three".

For Aristotle, then, the status of the being of numbers is determined by their natural meaning: the assertion that certain things are present in a specific number means only that *such a thing* is present in just this definite multitude (*Ph.* D 12, 221b14–15). This characterization of the manner of being number, however, presents the problem of how to account for the purely intelligible quality of mathematical numbers. This is a problem for Aristotle because, unlike Plato, who posits the independence of the intelligible being of the unit from sensible beings, Aristotle's reliance on the natural meaning (revealed in the analysis of ordinary speech) of numbers precludes the supposition behind Plato's position. It precludes the *hypothesis* that the homogeneous, indivisible (and therefore unchanging) characteristics proper to the unit as the source (*archē*) of mathematical numbers have their basis in a manner of being that is separate from sensible things. Aristotle, instead, articulates the manner of being belonging to these characteristics as arising "from abstraction [*ex aphaireseōs*]" (*Metaph.* K 3, 1061a29), from being "lifted off", "drawn off" or, in other words, from being "abstracted" from sensible beings. The mathematical objects (*ta mathēmatika*) studied by mathematical science (*epistēmē*), which in their being are not detached from sensible beings, are therefore nevertheless studied *as if* they were detached or separated. In line with this, Aristotle holds that "each thing may be viewed best in this way – if one posits that which is *not* separate *as separate*, just as the arithmetician and geometer do" (M 3, 1078a21–3).

How is it that someone who thinks mathematical objects is able to do so as separate from sensible beings, even though they are not separate? Aristotle's answer to this question arises by considering how the "single parts" (*merē*) of sensible beings are taken hold of in *logos*. When the aspects of a sensible thing are distinguished in speech one after the other from the concrete context of their being, a context without which they would not exist, for example, "this" "round" "white" "column", it is apparent that the nexus of being that links all the parts together is disregarded in a manner that allows each part to be singled out and apprehended separately. This "disregarding of" establishes a new mode of seeing that allows something *in* sensible beings to come before its regard in a manner that, for all their variety and transitoriness, is unchanging. As such, it remains always in the same condition and therefore satisfies the demand that for Aristotle, as for Plato, must be satisfied for a being to be an object of science.

The lifting off characteristic of abstraction expresses nothing other than the "disregarding of" that makes possible the articulation in *logos* of the single parts of a sensible thing, a disregarding in which sensible beings are deprived of their sensible qualities and individual differences. In a manner of speaking they shrink, becoming mere independent parts of bodies or mere bodies themselves, such that a demonstrative discipline becomes possible, one that, as it were, "reads off" such independent parts or bodies their arithmetical and geometrical aspects, namely, how many or how extensive they are. When the theoretical mathematician, moreover, in making that which comes into view in abstraction as the subject matter of study, no longer views what has been abstractedly lifted off as having its basis in mere bodies but views it as a part of them that in its own right is independent, such parts become "neutral" monads. Thus the mathematician "studies things after having stripped away everything perceptible ..., and this leaves behind [in the case of arithmetic] only what is of some amount" (*Metaph.* K 1061a28; 1061a32–3). To posit that mathematical things "*are* as separate natures" (M 2, 1077a17–18) is therefore contrary to truth, because "it is [only] the *supposition* of their being that way" (1077a18–19) that is necessary for mathematical knowledge, while "in truth they are derivative" (1077a20). It is therefore not an *original* separation but a *subsequent* indifference to the dependence on sensible beings that characterizes the manner of being proper to pure numbers. The task of determining how this manner of being is itself to be understood, however, belongs not to mathematics but to "first philosophy" (*prōtē philosophia*) (K 4, 1061b25–7) alone. This is the case because mathematics simply has to "accept [*lambanetai*]" (*An. post.* A 10, 76a33) the manner of being of the various *original* abstract beings that make up the *pregiven* contents of arithmetic and geometry, for example, the "one", the "straight", the "triangular" and so on, and deal with them only in so far as their non-contradictory connections are demonstrable.

It follows for Aristotle from the abstract manner of being proper to the monad that the Platonic solution to the problem of the unity of a number – that is, to the question how the "many" can be understood as "one" at all – is untenable. In the first place, it is untenable because the positing of a "common thing" (*koinon*) above and *alongside* the multitude of units supposedly unified by the integrity of its *genos* attributes unity to something that, properly speaking, cannot be one at all. It cannot be one, because what is meant in speaking of a number is precisely something that is *more* than one thing. Things are one by immediate contact, mixture or the placement of their parts, none of which is possible when it comes to the monads in the dyad, triad and so on (*Metaph.* M 7, 1082a20–23). Rather, "just as two human beings are not some one thing other than both, so too must it be with the units" (1082a23–4). In the second place, Aristotle complains that on account of *what* numbers are one, "no one says anything" (L, 1075b34).

Plato's view of the generic unity of numbers is the consequence of the supposition of the detachment and therefore independence of intelligible monads from sensible beings. This supposition removes the basis for appealing to the natural articulation of ever different and divisible sensible beings to account for the *origin* of the delimitation and unification of single numbers. Having eliminated this ultimate foundation of all possible unity, the "separation" (*chorismos*) thesis seduces the one who posits it into embracing the view that the possibility of collecting together *two* monads in *one* number has to be the effect of an original and therefore independent *genos* or *eidos*. Thus, for Aristotle, a number is precisely not *one* thing but a "heap" (*sōros*) (H 3, 1044a4; M 8, 1084b21–2; H 6, 1045a8–10[4]) of sensible beings or abstract monads. A number, therefore, is precisely *nothing more* than these parts, "for a number is only what has been or can be counted" (*Ph.* D 14, 223a24–5).

This last point is crucial to Aristotle for understanding properly the soul's pre-knowledge of all possible numbers, which, following Plato, could be called a "stored possession [*ktēsis*]" (*Tht.* 197b), in contrast to a "possession in use [*hexis*]" (*An. post.* A I, 71a13–28). Because a number is something that coincides with what is counted, the "pure" intelligible structures available to the soul prior to counting, that is, structures "indifferent" to the determinate qualities of sensible beings, must not be spoken of as *one thing* that, in turn, points to a "common thing" such as should be understood as a whole above and outside of the multitude of counted objects (*Metaph.* N, 1090a17–18). To the contrary, because the availability of such structures originally becomes known *in* counting, it is likewise rooted in the exercise of counting sensible multitudes and extracting from them, *ex aphaireseōs*, "pure" monads. As a consequence, numbers of "pure" monads involve, no less than numbers of sensible beings, "heaps": in this case, "heaps" of "pure" monads. They are therefore "one" only in the sense that something can be said to extend "over the whole [*katholou*]" (*An. post.* B 19, 100a6–8), which rules out their being "one thing" any more than numbers of sensible beings are "one thing" (*Metaph.* M 4, 1079a34–6).

Aristotle's answer to the question that he maintains is unanswered in Plato's generic account of number, namely, *what* it is that is responsible for the unity proper to number, begins by posing it only for *actually* counted multitudes. Such multitudes, as multitudes of homogeneous ones, make up a unity in so far as each multitude is measured by its own one. Thus Aristotle writes:

> We speak of one and many in just the way one might say one and ones, or a white thing and white things, or speak of the things measured off in relation to their measure; in this way, too, manifold things are spoken of, for each number is many because it consists of ones and because each number is measured by the one, and is many as opposed to the one and not to the few. In this sense, then, even two are many, but this not as a multitude having an excess either in relation to anything or simply, but as the first multitude.
>
> (I 6, 1056b23–4)

Counting presupposes the homogeneity of that which is counted, which means that in counting one and the same thing is fixed on, such that its definite amount is arrived at only after *one and the same thing* has been counted over. The "one", then, does *not* have priority in counting as the superiority of a genus over a species (which is how Aristotle thinks the one functions for Plato), but rather in its character as the "measure" (*metron*) by which the definite amount of a multitude is determined. The one is not a "common thing" (I 1, 1053a14) over or alongside things, for "[i]t is clear that the one signifies a measure" (N 1, 1087b33). The "being one" of sensible beings marks both the possibility of their being counted and the *indivisibility* of the "one" that, in so far as it functions to supply the measure of what is counted, is "one sensible thing" and therefore undivided. For example, the "being *one*" of each apple in a number of apples is not divided and therefore does not have a division, even though each apple as a sensible being can be divided, as can any other sensible being. Indivisibility therefore belongs to what is counted only in so far as it is the origin of the measure of the count, because "whatever does not have a division, in so far as it does not have it, is in that respect called one" (D 6, 1016b4–6). Any specific number is therefore "a multitude measured by the one" (I 6, 1057a3ff.). As such, its "thinghood" is the multitude of units as such, in the precise sense of the "how many" it indicates. Thus thinghood is understood here by Aristotle to be derivative, in so far as that *what* each number is, is not something that is separate or detached from the definite amount of homogeneous units it delimits. Thus, for example, "six" units are not "two times three" or "three times two" units, but rather precisely "once six" (D 14, 1020b7ff.). For Aristotle, then, there is no such thing as *the six*, with an intelligible being that would be distinct from the many hexads that delimit this or that multitude of "once six" units.

The "indivisible by anything [*pantê adiaireton*]" (I 1, 1053a1ff.) and "most exact [*akribestaton*]" (1053a1) status that the arithmetician understands the "unit" (*monas*) to possess arises for Aristotle on the basis of the elevation of a habitual procedure to the rank of *epistēmē*. The habitual expression of the sensible beings in every count in terms of their "being one" – for example, instead saying "one apple, two apples, three apples", what is said is rather "one, two, three" (M 7, 1082b35) – points already to the purely arithmetical status of sensible beings as countable material. When this status is abstractedly "lifted off" sensible beings, the mathematical "unit" originates. And it originates as nothing more than the character of being a measure as such, a character expressed through its indivisibility and exactness. The character of the one as measure is what is responsible for the universal applicability of "pure" numbers, namely, of the applicability of the "unit" to any arbitrarily countable being whatsoever. The "unit" is so applicable precisely because its manner of being is *not* separate from the sensible beings that are the source of its abstracted *origin*. Hence it is only because sensible beings, *as* the *kind* of beings that they are, are one and indivisible, that the arithmetician – having already abstractedly posited the "unit" as totally indivisible – is able to then see what always follows from any given sensible being in so far as it is subject to being counted or calculated with as a "unit". Thus, for example, a human being as the kind of being it is, namely *as human being*, is one and indivisible and, as such, the *abstract* "unit" (*monas*) is applicable to it (M 3, 1078a23–5).

FOUR

Origin of the task of pure phenomenology

The descriptive psychological formation of the concept of number

Husserl's pure phenomenology is driven by the goal of making philosophy a rigorous science. By "science" he understood a method of research capable of generating possible true and false propositions on the basis of evidence. By "rigorous" science he understood a science that had advanced to the point of being in the possession of a methodology whose basic concepts and criteria for distinguishing true from false propositions were sufficiently demonstrated to permit an ongoing research agenda available to and embraced by a community of researchers. And by "evidence" he understood the legitimizing source of scientific and philosophical concepts in an experience more original than, but nevertheless related to, their conceptuality. The signal importance of this goal in Husserl's formulation of pure phenomenology cannot be overestimated at any stage of its development. It composes both the most basic intention of his thought and the standard by which he measures the success or failure of its development at any given time.

Husserl did not originally set out to establish a new science whose status as rigorous science would lead to a reform of philosophy. His initial goal was the more modest one of clarifying the most basic concept of arithmetic, number, within the context of a pre-existing philosophical method, that of his teacher Franz Brentano. Brentano's method sought to account for the formation of concepts on the basis of their origin from what appears to perception. He distinguished two kinds of perception, inner and outer, each derived from the nature of the contents that are perceived: psychic in the case of inner perception and physical in the case of outer perception. Brentano's method sought to describe concept formation exclusively by appealing to what appears to perception in either kind of perception, the appearing of which he characterized as "intuition". Rather than explain what so appears in either inner or outer intuition by hypothesizing its genesis in a physical cause that does not appear but is nevertheless responsible for what does appear, Brentano's method was animated by the goal to describe the contents of inner and outer appearances by strictly attending to their basis in intuition. Because in either inner or outer intuition the appearance of the content that appears involves not just the physical or psychic content of perception, but the awareness of the perception perceiving its content, Brentano understood both kinds of contents as "phenomena" that are related to this awareness, an awareness he termed "consciousness". The descriptive method of investigating the physical and psychic phenomena of consciousness was designated "descriptive psychology" by Brentano.

Brentano characterized physical phenomena as sensible qualities and their complexes and psychical phenomena as psychical acts directed towards the contents of consciousness. He termed the "appearing" character of these contents "presentation" (*Vorstellung*) and held that the defining trait of the psychic phenomenon is "the directedness to an object" of its act. Brentano used the Scholastic concept "intentionality" to denominate the psychic phenomenon's reference to an object and he maintained that the object intended by this reference has "intentional inexistence" in the presentation. The context for his idea that the object of a psychic presentation somehow less than fully exists is Aristotle's account of perception in *On the Soul*, which (as we have seen) characterizes perception generally as receptive of the *eidos* but not the material of the sensible thing.[1] Brentano therefore identified the object of a psychic presentation with the "formal" content of perception. Physical phenomena, which he understood as the primary contents of psychic phenomena, do not contain within themselves such a content. Thus, for Brentano, outer perceptions do not have a conscious content but are directed towards "outer" contents, even though such perceptions are nevertheless contents of psychic acts. Consciousness, according to Brentano, is therefore immediately directed towards these outer contents and only secondarily directed towards itself. Concepts arise for Brentano when a conscious act turns reflectively towards its contents and isolates the common element of several concrete phenomena of inner or outer intuition. Concepts are therefore generated in an abstraction assisted by reflection. The common element is responsible for the generality of the abstracted concept (the *abstractum*), which is therefore understood as the universal in the thing (*universum in re*).

Husserl's investigation of the formation of the concept of number in his first published work, the *Philosophy of Arithmetic* (subtitled "Psychological and Logical Investigations"), sought to establish its psychological genesis following Brentano's method. He was therefore guided by the Brentanian principles that no concept can be thought without an intuitive foundation in either inner or outer perception, that the determinate or "concrete" phenomenon of either kind of perception is given in inner perception, and that the formation of general concepts arises on the basis of an abstraction from that act. Husserl's question, then, was: what is the psychic act that provides the basis for the abstraction from which the concept of number arises? For him the concept of number exhibits three characteristics that distinguish it from singular concepts and the relations formed on the basis of inner or outer presentations. First, and most important, number concepts are multitudes and therefore the concept of number and its species, the number concepts, are determinations of the more general concept of multiplicity. Second, the multitude that composes number falls under the abstract concept of what Husserl calls "collective combination" (*kollektive Verbindung*), which is the most important part of the concept of multiplicity. Collective combination is responsible for bringing into relation the items that are related when a number is arrived at through counting, and it is expressed linguistically by the conjunction "and". And third, there is the concept of the "something" (*Etwas*) and the closely related "one" or "unit", which is that part of the concept of multiplicity and number responsible for any arbitrary thing whatever being countable and therefore for the articulation of the amount of more than one thing by a number concept.

While the principles of Brentano's descriptive psychology have the resources to account for the concept formation of the singular concept of "something" and the closely related concept of "one", they come up short in the case of accounting for the formation of the plural concept of multiplicity. This is because for Brentano the relations between presentations are intuited as already there in the phenomena and therefore as being on the same "level" as the presentations they relate. The nature of the relations is therefore dependent on the nature of their relational terms, such that the contents of these terms determine their relations. Husserl designates relations of this type as "primary" and characterizes them as "content relations". He distinguishes four kinds of these relations, none of which can account for the collective combination responsible for the relation of multiplicity and closely related number concepts. Thus there are primary relations between physical parts (e.g. spatial continuity), between "metaphysical" (Brentano's term) parts (e.g. extension and colour), between logical parts and wholes (e.g. genus and species), and between the characteristics of sense-perceptible qualities (e.g. equality, similarity).

All of these relations hold immediately with the intuition of the related parts or terms and are therefore intuitively given on the same level as what is related. In the case of the collective combination, however, that which is responsible for the relation among the contents cannot be found in the presentations of the related contents. The natures of these contents do not in any way entail or otherwise include in their presentation being related as a multitude. Each of the contents related in a multitude need not have anything in common in order to belong to the unity of the multitude, what Husserl calls an "assemblage" (*Inbegriff*), and even if they do have something in common, their commonality is manifestly not what is responsible for their being a part of the multitude. According to Husserl, "the related contents and the relation thus form, as it were, contents of distinct levels" (PA, 73/70). He calls such non-primary relations "psychical" and he considers collective combination as such a relation. Husserl characterizes it as "not intuitively given *in* the presentational content, but instead as having its subsistence only in certain psychical acts" (PA, 77/73). His answer to his Brentanian question – What is the psychic act that provides the basis for the abstraction from which the concept of number arises? – is therefore the act of collective combination. Collective combination is the psychic act of combining any arbitrary things whatever, for instance, in Husserl's example taken from Leibniz, "a tree, a feeling, the moon, and Italy", not in so far as they are this or that kind of object but in so far as they are "anything whatever" (*irgend Etwas*). The *concept* of collective combination, which like other concepts is general but unlike them is also materially empty and therefore *formal*, originates then in an abstractive reflection that is directed towards the act of collective combination that is responsible for relating otherwise discrete presentational contents into a multitude.

The multitude generated by the act of collective combination has the structure of "anything whatever, anything whatever, anything whatever, ...", or, more succinctly, "one, one, one, ...". The formal relatedness of the parts of the multiplicity is expressed by the conjunction "and", as in "anything whatever and anything whatever and ...", or "one and one and one ...". The multitude that arises in collective combination is unlimited, in the precise sense that the concept of multiplicity that it falls under is indeterminate, meaning there is no upper limit imposed on the combination of items composing a multitude. The imposition of limits on a multitude and therefore the generation of delimited (or, equivalently, determinate) multitudes results in the cardinal numbers, beginning with the first number, the number two, as "one and one", then three, as "one and one, and one", and so on.

The formation of the formal concept "anything" and therewith the concept of "one" or "unit", which are parts of the concept of multiplicity, occurs according to Husserl on the basis of an abstractive reflection that is directed to a less complex act than the act that yields the concept of collective combination. Abstractive reflection on the act of presentation yields the concept of "anything", and the formal concept of "one" is abstracted in turn from this materially empty formal concept.

Husserl's critique of the psychologism in *Philosophy of Arithmetic*

The first volume of Husserl's second major work, *Logical Investigations*, titled *Prolegomena to Pure Logic*, contains a devastating critique of "psychologism", which is the term Husserl uses pejoratively to refer to the assumption that the reality of mental facts has cognitive priority over all other dimensions of reality. A theory of knowledge based on this assumption supposes that the mind (or, equivalently for this theory, the psyche) is that part of nature responsible for the origin of all ideas and relations and that therefore the proper study of knowledge begins with the psychological investigation of the natural laws governing the mind. Husserl's critique of psychologism has two foci. First, he demonstrates that the significance of the ideas and relations that compose objective knowledge is *ideal* in the precise sense that its ideal character presupposes units of meaning that, according to strict necessity, cannot be otherwise. (For example, the identity of something cannot both be what it is and be something else, a relation must relate at least two items, a part must be related to a whole, and so on.) And he then shows that the significance of the idea of mental or psychic reality is contingent in the precise sense that, as a part of nature, the concept of its reality presupposes facts that can always in principle be otherwise. (For instance, from the fact that the threshold of hearing has a lower and an upper limit that can be measured, it does not follow that these limits cannot be otherwise; for example, different individuals may, and in fact do, exhibit different thresholds.) Second, he argues that the natural science charged with the task of investigating psychological reality, empirical psychology, presupposes cognitive meanings that are ideal (such as the law of non-contradiction, the "equality" of measurements that yield the same numerical results, and so on).

From what is established in his first point of focus, Husserl draws the conclusion that a theory of knowledge cannot appeal to the contingency of mental reality as the origin of ideal meaning without contradiction. In a word, Husserl argues that contingent facts cannot account for the necessity that belongs to ideal meanings, because the concept of contingency excludes the concept of necessity. And from what is established by his second focal point, Husserl argues that the theoretical claim that all the ideas and relations that compose knowledge have their basis in – and are therefore relative to – the empirical reality of the mind, is self-contradictory. It is self-contradictory because the psychological commitment to the contingent nature of the mind brings with it the theoretical commitment to knowledge claims that are *not* necessary, while the cognitive commitment to the claim that *all* knowledge is a certain way brings with it the theoretical commitment to knowledge claims that *are* necessary.

It is commonly assumed that Husserl's critique of psychologism in the *Prolegomena* has as one of its targets the psychological orientation of his investigations in *Philosophy of Arithmetic*. However, the kind of psychologism criticized in the *Prolegomena* is not to be found in *Philosophy of Arithmetic* (see Mohanty 1974; Willard 1980: 46–7). Nowhere in that work does Husserl claim that the ideal concepts of logic or mathematics originate in the empirical reality of the mind or that ideal concepts are really psychologically contingent facts. The orientation that pervades Husserl's *Philosophy of Arithmetic* clearly holds that knowledge involves necessity and that the concepts that are responsible for this necessity are *not* psychological in the crude empiricistic sense that is criticized in the *Prolegomena*. When Husserl does appeal to psychological acts it is to account for the formation of certain concepts whose objectivity is never in doubt, for example, the formal concept of "anything" and the related concept of "one", or for the formation of physical, metaphysical, logical and arithmetical relations whose objectivity, again, is never in doubt. In the case of Husserl's descriptively psychological investigation of the presentations whose sense perception is appealed to as the basis for the reflective abstraction that yields the general concepts and relations in question, it is again clear that Husserl is not claiming that these concepts and relations are psychological because of their formation in psychic acts.

There is one place in the *Philosophy of Arithmetic*, however, where it is clear that Husserl does not merely appeal to psychic acts in order to clarify the formation of a general concept or relation, but actually understands the concept of a relation in question as generated by a psychic act, and that is the case of the collective combination. But even here Husserl is not claiming that the concept is a psychic act. Rather, his claim is that the abstractive basis for the concept of collective combination is the putative result of the *act* of collective combination, namely the combination into a "whole" of items that otherwise need not be related in any way. Thus Husserl's claim is that by an abstractive reflection on the whole supposedly generated in the psychological act of combining things into a whole, a general and formal concept is generated, namely, the concept of collective combination that is the most important part of the general and formal concepts of multiplicity and number. Unlike, therefore, the abstraction responsible for the concept of a primary relation, which isolates an element that is common to and shared by several concrete presentations, the abstraction that yields the concept of collective combination involves the "the reflection upon the peculiar – and, in its peculiarity, quite noticeable – manner of unification of contents, as it shows up in every concrete assemblage" (PA, 21/20). The unification presented in the assemblage involves a relation that is unlike a primary relation, in that it is present as "something *more* and over and above the single parts" (Husserl 2005: 285). Husserl thus speaks of the unification at issue as a "whole", and holds that "precisely that which makes the whole and which would have to be noticed to allow us to speak of a whole, i.e., the combination of the parts" (*ibid.*), originates in the *act* of collective combination. And it is precisely in this claim, made repeatedly in the *Philosophy of Arithmetic*, that Husserl himself locates that work's psychologism.

In a 1913 discussion of the development of his thought subsequent to the *Philosophy of Arithmetic*, Husserl zeroes in on the shortcomings of the latter's appeal to "psychological reflection in Brentano's sense" (ILI, 126) to account for "the unity of a collection", the "concept of unity" (*ibid.*), and, finally, "the concept of cardinal number". Significantly, Husserl acknowledges "[t]he unity of a collection is no material [*sachliche*] unity, grounded in the collected items" (*ibid.*), and that therefore there was "certainly something correct" in his view that "the presentation of a collection was supposed to arise out of the collective combination". However, he now explicitly denies the ability of the "'reflection' upon the act of collecting" (ILI, 127) to yield the *unity* of the collection, because "from the reflection on acts" of collecting "the concept of collecting … is all that can result" – not the concept of the unity of the collection. Indeed, Husserl reports that "doubts unsettled, even tormented" him "already in the very beginnings" regarding the question "is the concept of cardinal number not something essentially different from the concept of collecting?", doubts that "then extended to all categorial concepts as I later called them and finally in another form to all concepts of objectivities of any sort whatever" (*ibid.*).

From logical psychologism to pure logic

Husserl's response to what he called *Philosophy of Arithmetic*'s "logical psychologism" was to embrace a form of "Platonism"[2] that completely separates the "ideal unities" belonging to the content of the general and formal concepts of mathematics and logic from the act of their being thought. As he put it in *Investigation I* of the second volume of *Logical Investigations*:

> As numbers … neither spring forth nor vanish with the act of enumeration, and as the endless number-series thus represents an objectively fixed set of general objects, sharply delimited by an ideal law, which no one can either add to or take away from, so it is with the ideal unities of pure logic, with its concepts, propositions, truths, or in other words, with its meanings. They are an

> ideally closed set of general objects, to which being thought or being expressed are alike contingent. (LI, 333)

The proper meaning of the claim Husserl makes here, to the effect that the contents of both mathematical and logical meanings are *independent* of their being thought or expressed, remains a point of contention to this day among interpreters of his thought. They find it understandably difficult to harmonize this view with Husserl's later one that the acts and objects of consciousness are always in "correlation" with one another, such that an act of consciousness (such as thinking) without an object (such as an ideal unity of pure logic), and the converse, is impossible to conceive. The context for what Husserl must mean here by "being thought or being expressed" includes the fact that his critique of psychologism in the first volume of *Logical Investigations* (the *Prolegomena*) did not prevent him from characterizing the method used in the second volume's investigations as "descriptive psychology". Despite the distance of the method used there from Brentano's intuitionism, whose account of concept formation is limited, on Husserl's view, by its exclusive appeal to what is given in conscious *acts per se*, Husserl nevertheless presented his investigations of logic under the banner of "psychology". The answer to the question how, given the critique of psychologism in the *Prolegomena*, Husserl thought psychology was still able to contribute anything to logical investigations contains the key to understanding the enthusiastic embrace of a species of Platonism expressed both by the quote above and by that work.

The short answer to this question is that Husserl did not consider psychologism and psychology as the same thing. The long answer is that Husserl initially[3] thought that a descriptive psychology, purified of psychologism, would be adequate to the task of clarifying the formation of the concepts of pure logic. Thus Husserl endeavoured to retain the Brentanian commitment to the descriptive investigation of the immanent contents of consciousness, but with the decisive difference that instead of limiting these contents to Brentano's understanding of psychic acts, Husserl now understood the contents of consciousness to include the *objects* of these acts. That is, Husserl sought to expand the notion of the content of the presentation of psychic acts beyond Brentano's "immanentism", which was limited by Brentano's understanding of the acts' intentional directness to "contain" their objects as their intrinsic parts. Husserl therefore sought to employ "descriptive psychology" in the service of a "phenomenology" of the complete psychic act. Thus, in addition to its intrinsic parts recognized by Brentano's descriptive psychology, Husserl held that to the act there belongs an "intentional content", which, while inseparable from the act's contents, nevertheless was irreducible to the act's intrinsic, or to say with Husserl, "real" (*reell*)[4] contents.

Husserl's attempt to purify descriptive psychology from psychologism therefore attempts to distinguish *in* the psychic act itself the properly psychological presentation from the properly objective, intentional presentation. Thinking and expression, on this understanding, would belong to the act's intrinsic contents, whereas the ideal meanings of pure logic would belong to the act's objective, intentional presentation. Not being an intrinsic part of the act, the "content" of the objectivity proper to the ideal meanings of pure logic is something to which the psychic acts of thinking are incapable of contributing anything. After all, precisely the claim that the *act* of collective combination contributed something to the *concept* of the unity of collective combination is what Husserl had himself identified as the psychologism of the *Philosophy of Arithmetic*.

From within this context, then, Husserl's separation from psychologism and the embrace of Platonism is understandable. But it is not defensible, as Husserl eventually came to realize, on grounds internal to his own understanding of the intentional essence of the psychic act. Whereas Brentano spoke of psychic acts in terms of both their "directedness towards an object" and that object's "intentional inexistence", Husserl characterized the psychic act as a whole in terms of its "intentionality", which included for Husserl its moment of consciousness. Above all, for Husserl, the intentionality belonging to the "act" character of the psychic act did not signify volitional doing or any other kind of concentrated activity, but the being related to and having of an intentional object that characterizes conscious "lived-experience" (*Erlebnis*). ("Lived-experience" is Husserl's technical term for that which is presented when both inner and outer perceptions are apprehended in descriptive psychology's – and, then, pure phenomenology's – methodical reflections.) Husserl did not conceive this relation as being between two things, the intentional act and the intentional object, but rather as that which obtains when one thing, "intentional lived-experience", is grasped according to its essence. Thus he writes, "If this lived-experience is present, then *eo ipso* and through its own essence (we must insist) the intentional 'relation' to an object is achieved, an object is 'intentionally present'" (LI, 558).

Husserl's description of intentionality's essence involves, on the one hand, the "quality" of the act, and, on the other, its "matter". By quality or, equivalently, "act character", Husserl described the manner of the intentional act's being directed towards and therefore "conscious of" the intentional object. This manner is an intrinsic part of the act and must always be manifest in some fashion, such as judging, wishing, doubting, questioning. The matter, on the other hand, is not an intrinsic (*reell*) part of the act but its intentional content. The matter refers to the identical meaning that shows up in acts possessing different act characters that refer to the same object. This content is responsible both for directing the act to the *object* referred to by the meaning and for its being so directed such that the same object can, in turn, be referred to by different matters (meanings). For example, one act may judge that Edmund Husserl is the Master, another may wish that Edmund Husserl is the Master, and still another may doubt that Edmund Husserl is the Master. These acts have different qualities (judging, wishing, doubting) but all present the same matter, which, in turn, forms a presentation of the same object (Edmund Husserl). Moreover, the object referred to by this same matter may also, in turn, be referred to by different matters, as in the case where two acts with the same quality but different matters nevertheless intend the same object, for instance, acts that present the "founder of pure phenomenology" and the "author of *Philosophy of Arithmetic*".

Husserl's descriptive psychology therefore distinguishes between: (i) the intrinsic contents of the intentional act, which are those processes that are properly "immanent" to the act; (ii) the act's intentional meaning contents, which are not immanent to the act's processes but nevertheless still immanent to consciousness and, moreover, "objectively" so (i.e. they have the status of presentations to which the intrinsic contents of the intentional act are directed); and (iii) the intentional object proper, which is not a part of consciousness but nevertheless that towards which consciousness is ultimately "intentionally related". He also (within the context of his descriptive psychology) refers to (i) as the intentional act's "phenomenological" contents, and to (i) and (ii) as the act's "intentional essence". Husserl's identification of the phenomenologically proper dimension of the act with its intrinsic contents effectively excludes the intentional content from its methodological purview and therefore that part of the act that presents the meanings proper to pure logic. Thus, strictly speaking, in Husserl's attempt to investigate the intentional essence of consciousness within the framework of a phenomenological method understood as a descriptive psychology purified of psychologism, the investigation of that part of the intentional essence responsible for lived-experience having an objective meaning and reference beyond consciousness strangely falls outside phenomenology. Thus the conviction that drives Husserl's separation from psychologism, namely the independence of the content of the meaning belonging to the ideal unities of pure logic and mathematics from the psychological processes of being thought and expressed, is incapable of being systematically investigated by the phenomenological method of descriptive psychology.

From pure logic to pure phenomenology

Husserl, of course, eventually recognized this. And his response is telling. Rather than reassess the wisdom of effecting the methodical separation from psychologism by embracing a "pure logic" that is ideal in the Platonic sense, he reformulated the phenomenological method in a way that sought to purify it of its psychological "presuppositions". He did so to the end of rendering its method capable of investigating that part of consciousness's intentional structure that he was convinced is relevant to the presentation of pure logic's objective meanings. Thus Husserl sought to remove the psychological presupposition that limited phenomenological reflection to the description of the intentional act's intrinsic (*reell*) contents, and thereby to expand phenomenology's subject matter to include the act's intentional contents. The resulting method, "pure phenomenology", would therefore retain descriptive psychology's methodical commitment to clarifying what appears without recourse to causal explanatory hypotheses, while also freeing itself from the presupposition of the psychological origin of the phenomenon. Phenomenology's commitment to remaining free from these two presuppositions – hypothetical speculations about the cause of the phenomenon's appearing and the psychological interpretation of the essence of intentionality – is then formulated by Husserl as its "principle of presuppositionlessness" (LI, Intro. §7).

Husserl's formulation of pure phenomenology, however, owes another debt to his critique of the *Philosophy of Arithmetic*'s psychologism besides the Platonism that he embraced in order to establish the ideal integrity characteristic of the unities of mathematics and pure logic. His notion of a signitive dimension belonging to intentionality and therefore a signitive dimension belonging to the intentional act's matter is a direct outgrowth of that work's understanding of "symbolic" presentations. The project of accounting psychologically for the genesis of the cardinal number concept in that work was a part of the larger project of tracing the origin of the "symbolic" concepts and operations of universal (as Husserl called it) or equivalently formal arithmetic back to the "authentic" numbers of elementary arithmetic and their operations. Husserl began the *Philosophy of Arithmetic* with the thesis of the "logical" equivalence of the authentic and symbolic concepts of number, that is, of (respectively) numbers whose presentation includes the intuitive and therefore direct presentation of the items enumerated and those that present these items indirectly, through the mediation of sense-perceptible symbols. By their logical equivalence he understood the identity of the objects – multitudes of units – referred to by each concept of number, and the origin, and therefore "foundation", of formal arithmetic's operations with the symbols of these multitudes in the operations on the numbers that present the arithmetical multitudes directly.

Husserl attempted to establish this foundation by showing that formal arithmetical concepts and operational relations have their basis in the psychologically conditioned idealization of authentic numbers and operations. That is, he tried to show that the symbolic concepts and operational relations grow out of ideal concepts and relations that arise owing to the limited power of the human mind to count and calculate with large numbers. Instead of authentically presenting the multitudes of units whose unity composes the contents of the number concepts, their indirect presentation via ideal concepts was initially supposed by Husserl to account for the identity of the logic of formal arithmetic with that of elementary arithmetic. However, in the course of his investigations he realized that formal arithmetic's operations have their basis in the "rules of the game" that govern its manipulation of sense-perceptible symbols and not in these symbols' indirect reference, through idealized concepts, to the contents of the authentic concept of number. If the criterion for logical equivalence is that of different concepts referring to the same object, as Husserl presented it in the *Philosophy of Arithemtic*, then the authentic number concept of elementary arithmetic and the symbolic number concept of formal arithmetic are *not* logically equivalent. Husserl drew this conclusion because the former refers to determinate amounts of multitudes of units, whereas the latter can no longer be said to refer to anything other than itself as a sense-perceptible symbol and, thus, it cannot be said to possess its conceptual status on the basis of its "objective reference" (i.e. reference to the objects of "authentic" arithmetic, namely delimited multitudes of units). Thus Husserl concluded that formal arithmetic's symbolic presentations derive their cognitive status as a function of their place in the rules of the game that govern the symbolic calculus, and not from any "logic" originating in concepts.

Three defining characteristics of Husserl's pure phenomenology can be traced to his response to the collapse of his original presupposition that authentic and symbolic number concepts are logically equivalent. First, the notion of "symbolic presentation" is reworked in light of the fact that it does *not present* the object towards which it is directed, but only indirectly refers to it, if at all. Properly speaking, what the *Philosophy of Arithmetic* called a symbolic presentation is really then a "symbolic *representation*", in the precise sense that its immanent content is structurally different from the presentation of the content that it represents. Husserl now attributes intentionality to the acts that are responsible for symbolic representations (what, eventually, are referred to simply as "representations"), and, indeed, in articulating their intentional structure he first formulates a defining characteristic of the pure phenomenological concept of intentionality, namely, the character of the "intention" as an intuitively "empty" content of consciousness. Second, closely connected with his formulation of a representational act of consciousness whose immanent content is an empty intention, Husserl articulates another defining characteristic of the pure phenomenological concept of intentionality, that of the "fulfilling" act that presents in intuition the object whose "meaning" (*Meinen*) is merely intended by the act of an empty intention. And, third, Husserl separates the idea of pure logic from the instrumentality of the symbolic calculus. He therefore sharply distinguishes the latter's source in the "rules of the game" from the source of the *concepts* that properly belong to pure logic's formal meanings and relations.

FIVE

Pure phenomenology and Platonism

The simple givenness of ideality

The account of the origin and development of Husserl's pure phenomenology so far has identified two important contexts for grasping as a "task" the significance of both his formulation of its method and the achievement of its goals. First, his realization of the shortcomings of a more or less orthodox adherence to the principles of Brentanian descriptive psychology for providing an adequate account of the concept of number formation generated the task of reforming these principles in a manner appropriate for the investigation of the ideal meanings that are operative in mathematics and pure logic. Second, his realization that even a reformed descriptive psychology operated with a fundamental presupposition that prevented the proper methodical access to the ideal meanings of mathematics and pure logic generated the task of reformulating the descriptive moment of descriptive psychology as a pure phenomenology dedicated to providing such access. The task-oriented character of "pure phenomenology" thus signals that it is not a finished philosophical system but a method of research and, above all, that a research agenda drives its methodology.

The research agenda of the *Logical Investigations* is the investigation of the intentional concept formation, or "constitution" (Husserl's preferred word), of the ideal meanings of mathematics and pure logic, the general status of which he termed "ideality". Rather than focus on resolving the problem in the *Philosophy of Arithmetic* that led to his rejection of psychologism, the "constitution" of the objective unity of the concept of whole that is characteristic of a multitude, namely, the concept of the collective combination, Husserl's investigations in the *Logical Investigations* focus on the problem of the constitution of ideality *per se*. In line with this, they also contain a sketch of the basic contours of the domain of pure logic: what – under Leibniz's influence – he termed in the *Logical Investigations* and henceforth the pure *mathesis universalis*. Like his embrace of Platonism, Husserl's articulation of the idea of a pure *mathesis universalis* does not follow from the results of concrete phenomenological investigations. Rather, once he becomes committed to the idea, the task of accounting for its phenomenological "foundation" becomes a part of phenomenology's research agenda. In the case at hand, Husserl envisages the pure *mathesis universalis* as the complete theory of all possible theory forms, that is, the theory of theories that establishes the unity of the heretofore separate theories of formal logic and formal mathematics.

Husserl's Platonism did not conceive the ideality of the meanings of mathematics and logic to be analogous in their structure or mode of apprehension to the structure and perception of sensible things. He thus did not consider abstract objects such as universals as things possessing the same mode of being as the individual things that exist in time and space. He did not, in other words, "hypostatize" ideality as having the same kind of being as non-ideal things. Nor (as is still commonly thought) did he draw from the fact that the intrinsic content of psychic acts is incapable of contributing anything to ideal meanings' content the conclusion that ideal meaning *per se* has being independently of minds of any type. Intentional acts for Husserl are *not* mental in the way that qualities of the mind have been understood to be mental since Descartes, namely, as properties of a thinking substance that is separate from corporeal substance and therefore severed from the "objective" reality of the world. The intentional act already *includes* its "object" for Husserl, although not, as we have seen, as an intrinsic part of this act but as its "intentional content". As the act's objective referent, the object's intentional content is irreducible to that of the act's, even though it is inseparable from the act by virtue of the act's intentional directedness towards its content.

Despite the cumbersome terminology of "act" and "act content" that saddles Husserl's pure phenomenology at this stage, his position is clear enough: within the immanence of the intentional act as a whole the objective referent of that act presents contents that cannot be reduced to the act's partial immanence and that therefore "transcend" it. Husserl eventually (in *Ideas I*) restricted the term "act" to consciousness's mode of directedness towards its object, thus distinguishing it from the object towards which it is directed. By terminologically distinguishing more sharply the intentional "act" from its "intentional object", the cumbersome talk of the latter being a non-intrinsic (*reell*) part of the former is therefore avoided.

But even with the old terminology, Husserl's analyses demonstrate time and again that, in his words, "My so-called 'Platonism' does not consist in some sort of metaphysical or epistemological substructures, hypotheses, or theories but rather in the simple reference to the type of original 'givens' which usually, however, are falsely explained away" (ILI, 118). The "simple reference", as Husserl puts it here, to the "original 'givens'" of ideal objects is, however, embedded in acts of abstraction that isolate the categorial features of sense-perceptible things *and* in acts of "ideating" abstraction that isolate the ideal contents of the categories themselves responsible for these features. Both types of abstraction occur in acts of "phenomenological" reflection that are driven by the cognitive intention of providing evidence that delivers what Husserl metaphorically characterizes as the full "bodily presence" (*Leibhaftigkeit*) proper to the category's ideality. And the termination of the intentional "regard" belonging to the "simple reference" of each type of abstraction in the acts of fulfilment that present the original givenness of their respectively apprehended categorial objects, what Husserl calls "consciousness of fulfilment", is termed by him "categorial intuition".

Phenomenological reflection as distinct from empirical introspection

By "phenomenological" reflection Husserl understood something radically different from the "inner perception" of the British empiricists and of his own Brentanian legacy. Husserl came to view the empirical distinction between inner and outer perception as something that is determined on the basis of the presupposition that there are objects whose being is either "inner" or "outer" in relation to the mind. Thus, on this view, the criterion that determines a perception as "inner" is its direction towards an object interior to the mind, while the criterion for an external perception is its direction towards an object external to the mind. However, the appeal to the presupposition of the reality of the mind as a criterion for making phenomenological distinctions violates Husserl's pure phenomenology's principle of presuppositionlessness, because such a presupposition is based in speculation about the mode of being of objects in relation to the being of an equally speculative object, the mind. The criterion employed by Husserl in order to determine non-speculatively the interiority and exteriority of perception, on the contrary, has its basis in distinctions originating in intentionality. Thus, on the one hand, the interiority of inner perception is determined by the contents of perception belonging to the same act that intends them, which is made manifest by their presenting themselves in a manner that is inseparable from the intending act. On the other hand, the exteriority of outer perception is determined by the contents of perception not belonging to the intending act, which is made manifest by their presenting themselves as unities that remain constant in multiple acts or as a single intentional object presented in multiple perspectives. Husserl's "intentional" account of the distinction between inner and outer perception therefore represents a radical break with Brentano's division of psychical and physical phenomena along the lines of their respective inner and outer presentations in sense perceptions. In Husserl's account, not just the psychical phenomenon but the physical phenomenon as well are characterized by the intentional directness of perception and the presentation of intentional objects. And Husserl's intentional account of inner perception dissociates from phenomenological reflection once and for all the empiricistic concept of "introspection", that is, the idea that the inward directedness of reflection has as its content the real "inner" contents of a particular mind.

Both inner and outer perception compose aspects of what Husserl refers to as "lived-experience" (*Erlebnis*), that is, the "experience" that is made available to pure phenomenological reflection as it is "lived", in contrast to "experience" (*Erfahrung*) as it is quantified and otherwise treated as a value-neutral datum by empirical methods of investigation. Husserl therefore sharply distinguishes pure phenomenological reflection from both "empiricistically" conceived inner perception (introspection) as well as from his own, pure phenomenological account of inner perception. Phenomenological reflection is itself a kind of lived-experience, albeit a "higher"-level one than that which characterizes lived-experience's natural course. In its natural course, lived-experience is directed towards its intentional objects, immanent in inner perception and outer or, equivalently, "transcendent" in outer perception. Husserl accordingly characterizes the natural "direction" of lived-experience as "straightforward", as it is *directly* oriented towards the *object* of lived-experience, whether inner or outer, rather than towards lived-experience's content as an experience. Phenomenological reflection, in contrast, is directed towards the *content* of lived-experience. Husserl characterizes this direction as "unnatural", because its concern is not with the seemingly direct contact and relation to things that perception provides; rather, phenomenological reflection is driven by the cognitive concern to provide philosophical "legitimization" for the implicit and explicit cognitional claims that issue from lived-experience's straightforwardness.

Each progressive stage of Husserl's phenomenology targets a different, albeit related, threat to the integrity of knowledge that, on his view, "demands" a philosophical response whose aim is to establish once and for all the legitimization of cognition. All the threats, however, lead back to the first threat that Husserl confronted and vanquished with the establishment of pure phenomenology, namely "empiricism". Empiricism is the original source of both psychologism and the radical scepticism that follows from its claim that all ideas and cognitive relations arise in sense perception's most basic components, sensations. The unnatural direction of phenomenological reflection is therefore "motivated" by the concern to overcome empirical scepticism by providing a phenomenological critique of knowledge that establishes the cognitive legitimacy of ideality. And it endeavours to establish this by tracing ideality's origin, which is to say, its "constitution", back to the intentional lived-experiences in which ideality is "given".

The account of intentionality's essence therefore occurs within the context of the "immanence" proper to phenomenological reflection, which, in contrast to the perceptual immanence characteristic of "inner perception", is reflective in a methodically rather than perceptually driven sense. Specifically, pure phenomenology's principled commitment to "presuppositionlessness" limits the scope of the reflection whose reflected content presents the content of lived-experience to precisely what is given in the *reflected* presentation of this content. The phenomenological description made possible by phenomenological reflection therefore limits itself to articulating what is given as *immanent* to its reflective "regard". "Regard", in turn, is the term used by Husserl to describe the consciousness that belongs to the intentionality characteristic of reflective lived-experience. The appeal to objects that cannot be exhibited immanently before this regard and the presupposition of a non-apparent cause in order to explain what is exhibited are both ruled out by pure phenomenology's commitment to presuppositionlessness. Indeed, so fundamental is pure phenomenology's methodical commitment to basing its cognition in what is immanently given to reflection and therefore intuited that Husserl enshrines it as his phenomenology's "principle of all principles" in section 24 of the first book of his *Ideas Pertaining to a Pure Phenomenology and to a Phenomenological Philosophy* (*Ideas I*): "that *everything originarily* (so to speak, in its 'full embodied presence' [*Leibhaftigkeit*]) *offered* to us *in 'intuition' is to be accepted simply as what it is presented as being*, but also *only within the limit in which it is presented there*" (43–4).

Husserl's self-understanding of his so-called (and he himself, as we have seen, so calls it) "Platonism", then, is that it is based in the "simple reference" to "original givens" that appear before pure phenomenology's methodically reflective regard. Because it can make absolutely no sense to characterize the status of the "being" of these givens as existing independently of the "mind" (understood as consciousness), it would seem that only a very superficial acquaintance with Husserl's phenomenology could lead to the claim that his talk of the apprehension of ideal objects in categorial intuition entailed the view that such objects exist independently of consciousness; that is, that such talk committed him to a robust Platonism. Of course, this, which is Husserl's view of the matter, assumes that his actual concrete analyses of ideality are consistent with his methodological principles. Three details that emerge from these analyses, however, complicate the simple affirmation that they are indeed consistent in this regard. First, Husserl speaks of the acts of intentional meaning as "instantiating" ideal objects, which objects, in turn, are designated as "species". Second, he characterizes the unity and validity belonging to categorial ideality as "already there" before it is apprehended in thought. And third, his account of the "intentional object" does not always make it clear whether he is referring to the immanent object that is properly a content of intentionality's reference to an object or to an objective referent of this reference that transcends all intentional immanence. This last complication is the most serious. Husserl came to recognize the ambiguity of his treatment of the "intentional object" and responded by reformulating pure phenomenology as a "transcendentally" pure phenomenology. This by no means uncontroversial development of pure phenomenology, as we shall see, was Husserl's attempt to respond philosophically to the deeper issues raised by the intentional object's ambiguity as both an immanent and transcendent object of consciousness.

The complication connected with Husserl's account of the species character of ideality grows out of his critique of Locke's and Hume's empirical theories of abstraction. Both theories, albeit in different ways, falsely explain away ideality's original givenness. In the case of Locke, abstraction is said to generate ideal objects through the mind's selective inattention to the specific qualities of individual objects. The resulting "abstract" object is supposed to be general and therefore to possess the capacity of representing all the objects of the kind from which it is abstracted. Hume's theory appeals to the association of the similarity between particular objects that is presented with their perception to account for the basis of individual perceptions functioning in a manner that nevertheless represents general meanings. Hume maintains that this is accomplished in two steps. First, the customary association of ideas that are similar allows the imagination to recall the similarity in question whenever it is confronted with a particular idea from among the previously associated ideas. Second, while remaining attentive to this similarity, the imagination "annexes" to it a particular word that refers only to the similarity among ideas, and this term thus functions in a manner to signify non-particular meaning. Husserl argues that in both theories the empirical presupposition that only sensations are capable of being experienced leads their authors to explain away something that is manifestly given – although, of course, not in sensation – in lived-experience, namely, the ideality of the species. In Locke's case, the very recognition of the need to account for the origin of the general idea of things signals that this idea is already an object of his lived-experience. In Hume's case, the recognition of the similarity between perceptual objects signals that there is already available to his lived-experience a general idea whose guidance is responsible for the similarity as such to be recognized in the first place.

Categorial intuition

Once the empiricist's presupposition that experience is composed exclusively of sensations is exposed as lacking justification by the unprejudiced reflection on the contents of lived-experience, Husserl maintains that, in addition to the perceptual quality of the act, its categorial quality can be discovered in these contents. The intentional quality of the perceptual act is directed towards the sense perception of individual objects; the categorial quality is directed towards the general idea that is their species. In sense perception the intentional reference belonging to the act's quality is directed towards *this* concrete individual thing or a property or part of the thing. In the categorial "perception" or, equivalently, "intuition", the intentional reference is directed towards the "idea", which is the "species" content of the here-and-now reference belonging to the sense perception's intentional reference. Thus to the concrete reference to *this* red car that intends something individual there belongs the categorial reference to the red meant not as an individual but as a species. In fact, Husserl describes the relation between the unity and ideality of the species and the matter of the individual categorial act that intends it as being the "same" as the relation between "this red" and "redness in general"; as "this red" is related to an "instance of" (*ein Einzelfall von*) "redness in general", so, too, is the matter of the individual categorial act related to the universal idea of the species red.

Husserl understood instantiation as a primitive "logical" relation, and thus not as the individual act having the meaning of being an "example" of the universal idea. The act's meaning therefore does not "exemplify" the universal idea as a whole but rather presents a partial moment of this whole to this act's intentional reference towards it. Because the categorial act is not given independently of the individual perceptual act, but is based on it in a relation of "higher" to "lower", the intentional apprehension of the categorial content is not an instance of the kind of intellectual intuition criticized by Kant. That is, it is not an act that is independent of sense perception and that therefore apprehends universals the way that sense perception apprehends individual things. It is rather an act that directs itself to an aspect of what is already given in the lived-experience of the concrete perceptual act's matter but that is not apprehended as such by that act. Husserl characterizes as "abstraction" the explicit act of intending the matter of the act given in the intentional meaning of the perception, although he differentiates it from both the empiricist's philosophical account and his own earlier descriptive psychological account. Unlike the empiricist's account, pure phenomenological abstraction does not generate the universal either by extracting it from the individual thing (Locke) or by attaching a particular term to a perceived similarity (Hume) in order to yield a universal significance. And, unlike abstraction in his earlier account, pure phenomenological abstraction does not generate the concept from a reflection on the act of its presentation.

Rather than generate its object, pure phenomenological abstraction makes it manifest in an act that highlights the givenness of the species's instance in the perceptual lived-experience of the individual thing, and it does so via a change in the act character (quality) of the act. Instead of straightforwardly intending the individual object in an act of sense perception, the intention of the act is redirected from the individual thing that composes the object of its intention to the contents of that intention. These contents include both sensations immanent to the act and the act's matter. The sensations, according to Husserl, are "lived through" during perception and thus not a proper part of the perception's intentional object; it is the "red" of the car that is perceived, not the sensation red, which appears only as the reflected content of an act of phenomenological reflection. And the act's matter, which is likewise "lived through" during perception, is what appears when the act of phenomenological reflection directs its intention away from the act's sensation contents towards its meaning contents. So long as the meaning contents of individual acts are the objects of the abstractive intention, the meaning that appears has the status of an instance of the species themselves. However, according to Husserl, a still higher-level abstractive act is possible, one of "ideating" abstraction, which shifts its intention away from the givenness of the matter in this or that individual act and instead intuits the ideal meaning of the species "itself". The ideal meaning of the species is thereby given to the "simple reference" of this intuition; it is given as the unity that "runs through" (and is therefore common to) its various "instances", which are made manifest in the ideative act's reflective encompassing of a multitude of individual abstractive acts.

Husserl's elaboration of the manner in which ideality is grasped leads him to extend its scope beyond that of the universality of the species to include the relations between ideal objects (categorial relations) and the unity of the complex categorial object that is composed as a whole from among these relations. His elaboration also leads him to expand the dimension of the intentional act that is responsible for its "reference" to the intentional object beyond the reference accomplished by its matter to include in this dimension the directedness that belongs to the individual perceptual act. Both elaborations challenge the capacity of the putative paradigmatic status of the universal's instantiation in an individual act to account for all ideal meaning and for all references to the intentional object.

The extension of ideality beyond the species follows Husserl's characterization of what he terms the categorial "state of affairs" (*Sachverhalt*), which is a categorial unity whose parts can be perceived in sense perception but whose whole can be *apprehended* only in their relations and unity, which patently cannot be made manifest in sense perception. The intuition of the state of affairs, like that of the species, has its basis in the individual act of perception. But unlike the universality of the species, which can be apprehended in a "simple" act of categorial intuition – that is, in the act of ideative abstraction that presents and grasps the "embodied presence" of the species – the apprehension of the state of affairs occurs in an act that is considerably more complex. For instance, the apprehension of the species white that is instantiated in the individual act of the perception of a white sheet of paper develops on the basis of singling out the partial perception of the "white", which is then ideatively abstracted in a manner that yields the unity of the species common to all the individual perceptual acts of the white. The apprehension of the state of affairs "the paper *is* white", or "I see *that* the paper is white", however, does not occur in the ideation of the unity of the species white. According to Husserl, it occurs in a relation among acts that brings about something more than the categorial intuition of the species white, namely, in that relation that brings about the categorial intuition of the paper's *being* white. This intuition occurs in a complex of related acts, one of which is perceptual, another that is a judicative, and a final one that is categorial. In the example of the state of affairs "the paper is white", the act of perception is characterized by its sensible intuition of the paper and the white. The act of judgement is characterized by its making explicit the paper's relation to the white, namely, that the paper is white. And the categorial act is characterized by its apprehension, as an object in its own right, of the "*is*" that is formed in the judgement relation, namely, its intuition as a categorial object.

Husserl's analyses show that the intentions of these acts are not the same: one intuits the sensible givenness of the paper and white; the next *relates* the sensibly given paper and the sensibly given white; and the final act intuits as an object the judgement intention itself that relates the paper and the white. Husserl's description of the relation between these acts is guided by his formal account of the various possible "foundational" relations between the parts and whole of an intentional object. Each act and the intentional relations that compose it involved in his account of categorial intuition, beginning with the perceptual act, provides what Husserl characterizes as a "one-sided" foundation for the next act. By this he means that the act of judgement occurs on the basis of the perceptual act and the categorial act on the basis of both the judicative and perceptual acts. Thus the presentation of an act of judgement requires the presentation of an act of perception and that of categorial intuition requires that of the judgement and perceptual acts, but not conversely: perception does not require judgement and judgement does not require categorial intuition. Given the importance of foundational relations for both Husserl's account of categorial intuition as well as for the descriptive analyses at work in each and every stage of his phenomenology, a closer look at their basis in his analysis of the relations between parts and wholes is in order.

Parts and wholes: foundational relations

Husserl calls anything that can be distinguished in an intentional object as a whole a "part", and he further distinguishes such parts into "pieces" and "moments". The part or parts of the whole of an intentional object that can be presented independently of it are respectively characterized as a "piece" or "pieces" of this whole. For example, a leg of a chair broken off from the chair can be presented in perception independently of the perception of the chair as whole. That part or those parts of an intentional whole that cannot be presented independently of the presentation of it as a whole are called its "moment" or "moments". For example, the species white cannot be presented independently of the generic species colour, and is therefore a moment in this generic species. The presentation of the generic species colour is therefore characterized by Husserl as the foundation for the presentation of the species white: white cannot present itself or appear without colour and therefore the appearance of white is necessarily "supplemented" by the appearance of colour. Because, however, the generic species colour can appear independently of the species white, colour is not founded in white and does not require the appearance of white as its "supplementation" in order to appear. The "foundational" relation between the moment white and colour is therefore "one-sided". The generic species colour, though, does need some one or more species of determinate colours in order to appear, which illustrates what Husserl characterizes as a "two-sided" or "reciprocal" foundation relation: the appearance of the various species of colours requires the supplementation of the generic species's colour's appearance and is therefore founded in this generic species, and this species itself requires the supplementation of the appearance of one or more species of colour for its appearance.

As we have seen, in the categorial intuition of the state of affairs "the paper is white", the "white" and the "paper" appear in an act of sense perception, which provides the foundation for the act of judgement that relates the paper and the white as the state of affairs "the paper is white"; and both of these acts, in turn, provide the foundation for the act of categorial intuition in which the *being* proper to its state of affairs appears and is therefore intuited. According to Husserl, the way in which the "*is*" and therefore the "*being*" of the paper's whiteness appears is something that occurs in neither the act of judgement that relates them nor in the act in which the "evidence" relevant to the judgement appears, but only in the "coincidence" (*Deckung*) of these two acts. And it is precisely the *intentionality* characteristic of this coincidence that is intuited and that therefore appears in the categorial act proper, as that which constitutes the "object" of the categorial intuition of the *being* proper to the state of affairs. The intentionality that composes this coincidence thus becomes a categorial object in its own right, namely, something that appears to the regard of a perception and hence in an intuition that yields what appears in excess of what appears in sense perception. Therefore, on Husserl's view, the object that appears in the coincidence of acts is categorial and its apprehension deserves the title "categorial intuition". As Husserl puts it, when the "signitive" intention of the act of judgement that refers "emptily" to its intentional object (in this case, to the copula relation "is" that relates the paper and white) coincides with the act that presents the evidence that fulfils the signification's intention, the intentionality proper to the coincidence of the signification with what is signified presents the *being* proper of the state of affairs composed of the relation *that* the paper is the white.

The fact that the intentionality *itself* characteristic of this coincidence has neither sensible qualities nor categorial features belonging to the perceptual object leads Husserl to conclude that the "*being*" of the state of affairs is not a property of the object of perception. "Being" in this context, however, is nevertheless something that "appears", and it does so to the higher-level intention that is directed to the intentionality that encompasses the categorial relations that fulfil the empty signitive intention of these relations and that belong thereby to the *ideal* structure of the perceptual object.

Finally, Husserl's attention to the distinction between indefinite and definite significations uncovers a "meaning" that refers to the intentional object that is not derived from the meaning instantiated in an act. The meaning of "this" when it signifies not just "something being pointed to" but "this computer in front of me", together with the content of this concrete reference, is something that cannot be derived from my act's instantiation of the indeterminate meaning of "this". Rather, what is responsible for the meaning of this signification is the individual perceptual act that refers to something whose givenness completes the act's specific "form" of intending its object.

Phenomenological "thematization" and Husserl's "so-called" Platonism

What, then, about Husserl's Platonism? Do the analyses of instantiation, abstractive ideation and categorial intuition maintain more than Husserl's methodical principle of presuppositionlessness allows, and appeal to ideality as an extra mental reality? Is Husserl therefore guilty of what everyone – except, it has to be noted (and shortly elaborated on), Plato and Aristotle – understands by the term "Platonism"? Four things must be noted before answering this question. First, what Husserl's analyses present here is stronger than the claim that the contents of psychic acts are "contingent" *vis-à-vis* the intentional content of ideal meaning; they are claiming that the content of ideal meaning itself is something that is presented in acts, and, moreover, presented in them in an objective manner. Additionally, they are claiming that this presentation is apprehended directly and therefore intuitively by yet another act that brings together the content of what the initially "objectively" empty signitive intention was directed towards, namely, the categorial content, and this content *itself*. Second, Husserl's reintroduction of "acts" in connection with the presentation of ideal meaning invited the critical interpretation that after rejecting psychologism in the *Prolegomena* he had "relapsed" into it in the second volume of the *Logical Investigations*. (This was an invitation that many would accept.) Third, Husserl uses a series of terms that originate in psychology – "thematize", "thematized", "thematic" and "thematization" – to characterize the relation between the pure phenomenological reflective act in which the categorial meaning is apprehended and the reflected content that yields that meaning. And, finally, fourth, Husserl characterizes the pure phenomenological "mode of givenness" of the reflected categorial meaning to the reflection in which it is given as "already there".

These last two points present a crucial aspect of Husserl's method of "phenomenological description" that is at once novel and the key to its cognitive pretensions. It is useful to recall that, in general, the descriptive moment of the phenomenological method is employed because the appeal to sense perception and sensible concepts cannot account properly for important aspects of cognition. These aspects include both the contents of cognition and the cognitive process itself that are at stake in Husserl's critique of psychologism and his subsequent investigation of the ideal cognitional contents belonging to pure logic. It is within this context that Husserl employs the term "thematize" to describe phenomenological reflection's capacity to bring to methodical awareness the straightforwardly "lived" contents of lived-experience; "thematized" to describe the condition of the lived-experience as a whole that is now before this methodical awareness;

"thematic" to describe the condition of the specific content of thematized lived-experience now before this same methodical awareness; and, finally, "thematization" for the entirety of this methodically reflective process.

That which is thematized together with its specific thematic content is characterized as presenting itself to reflection's methodical awareness with a "mode of givenness" that Husserl describes as "already there" or as "always already there" (*immer schon da*). Above all, what this descriptive term indicates is that coincident with its thematization, lived-experience does not present itself as coming into existence for the first time but rather as something that has been going on "prior" to its being thematized. The "priority" here, however, is not temporal, if by that term something is meant that is datable in terms of that modality of time that comes before the present, namely the "past". It is rather "descriptive" in the precise sense that any phenomenological claims about the content of lived-experience *before* it was reflected have to be investigated on the basis of lived-experience's appearance in the reflected content of phenomenological reflection subsequent to its thematization. This means, for instance, that the temporality of lived-experience can be investigated phenomenologically only on the basis of its thematization by methodical reflection, and not the reverse; namely, that the concepts belonging to the temporality of lived-experience can be employed in a phenomenological investigation of unthematized lived-experience.

The descriptive subtlety at play here in thematization and the mode of givenness of the thematized is decisive for understanding Husserl's appeal to acts in his account of the "simple reference" to the "original givens" of ideal meanings. The categorial relations and categorial "being" that compose these meanings, as "original givens", are given as "already there", prior to the advertence of the thematic intention of phenomenology's methodical reflection. This reflection, guided by the cognitive goal of accounting for the ideality of the concepts and relations belonging to the significations that "emptily intend" them in the judgements of pure logic, therefore makes their phenomenological investigation possible. And their mode of givenness, as "already there", eliminates once and for all, so Husserl thought, the absurd understanding that the "unnatural" act of their reflective thematization should in any way contribute anything of its "act character" to the phenomenal content of their ideality.

One philosopher who agreed with Husserl on this point was Martin Heidegger. Whatever the problems Heidegger had with Husserl's phenomenology, and they were to become both legion and very severe, he credited Husserl's account of categorial intuition with making possible the rediscovery of the genuine ancient Greek meaning of the *eidē* and the meaning of Being guiding their conception. And it was precisely Husserl's account of the ideal object as something given in a manner that preserves its integrity despite the fact that it is thought and expressed, and whose intuitive presentation and therefore "givenness" itself made manifest its "Being", that Heidegger found so profound in this regard. Indeed, Heidegger, who was rarely given to autobiographical statements about the influences on his thinking, consistently credited Husserl's Sixth Logical Investigation with providing a decisive clue for his own thinking about the unity of the meaning of Being, given its manifold ways of being spoken about.

We shall have occasion to discuss both Heidegger's assessment of Husserl's importance for understanding ancient Greek philosophy and his fundamental criticism of Husserl's transcendental phenomenology. However, the issue of the ambiguous status of the intentional object in Husserl's pure phenomenology still needs to be taken up in connection with the issue of his so-called Platonism, as does this Platonism's relation to the "Platonism" at issue in the historical Aristotle's dispute with Plato over the manner of being of the ideal being of the *eidē*.

SIX

Pure phenomenology as the transcendental-phenomenological investigation of absolute consciousness

The transcendental-phenomenological reduction

The ambiguity of the status of the intentional object, as both the immanent content of the act of intentionality and as this act's extra psychic and therefore transcendent referent, is resolved in one bold stroke with Husserl's formulation of the phenomenological reduction. The reduction accomplishes this by radicalizing pure phenomenology's methodical commitment to presuppositionlessness, a commitment that, as we have seen, is realized by the restriction of phenomenological description to that which appears as the reflected and therefore immanent content of phenomenological reflection. The phenomenologically reductive radicalization of pure phenomenology's methodical commitment and reflective character has three reciprocally founded moments: the "bracketing" of the "index of existence" of that which appears to phenomenological reflection, the suspension or "*epochē*" of the belief in this existence, and the "reduction" proper that follows from these first two moments, in which the reflected phenomenon is presented to phenomenological reflection with the effective "neutralization" of the distinction between its "immanent" and "transcendent" *objectivity*.

Husserl's notion of "bracketing" is borrowed from symbolic mathematics, where enclosing a mathematical expression in brackets indicates its operational precedence over the expressions surrounding it. His notion of "existential index" refers to the "taken-for-granted" status of the "existence" (as either a transcendent or immanent object) of the reflected content as it is initially given to phenomenological reflection. In the case of the bracketing of the existential index of the reflected content, Husserl characterizes the "operational precedence" as one of "putting out of play" the *question* of this content's existential status, that is, the question of whether it is *really* transcendent to experience or not. This question arises naturally, according to Husserl, because not only does the reflected content of *phenomenological* reflection present itself as "having already been there", prior to its reflective thematization, but also the reflected content of any reflection whatsoever so presents itself. And there is, according to him, a natural inclination to take it for granted that the priority of the reflected content to its reflective thematization entails its *existence* as an object that is transcendent not just to the act of reflective lived-experience but to any lived-experience whatsoever. This inclination is at the root of what Husserl describes as the "natural attitude", which involves both the "thesis" that the objects of lived-experience exist in a world that is "external" and therefore "transcendent" to their lived-experience and the corresponding belief in the "truth" of this thesis. The belief in the truth of the thesis of the world brings with it the uncritical acceptance of these objects as *being* just the way that they are given in lived-experience. Husserl terms the intentional act responsible for this thesis and the belief that affirms it a "positing" act, and he characterizes it as *intending* the object towards which it is directed as "actually existent, that is, as *transcendent* to the intentional act that intends it".

The bracketing moment of the phenomenological reduction, then, presupposes the pre-phenomenological operation of the natural attitude and its positing of the existence of the intentional object; by putting the thesis moment of this natural positing in "parentheses", phenomenological bracketing signals the methodical intent to neutralize operationally the result of its positing. The neutralization proper occurs with the "suspension" of the belief that affirms the thesis moment of the natural attitude, which Husserl designates using the Stoic term for withholding judgement and assent, *epochē*. The *phenomenological* reduction that follows from the bracketing and *epochē* of the content of phenomenological reflection yields a reflected *phenomenon* whose appearance – as an intentional content – to this reflection encompasses the natural "meaning" (*Sinn*) of the *objective* distinction between "immanent" and "transcendent". That is to say, because the phenomenological reduction changes (as Husserl sometimes puts it, drawing again from mathematical techniques to explain crucial phenomenological moves) the "sign" of the index of existence that is inseparable from the intentional object, this object's designation as either "immanent" or "transcendent" to intentionality becomes methodically irrelevant so long as the reduction remains in effect.

At stake in the methodical irrelevance of the intentional object's immanent or transcendent *being* is what Husserl refers to as the "nuance" of the phenomenological reduction, whereby a change in the manner of "intending" the intentional object brings about a corresponding transformation of the manner of its appearance. When this manner of intending follows the natural tendency to affirm the existence of the intentional object, the natural attitude is in effect and this object appears as something transcendent to and therefore independent of the act of intentionality that intends it. While in this attitude, it makes sense to question whether the proper philosophical status of the intentional object that appears is as something that is really transcendent to or only merely immanent to the intentional act to which it appears. But it cannot make any sense to question the philosophical status of the intentional object in this way once the phenomenological reduction is in effect, because the manner of intending it no longer posits its existence; yet – and precisely this is what Husserl maintains is the *nuance* of the reduction – the intentional object as a content of phenomenological reflection continues to appear just as it did prior to its being reduced, save for what is manifest in its appearance being now taken as the meaning (*Sinn*) instead of the being of what appears. The manner of intending the intentional object that takes what it appears to manifest, in its presentation, as the meaning rather than the existence of what appears – which is to say, that takes what appears (the phenomenon) to be coincident with the *meaning* proper to what appears – is characterized by Husserl as the "phenomenological attitude".

Analytical misunderstandings of the transcendental-phenomenological reduction

When Husserl's account of the phenomenological reduction is taken out of its *phenomenologically* reflective context and considered solely on the basis of the contextless analysis of the significance of the terms he uses, his claim that the phenomenological reduction effects the transformation of the intentional object into an intentional content and then into an intentional meaning becomes "analytically" meaningless. For when its reflective phenomenological context is disregarded, the significance of the concept "intentional object" seems to be necessarily that of an object that, *qua* its being intended, is *not* a real part and therefore *not* a content of the intentionality that intends it; in addition, the significance of the concept of "intentional content" seems to be that of a part of intentionality; and, finally, whatever the significance of the concept meaning (*Sinn*) may be, the significance of its identification with all that appears to intentionality cannot but seem to be meaningless. On this interpretation of the phenomenological reduction, Husserl's thought seems hopelessly confused, as the significance of his concept of intentional content putatively identifies *real* objects with *meanings* (which, on this interpretation, signify *concepts*). The seeming analytical confusion on Husserl's part in evidence here, moreover, is only compounded when the referent of the appeal to a change of "attitude" in his account of the phenomenological reduction is taken to be a psychological disposition. For now it appears that the confusion is based in Husserl's relapse into psychologism or into something far worse, German idealism, as we shall see when Husserl's account of absolute consciousness is considered.

A closer look, however, at the reflective phenomenological context for each moment of Husserl's claims and its impact on their significance discloses that he is grappling philosophically with something more fundamental than the question of the contextless significance of concepts. The significance of his claim that, subsequent to the phenomenological reduction, the intentional object is operationally equivalent to the intentional content is not the analytical understanding of this claim, namely, that the contents belonging to the concepts of intentional object and intentional content are identical. Rather, Husserl's claim signifies that the locus of all possible *evidence* in support of any claim about the transcendent *existence* of the *objective* referent belonging to intentionality can be found only in the reflectively thematized intentional *content* of this referent, the direct *ontological* inspection of its putative *object* being ruled out by its givenness in lived-experience. The context within which Husserl makes this claim, as we have seen, is both his critique of empiricism, which establishes that evidence for the properly speaking *objective* aspect of cognition cannot be found in sense intuition (including inner perception), and his critique of the descriptive psychological concept of "intentional immanence", which establishes that the immanent content proper to intentionality includes an "object" that is not a real (*reell*) part of the intentional act. The phenomenologically reductive claim in this regard, then, amounts to the claim that there is an insuperable epistemic condition for access to evidence in support of positive knowledge claims about objects that are independent of and therefore transcendent to the lived-experiences that putatively encounter such objects, and that this condition is the phenomenologically reflective thematization of a specimen of such lived-experience.

The significance of Husserl's claim that the reflectively thematized intentional content of such lived-experience, subsequent to the phenomenologically reductive neutralization of its index of existence, is coincident with the *meaning* of what appears as this content likewise is not the analytical understanding of the claim, namely, that the *being* of the real object of intentionality is *conceptual*. Rather, its significance is that the *intuitive* evidence for any claim about the real being of the object of intentionality is not only exhausted by what appears as the reflectively thematized intentional content of lived-experience, but that what so appears manifests the only possible basis for meaningful claims about its real being. That is, Husserl's position is that only knowledge claims backed by intuitive evidence are meaningful and that the sphere of such meaning is restricted to precisely that which is manifest as the phenomenologically reduced appearance of the reflectively thematized intentional content.

Five elements of Husserl's enduring philosophical self-interpretation of the transcendental-phenomenological reduction

The resolution of the ambiguity of the status of the intentional object brought about by Husserl's formulation of the phenomenological reduction inaugurates the second stage of his pure phenomenology. His philosophical self-interpretation of the significance of the initial results of the reduction in his *Ideas I*, the major work in which he articulated the significant advances in his thinking and formulation of a pure phenomenology since the *Logical Investigations*, is crucial for understanding not only this stage but all subsequent stages of his pure phenomenology. Notwithstanding the significant developments that characterize these latter stages, five elements of Husserl's philosophical self-interpretation in *Ideas I* remain constant throughout this development.

First, the phenomenological reduction makes accessible to philosophical cognition a region of being heretofore undiscovered and therefore unknown to philosophy and science, namely, transcendentally pure and absolute consciousness. By doing away with the ontological distinction between immanent and transcendent objects and thereby reducing their indexes of existence to the *phenomenologically* immanent mode of givenness or "how" of their appearance as phenomenologically reduced meaning, Husserl understood the consciousness to which the appearance of the phenomenon is given to be purified of all natural "transcendencies", including the transcendency of the general thesis of world itself; such consciousness, therefore, warrants for Husserl the designation "transcendental" consciousness. Moreover, Husserl understood the reductive change of "sign" with respect to existence – accomplished by what, in light of the preceding consideration, he most properly called the *transcendental*-phenomenological reduction – to be, in principle, comprehensive. Thus he understood all cognitive claims seeking legitimization, including, of course, phenomenology's cognitive claims, as relative to what he considered to be the sole possible source of intuitive evidence proper to their *meaning* as knowledge claims: the transcendentally pure consciousness in which all meaning has its source and which is therefore *itself* the "absolute" source of any possible meaning.

Second, on Husserl's view, for phenomenological cognition to become philosophical it has to satisfy the criterion of necessity and for it to be necessary it has to apprehend (as noted earlier) the "essence" or equivalently the "*eidos*" of its phenomenologically reduced subject domain. Hence, in addition to the transcendental-phenomenological reduction, phenomenological cognition requires an "eidetic reduction", the goal of which is to uncover and apprehend the essential, or *a priori*, structure of the phenomenon under investigation. The methodical process of eidetic reduction is isomorphic with that of abstractive ideation, save for two significant innovations. First, whereas, as we have seen, ideation is limited to isolating and apprehending logical species, the scope of ideality investigated by the eidetic reduction's methodical "essential seeing" or "eidetic intuition" is expanded to include, in addition to logical ideality, the ideality of the material and formal regions of being and, as well, of phenomenological "being". Husserl characterized a material region of being as the highest generic unity belonging to a class of individual objects and the formal region as the forms and laws of combination that belong to any object whatsoever. And the ideality of phenomenological being encompassed for him all the eidetic structures and processes of transcendental absolute consciousness responsible for the constitution of meaning. Second, while the process of abstractive ideation is limited to the apprehension of the species as a commonality encompassing a multitude of individual acts, the eidetic seeing proper to the eidetic reduction apprehends the *eidos* on the basis of a multitude of imaginatively generated variants of exemplars belonging to the region of being under investigation. Husserl refers to imaginative generation of exemplars generally as the "eidetic variation" and specifically as "free fantasy" or "imaginative variation". Given its systematic importance for phenomenological cognition, it is noteworthy that Husserl's most complete accounts of it are not to be found in any of the introductions to phenomenology published during his lifetime, but are only in the posthumously published *Phenomenological Psychology: Lectures, Summer Semester 1925* (1968) and in *Experience and Judgment* ([1939] 1985).

Third, Husserl understood the essential structure of transcendental consciousness to be intentional and its intentionality to manifest a "strict" *a priori* correlation with the world. One significant implication of this is that the meaning of any world phenomenon, including the phenomenon of the world as whole, is, for Husserl, in principle, traceable to its source in intentionality. The phenomenological analyses that trace phenomena to their source in the transcendental intentionality of absolute consciousness are called by him "constitutive", and phenomenology as a whole is defined by the project of tracing all "constituted" meaning to this source. Indeed, it is within the context of the "infinite task" that defines this project that

Husserl's phenomenological battle cry, "Return to the Things Themselves", is to be understood.

Fourth, Husserl understood the lived-experience whose thematically reflected content is subject to the transcendental-phenomenological reduction to have its natural foundation in the psyche, which he also understood to be a part of nature and therefore of the world. As a consequence, it is not just the transcendencies of the objects in the world and the world as a whole that need to be subject to the reduction in order to secure the region of transcendental absolute consciousness; the transcendency of the psyche's existence also needs to be reduced. Because of this, Husserl maintained that it is also possible to investigate systematically the eidetic structure of lived-experience without having reduced the psyche's natural existence. Such an investigation, despite being an eidetic investigation, would occur in the natural attitude and have the status of a phenomenological psychological enquiry. The conclusion Husserl drew from this is that phenomenological psychology and transcendental phenomenology are parallel sciences, and that to this cognitive parallelism there corresponds the parallelism of their subject matters: the natural psyche, on the one hand, and, on the other, transcendental absolute consciousness.

Fifth, Husserl's investigation of the eidetic structure of intentionality led him to make fundamental distinctions that resulted in recasting to a large extent the terminology employed in the *Logical Investigations*. The first and most fundamental distinction concerned the structure of intentionality as the directedness of consciousness to an object, which, as we have seen, was termed "act" in the *Logical Investigations*. Husserl's investigation of the intentional structure belonging to lived-experiences other than those that characterize the cognition of categorial objects and their relations led him to distinguish between such acts, which are thematically related to their intentional objects, and those that are not so related. Husserl characterized this difference in mode of intentionality in terms of "actionality" (*Aktualität*): he therefore designated thematic intentionality as "actional" (*aktuell*) and non-thematic intentionality as "non-actional". Terminologically, this distinction is reflected by Husserl's abandonment of "act" to signify intentionality as a whole, using it instead to refer to the "consciousness of" aspect of intentionality. To signify intentionality in its actional modality, Husserl now employed the Cartesian terms "*cogito*" and "*cogitatum*" to refer, respectively, to the thematic intending and the thematized intentional object that are its essential characteristics. He then introduced the Greek terms, *noēsis* and *noēma*, to refer to the two moments characteristic of the essential structure of intentionality *per se*, its conscious directedness towards (*noēsis*) and corresponding intentional object (*noēma*), either moment of which may be structured actionally or non-actionally. In connection with these intentional distinctions and terms, Husserl introduced the descriptive term "horizon" to refer to the manner in which the non-actional *noēsis* and *noēma* appear in relation to the *cogito*'s and *cogitatum*'s manner of appearance. And, finally, Husserl identified two horizonal limits that eidetically structure intentionality as such: the noetic horizon of inner time consciousness and the noematic horizon of the world. Both of these horizons exhibit an eidetic structure that limits their appearances to non-thematic and therefore non-objective modes of givenness.

Husserl's non-Platonistic and non-Cartesian philosophical self-interpretation of phenomenological being

Because these five elements of Husserl's philosophical self-interpretation remain constant throughout the development of his phenomenology, its relation to Platonism, both as it is traditionally understood and as it is presented in Plato's writings and in Aristotle's critique, may be provisionally assessed at this point. (The definitive assessment of the relation of Husserl's philosophical self-interpretation to Plato's and Aristotle's thought will occur at the end of this work, where it will be possible to consider it from the perspective of the entirety of the development of Husserl's thought.) According to the traditional formulation of the Platonistic conception of the nature of ideal beings, claims about *eidē* are analogous to claims about real physical objects and their relations, with the one decisive difference that *eidē* are neither physical nor individuated spatiotemporally and, thus, not perceived sensuously. Platonism therefore posits the thesis of an ideal world of entities – *eidē* – that are both separate (*chōriston*) from, and the cognitive and ontological foundations for, the real world of physical things possessing spatiotemporal properties. Husserl's account of the *a priori* correlation between the reduced phenomenon of the world and the intentional structure of transcendental absolute consciousness rules out, once and for all, the legitimacy of the charge that his transcendental phenomenology presupposes the *eidē* as the foundational entities of traditional Platonism. Nowhere does Husserl's phenomenology posit any kind of meaning, including the ideal meaning of logic and mathematics, as having being, or having a being, that is independent of its givenness as a reflected phenomenon and, therefore, as separate from the latter's foundedness in an individually given lived-experience. This also holds, of course, for the *eidē* that structure the phenomenological cognition of the meaning that appears to and is constituted by transcendental absolute consciousness. However, Husserl's philosophical interpretation of the latter as a region of being in its own right, albeit of "phenomenological being", gives rise to the problem of the *philosophical* meaning of the *being* that is appealed to by Husserl and continues to plague his transcendental phenomenology to this day. This problem concerns how to understand both Husserl's references to "being" subsequent to the transcendental-phenomenological reduction and the relation between "phenomenological being" and the being that is "put out of play" by the reduction itself.

There is a standard interpretation of this relation that maintains that Husserl's self-interpretation of phenomenological being is limited by his uncritical appropriation of the Cartesian concept of being, which equates the *truth* of being with its *being known*. Thus, on this view, despite the undeniable differences between Husserl's phenomenology and Descartes' first philosophy, Husserl's transcendental-phenomenological formulation of phenomenological being shares Descartes' presupposition that the "intuitive" immediacy and consequent transparency of the *cogito* accords it both its *epistemological* and *ontological* priority over the world. Both of these priorities are supposed to be based in the certitude of the *cogito* that results from its unmediated self-apprehension. The dualism of the being of consciousness and the being of the world therefore necessarily follows from this presupposition, with the unavoidable consequence that the phenomenological being of Husserl's transcendentally reduced consciousness cannot avoid suffering the same fate as that which *being* suffers in all philosophies of consciousness, which is the reduction of its primary meaning to that of a "subjective" phenomenon.

There are two fundamental problems with this interpretation, both of which have their source in a view of Descartes' philosophy that is too general to do justice to the details that are crucial to the critical claims it makes about Husserl's phenomenology. First, the "intuitive immediacy" of the *cogito* is not what is fundamentally responsible for the transparency of its *cogitationes*, that is, for the privileged epistemological warrant linked with the Cartesian philosophy of "clear and distinct" perception. The deceptionless manifestation of the *cogitatum* – so long as it is not judged, in accordance with Descartes' stipulation, to image or otherwise point to a being that is transcendent to the *cogitatum*'s mode of being as a part of the *cogito* – is not established by Descartes solely on the basis of criteria intrinsic to the nature of the *cogitatum*'s appearance. Rather, for Descartes, it is a transcendent principle grounded in a transcendent Being that guarantees the transparency of clear and distinct perception of the *cogitatum*, the manifest goodness of God and the ungodly inconsistency that would have to characterize God's ever bringing it about that a clear and distinct perception should prove deceptive. Thus, second, this means that the attempt to understand being in Descartes' philosophy as a completely subjective phenomenon, that is, as what clearly and distinctly appears in thought as the *cogitatum*, is misguided. Because the possibility of being deceived by what *appears* in a clear and distinct perception remains until the *metaphysical* establishment of its incorrigibility removes it, the clarity and distinctness of what appears is incapable of *independently* establishing either the meaning or the being of anything that is transcendent to the *cogito*. Moreover, what the principle of God's goodness guarantees is *not* that the *cogitatum*, as it appears in clear and distinct perception, is somehow related to the *being* of something that is transcendent to this appearance, but only the ontologically much weaker claim that there can be no deception in this perception *so long as no judgement is made that the content of the perception contains a true reference to a transcendent being.*

The precedent for the presupposition that the phenomenon itself is capable of establishing the truth of the being of something, and of its doing so independently of the appeal to an additional principle or transcendent Being, which is the presupposition that guides Husserl's understanding of the phenomenon, therefore cannot be found in Descartes' philosophy. Indeed, as we have seen, this presupposition occurs first in Aristotle, and it occurs within the context of his critique of the status of the phenomenon in Plato's philosophy.

The phenomenon in Plato and Aristotle and in transcendental phenomenology: preview

As already mentioned, Aristotle situates his account of the phenomenon, that is, of the appearance as *phantasma*, in critical contradistinction to Plato's account of the same. For both thinkers *phantasia* is what is responsible for the soul's capacity to see the *phantasma*, that is, for the soul's *seeing* of the appearance. However, Aristotle rejects Plato's connection of *phantasia* with sensible judgement (*doxa*), that is, with assertion and denial in sensing, and, therefore, Plato's identification of *phantasia* with sense perception. Aristotle's ground for this rejection is that the appearance that is illuminated by *phantasia* is independent of such judgement. For Aristotle, the *phantasma* is precisely what the soul sees when the sensible being responsible for sense perception ceases to act on it. What is seen, on Aristotle's view, has a twofold manner of being, which, accordingly, can been seen as either something in its "own right" (*kath' auto*), as a thing beheld and therefore as a certain "thought" (*noēma*), or as "being of something", as a certain kind of likeness or reminder of things that are absent. In either case, what the soul sees according to Aristotle is a pure appearance, the content of which is untouched by judgement. The twofold being of the *phantasma*, and the two ways of seeing it, are the original philosophical precedents for Husserl's presupposition that the reflected phenomenon, when reductively deprived of its index of existence and transformed thereby into a transcendental phenomenon, does not suffer any loss of *phenomenal* content but remains just as it was before, save for the neutralization of its index of existence. And it is precisely this presupposition that is behind the most crucial claim at work in Husserl's phenomenology, namely, that the transcendental reduction does not change the *content* of what is reduced, but only its existence status.

Aristotle, of course, unlike Husserl, was not in a position to appeal to metaphors drawn from symbolic mathematics to explain the twofold being of the same phenomenon. But Aristotle's illustration of this twofoldness makes the same point as Husserl's metaphors by comparing the *phantasma* to "what is drawn on a tablet". Thus, just as the drawing is both a figure and a likeness, although what it is to *be* each of these two things is not the same, so, too, the bracketed and unbracketed phenomenon are the same, although what it is to *be* each of them is not. To be sure, Aristotle does not understand the two ways of seeing the *phantasma* as Husserl does, namely, as the result of a methodical procedure oriented toward the goal of the evident apprehension of all objects, including the *being* of what is. Nevertheless, Husserl's claim that the reductive neutralization of the natural phenomenon yields a transcendental phenomenon that is effectively *transparent* with the natural phenomenon presupposes both the twofold being of the phenomenon that is made explicit in Aristotle's argument and the consequence that he draws from this: that – in accordance with this twofoldness – the soul sees it in one of two ways. Indeed, these two ways of seeing are themselves remarkably similar to Husserl's description of the natural and transcendental-phenomenological attitudes. As we have seen, the natural attitude sees the phenomenon in terms of its index of transcendency, its reference to an object not given in the phenomenon, which tracks Aristotle's account of seeing the *phantasma* as a reference to something absent; and the transcendental attitude sees the phenomenon strictly in terms of what is given in its appearance, which tracks Aristotle's account of seeing the *phantasma* as something in its own right.

The philosophical proximity to Aristotle's notion of the *phantasma* of Husserl's presupposition that the transcendental phenomenon is of a nature to establish the truth of the being of something does not, to be sure, suggest that Aristotle conceived anything remotely approaching the specific task Husserl sets for transcendental phenomenology. That is, it does not suggest that Aristotle conceived the investigation of the soul's seeing the *noēma* in the service of accounting for the *evidence* that establishes the *phantasma*'s reference – when it is seen as a *likeness* – to the absent thing. But what this proximity points to is that Husserl's account of the transcendental phenomenon shares the basic ontological presupposition that is implicit in Aristotle's account of the *phantasma*, namely, that it is able to provide an incorrigible appearance of *what is*, that is, an appearance whose content is in complete fidelity with its source and therefore cannot be corrected *vis-à-vis* its origin. For both thinkers, the phenomenon's incorrigibility in no way implies the freedom from falsehood: if the original proves false, then so too will its phenomenon, since, for Husserl as for Aristotle, the incorrigibility at issue has its basis in the phenomenon's fidelity to sense perception. Finally, Husserl also shares Aristotle's view that one aspect of the *phantasma*'s incorrigibility is also coincident with the freedom from falsehood, namely, the *phantasma*'s reception of the sense impression. For Husserl as for Aristotle, there can be no falsehood in the *appearance* to the soul (Aristotle) or consciousness (Husserl) of the putatively most basic sense qualities, the impressions of colour, sound, smell, taste and touch that compose the objects of the proper senses.

In addition to the precedent for the basic ontological assumption of Husserl's transcendental phenomenology that is provided by the twofold being of the *phantasma* in Aristotle's thought, Husserl's phenomenological account of the intuition of *eidē* has as its precedent Aristotle's view that the presence to thought of *eidē* requires *phantasmata*. For Husserl, as has been mentioned, the intuition of *eidē* likewise requires phenomena that refer to but do not posit the existence of beings. Husserl calls the latter "images" in his account of the free fantasy or eidetic variation proper to the eidetic reduction that brings about eidetic seeing, because having been neutralized, such phenomena no longer *posit* being even though they still *present* it, albeit in a non-positional way. There is, however, a decisive difference between Husserl's and Aristotle's accounts of the exact relation of, respectively, *phantasmata* and images to *eidē* that can be discerned in these accounts, despite (as has been noted) the notoriously cryptic nature of Aristotle's texts on this topic. The difference concerns Husserl's view that manifold images (generated by free fantasy or eidetic variation) are necessary to discover and then intuit an *eidos*, which contrasts sharply with Aristotle's view that a single *phantasma* is sufficient to illuminate an *eidos*. And, with this difference, Plato's precedence for Husserl's account of both the *seeing* and the *being seen* of the "manner of being" proper to the *eidos* comes into view.

As we have seen, Plato's account of the *phantasma* occurs within the context of appearances in general, understood as what "looks" like something, "images" (*eidola*), which are further specified according to whether they have the status of "likenesses" (*eikones*), that is, appearances that *are* like something, or "apparitions" (*phantasmata*), that is, appearances that only *seem* to be like something. Moreover, his concern is with the invisible images that occur in the medium of *logos*, through which appear both the *beinghood* of things, when the word images are likenesses, and Not-Being, when the word images are apparitions. Plato's specific concern is that because Not-Being is something that appears, the distinction between appearances that are likenesses and appearances that are apparitions cannot simply be assumed to be apparent at the start of a philosophical investigation; rather, this distinction is something that must be established by the dialectical investigation into the truth of the originals that are presupposed by all images, namely the *eidē*. Thus, for Plato, *seeing* an *eidos* requires the traversal of a multitude of images and their division into likenesses and apparitions. This division is made on the basis of, respectively, whether an image's reference to the *eidos*'s unity of a multitude is consistent with the appearance of unity itself and is therefore one and limited, or whether it is inconsistent with the appearance of unity itself and therefore belongs to an unlimited multitude. Very significant in regard to this distinction is that the appearance brought about by sense perception (*phantasia*) is divided under the heading of *phantasma*, because what appears through the senses only *seems* to be what is responsible for the thing that appears. In truth, it is not the sense qualities of the thing but the invisible and therefore non-sensible *eidos* that is responsible for what the thing *is* that appears through the senses.

The precedent that Plato's account of the *seeing* of *eidē* sets for Husserl's account of eidetic intuition is twofold. On the one hand, for Plato as for Husserl, the seeing of an *eidos* occurs on the basis of a multitude of (Plato) or manifold (Husserl) appearances that yield the *eidos*'s unity. On the other hand, for both thinkers the seeing of an *eidos* presupposes the purification of sense perception from the many appearances through which its unity appears. Aristotle rejects both of these presuppositions, as already noted, in his critique of Plato's account of the manner of being of the *eidē*. Thus, for Aristotle, seeing the *eidos* does not presuppose a multitude; seeing the unity of an *eidos* does not look to a "common thing" (*koinon*) that is a "one over the many" but to the "common thing" that unites the soul's knowledge and the thing known. And neither, too, for Aristotle does the seeing of an *eidos* require the soul to prescind from sense perception, as the *intelligible eidos* is to be found – admittedly, somehow, in a manner none too clear in Aristotle's texts – nowhere else than in the sensible *eidos*.

For Plato the *being seen* of the *eidē*, in turn, requires that the most basic presupposition of the *logos* that guides the *seeing* that traverses and divides into two (as "likenesses" and "apparitions") their appearances, namely, the presupposition that what is *being seen* – the *eidos* – is one, be pushed aside.

Once this presupposition is pushed aside, *logos*'s invisible word images are no longer taken as fundamental *likenesses* of the *eidē* that they nevertheless continue to refer to, which permits the *eidē* to appear in their own right, albeit without the clarity afforded by *logos*'s most basic presupposition that what it is about and therefore *seeing* is one. As such, the *eidē* are manifest as multitudes of non-homogeneous and therefore unique units that are united, on the one hand, by other, separate, non-homogeneous and unique units, and, on the other hand, by the separate unity in beinghood of the two capital, non-homogeneous and most opposite units, Rest and Motion; and the appearances and therefore *being seen* of these *eidē*, in turn, are generated by the two supreme *eidetic* principles, the Same and the Other.

Plato's account of the *being seen* of the *eidē* sets the precedent for Husserl's lasting conviction that transcendental phenomenology is a foundational science and that this foundation is secured by the *being seen* of the *eidē* as they appear to eidetic intuition. Moreover, the *aporiae* that beset Plato's attempts to articulate the being proper to the *eidē*, given the weakness of the *logos* in the face of the peculiar one over many being that is characteristic of both the unity of numbers and the community or participation of *eidē* with one another, are likewise encountered by Husserl. Thus, on the one hand, there is Husserl's encounter with the peculiar "one over many" unity of cardinal numbers, which defeated his descriptive psychological attempt to account for its logical ground. (Indeed, as we shall see, the fairly common assumption that Husserl's account of the categoriality proper to pure logic and the closely related phenomenological theory of judgement is able to accomplish what his descriptive psychology could not in the case of providing a logical foundation for the unity of cardinal numbers turns out to be unfounded on closer examination of his later work.) While, on the other hand, there is Husserl's lifelong struggle to ground phenomenologically not only ideality's unity in relation to the manifold of lived-experiences in which it is given, but to ground as well the "phenomenological" mode of being of ideality itself, as a self-identical unity whose meaning is completely independent of the manifold in which it is necessarily given. These two foundational problematics are not the same, as is also commonly assumed. The first concerns the foundation of the *eidetic seeing* that makes possible *seeing* an *eidos* as a unity that encompasses a manifold; the second concerns the foundation of the *eidos*'s *being seen* as a self-subsistent unity in any moment of the manifold that presents its appearance to eidetic seeing.

This assessment of the precedent that Aristotle's account of the *phantasma* provides for the basic ontological assumption of Husserl's transcendental phenomenology as well as of the precedent that Plato's account of the seeing and being seen of the *eidē* sets for Husserl eidetic reduction is necessarily provisional at this point. Its aim, however, is to prepare the basis for establishing something more than the existence of an external relation between the philosophical content of these precedents and Husserl's transcendental phenomenology. Once our discussion of the development of Husserl's phenomenology is complete, we shall establish the direct connection of these precedents, in the guise of their "sedimentation", with the most basic philosophical presuppositions of Husserl's transcendental phenomenology. Moreover, we shall establish that, in contrast to the presuppositions guiding the criticisms of transcendental phenomenology presented by Husserl's two most prominent critics, Heidegger and Derrida, Husserl's phenomenology and therefore his thought alone has the resources both to recognize and to appropriate critically its own presuppositions.

SEVEN

Transcendental phenomenology of absolute consciousness and phenomenological philosophy

Inadequate and adequate evidence: the Leibnizian precedent

In addition to these five characteristic and enduring basic elements of Husserl's initial philosophical self-interpretation of the significance of the transcendental reduction, other aspects of his initial self-interpretation are either modified or significantly recast in the course of his phenomenology's development. The revision and correction of previous claims is consistent with Husserl's self-understanding of phenomenology as rigorous science. Thus, in contrast to the cognitive pretension of a philosophical system, which is to endure fundamentally without change throughout time, Husserl understood phenomenological cognition to take place in concrete research devoted to specifically phenomenological problems, and to produce cognitive claims that are, in principle, revisable. The general heading of these problems is the previously mentioned analyses of constitution, which are then further specified on the basis of Husserl's ongoing phenomenological research. The second stage of the development of Husserl's phenomenology, which is coincident with what is sometimes called the "transcendental turn" of *Ideas I*, identified as the major areas of phenomenological research the constitution of the unity proper to phenomenon of the world, including that of the various material regions of objects, and the constitution of the unity of lived-experiences. In addition to these research areas, Husserl's third stage added the constitution of the genesis of meaning as well as the constitution of intersubjectivity. And, in the fourth and final stage of the development of his thought, Husserl introduced the constitution in history of meaning, including the *a priori* meaning of the formal sciences, as transcendental phenomenology's most pressing, if not most fundamental, problem.

The revisable, in principle, nature of phenomenological cognition in this or that problem area, however, is counterbalanced by Husserl's philosophical self-interpretation of the unsurpassable epistemological warrant of certain eidetic claims, a warrant that is established on the strength of the evidence on which they are founded. As we have seen, evidence in general is constituted for Husserl on the basis of the coincidence of empty intentions with fulfilling intentions, a coincidence that is itself the fulfilment of the reflective intentionality operative in phenomenological cognition that thematizes the previously straightforward directedness of cognitive and generally meaningful lived-experiences. Husserl, however, further refines the phenomenological notion of evidence in terms of its strength and scope, and, following Leibniz, he introduces criteria for distinguishing fundamentally these determinations of evidence. Because Husserl uses Leibniz's most basic terms, while, of course, modifying them to suit his purposes, it is worthwhile to review briefly their original context and meaning for Leibniz.

Leibniz (1684) provides a set of criteria for determining the degree of perfection belonging to the "cognitive awareness of things" (*cognitio*), beginning with the least amount of perfection and ending with the ideal of perfect cognition. The criteria are introduced to mediate the controversies over true and false ideas generated by the employment of Descartes' criterion of "clear and distinct" for the recognition of truth. Leibniz's criteria address the basis for distinguishing "obscure" from "clear" *cognitio*, and then "clear and confused" from "clear and distinct" *cognitio*, and then, again, "distinct and inadequate" from "distinct and adequate" *cognitio*, and, finally, "adequate and blind or symbolic" from "adequate and intuitive" *cognitio*. Obscure *cognitio* is not able to recognize the thing represented, while clear *cognitio* is able to do so. Clear *cognitio* is confused if it is unable to articulate the determinations that distinguish the thing represented from similar things, and distinct when it is able to enumerate, one by one, such determinations. Distinct *cognitio* is inadequate when not all of the determinations that compose its representation of the thing are distinctly represented, that is, when some of them are represented clearly but confusedly. *Cognitio* that is distinct and adequate would be capable of clearly and distinctly representing *at once* all of the determinations that compose the nature of the thing represented, which is a capacity Leibniz doubts humans have, given the lengthy analysis that is often involved, although on his view it is approached by the knowledge of numbers. Instead of clearly and distinctly representing all the determinations that compose the nature of the thing represented, signs are usually employed indicating that the knower has the power, at will, to produce such representations, in which case, for Leibniz, the *cognitio* is both adequate and blind or symbolic. When all the determinations that compose the nature of the thing are clearly and distinctly represented, or, as is the case for human *cognitio*, in so far as these determinations are clearly and distinctly represented, *cognitio* is adequate and intuitive.

Husserl borrowed Leibniz's terms "inadequate" and "adequate" to characterize the scope of the fulfilment of empty intentions, stipulating that inadequate fulfilment or evidence falls short of a complete coincidence of the intended meaning and that adequate evidence yields their total coincidence. This usage is very close to Leibniz's (a fact noted by Heidegger), although there is a profound and decisive difference in Husserl's understanding of the criteria for "symbolic" and "intuitive" in contrast to Leibniz's (a fact missed by Heidegger). Thus, on the one hand, Husserl follows Leibniz's understanding of the epistemic standard of "inadequate" to mark the incomplete manifestation of the essential determinations of something that is otherwise represented in cognition and therefore "known". On the other hand, both thinkers understand by "adequate" the standard that marks the complete manifestation of the essential determinations of the object of cognition. Husserl, however, departs significantly from Leibniz when it comes to the latter's claim that it is possible to have adequate cognition that is symbolic. For Husserl, this is impossible, because the mark of evidence is precisely its intuitiveness, and therefore symbolic representations, by definition lacking intuition, are intrinsically inadequate. Husserl also departs from Leibniz by employing the term "apodictic" to characterize evidence, assigning to it the Cartesian meaning of indubitable, which during the second stage of phenomenology's development he maintained is achieved only through adequate evidence.

Husserl's transcendental-phenomenological investigations of evidence are eidetic, and therefore seek to establish the eidetically necessary scope and limits of the intuitive fulfilment or givenness of the phenomena appropriate to the constitutional analyses of phenomenology's problem domains. The results of these investigations provide the framework for concrete constitutional research, and despite the fact that Husserl presents them as apodictic, he nevertheless eventually revised both his identification of apodictic evidence with adequate givenness and his initial self-interpretation of the philosophical significance of the eidetic difference in the givenness of the world and the unity of consciousness. His initial account of the latter contrasted the eidetic necessity of the inadequate and therefore imperfect givenness of the unity of world and all worldly objects with the eidetic necessity of the perfect givenness of the immanent contents belonging to lived-experiences. Husserl's reasons for making these initial claims, as well as his reasons for revising them, are rooted in the innermost dynamic that informs transcendental phenomenology's relation to phenomenological philosophy, a dynamic that plays itself out in the tension between what phenomenology presents as evidence and the philosophical significance of this evidence that is advanced by Husserl's philosophical self-interpretations. A closer look at both the original appearance of this dynamic and its development will not only provide an account of the development of phenomenology from, as it were, the inside out, but will also uncover the internal consistency, or lack thereof, of the reasons behind each of Husserl's revisions and consequent attempts at self-correction.

Fact–essence distinction as guiding clue for Husserl's initial self-interpretation of transcendental phenomenology

Phenomenology's constitutional research requires what Husserl termed a "guiding clue" (*Leitfaden*) to constellate both the theme for its methodical reflections and a specimen of constituted meaning to serve as the point of departure for its constitutional analysis. The most fundamental guiding clue for the initial stage of transcendental phenomenology is the "fact–essence" distinction, which guides Husserl's articulation of both the contradistinction of phenomenology's status as a science of essences to all sciences of facts and his initial account of the transcendental-phenomenological region of absolute consciousness. The next stage of transcendental phenomenology is characterized by the dominance of two guiding clues: the Cartesian-inspired "idea of first philosophy" and the clue, internal to phenomenology, of the function of "sedimented" meanings and their "hidden" intentional accomplishments in the constitution proper to all being and meaning. And, finally, in its last stage, Husserl's transcendental phenomenology is guided by the existential crisis occasioned by philosophy's lack of rational unity, which provides the clue for extending the scope of phenomenological reflection, in the search for this unity, to both the historical constitution of meaning and this meaning's constitution as historical.

The "fact–essence" distinction thematizes the existing sciences along the dividing line of sciences (natural and human) of facts, for example physics and history, and sciences of essences, for example geometry. Husserl articulates the basis of this division in terms of the essential distinction between fact and essence: factual sciences deal with objects, that is, *facts*, whose meaning includes the *essential* possibility of being otherwise, whereas sciences of essences deal with objects, that is, essences, whose meaning is *essentially* invariant and therefore excludes the possibility of being otherwise. Husserl also distinguishes two kinds of essences, exact and morphological, using as the criteria for this distinction both the intrinsic distinguishability proper to their conceptuality and the degree of precision defining their sphere of application. Morphological essences, owing to their origin in the *description* of sense perception, are intrinsically "vague", and, because the scope of their application is limited to the flux of things, they are "fluid".

Exact essences, in contrast, are intrinsically distinguishable and precise in their application, owing to their origin in what is "ideal". The ideal, for Husserl, is that which cannot be seen and therefore cannot be described, and, yet, that which, owing to its status as an ideationally generated "ideal limit", nevertheless yields an essence with an *exact* sphere of application.

Husserl applies these distinctions drawn from the existing sciences to classify the new science of transcendental phenomenology as a descriptive science of morphological essences, albeit as an *eidetically* descriptive science of *phenomenologically* morphological essences. This classification is rooted in the circumstance that the essences that transcendental phenomenology describes are not drawn from sense perception but from eidetic intuition, which means that the scope of their application is not to the flux of sensibly given things but to the flux of reflectively thematized lived-experiences. The fact–essence distinction at work here is responsible for Husserl's characterization of the "purity" of phenomenology as a science that excludes, as irrelevant for phenomenological cognition, all facts established by the factual sciences. These facts, together with the sciences that generate them, are thus placed in phenomenological "brackets" and "put out of play" so far as phenomenological research is concerned. (As mentioned, the forcefulness of Husserl's exclusion of facts and factual sciences in this stage of phenomenology's development, especially in connection with historical facts and the science of history, presents a powerful obstacle to the attempt to interpret Husserl's turn to history in the final stage of this development as a move that is consistent with the basic principles of "pure" phenomenology.)

Transcendental phenomenology, as the eidetic science of transcendentally reduced absolute consciousness, does *not* have as its subject matter the phenomenological being of the region of absolute consciousness, but that of the transcendental-phenomenological *essence* of the being of the region of absolute consciousness. As we have seen, this essence is intentional for Husserl, and, in accordance with intentionality's noetic–noematic structure, it follows that there is an essential two-sidedness to phenomenological research, in so far as constitutional problems peculiar to the *noēma* or to the *noēses* are investigated. And, as we have mentioned, Husserl first establishes the eidetic scope and limits of the evidence within which phenomenology's concrete analyses are to be conducted. In line with this, Husserl characterizes the eidetic structure of the evidence in which noematic and noetic phenomena are given. In the case of noematic phenomena, he distinguishes between the givenness of the individual objects of sense perception and the givenness of the "world horizon" within which these objects are given. In the case of noetic phenomena, he distinguishes between the givenness of manifold individual "streams" of lived-experiences and the givenness of their unity in a single stream of lived-experience.

Eidetic scope and limits of the evidential givenness of transcendent objects

Husserl's descriptions of the evidence in which the individual objects of sense perception are given find that they are always given from a "perspective" or "one-sidedly", for example from the front or the back, from up close or far away, and so on. This "perspectival" mode of givenness yields what Husserl characterizes as an "invariant", one aspect of the pure phenomenological significance of which is that the individual object of sense perception, or, more precisely, of the object of transcendently directed sense perception, can never appear in perception except as manifested through a perspective. The phenomenological status of this invariant is decidedly not that of a fact; were it a fact, the possibility of the object of a transcendently directed sense perception appearing "aperspectivally" could not be ruled out. But, in accordance with the eidetic reduction of the invariant in question, this possibility can be ruled out, because, in addition to the discovery of this invariant in the reflective comparison of manifolds composed of lived-experiences that are directed to the transcendent object of sense perception, the imaginative extension of this manifold brings about the eidetic insight that every conceivable transcendently directed sense perception presents its object perspectivally. The perspectival givenness of the transcendental phenomenon that yields the manifestation of the transcendent object, that is, the perspectival givenness of the phenomenal *meaning* (*Sinn*) of "transcendent object", therefore does not occur as a matter of fact but in accordance with an eidetic law. As such, the law in question prescribes that, in accordance with the strictness of eidetic necessity, the *evidence* that gives any actual or possible transcendent object is inadequate; this means that the transcendent object will always exceed the scope of the perspective from which it is given.

Husserl's descriptions of the givenness of the phenomenon of the transcendent object also uncover the invariant of its givenness within the "halo" or "horizon" of a manifold of unthematized phenomena of transcendent objects, each one of which, when thematized, is given perspectivally. The eidetic reduction of this horizon yields the eidetic insight into the "world-horizon", one aspect of the pure phenomenological significance of which is the non-objective and non-objectifiable mode of the evidence in which it is given. As such, the horizon of the world, in accordance with the strictness of eidetic necessity, is "always already there", as the – in "principle" (i.e. in eidetic principle) – unthematizable background of the perception of the transcendent phenomenon. The evidence in which the phenomenon of the world-horizon is given is, therefore, likewise, in accordance with the eidetic lawfulness established by eidetic seeing, inadequate, albeit not on the basis of its perspectivity but on the basis of the non-objective and in principle unthematizable character of its mode of givenness.

Eidetic scope and limits of the evidential givenness of immanent objects

In contrast to the essential inadequacy of the givenness of the noematic phenomena of transcendent objects and the horizon of the world, Husserl's descriptions of the *noēses* proper to the manifold of lived-experiences find that it is to their givenness that the invariant of not appearing perspectivally belongs. In radical contrast, then, with the essentially inadequate mode of givenness of something transcendent, Husserl characterizes the non-perspectival mode of givenness of a lived-experience as the simple seeing of something *absolute* and therefore "immanent" to the *noēsis* that perceives it. The eidetic reduction of this invariant yields the eidetic law that the givenness of something immanent cannot ever be presented perspectivally. The absolute givenness of something immanent, however, despite its absoluteness and therefore evidential perfection, cannot be equated with adequate evidence, owing to the flux that belongs to the *noēsis*'s essence. Husserl, however, maintains that the essential limit that marks the ability of perception to encompass the whole stream of *noēses* is radically different from the incompleteness that characterizes the perception of something transcendent. The incompleteness of the latter's givenness entails the impossibility of it ever being given in a manner that would include it as an intrinsic (*reell*) part of the intentionality in which it is given, that is, the impossibility of its immanent givenness; the incompleteness of the former's manner of givenness does not concern its lack of immanence *per se* but its limited scope *vis-à-vis* the movement intrinsic to the immanent content's givenness.

Noēsis–noēma correlation: unity in duality of *hulē* and *morphē*

In addition to the eidetic distinction belonging to their modes of givenness, Husserl characterizes the *noēsis* and *noēma* in terms of their essential correlation: each *noēma* has its *noēsis*, and, conversely, each *noēsis* its *noēma*. Phenomenology's constitutional research is therefore characterized by its description and fixing of the eidetic laws that govern this correlation. Husserl's initial investigation of this correlation, therefore, is also oriented towards establishing it as a framework for phenomenology's concrete analyses. Thus, on the one hand, Husserl investigates the noetic–noematic correlation that is constitutive of the sense perception of the transcendent object as a unity of meaning. On the other hand, he investigates the constitution of the unity of the flux of *noēses*, both in terms of its function to found the noetic–noematic correlation constitutive of the *noēma*'s transcendent unity and in terms of the peculiar "transcendence in immanence" that eidetically governs this unity itself.

Husserl describes the noetic–noematic correlation that is constitutive of the *noēma* proper to the transcendent object as a synthesis of *noēses* that "adumbrate" its perspectives. By adumbration he understands both the perspectival manifestation of the transcendent object, that is, its givenness in a manifold of *noēmata* – each one of which yields a profile of the perspective belonging to the *noēma*'s unity – and the noetic intending of these noematic profiles themselves. Husserl describes this intending as being mediated by a continua of sensations – colours, sounds, smells, tastes, touches – that belong to the intrinsic (*reell*) content of the perception, in so far as the intending "consciousness of" that essentially structures each *noēsis* "passes through" these sensuous contents as it intends each adumbrated noematic moment. To these "sensuous contents", which correspond much more rather than less to Aristotle's "objects" of the proper senses, Husserl gives the Aristotelian term *hulē*. Each adumbrated perspective through which the unity of the "transcendent object" is given, and so given as a meaning constituted by the manifold of intended *noēmata*, is described by Husserl as having the status of a remarkable "duality and unity" of sensuous *hulē* and intentive *morphē*. Husserl, therefore, describes the noetic–noematic correlation constitutive of the noematic unity "transcendent thing" in terms of intentive *morphē* "animating" or otherwise "bestowing meaning" on the sensuous *hulē* proper to sense perception. This process itself is described such that, from the manifold of correlated *noēses* and *noēmata* proper to the thing's perception, its unity as an object transcendent to both any given moment, and to the, in principle, infinite totality of noematic moments in which it is necessarily presented, is given.

Phenomenological temporal structure of the synthesis of manifold *noēsis* into perception of something transcendent

Husserl describes the relation among the manifold of *noēses* that constitute the *noēma* of the unity proper to the transcendent object as a "synthesis": each noetic phase or moment of the manifold that intends the *noēma* is connected in a unitary fashion to the other phases that compose the manifold. He describes the manner of synthesis as a noetic–noematic temporal duration, whereby to the noematic "temporality" (*Zeitlichkeit*) of the future, present (now) and past temporal phases belonging to the lived-experience of the transcendent object's adumbrations there corresponds the immanent perception of their temporality. Husserl describes the latter as a perceptual intentional structure composed of three reciprocally founded moments: the protentional consciousness of the future, the impressional consciousness of the now and the retentional consciousness of the past. He characterizes the immanent perception of the temporality belonging to the transcendent object as "internal time consciousness" (*inneren Zeitbewußtseins*), in order to distinguish it from the external or objective time measured by clocks and chronometers. The latter time is subject to the phenomenological reduction and therefore "put out of play" in the phenomenological cognition of time. However, Husserl characterizes the relation of objective time to phenomenological time as "somewhat analogous" to that of the relation between the noematic and noetic aspects of the adumbration of the transcendent object, in the sense of the relation between phenomenological time to objective time being comparable to the relation of the *hyletic* adumbrations of the object's perspectives to these perspectives themselves.

The internal time consciousness that synthesizes these adumbrations is therefore perceptual, and, as such, its thematization by phenomenological reflection is requisite in order for its mode of givenness to be described and eidetically fixed. Prior to this thematization, consciousness "lives" in the straightforward perception of objective time, unconcerned, as it were, with the mode of givenness of its perception. With the methodical thematization of objective time's phenomenological givenness, the perceptual intentionality composed of the reciprocally founded moments of the noetic–noematic correlation between protentions and the future, impressions and the now and retentions and the past becomes thematic. Husserl's descriptions characterize the relation of these moments in terms of the continuous flow of the modes of givenness of the phases of temporality that compose the duration of a lived-experience and the mode of givenness of the lived-experience itself in which the inception of the duration is given. Thus, on the one hand, Husserl describes, in its "purity", the temporal phase of a lived-experience that begins and ends while enduring in the interval, and he does so as a "stream" whose modes of givenness constitute a concretely filled continuum of past–present–future. On the other hand, he describes the modes of givenness of this duration itself as the continuity of "nows", whereby every actual "now" is supplanted by a new "now" that links up with the "now" just supplanted, such that each actual "now" when supplanted becomes a "just (gone) now", and thus a "now" in the process of receding and eventually vanishing into the "past". To this noematic continuum of ever-new actual "nows" Husserl correlates the noetic intending and animation of a *hyletic* impression, which functions as the limit-phase for the continuum of noetic retentions that are correlated, in turn, with the continuum of "just (gone) nows" constitutive of the "past". And, "in an opposite direction" from the continuum of "nows" that come "before" the actual "now", Husserl describes the continuum of "nows" coming "after", to which are correlated the noetic protentions constitutive of the future.

According to Husserl, these mutually founded moments that constitute the noetic–noematic structure of "phenomenological time" synthesize the perceptual phases of the transcendent thing into the unity of a single perception. This means, on the one hand, that neither the temporal phases past, present, future, nor the consciousness of these phases manifest an independent givenness. Rather, both the temporal phases and the consciousness of them are "co-given" as an inseparable configuration wherein the noetic intention that animates the actual now through its *hyletic* impression functions, in turn, as the limit for the horizonally given noetically intentional retention of just-past nows and protention of nows to come. Both the continuous succession of retentions of retentions of "just nows" and protentions of protentions "nows to come" are not on the "same" level as the continuous succession of ever-new nows, although their initial givenness as "just now" or "now to come" is a *part* of the perception. The latter are parts of perception in the sense that they are responsible for the constitution of perception's flux. Thus Husserl maintains that, in accordance with "essential necessity", the "actual now" is a *form* that persists for ever-new *hyletic* material, while the "just now" is a continuity of *forms* for ever-new contents. The distinction between "material" and "contents" is crucial in Husserl's account, as precisely the transition from material impression to intentional content is what for him least characterizes elements of temporal succession, the lived-experience of which is marked in his descriptions with the metaphors "flux" and "stream". (Presumably, too, the "now to come" would be likewise a continuity of *forms* for ever-new contents, although Husserl's descriptions often, as in this instance, focus on retention's role in the constitution of the succession of perception's flux.) According to Husserl, all of these forms of the "now" are "punctual", meaning that together they constitute, from the perceptual present, the flux of time. Husserl will later characterize the temporal whole of the perceptual present – which, of course, includes and therefore cannot be equated with the "actual now" or "now point" – as the "standing-streaming present". What is "standing" are the enduring now forms (i.e. the "actual now", "just-past nows" and "nows to come") and what is "streaming" are their ever-new material and intentional contents.

Phenomenological temporal synthesis of manifold lived-experiences into one stream of lived-experience

In addition to the "internal time consciousness" that synthesizes the phases of the perceptual manifold that constitutes the unity of the transcendent object (i.e. the phenomenological meaning of the transcendentally reduced transcendent object), and thereby constitutes a single stream of lived-experience, each single stream of lived-experience is itself connected in a unitary fashion with other streams of lived-experience. The syntheses that combine these single streams of experience into *one* temporal stream and *one* phenomenological time are described by Husserl as belonging to "original time consciousness", the mode of givenness of which is responsible not only for combining the *noēses* of the single streams of lived-experiences in a unitary fashion but also for the constitution of the manifold single streams of lived-experiences into *one noēsis* with *one noēma*. For Husserl, what holds for the internal time consciousness of single lived-experiences also holds for the whole stream of lived-experience. Thus, just as there can be no consciousness of the cessation of time in the case of single lived-experiences, as it is manifest that when the duration of one stream ends another necessarily takes its place, so too, no matter how diverse lived-experiences can be with respect to their essence, they are nevertheless constituted altogether as *one* temporal stream, and, therefore, as members of the *one* phenomenological time.

How, exactly, this primal synthesis of original time consciousness constitutes one encompassing stream of lived-experience that, as Husserl puts it in *Ideas I*, "cannot begin and end" (164), is something that he clearly did not work out in his published introductions to phenomenology; and it is also debatable whether he did so satisfactorily in his lectures and research manuscripts on time. This situation has given rise to much speculation and many complicated diagrams devoted to unravelling the nature and essence of what Husserl also characterized in *Ideas I* as "the great metaphysical consequences" (165) of the phenomenological insights into time. These insights concern the primal source of what, in relation to the transcendental absolute uncovered by the transcendental reduction, surpasses it as "what is ultimately and truly absolute" (163). These speculations, however, revolve around two related problems that Husserl addresses in his introductions, namely, that of the description and proper phenomenological essence of consciousness prior to its reflective thematization and that of the description and proper phenomenological essence of the "pure Ego's" relation to the stream of lived-experiences in its "infinite unity". A closer look at the statuses of these problems in Husserl's initial description and eidetic formulation of them in *Ideas I* is therefore in order at this point.

Pure Ego as the residuum of the transcendental-phenomenological reduction

One consequence of the transcendental-phenomenological reduction is that the "I" or "ego" that characterizes the human being in the natural attitude, and that does so as the real or empirical part of his or her empirically psychic and "subjective" being that is somehow bound up with all questions of personal identity and volition, is "put out of play" and thereby "excluded" as a source of phenomenological cognition. Subsequent to its reduction, the human ego, like all other beings posited by consciousness, is reduced in its meaning to a "merely intentional being". Nevertheless, Husserl finds that after the reduction an ego still belongs to each lived-experience that comes and goes, and that it does so necessarily. Husserl describes this ego as the source of the unifying intention – the unifying consciousness of – that is directed through every transient *cogito* to the objective something, the *cogitatum,* towards which it is directed. This unifying intention changes from transient *cogito* to *cogito*, vanishing with each as their streaming lived-experience elapses, while yet "shooting forth anew" with each new *cogito*, all the while unifying each lived-experience as *mine*. Husserl describes this unifying intention as the mine of the *cogito–cogitatum* as a "ray of regard", in order to capture both its directedness and essential connection to the essentially transitory lived-experience of which it is an intrinsic (*reell*) part. Because of the transitory character of the intrinsic parts or contents of each lived-experience, Husserl holds that the ray of regard's unifying intention cannot originate in them. As a consequence of this, he attributes the source of the absolute identity that each lived-experience manifests in so far as it is experienced as mine, together with the source of its directedness, to an Ego that, because it is not in any way an immanent content of the lived-experience itself, is *pure*.

Because the pure Ego is not in evidence prior to the transcendental-phenomenological exclusion of the world and the human empirical subjectivity that belongs to it, Husserl characterizes it as a "residuum" of the reduction. On account of its not belonging to the immanent contents of the phenomenon of lived-experience, Husserl characterizes the pure Ego as "a transcendency of a peculiar kind – one which is not constituted – *a transcendency within immanence*" (*Ideas I*, 110). He does not describe the pure Ego as a "constituted" transcendency because, unlike the transcendency of the unity belonging to the transcendent object, the transcendency of the pure Ego is not presented as a unity given though a manifold. The pure Ego is therefore neither constituted through the adumbrations proper to the intrinsic content of each noetic–noematic phase of a lived-experience (as is the unity of the transcendent object), nor through the immanent contents proper to the manifold of lived-experiences themselves. The pure Ego cannot be so presented, because its ray of regard belongs to the transitory immanent contents of each *cogito*, none of which endures beyond the cessation of a given *cogito*. Rather than be constituted by these contents, these contents, precisely because they are experienced as mine, point to a pure Ego that is transcendent to them. Indeed, they do so because the source of both the unity and essential character of this unity as mine cannot be founded in these contents themselves, as they are inseparable from the transitory essence of the *cogito*. For this reason Husserl's description of the pure Ego maintains that there is "an essentially different pure Ego for each stream of lived-experience" (*Ideas I*, 109).

The pure Ego's identity as something that extends beyond its transcendency in a single given stream of lived-experience is therefore something that Husserl maintains cannot be justified phenomenologically, because its givenness is not constituted through a manifold. Only in so far as "its immediate, evidently ascertainable essential peculiarity and its givenness along with pure consciousness extends" (*ibid.*) does Husserl "propose to count the pure Ego as a phenomenological datum" (*ibid.*). All theories, then, that exceed the limits of what can be evidently given in phenomenological reflection "undergo exclusion" (*ibid.*). Husserl especially has in mind here the neo-Kantian theories of the pure Ego, which argue, but without appeal to reflectively thematized evidence, that in order to account for the conditions that make possible what we do in fact have evidence for, namely, presentations that appear as "my" presentations, an "I think" *must* accompany all presentations. The rigour of Husserl's refusal to violate his phenomenology's principle of principles is particularly in evidence in his account of the pure Ego. The problem this rigour gives rise to is that of providing a phenomenological account of the pure Ego's relation to the "infinite unity" that belongs to the stream of lived-experiences. This problem has two interrelated dimensions, involving both the account of the pure Ego's unity in its role of not just encompassing this or that single *cogito* (as a transcendency within the immanence of a single lived-experience) but of encompassing all the *cogitationes* collectively (as a transcendency within the immanence of the manifold of *cogitationes*), and the account of the relation of the pure Ego's unity to the temporality that synthesizes the unity of lived-experiences (singly and collectively).

The pure Ego's horizon of reflection of lived-experiences: the eidetic lawfulness of temporal simultaneity

Prior to the emergence of the next stage of the development of phenomenology, Husserl characterized the pure Ego's relation to lived-experiences other than the one it is currently living out – in the actional (thematically intentional) mode of the *cogito* – as one of "belonging"; all of these other lived-experiences compose the horizon of the pure Ego and, in accordance with eidetic lawfulness, the pure Ego can turn to any one of them and convert it into an actional *cogito* or incorporate it into such a *cogito* as its immanent contents. Husserl describes these non-actional lived-experiences as the pure Ego's "horizon of reflection on lived-experiences", in the precise sense of the "field" of non-actional lived-experiences whose non-thematic and therefore non-objective intuition and "seeing" compose the horizon that is inseparable from the actionally modified *cogito*. According to Husserl, it is an "*eidetic law* that every lived-experience is an essentially self-enclosed totality of experiential processes not only with respect to temporal *succession* but also in regard to *simultaneity*" (*Ideas I*, 165). This means that each "now" of lived-experience has a horizon of lived-experiences that also have the same original temporal form of "now", and that each of these lived-experiences composes the original horizon of the pure Ego, the totality of which constitutes the original "now" of consciousness. This original horizon enters into the modes of the past in a unitary way, such that every "before" and "after", as modified "nows", embrace, respectively, what simultaneously "was" and what simultaneously "is to come". Husserl characterizes the intentional unity of these simultaneous successions as the "*whole* field of phenomenological time of the pure Ego – which, from any one of 'its' lived-experiences, it can traverse in accord with the *three* dimensions of before, after, and simultaneity" (*ibid.*). A significant consequence of this is that the following are necessary correlates: *one* pure Ego and *one* stream of lived-experiences fulfilled in regard to all three dimensions in an essentially connected manner that progresses with a continuity of content.

EIGHT

Limits of the transcendental-phenomenological investigation of pure consciousness

Intuition of the unity of the one, infinite, stream of lived-experience as an idea in the Kantian sense

Husserl's account of the unity of the lived-experiences that belong to the pure Ego in accordance with the primal form of consciousness, however, encounters a limit in the scope of the givenness of this unity to and by the pure "regard" of its (the unity's) reflection by the pure Ego. The essential incompleteness of the evidence in which the immanent contents of any lived-experience is given, which, as noted earlier, is a consequence of its mode of synthetic connection as a flux, means that "by essential necessity this whole connection is *never* given or to be given by a single pure regard" (*Ideas I*, 166). Nevertheless, Husserl maintains that it can be given in the manner of an *idea in the Kantian sense*. By this Husserl has in mind Kant's understanding of an idea as something that prescribes the rules that govern and therefore limit the thought of that which cannot be grounded in a perception unified by the categories of thought. Such "regulative ideals" were necessary for Kant, because, on his view, not all the objects of thought have limits determined by the intuition, or, what is the same thing for him, the sense perception of an object. According to Husserl, the whole of the in principle unencompassable synthetic connection of the three temporal dimensions of the one stream of lived-experience that belongs to the pure Ego can be "seized upon" by that Ego in the manner of an "idea in the Kantian sense". Husserl describes this "seizing" in terms of the process whereby the pure regard of the Ego reflects the immanent contents of any given lived-experience in a manner that progresses to the unregarded horizon pertaining to it, at which point it thematizes the contents of this horizon, progressing again to the horizon of these now-thematized and immanently given contents, and "so on", such that, in "a certain way", the unity of these contents is given as an "idea in the Kantian sense". The "certain way" concerns the manner of givenness of the unity, which is not given in the reflection on a single lived-experience but rather as the limitlessness in the progression of this lived-experience's givenness as a unity that conforms to and is thereby regulated by the *form* of the combination of its immanent contents with the immanent contents of other lived-experiences, a form that is reflected and intuitively grasped by the pure Ego's "ideational regard". The "ideation" that "sees" a Kantian "idea", then, does not lose the insight into the unity of its "content" (the infinite unity that connects the manifold of lived-experiences into the *one* stream of lived-experiences), even though the adequate givenness of this unity is, in principle, unattainable.

Eidetic limits of modifications of lived-experience: reflective acts and the unreflective originary temporal phase of the living-now

As we have seen, phenomenological description and eidetic cognition take place solely in – and therefore presuppose from the start – acts of *phenomenological* reflection. Husserl could not be more explicit about this: "The phenomenological method operates exclusively in acts of reflection" (*Ideas I*, 144), which means that "[o]nly through acts of *experiencing* as reflected do we know anything about the stream of lived-experience and of its necessary relationship to the pure Ego" (*Ideas I*, 150). Indeed, Husserl singles out the connection between acts of reflection and phenomenological cognition as belonging to the "most universal essential" peculiarities of the sphere of pure lived-experiences. Among the enduring implications of this peculiarity is the eidetic limit it imposes on the phenomenological cognition of lived-experiences in the "mode of *unreflectively lived conscious* lived-experiences" (*Ideas I*, 147). The methodical presupposition of acts of reflection in order for phenomenological cognition to take place therefore means that unreflected lived-experiences are *essentially* incapable of being *directly* apprehended in their "unreflected" mode. Thus cognitive access to unreflected lived-experiences can occur only through the mediation of phenomenological reflection, that is, only in so far as such experiences come before what Husserl calls "the reflective regard".

How, exactly, Husserl thinks that acts of reflection, which is to say, reflectively modified lived-experiences, are capable of apprehending unreflectively modified lived-experiences is something neither Husserl's critics nor many of his followers seem to appreciate adequately. According to him:

> [W]hen a lived-experience that at some particular time is actually being lived comes into the reflective regard it becomes given

> *as* actually being lived, as existing "now". But not only that: it becomes given as having just now *been* and, in so far as it was un-regarded, precisely as not having been reflected on. (*Ideas I*, 145)

In the natural attitude, it is taken for granted that the lived-experiences do not only *exist* when they are being reflected, but that they "were actually lived by us if in reflection on something immanent, there is awareness of them within *retention* ('primary' memory) as having 'just' been" (*ibid.*). However, when the phenomenological and eidetic reductions are put into effect, this taken-for-granted status is "bracketed" and undergoes a "transformation into exemplary cases of eidetic universalities that we can make our own in the framework of pure intuition and study systematically" (*Ideas I*, 146). Subsequent to these reductions, the taken-for-granted *existence* of lived-experiences that are not directly before the regard of reflection is "put out of play", which means, among other things, that the phenomenological description and fixing of the essential structure of such experience is *eidetically* limited to an account that does not extend beyond its givenness to reflection. As we have just seen, Husserl characterizes the limit of the givenness of a lived-experience in terms of its presentation as "just having now *been* and, in so far it was un-regarded, precisely as not having been reflected on". Two conclusions are immediately apparent from this account. First, Husserl does not *posit* un- or pre-reflective lived-experiences as being given *prior* to their reflective thematization by and, thus, their phenomenal exhibition to the regard of phenomenological reflection; rather, he describes the mode of givenness of the initial manifestation of a lived-experience to reflection as one in which it *presents itself* as "having just now *been*" and "not having been reflected on". Second, this mode of presentation of a lived-experience as a phenomenon, that is, as "having just now *been*", is therefore inseparable from the *phenomenon* of its temporality.

It follows from this first conclusion that, strictly speaking, there is no such thing as "pre-reflective" lived-experience or "pre-reflective" consciousness: lived-experiences and modes of consciousness that are not reflectively modified are incapable of *appearing* independently of their reflective thematization. Husserl's terminology reflects this, as he does not use the designation "pre-reflective" to refer to such lived-experiences and modes of consciousness.[1] Phenomenology's methodical access to unreflected lived-experiences is therefore *founded* on acts of reflection, while the phenomenological acts of reflection themselves are also *founded*, in turn, on lived-experiences that are modified at a "lower" reflective level than the reflective acts within which all phenomenological cognition takes place. Indeed, Husserl maintains that the eidetic structure of the relation of reflectively modified lived-experiences to those that are not so modified is such that while "[t]he already given lived-experience can itself already have the characteristic of a reflectively modified consciousness of something, so that the new modification belongs to a higher level, ultimately, however, we get back to lived-experiences that are absolutely un-reflected, together with their intrinsic (*reell*) and intentional data" (*Ideas I*, 148).

Reciprocal and asymmetrical foundational relations between reflectively and unreflectively modified lived-experiences

The "modifications" that "belong to *any* lived-experience as ideally inherent variations" (*Ideas I*, 149) in it are therefore investigated by Husserl's pure phenomenology and articulated by him in terms of the "totality of essential modifications that *any* lived-experience must undergo during its originary course and, in addition, the different kinds of variations that can be conceived ideally as effected on each lived-experience by means of 'operations'" (*ibid.*). Husserl characterizes every lived-experience as being what it is in an original generation of "an invariant essential type", namely, the "continuous flow of retentions and protentions mediated by a flowing phase of [its] origination, in which the living-now of lived-experience becomes conscious in opposition to its 'before' and 'after'" (*ibid.*). According to Husserl, the "impressions" that are exhibited in the origination of absolutely original lived-experiences are inseparable from perceptions of physical things, which means that these lived-experiences are "originary" in relation to all the ideally possible variations of lived-experiences that arise through the modifications brought about by the operations effected on each lived-experience. In general, Husserl characterizes these modifications as "re-presentations" (*Vergegenwärtigung*), in order to articulate that while they do indeed present the physical thing that is originally given in perception, they nevertheless do so in a manner that is not "original". Husserl therefore contrasts the presentation of the objects of perception in "primal lived-experiences" that originally generate every lived-experience "as a flux of becoming" with those lived-experiences that, being modifications of these original lived-experience, present such objects on the basis of the mediation of re-presentational operations. Moreover, he holds that these modifications, in accordance with strict eidetic necessity, ultimately lead back to the primal lived-experiences in which the object of perception is originally given.

Under the general heading of "re-presentations" Husserl includes the presentations given in recollection (memory contents connected with contents presently given in lived-experience) and anticipation, in fantasy (i.e.

images) and, of course, in reflection. Husserl therefore maintains that the modifications of lived-experiences brought about by the re-presentations generated by these operations ultimately lead back to certain primal lived-experiences, which, as a consequence of their being "absolutely" unreflectively modified, have "only *one*, but also a continuously flowing, *absolutely originary* phase – the moment of the living-*now*" (*Ideas I*, 149–50). Husserl understands each such originary lived-experience to be "concrete", in the precise sense of its independence, as an individual stream of lived-experience, from the givenness of the modifications that are founded on its absolutely originary givenness. However, because it is only through *reflectively* modified lived-experiences that anything can be known about the stream of lived-experiences generally, and, therefore, about any given concrete lived-experience, the independence characteristic of the concretion of any given lived-experience is relative. This independence is relative in so far as the *phenomenal* givenness of any lived-experience is "reciprocally" related to and therefore mutually founded on acts of reflection. Thus, for Husserl, the givenness of any one of the possible modifications that are ideally inherent in any concrete lived-experience is related primarily to actual lived-experiences lacking reflective awareness, because it can be seen at once that all reflective awareness, when taken in its full concreteness, is necessarily itself a lived-experience that lacks reflective awareness; as such, each reflectively modified lived-experience therefore "participates" (*Ideas I*, 150) in the primary modifications of the unreflectively modified lived-experience that generates every lived-experience.

On Husserl's view, however, the reciprocally foundational relation between reflectively and unreflectively modified lived-experiences is not symmetrical. On the one hand, the ideally possible operations that can be brought to bear on any lived-experience "are repeatable *ad infinitum*, as they can also be performed on the modified lived-experiences" (*Ideas I*, 149). On the other hand, the primary modifications proper to the absolutely originary phase of lived-experience, the moment of the living-*now*, are *one* in their concreteness and therefore incapable of repetition. The reflective modification that exhibits the modifications that are founded on these primary modifications, which is to say, founded on the original consciousness of time, therefore do not "repeat" this original consciousness when it thematizes and brings it to givenness. Rather, reflection thematizes the original consciousness of time and in so doing exhibits it as a phenomenon, that is, as something that presents itself as having already been there and, as such, as going on before its reflected manifestation to and by the regard of reflection.

Reflectively thematizing a lived-experience and attending to its manner of givenness as already going on and therefore "having been", prior to its being "adverted to" by reflection, however, is one thing; bracketing the "natural attitude's" positing of its existence when it is not being reflected, in order (i) to exhibit and describe the "how" of the temporality of its appearance as "unreflectively" modified, and (ii) to unfold or otherwise articulate its eidetic structure, is quite another. As mentioned, what is at issue here is the phenomenological account of original time consciousness's primal synthesis of manifold lived-experiences into *one* encompassing stream of consciousness. As also mentioned, the incomplete status of Husserl's analysis of this problem has given rise to speculative attempts by others to resolve it. On the basis of Husserl's account of the reflective modification of lived-experience presented here, one such attempt (which is quite prevalent today) can be rejected as "un-phenomenological", in so far as it transgresses the basic methodical principles of Husserl's pure phenomenology. Because these principles do not undergo fundamental revision in the course of the development of Husserl's thought, it is appropriate to point out precisely how this speculative attempt to account for the unity of consciousness deviates from phenomenology's basic principles.

Equivocation of the "given" as the source of phenomenologically unwarranted speculations about the temporality of so-called "pre-reflective" self-awareness

The attempt is based on the claim that internal time consciousness is initially and most originally "given" in an implicit and "pre-reflective" manner, as a streaming self-awareness that not only manifests itself as a unity, but also functions to account for the unity of the manifold of temporally streaming lived-experiences that are "constituted" in reflectively thematizing acts. According to this account, then, there is not, as Husserl thought, a problem of unifying the manifold *noēses* into *one* streaming *noēsis*. The pre-reflective self-manifestation of internal time consciousness does not divide itself along the lines of the givenness of an act as a temporal unity and the manifestation of its synthesis of the flow or stream of temporal duration. Rather, this division itself is the result of the thematization, by a reflection, of the inner time consciousness that – "prior" to its thematization – is one with pre-reflective self-awareness. This thematization, then, is the source of the initial distinction between the givenness of the temporal act and the manifestation of the flow constituted by this act. Hence this account concludes that the reflective thematization of acts as discrete temporal unities that stream into one another does not constitute a temporal flow that is "separate" from the original givenness of the absolute, pre-reflective flow of lived-experience; rather, it only manifests differently "one and the same" original self-manifestation of the flow. Thus there are not, as Husserl thought, manifold temporal streams of lived-experiences that are encompassed and therefore unified by one, absolute, stream of lived-experience. On the contrary, there is only one stream that is manifested in two different ways, in accord with either its pre-reflective unity or its reflectively thematized multiplicity.

Two speculative moments are identifiable in this account of the original temporality putatively belonging to pre-reflective self-awareness. The first is the result of the equivocal employment of the term "given". The claim that self-consciousness is originally "given" in an implicit and pre-reflective manner presupposes, as we have seen in the discussion of the basic principles of pure phenomenology, that a lived-experience is "given" to the methodically reflective – and therefore cognitively interested – regard of the phenomenologist. Only the evidence "given" to this reflectively modified lived-experience can legitimize the phenomenologically cognitive claim that – in its full concreteness – the phenomenon of lived-experience is originally and absolutely not modified reflectively. The failure to keep these two mutually foundational but nevertheless radically different senses of the "given" distinct leads to the equivocation that is behind the claim that the original givenness of internal time consciousness is, *tout court*, "pre-reflective". Once this claim is invoked, all claims made about the "pre-reflective" manifestation of self-awareness lose their phenomenological value, as they issue from the collapse of the distinction and reciprocal foundational relation between the reflective and unreflective senses of the "given". Such claims, therefore, *presuppose* what for Husserl is a phenomenological impossibility: direct – that is, not mediated by reflectively modified lived-experience – cognitive access to unreflectively modified lived-experience. From the methodical standpoint of Husserl's pure phenomenology, these claims cannot but have the cognitive status of speculations, as they neither have nor can have a basis in phenomenological evidence. The claim, then, that the *multitude* of reflectively thematized *acts* of temporally streaming lived-experiences is but a different manifestation of the *unity* belonging to the only, and, therefore, the *one* original stream of conscious lived-experience, namely, pre-reflective self-awareness, cannot but have the status of a phenomenologically unwarranted speculation.

The second speculative moment in the account of the original temporality of consciousness under discussion follows naturally from the first, as it presupposes the fundamental opposition between the givenness of pre-reflective and reflective lived-experience that arises from the equivocation of the two phenomenological senses of the given in the first moment. Once this opposition is posited, all claims made about the original *unity* of the temporal streaming of consciousness "prior" to reflection, claims that are prefaced by still other claims that set absolute limits for what *reflective* consciousness can capture with respect to consciousness's pre-reflective unity and immediate self-consciousness, cannot but be seen as speculative from the standpoint of the most basic methodical principle of Husserl's pure phenomenology. The reason for this is profoundly simple, as this principle holds, as we have seen, that "only through acts of *experiencing* as reflected do we know anything about the stream of lived-experience". Therefore the setting-in-relation of unreflectively modified and reflectively modified lived-experiences is itself a "new" phenomenon, and one that presupposes the givenness of both terms of this relation to the regard of a methodically higher-level reflection that encompasses them both. Any claim about the "being" of lived-experience "prior" to its reflective thematization must therefore presuppose its givenness to reflection in this sense. For instance, the claim that the "reflective" distinction between the constituting act of internal time consciousness and constituted temporality of successive phases of time does not capture the act's "pre-phenomenal being" because the latter's unity does not admit this distinction can only be made evident on the basis of a higher-level "phenomenological" reflection to which is *given* precisely the collapse of the distinction between "constituting" act and "constituted" flow in the act's pre-phenomenal being.[2]

Relatedness of the stream of lived-experiences to the empty pure Ego

As mentioned, Husserl's analysis of the constitution of the pure Ego contrasts its distinctive "transcendency within immanence" with the constitution of the transcendent object. Unlike the latter, which is constituted as a unity that is given through both a manifold of phases within a single lived-experience and through a manifold of lived-experiences themselves, the unity of the pure Ego is not constituted through a multiplicity. Thus Husserl, in his initial philosophical interpretation of this aspect of the pure Ego's givenness, refuses to speculate about its unity beyond what he thinks can be maintained on the basis of its givenness in the immanence of lived-experience. Its "purity", above all, is interpreted by him as its absence of immanent content, beyond its function as the source of the "ray of regard" animating, as it were, each transient stream of the *cogito*. One consequence of this, as we have seen, is Husserl's conclusion that there is an essentially different pure Ego for each stream of lived-experience. However, this apparently does not mean for him that there is a plurality of egos, as he notes that reflection on the stream of lived-experiences provides knowledge of the "necessary relatedness" (*Ideas I*, 150) of this stream to the pure Ego. Moreover, such reflection allows us to know that this stream "is a field of free accomplishing of *cogitationes* belonging to one and the same pure Ego; that all lived-experiences of the stream are the Ego's precisely in so far as it regards or can direct its regard 'through' the stream to something other than the Ego" (*ibid.*).

Such reflective knowledge of the pure Ego, however, does not mean for Husserl – at this stage of his phenomenology – that it "can be taken *for itself* and made into the object of a *proper* investigation" (*Ideas I*, 160). Apart from its "modes of relation" and "modes of comportment" made manifest by the *cogito*'s being directed to its object, being busied with it, taking a position towards it, or undergoing and suffering it, the pure Ego "is completely empty of essential components, has no content that can be explicated, is indescribable in and for itself: it is pure Ego and nothing else" (*ibid.*).

NINE

Phenomenological philosophy as transcendental idealism

Phenomenology as transcendental theory of knowledge: criticism of transcendental experience and knowledge

The third and next to last of the four stages in the development of Husserl's phenomenology, as previously mentioned, has two guiding clues: the Cartesian-inspired idea of first philosophy and that of the function of the passive constitution of meanings and their hidden intentional accomplishments in the constitution characteristic of all meaning and being. Under the guidance of the idea of first philosophy Husserl reinterprets the very meaning of transcendentally pure phenomenology as transcendental philosophy. Phenomenological science, as the science devoted to the concrete explication of transcendental consciousness and the fixing of the eidetic laws governing its absolute being, is now understood as having an intrinsically philosophical meaning. The third stage of Husserl's phenomenology thus overcomes the hesitation of its second stage to characterize the science of phenomenology as a science that is necessarily philosophical, as opposed to an eidetic science whose cognitions possess a philosophical significance and are therefore of some service to philosophy. What allows Husserl to interpret transcendentally pure phenomenology's proper meaning as transcendental philosophy is the phenomenological idealism that he now identifies with phenomenology's innermost self-understanding. It is this conception of a phenomenological science that, as Husserl puts it, is "destined to become *philosophy*" (CM, 67). It is so destined in so far as a phenomenological philosophy and phenomenological idealism are the "only possibilities" (CM, 120) from which is constituted "a philosophy as common to 'all of us' who mediate together – ideally, a single *philosophia perennis*" (*ibid.*).

Phenomenological philosophy as transcendental idealism assumes for Husserl the guise of a two-staged transcendental theory of knowledge, the first stage of which is characterized by the exploration of the realm of being that is accessible to transcendental self-experience and the second by the criticism of both this experience and of all transcendental cognition. Seen within the context of Husserl's articulation of this two-stage structure, what we are calling both the second and third stages of his development fall within the stage of the transcendental theory of knowledge that he identifies as the criticism of transcendental self-experience. Such criticism is concerned with the determination of the range and limits of apodictic evidence, but not with its modes. By a "mode of apodicticity" Husserl understands the manner of givenness itself of the evidence that provides the foundation for phenomenological cognition. Consideration of the modes of apodicticity falls under the heading of the criticism of transcendental knowledge, a criticism that "also demands a criticism" (CM, 178), "owing to phenomenology's essential relation back to itself" (*ibid.*), which is to say, to its methodology's self-reflective commitment to critical justification of all presuppositions. Prior to the criticism of transcendental knowledge, phenomenology is, in Husserl's words, "*still infected with a certain naïveté* (*the naïveté of apodicticity*)", even though it nevertheless "contains the great and most characteristic accomplishment of phenomenology, as a refashioning of science on a higher level" (*ibid.*). We shall see below that it is not until what we are calling the fourth and final stage of the development of phenomenology that Husserl takes the first steps of a criticism of transcendental-phenomenological knowledge demanded by its method. And we also see that these steps lead not to "endless regresses that are infected with difficulties of any kind" (*ibid.*), but to the self-critical recognition on Husserl's part that the mode of the apodicticity that characterizes all meaning and cognition, including, therefore, the meaning of phenomenology as transcendental philosophy and the evidence that grounds its cognitions, is inseparable from its intentional history. In radical contrast with the content of empirical history, namely, datable facts and events, the last stage of Husserl's development of phenomenology understands (as we have mentioned) the phenomenological meaning of history as the interweaving of the original accomplishments of transcendental subjectivity and the forgetfulness constitutive of their sedimentation.

Transcendental subjective syntheses responsible for constitution of the meaning and being (and non-being) of all that is

Under the guidance of the function of passively constituted meanings, together with the hidden intentional accomplishments that generate them, Husserl establishes that the full scope of phenomenological constitution is responsible for not only the entirety of the meaning that renders intelligible all that is, but also that phenomenological constitution is responsible for the very being (or non-being) of everything that is meaningful. That is, not just the "meaning" (*Sinn*) of the transcendency of the world and the objects in it are understood by Husserl to be correlates of and therefore inseparable from the constitutive accomplishments of transcendental subjectivity, but also their very "actuality of being" (*Seinswirklichkeit*) (CM, 97) is now maintained by him to be the accomplishment of transcendentally subjective syntheses. Thus, in what can only be experienced as a shocking statement by those who take their phenomenological bearings from Husserl's development prior to his "transcendental turn", he writes:

> The "object" of consciousness, the object as having identity "with itself" during the flowing lived-experience, does not come into this experience from the outside; on the contrary, it is included as meaning in the lived-experience itself – and thus as an "*intentional accomplishment*" of the synthesis of consciousness. (CM, 80)

The clues of passively constituted meanings and their hidden intentional accomplishments are behind Husserl's self-interpretation of phenomenology as phenomenological idealism, in so far as they lead him to the discovery of a second kind of synthesis besides that of the multiplicities of actual and possible consciousness directed towards objects as poles; namely, they lead to the discovery of a synthesis that belongs to the transcendental Ego as an identical pole of its acts. In marked departure from his previous account of the pure Ego as an identity that is empty of essential content, Husserl's account of the transcendental Ego maintains that it "*is not an empty pole of identity*, any more than any *object* is such" (CM, 101). Rather, in addition to functioning to embrace the multiplicities of the *cogitationes* collectively as *cogitationes* belonging to it as an identical Ego, the transcendental Ego possesses abiding properties. These properties arise in accordance with "a law of 'transcendental generation'" (*ibid.*), whereby every act possessing a *new* objective meaning yields "*a new abiding property*" of the transcendental Ego, such that by its own active generating, the transcendental Ego constitutes itself "as *identical substrate of Ego-properties*" (*ibid.*). And in the most remarkable departure from his previous account of the pure Ego, Husserl distinguishes from the Ego as pole and the Ego as substrate yet another dimension of the transcendental Ego, its full concretion. The transcendental Ego in its full concreteness is designated by Husserl with the Leibnizian term "monad", and its concreteness is characterized as composed of "the flowing multiformity of his intentional life, along with the objects meant – and in some cases constituted as existent for him – in that life" (CM, 102).

The transcendental Ego as a pole of identity, substrate of habitualities and monad is not only characterized by Husserl as possessing essential content, but the problem of phenomenologically explicating the monadic Ego, in which is included "the whole of actual and potential conscious life" (*ibid.*), is now characterized by him as having to "include *all constitutional problems without exception*" (CM, 102–3). And Husserl draws from this the conclusion that "the phenomenology of this *self-constitution* coincides with *phenomenology as a whole*" (CM, 103), which means that the third stage of Husserl's development of phenomenology assumes the guise of an egology or, equivalently, a monadology. The latter is a term that he acknowledges he uses deliberately to suggest Leibniz's metaphysics. The reasons that Husserl invokes Leibniz will become apparent shortly, when we discuss Husserl's solution to the problem to which phenomenology's ego-based theory of knowledge gives rise, namely, the spectre of being unable to account for the constitution of the world's "objectivity", as a world that is identically the same for all subjects. According to Husserl, to the very meaning of "objectivity" and therefore to the world's "objectivity" there belongs the experience and knowledge of something that is experienced and known to be identical by a plurality of subjects. Because the phenomenological theory of knowledge is based in the reduction of all experience and knowledge to a putative foundation in an Ego, and because the latter necessarily appears as a *solus ipse* (himself alone), it seems – at least on the surface – that this theory suffers from the defect of *solipsism*; that is, from the inability to account for the existence of the other Egos whose mutual coexistence is a necessary condition for the constitution of the objectivity of something, and, in the first instance, of the world's objectivity.

Husserl's response to phenomenology's appearance as a solipsism is to show that, despite all appearances, the phenomenological theory of egological constitution is nevertheless able to account for the constitution of the meaning and being of other Egos. Husserl shows this by exhibiting how, in practice, phenomenology is able to explicate the constitution of, first, the meaning and being of an Alter Ego, and then, of a plurality of Egos. To appreciate properly how Husserl thinks that the transcendental Ego can constitute a plurality of Egos and thus the intersubjective being upon which all objectivity has its foundation, the phenomenological evidence that led him to revise his view of the pure Ego as an identity without essential content must be carefully considered.

The pure Ego's concretization as monad: the essential connection of the content of the transcendental Ego's horizon with its intrinsic being

Husserl's initial view of the pure Ego as lacking essential content is based, as previously noted, in his account of the scope and limits of the evidence though which it becomes manifest. This evidence is manifest to reflection, and exhibits the pure Ego as the identical source of each essentially transient "ray of regard" that animates a given, and equally transient, lived-experience whose consciousness is *actionally* modified and thus exhibits the modality of the *cogito*. The peculiar status of such animation, as mentioned above, is characterized by Husserl as a "transcendency in immanence", in the recognition that while the regard's conscious intention belongs to the immanent contents of the *cogito*, it nevertheless exceeds them in its function to render thematic its (the *cogito*'s) object (*cogitatum*). Despite its transcendency, however, the evidence in which the ray of regard is manifest perishes with the expiration of the transient stream of the lived-experience to which it belongs. Husserl drew two conclusions from this state of affairs. First, each ray of regard must have a source in something other than the manifold of transient streams of lived-experience, namely, in the pure Ego that "shoots forth anew" an essentially different ray of regard in each lived-experience animated by it. Second, that this pure Ego, other than its status as the source of the essentially different rays of regard animating the manifold of actionally modified consciousnesses that "belong" to it, is empty of essential content.

The question before us now is what considerations led Husserl not only to come to view the pure Ego as the possessor of essential content, but also to reformulate phenomenology as a whole in terms of the self-explication of the monadically concrete Ego. The answer is "recollection" – or, rather, a deepened understanding of its scope and capacity as a "re-presentation" to make present again (*vergegenwärtigt*) the objects of past experiences and these experiences themselves. Husserl's deepened understanding of recollection goes beyond previously perceived objects or one of the Ego's past lived-experiences to include its capacity to make present the essential connection between the structure and content of the Ego's present lived-experience and that of contents belonging to its horizonal lived-experience. In Husserl's account of the pure Ego as a pure identity and nothing more, the non-actional lived-experiences that composed the essential horizon of its actionally modified lived-experiences were described as "belonging" to the Ego. By this Husserl meant that the pure Ego, in accord with eidetic lawfulness, could always turn to any one of the non-actional lived-experiences and convert it into an actional *cogito* or incorporate it into such a *cogito* as its immanent content. But it also implied that, prior to the Ego's advertence and actional modification of the lived-experiences that compose its horizon, these lived-experiences do *not* belong to it. This is implied because other than the transient – and therefore non-essential – ray of regard (that issues from the pure Ego) whose transcendency in immanence animates (*qua* its actional modification of consciousness) each lived-experience in the mode of *cogito*, Husserl could find no evidence for the pure Ego's existence, other than its empty identity as the source of these rays of regard.

All of this changes with Husserl's discovery that the non-actional lived-experiences that compose the horizon of actionally modified consciousness belong to the essential content of the Ego prior to either their actional modification or their inclusion in a consciousness that has been so modified. They belong to the Ego as "a *realm of the innate 'apriori'*, without which an ego as such is unthinkable" (CM, 114). Husserl characterizes this innate *a priori* as a realm of *passive* syntheses that generates both the objects that are already there (and therefore function as pregiven "material") for the *active* synthesis accomplished by the Ego in the mode of the *cogito* and as a realm that generates the Ego *itself*. The passive syntheses that generate the Ego "produce a unity of *universal genesis of the ego*" (CM, 109), a unity that according to Husserl is responsible for both the succession and simultaneity of the lived-experiences that constitute the single multiformity of the Ego's concrete intentional life. Thus Husserl can now write that "[o]nly through the phenomenology of genesis does the ego become understandable" (*ibid.*).

Husserl's evidence for these remarkable claims is rooted in the Ego's capacity to, at any time, interrogate a given horizon and ask "*what 'lies in it'*" (CM, 82), and thus "*explicate* or unfold it, and '*uncover*' the potentialities of conscious life at a particular time". This explication is accomplished in "awakenable recollections", to which there belongs "as horizon, the continuously intervening intentionality of possible recollections (to be actualized on my initiative, actively), up to the actual Now of perception". The horizons are thus "'predelineated' potentialities", the form of which "has its 'history'" (CM, 112) in so far as these potentialities are the accomplishments of passive syntheses. Husserl therefore maintains that:

> without putting ourselves back in the realm of passivity … the meditating ego can penetrate into the intentional constituents of experiential phenomena themselves … and thus find references leading back to a "history" and accordingly making these phenomena knowable as formations subsequent to other, essentially antecedent formations. (CM, 113)

Husserl holds that by following the chain of intentional references in which are awakened historically ordered recollections, "we soon encounter eidetic laws governing a passive forming of perpetually new syntheses (a forming that, in part, lies prior to all activity and, in part, takes in all activity itself)". And he also maintains that this forming is itself something that "points back to the 'primal instituting' of this form".

The universal principle responsible for the passive syntheses generative of the transcendental Ego: association

The universal principle of passive synthesis is association, by which Husserl understands not what he considers to be the naturalistic distortions of the genuine intentional concepts of association but "the conformity to eidetic laws on the part of the constitution of the pure Ego" (CM, 114). The pure Ego here is the concrete monadic Ego, to which belongs not only the objects meant and constituted as existent (or nonexistent) by its transcendental subjectivity but also the substrate of the habitualities that are constituted by its positing of these objects. At issue in the pure Ego's genesis are what Husserl refers to as the "eidetic laws of compossibility" (CM, 109) that govern "the existence and possible existence together" of manifold streams of lived-experiences whose simultaneity and succession "constitute the intrinsic [*reellen*] contents of the transcendental Ego's being". The universal form of the Ego's genesis is time, understood as the unity form of both the streams of lived-experience that begin and end and of the one stream of lived-experiences that constitutes the singularity of the Ego's intentional life. Because the transcendental Ego's genesis not only occurs in time but also occurs in time now understood as the formal regularity pertaining to a universal genesis, Husserl draws the conclusion that "the ego constitutes himself in, so to speak, the unity of a 'history'". All the particular phases of the multiplicities belonging to each single lived-experience, as well as the multiplicity of lived-experiences themselves, have their respective places in the successively and simultaneously ordered unity of the universal genesis of the Ego.

Under the heading of "compossibility" Husserl is addressing the problem, unresolved in the second phase of his phenomenology, of precisely how the temporal syntheses accomplish the unification for which they are responsible, namely, the unification of the manifold of transient lived-experiences into one streaming lived-experience belonging to the pure Ego. His answer, association, does not – on his view – signal a relapse into the empirical theory of association, the Humean concept of which he criticized in the *Logical Investigations* on the grounds that it is unable to provide a satisfactory account of the origin of the non-particular meanings presupposed by logic and by cognition generally. Rather, the phenomenological treatment of association is distinguished from the empirical theories by its focus on the eidetic lawfulness that governs the givenness of a similarity from a multitude of distinct phenomena. Specifically, Husserl maintains that similarity is constituted from a multitude composed of a minimum of two intuitive data presented to a consciousness whose intentionality (i) encompasses them in their mutual distinctness and (ii) intends the similarity that exceeds this distinctness. The similarity here is purely passive, in the precise sense that it appears to consciousness whether or not it is noticed; what is presented as similar in the appearance of similarity is what Husserl calls "an overlaying of each [intuitively prominent datum] with the objective sense of the other" (CM, 142). With this overlaying of sense "there takes place an association at a higher level" (CM, 147), namely, a "*fusion*", whereby the appearance of the one intuitively prominent datum is "supplemented" by the appearance of the other. This supplementation accommodates the sense of the one datum to the other, such that each appears as the analogue of the other, with the result that these analogous senses "*found phenomenologically a unity of similarity*" (CM, 142). Because at least two distinct (intuitively prominent) data are eidetically requisite for an association, Husserl refers to this primal associative form as "pairing".

Husserl's published writings do not provide phenomenological details in support of his claims about the passive character of the syntheses constitutive of time, especially (as one would expect from his remarks here) about the relation of these syntheses' universal principle of association to the constitution of the streaming succession and simultaneity of temporality and to the multiple modes of the internal time consciousness of these temporalities. He does, however, work out in detail precisely how the basic structure of association, pairing, functions in the constitution – "in my monad" (CM, 154) – of the meaning and being of, first, the other Ego, and then, other Egos. In order to understand precisely how Husserl thinks the Ego "can experience what is constituted in me as nevertheless other than me", and how, related to this, "I can identify a Nature constituted in me with a Nature constituted by someone else (or, with the necessary precision, how I can identify a Nature constituted in me with one constituted in me *as* a Nature constituted by someone else" (CM, 155), the account of the distinction he makes between the psychophysical human Ego, the factical transcendental Ego, and the *eidos* transcendental Ego needs first to be addressed.

TEN

The intersubjective foundation of transcendental idealism: the immanent transcendency of the world's objectivity

Eidetic analysis of the self-constitution of transcendental Ego

In the second stage of Husserl's phenomenology, the distinction (as we have seen) between the empirical Ego and pure Ego is made. To the being of the former the "index of existence" that characterizes all the objects given in the natural attitude remains inseparable, while to the being of the latter this index has been annulled subsequent to the phenomenological reduction. The result of this reduction is the "merely intentional" being of the essentially empty pure Ego. In Husserl's third stage of phenomenology, the discovery of the pure Ego's concreteness complicates considerably the phenomenological status of the Ego. Husserl speaks, first of all, of the Ego as "himself *existent for himself* in continuous evidence; thus, in himself, he is *continuously constituting himself as existing*" (CM, 100). By the "Ego" here he evidently means the transcendental Ego, as his marginal note to this passage reads "Transcendental Self-Constitution". He also speaks of "I, the reduced 'human Ego' ('psychophysical' Ego)" (CM, 129), who is constituted, "accordingly, as a member of the 'world' with a multiplicity of 'objects outside of me'". And, again, he refers to "the transcendental Ego, who constitutes in his constitutive life everything that is ever objective for me – the Ego of all constitutions, who exists in his actual and potential life-processes and Ego-habitualities and who constitutes in them not only everything objective but also himself as identical Ego" (CM, 130). Finally, there is the "eidos Ego", which Husserl characterizes as follows:

> After transcendental reduction, my true interest is directed to my pure Ego, to the uncovering of this factical Ego. But the uncovering can become genuinely scientific, only if I go back to the apodictic principles that pertain to this Ego as exemplifying the eidos Ego; the essential universalities and necessities by means of which the

> fact is to be related to its rational grounds (those of its pure possibility) and thus made scientific (logical). (CM, 106)[1]

The appearance evident here of seemingly multiple Egos has given rise to two basic interpretative tendencies among phenomenologists. One maintains that the appearance of more than one Ego, for example, of a human or psychological Ego and the transcendental Ego, is the result of the one and only identical Ego being apprehended in two different attitudes, the natural and the phenomenological. The other basically elides Husserl's talk of an Ego or Egos altogether in connection with phenomenological constitution and replaces such talk with the contrast between the "first-person" perspective in which the subject is given and the "third-person" perspective in which objects are given. Both of these tendencies, however, make it difficult (albeit for different reasons) to address a key aspect in Husserl's account of the transcendental Ego's self-constitution in evidence in the distinctions noted directly above. Specifically, this aspect concerns the essential distinction at work in his account of the transcendental Ego as the constitutive source of all objects, as well as the source of the multiplicity that unites these objects themselves as unities of meaning and existence that belong together. The latter multiplicity, according to Husserl, includes the Ego itself as an empirical or worldly object among other objects, and all of these objects are characterized by Husserl as belonging to the concrete essence of the constituting Ego as an inseparable internal determination – but *not* as an identity. Husserl characterizes the transcendental Ego as a "self-constitution" involving two essentially distinct aspects that are nevertheless united in determining it as a whole. Thus, on the one hand, there is the constituting dimension of the Ego, which is responsible for the constitution of its own meaning and being as an object among other constituted objects, and, on the other hand, there is the constituted meaning and being of the Ego itself so constituted, which is phenomenologically accessed as the *reduced* human Ego. Husserl therefore asks "how I, the human Ego reduced to what is purely my own and, as thus reduced, included in the similarly reduced world-phenomenon and, on the other hand, I as transcendental Ego are related to one another" (CM, 131).

The first interpretative tendency's claim that there is one and only one Ego, and that this Ego is the *identity* that constitutes itself as the unity underlying different manifolds of lived-experiences – one psychological, the other transcendental – and therefore is unable to account for the essential difference that Husserl maintains characterizes the transcendental Ego as *both* a constitutive *accomplishing* and as a constitutive *accomplishment*. While both modes of the transcendental Ego are unities, the unity of the former, according to Husserl, is a generative unity, in the exact sense that its unity functions to constitute both the units that compose the multitude of objects "external" to the transcendental Ego that generates them and the unity of the multiplicity itself that encompasses this multitude as precisely a multitude of constituted objects. In other words, the constituting modality of the transcendental Ego responsible for the constituted meaning of objects, and, in so far as they possess being, their constituted being, is distinct from the constituted meaning and being of the mode of the Ego constituted by it. Husserl characterizes the unity of the constituted mode of the transcendental Ego – as a constituted unit among a multitude of other constituted units – as "mundane". By this he does not mean the empirical or human Ego *per se*, but this Ego as a reduced phenomenon, which is constituted by the transcendental Ego through "a *mundanizing self-apperception*" (CM, 130). Husserl characterizes the "mundanization" involved here by saying that "everything included in the ownness belonging to me transcendentally (as this ultimate Ego) enters, as something *psychic*, into 'my psyche'". Whatever phenomenological and philosophical difficulties Husserl's account here may involve, it is clear that for him *both* of these modes of the Ego presuppose the phenomenological attitude, as is evident by his characterization of the "mundane" Ego as the *reduced* human Ego. The Ego that is the focus of the natural attitude is therefore the Ego *prior* to the reduction at issue in Husserl's account here, namely, the human (psychophysical) Ego. Talk of an identity of the Ego across the natural and phenomenological attitudes therefore makes sense with respect to the human Ego and the reduced mundane Ego. The distinction, however, between the mundane Ego, accessed as the constitutive accomplishment of the transcendental Ego, and the latter as the constituting source of this accomplishment, is a distinction that is made *within* the phenomenological attitude. It is therefore not properly a distinction that has its basis in the difference between the natural and phenomenological attitudes.

To interpret as identical the aspect of the Ego's self-constitution that is constituting and that aspect that is constituted, and to ascribe the difference between them as only an apparent one, determined by the character of two different apprehending attitudes, leaves out of the account the difference in the descriptive character of the unity belonging to each of these egological dimensions that informs Husserl's account. The transcendental Ego, as the generative source of the meaning and being (or non-being) of the manifold objects that belong to the world and are therefore outside of "me" as the mundane Ego that is constituted as a member of this world, is "one" in the sense of the unity that encompasses a multitude. Such a unity, as the unity of a multiplicity, is essentially different from the unity of the items that make up the multiplicity, which, in this case, are the constituted objects belonging to the world. Each of these worldly items – *including the reduced human Ego* (or the terminologically equivalent mundane Ego) – is "one" among the other objects belonging to this world, each of which, as a member of this multiplicity, is likewise itself "'one". In precisely this sense, as members of a multiplicity, the constituted units are comparable in a way that the Ego responsible for their constitution is not, for the constituting Ego's unity is precisely such as to not admit its comparison with other units, neither those it constitutes nor those of other putative constituting Egos. The constituting Ego's unity is incomparable with the unity of the objects it constitutes, because the being one of each of these objects is a one among a multitude of other objects, each of which is likewise one, while the constituting Ego's unity is precisely such as to not be a one among a multitude of objects. Likewise incomparable is the constituting Ego's unity in relation to other constituting Egos, any one of which, as we shall see, is necessarily given to the constituting Ego in a mode other than that of the constituting Ego's own self-givenness as the unmediated source of all constitution.

To elide all reference to an Ego as either a constituting or constituted phenomenon in Husserl's account of transcendental subjectivity and to refer, instead, to the "first-person" perspective of his account of subjectivity, is to leave out of the account the role Husserl assigns to the Ego as a constitutive source of meaning and being (or non-being) and to fail to confront the fundamental phenomenological problem of egological unity. As we have seen, Husserl's engagement with subjectivity is fundamentally reflective, not first-personal. While the first-person singular – "I" – and first-person plural – "we" – figure in Husserl's investigation of the being and structure of subjectivity, each as a unit of meaning is not only maintained by him to be constituted by a dimension of subjectivity that is not unequivocally first-personal, but also each is characterized as being uncovered as a reflected phenomenon by a phenomenological reflection whose proper subject can only be said to be "I" by equivocation.

From the shortcomings of these interpretations it does not, of course, follow that Husserl's account of the status of the transcendental Ego in phenomenology is consistent, let alone phenomenologically and philosophically compelling. However, the problem that neither interpretation can capture adequately is precisely the problem that Husserl endeavours to solve in the third stage of his phenomenology, namely, how the transcendental Ego can constitute a meaning and being (and non-being) that, *qua* this meaning and being, transcends the meaning and being of the subjectivity that is its constitutive source – *while nevertheless being inseparable from this source's subjectivity*. Husserl's term for the transcendence in question here is "immanent transcendency", which is similar to the term "transcendency in immanence" that he used in the second stage of his phenomenology to characterize the pure Ego's structural relation to the transient stream of lived-experience that has been actionally modified by it. The phenomenon indicated by "immanent transcendency", however, is radically different, as it concerns not the pure Ego's relation to manifold lived-experiences that come and go but rather the relation of the object constituted in such experiences to this Ego now characterized as it constitutive source. Specifically, it concerns that object's meaning and potentially its existence as an ideality whose synthetic unity, on the one hand, is "*'external' to my own concrete Ego* (but not at all in the natural spatial sense)", while, on the other hand, "it is *still a determining part of my own concrete being*, the being that belongs to me as concrete Ego" (CM, 136).

Husserl's account of the constitution of the meaning of the intentional object as an identity, as we have seen, describes it as the correlate of multiplicities of modes of consciousness that belong together synthetically. Among these multiplicities, Husserl maintains, there are syntheses that are verifying, in the precise sense that their intention is directed towards making evident and having as evident the meant object. When such syntheses take place, the meant object has the evident characteristic "existing", and when they fail to take place it has the evident characteristic "non-existing". As such, these synthetic occurrences are characterized by Husserl as higher-level intentionalities than those in which the intentional object's meaning is constituted, and are described by him "as acts and correlates of 'reason', essentially producible by the transcendental Ego, which pertain (in exclusive disjunction) to all objective senses" (CM, 92). Thus, for Husserl, "*reason and unreason*, as correlative titles for being and non-being" (CM, 91), become "an all-embracing theme for phenomenology". And, with the development of his notion of the pure Ego to include the concretion of the transcendental Ego as monad, this theme is seemingly threatened by his claim that transcendental phenomenology is transcendental philosophy and that, as such, it has the ability to solve the problems connected with the possibility of objective knowledge.

Transcendental phenomenology's appearance as solipsism

The basis of this threat, as mentioned, is transcendental phenomenology's appearance as solipsism, in so far as the very notion of "immanent transcendency" seems to be a contradiction in terms. "Transcendent" and "immanent", as conceptual opposites, are incapable of being combined, as the former refers to the status of something that is independent of the being of the subject and the latter to something that is included in the subject's mode of being. Husserl's response to this threat and the seeming contradiction that composes it is twofold. On the one hand, he explicates the very meaning of "objectivity" to show that it *includes* a reference to subjectivity, albeit subjectivity in the plural, in so far as the very meaning of the objectivity of anything is inseparable from the conviction that it is the same for *all* subjects. On the other hand, he makes a distinction between the "immanent transcendency" of the meanings constituted by and therefore belonging to the concrete transcendental Ego whose transcendental experience has been reduced by a phenomenological abstraction to what intrinsically belongs to it, and the "immanent transcendency" of the meanings constituted by this Ego but that nevertheless do not intrinsically belong to it.

To the first "immanent transcendency" there belongs what Husserl characterizes as the "'*primordial' transcendency*" (CM, 136) of the world, namely, the world as a constituted unity that "*is inseparable from the original constitution itself*, with the inseparableness that characterizes an immediate *concrete* oneness" (CM, 134). Where and in so far as this concrete oneness obtains, Husserl maintains, "not only the constitutive perceiving but also the perceived existent belongs to my concrete very-ownness". Included in the primordial transcendency of the transcendental Ego's concrete ownness are sensuous data constituted as the Ego's immanent temporalities, the Ego as mere Ego pole and as its habitualities, transcendent objects as unities belonging to multiplicities of sensuous modes of appearance, and the body as it is lived (*Leib*) – in contrast to the body as one object among the other objects that belong to the objective world – that belongs to this Ego. To the second "immanent transcendency" there belongs the intrinsically first non-Ego – namely, the other Ego – which makes possible the constitution of an objective nature and the whole objective world, as a nature and world identically there for an Ego-community that "includes me" (CM, 137). This other Ego, together with others like it, become "constituted (in my sphere of ownness, naturally) as a community of Egos existing with and for each other – *ultimately, a community of monads*, which, moreover, (in its communalized intentionality) constitutes the *one identical world*" (*ibid.*).

By means of what Husserl characterizes as the "communalization" of constitutive intentionality, the multiplicity of transcendental Egos that make possible the objectivity of nature and the world – a multiplicity that he terms "transcendental intersubjectivity" – comes itself to have "an *intersubjective* sphere of ownness". And because of this, Husserl maintains that "the objective world does not, in the proper sense, *transcend* that sphere or that sphere's intersubjective essence, but rather inheres in it as an 'immanent' transcendency" (*ibid.*). Husserl explicitly connects *this* sense of immanent transcendency with the transcendental idealism of phenomenology, and therefore maintains that the "objective world as an *idea*" (CM, 138) is essentially related to intersubjectivity, as its "ideal correlate". Thus the idealism of phenomenology concerns precisely the constitution of the world's objective status in the intersubjectively communalized experience of a multitude of transcendental Egos, a multitude that, in the "ideality of endless openness", is itself constituted on Husserl's view, as we have seen, in the transcendental Ego's sphere of ownness.

The Leibnizian problem of the Other in transcendental phenomenology

Before turning to Husserl's accounts of the intentional explications that "actually execute the transcendental idealism of phenomenology", two things need to be pointed out. First, the transcendental Ego described in Husserl's account of the inseparability of its self-constitution and the objective world's constitution is the "*all embracing eidos, transcendental Ego as such*, which comprises all pure possibility-variants of my factical Ego and this Ego itself qua possibility" (CM, 105–6). Second, the Leibnizian metaphysical context deliberately invoked by Husserl's account of the communalized experience of a multitude of transcendental Egos, as essentially involving "*a 'harmony' of the monads*" (CM, 138), each one of which is a particular subject "equipped with mutually corresponding and harmonious constitutive systems", calls attention to a non-Cartesian metaphysical problem that Husserl thinks his phenomenology can solve. Specifically, the Leibnizian problem invoked by Husserl's terminology is that of establishing the objectivity and unity of the world in the face of the manifest plurality of other minds with uniquely subjective "points of view", which is radically distinct from the Cartesian problem of establishing the existence of other minds, since for Leibniz the existence of not just one other mind but of a plurality of them is assumed from the outset.

Because Husserl's descriptions of the transcendental Ego are eidetic, they do not have "empirical" significance, as signifying "factical occurrences in the factical transcendental Ego" (CM, 104). Rather, they have the significance of essentially determined and therefore essentially necessary descriptions of "a *purely possible Ego*, a pure possibility-variant of my *factical Ego*" (CM, 105); or, as in the case of the eidetic description of perception, they are descriptions of "free variations" that start out "by imaging this Ego to be freely varied", such that "the problem of exploring eidetically the explicit constitution of any transcendental Ego whatever" is set. Because in either case "the variation being meant is an evident one, accordingly as presenting in pure intuition the possibilities themselves as possibilities, its correlate is an *intuitive and apodictic consciousness of something univer-*

sal". This means for Husserl that "the eidos itself is a beheld or beholdable universal, one that is pure, 'unconditioned' – that is to say: according to its own intuitional sense, a universal not conditioned by any fact". Moreover, it means that the *eidos* "is *prior to all 'concepts'*, in the sense of verbal significations; indeed, as pure concepts, these must be made to fit the eidos" (*ibid.*). We have already had occasion to remark that the precedent for Husserl's formulation of the "being seen" of an *eidos*, which is patently evident in this passage, is Plato's arithmological account of the *eidē*. Here, in anticipation of our discussion of the significance of this for both Husserl's thought and its Heideggerian and Derridean critiques, we call attention to perhaps Husserl's clearest statement that to the intuition (seeing) of an *eidos* there is correlated the *eidos* as something "beheld" and, therefore, something "being seen".

Husserl makes it clear that "in the transition from my Ego to an Ego as such [i.e. an *eidos* Ego], neither the actuality nor the possibility of other Egos is presupposed" (CM, 106). He also makes it clear why this is the case: "I phantasy only myself as if I were otherwise; I do not phantasy others" (*ibid.*). How, then, does Husserl think that the constitution of the other Ego, which is necessary for phenomenology to overcome the semblance of solipsism, can be accounted for in an eidetic analysis founded in "my" transcendental Ego? The answer is that Husserl does not think that the other Ego, in either the guise of the other pure Ego (the other Ego who does not yet have a worldly sense) or the other Ego as monad (the other Ego as a world-constituting concrete transcendental Ego), is constituted as a variation of the perception of my own Ego, which is what the other Ego would have to be in order to be constituted in a fantasy of *my* Ego. Rather, for Husserl the very meaning of the other Ego as *other* precludes precisely the mode of access to its constitution that takes it departure from the experience of my Ego. The mode of access is rather, as it always is for Husserl's phenomenology, the "transcendental clue", ultimately traceable to the straightforward consciousness of something and the examination of its noetic–noematic structure. In the case at hand, the transcendental clue is "the experienced other, given to me in straightforward consciousness and as I immerse myself in examining the noematic–ontic content belonging to him (purely as correlate of my cogito)" (CM, 123). The problem of the other Ego for Husserl is therefore clearly not that of establishing that the other Ego exists; Descartes' worry that his *cogito* may be all alone is not Husserl's. Husserl's problem is the subtler one of accounting for how the very meaning of the other Ego, as *other*, that is given in my experience can nevertheless arise in a constitution that essentially and necessarily is constituted in *my* transcendental Ego, as the constitutionally "primal" monad.

Leibniz's importance for Husserl's account of phenomenology as a transcendental idealism, which is signalled by Husserl's invocation of Leibniz's notion of the "monad", can be established by a brief consideration of the three aspects of Leibniz's "Monadology"[2] that are at stake in all of Husserl's "deliberate suggestions of Leibniz's metaphysics" (CM, 176–7). The first aspect is the multiplicity and diversity of Leibniz's monad, the second is the reason why, despite the many different universes that correspond – one to one – to this multiplicity and diversity, for Leibniz they are only perspectives of one single universe, and the third and last is the pre-established harmony that Leibniz maintains is responsible for the *a priori* rather than contingent status of this reason.

Leibniz's monads, as the very term "monad" suggests, are irreducible unities, which nevertheless enter into composites. Each monad possesses the minimal quality of involving a multitude in its unity, which he calls perception. Among monads, only some possess "apperception, or consciousness" (Monadology, 14), which should be distinguished from perception, otherwise all monads will be thought to be minds, which Leibniz thinks is Descartes' mistake. And even fewer possess the maximal quality of "*reflective acts*, which enable us to think of that which is called 'I' and enable us to consider this or that in us" (30). No two monads are identical, each possessing "different points of view" (57), but all are nevertheless related to each of the others in an interconnection or accommodation "that express all others" (56). Each monad is therefore "a perpetual, living mirror of the universe", which, despite there being as many universes as monads, is viewed as the *same*. That is, even though each monad's point of view, when "multiplied perspectively" (57), yields an infinite multitude of universes as a function of the different perspectives expressed by each, these perspectives are but the perspectives of a "single universe" (*ibid.*). The harmony that unites the infinite multitude of diverse monads into a regulated whole has its basis in "apriori reasons" (60), and is therefore "pre-established" (78) between all monads, "since they are all representations of a single universe". Finally, the source of *a priori* reasons is God, because it must be recognized by reflective acts that no contingent ratiocination is capable of accounting for the original unity of the truths of these ultimate reasons, and because each truth rules out, in principle, its opposite, thereby establishing its necessity. As the source of these truths, God must be a "unique" (incomparable) being whose existence is both possible, because it is conceivable without contradiction, and necessary, because otherwise the ultimate reasons would have to be thought without an origin, which *is* a contradiction.

The Leibnizian context of Husserl's monadology is especially evident in Husserl's account of the following: the '"unity in multitude" that structures egological perception; the distinction between perception and apperception in the transcendental Ego's self-constitution (and, as we shall see, in the transcendental Ego's constitution of the other Ego); the status of the objective world as a single unity, despite the intersubjective multitude of the concrete and therefore factically diverse transcendental Egos that constitute it; and, finally, the harmonious course of transcendental experience that characterizes the intersubjective community of Egos' constitution of the one and only objective world. Indeed, Husserl holds that:

> Leibniz is right when he says that the infinitely many monads and groups of monads are conceivable but that it does not follow that all these possibilities are *compossible*; and, again, when he says that infinitely many worlds might have been "created", but not two or more at once, since they are incompossible. (CM, 167)

Compossibility is Leibniz's term for the actual coexistence of two or more realities whose existence is possible, that is, conceivable without contradiction. As mentioned, Husserl initially employs this term to refer to the existence and possible existence together of the transcendental Ego's successive and simultaneous streams of lived-experiences. Husserl's agreement here with Leibniz does not extend, of course, to what Husserl considers Leibniz's "metaphysical construction" (CM, 177), which grounds both the selection of compossible monads and the incompossibility of more than one world in theoretical "presuppositions or helpful thoughts drawn from the historical metaphysical tradition". Rather, Husserl's phenomenological transcendental idealism, despite being presented as a monadology, "draws its content purely from phenomenological explication of the transcendental experience laid open by transcendental reduction" (*ibid.*).

With the Leibnizian context in view, we can see that the other Ego is of importance for Husserl, above all, to establish the community of Egos necessary for the intersubjectivity presupposed by the objectivity proper to the world's meaning. And, by keeping this context in view, we shall also see Husserl's account of the phenomenological basis for metaphysical implications of phenomenology as a transcendental idealism. Specifically, he holds that the foundation in ultimate cognitions provided by phenomenology establishes the impossibility of even the conceivability of the coexistence of two or more separate pluralities of monads, "i.e., pluralities *not in communion*" (CM, 166) and, correspondingly, the "pure absurdity" of separate groups of monads constituting *two* spatiotemporal worlds that are "separate ad infinitum".

The constitution of the meaning and being of the other Ego as pure Ego and concrete transcendental Ego (monad) in "my" transcendental Ego

The key to Husserl's account of "my" transcendental Ego as the source of the plurality of monads and the *a priori* harmony that governs both the meaning and existence of their interrelations is the peculiar phenomenological abstraction that separates off from the immanence of the Ego everything given to it by transcendental constitution as "'alien' and 'other'" (CM, 127), including other ego-subjects and "everything '*other-spiritual*'". By the latter Husserl understands both the world as it is there for others at a given time, what he calls the "surrounding world", as well as the world that is given for everyone at any time, the objective natural world. Subsequent to this abstraction, the Ego's transcendental experience is reduced to what, taken concretely, is inseparable from its experience. As mentioned, this primordial experience includes the transcendencies in immanence of the Ego's sensuously constituted immanent temporalities, the Ego as the pole that acquires enduring habitualities, unities of sensuous modes of appearance, and the lived-body "'in' which I '*rule and govern*' *immediately*" (CM, 128). Despite the meaning-exclusion of everything alien, Husserl maintains that the reduction to the transcendental Ego's ownness "leaves us a *kind of* 'world' still, a nature reduced to what is included in our ownness and, thanks to the lived-body, a nature that includes a psychophysical Ego with 'body and soul' and personal Ego as utterly *unique* members of this reduced 'world'" (CM, 129). Husserl refers to this world as "primordial nature" (CM, 149), and stresses that "[b]ringing to light my lived-body, reduced to what is included in my ownness, is itself a part of bringing to light the *ownness-essence* of the objective phenomenon: '*I, as this man*'" (CM, 128).

The lived-body is the key to how Husserl thinks that "every *consciousness of* what is other, every mode of appearance *of* it, belongs" (CM, 131) to the transcendental Ego's ownness. The physical body of the other Ego appears in the sensuousness that is inseparable from the experience of the concrete transcendental Ego's lived-body, which is to say, in the sensuousness of this Ego's self-apperception as a mundane Ego to which a lived-body essentially belongs as "my" lived-body. Husserl describes what appears in the transcendental Ego's concrete experience *as* the body of the other Ego, and not as a body that is "merely an indication of someone else" (CM, 151). His description is based on the fact that "we are not dealing here with a temporal genesis of such experience, on the basis of a temporally antecedent self-experience", but rather with "only a precise explication of the intentionality actually observable in our experience of someone else". The results of this explication uncover three basic dimensions at work in the constitution of the alien: (i) the constitution of the other Ego as the pure Ego belonging to the other's body experienced in the immanence of the transcendental Ego's sphere of ownness; (ii) the constitution of the *objective* transcendency of the world, as the one and the same world there for the Ego community that includes "me" as a pure Ego; and (iii) the constitution of the monad community as the transcendental intersubjectivity whose collective constitutive intentionality is responsible for the objective world's meaning and being as an objective transcendency.

The crucial aspect belonging to the initial constitution of the other Ego as the pure Ego belonging to the experience of someone else's body is the passive associative "pairing" of my lived-body with the experience of another physical body. Based on the *perception* of the similarity between my lived-body, "which is always there and sensuously prominent" (CM, 143), and my perception of a different body, an overlaying of the meaning of my lived-body as a psychophysical unity with the meaning of the body appearing in my perceptual field occurs. As already mentioned, the resulting passive association yields a "fusion" of meaning, which presents a unity of similarity at a higher level than the perceptual similarity of the two distinct intuitive data involved (my lived-body and the physical body in my lived-body's perceptual field). Husserl characterizes the associative unity as "apperception" or more precisely '"appresentation". He does so because the meaning content in question, although co-given with perception, is strictly speaking not constituted perceptually but in an "*intentional modification*". Whatever can become *originally* presented and evidently verified "is something *I* am; or else it belongs to me as peculiarly my own", whereas whatever "is experienced in that founded manner that characterizes a primordially unfulfillable experience – an experience that does not give something itself originally but that consistently verifies something indicated – is 'other'". The other Ego, *qua* its very meaning and being as other, is something that cannot be originally given in *my* experience. Its meaning constitution therefore necessarily involves the modification – rather than the variation or extension – of my experience. This modification concerns both my transcendental Ego, "which is the first to be objectivated" (CM, 144) as a (mundane) Ego, and my primordial "world", each of which is "appresented, in an analogizing modification", with the other Ego.

The appresentation of the other Ego – in an analogizing modification – as an analogue of myself as a mundane Ego, constitutes both "my" self as *mine*, "by virtue of the contrastive pairing that necessarily takes place" (*ibid.*), and brings about the constitutionally secondary transcendency of the objective world. Moreover, the analogizing modification of my primordial "world" appresents "*his* primordial world, and then his fully concrete Ego", which is to say, "'in other words, *another monad* becomes constituted appresentatively in mine" (*ibid.*). The analogizing appresentation responsible for these three interrelated and interdependent aspects of the constitution of the objective transcendency of the world takes place in what Husserl refers to as a "*combination* (*Verbindung*) accomplished through the medium of representation" (CM, 155).

Combination (*Verbindung*) founded in recollections as the source of the objectivity of the meaning and being of the other Ego

Combination in general brings about the constitution of an identity whose unity as "the Same" is accomplished by an identifying synthesis that unites a multitude of repeated representations, each of which is "separate from the others", into the evident consciousness of an identical intentional object. Because each of the lived-experiences is a "*separate conscious lived-experience*", the "object immanent in them" is so "only as something non-intrinsically (*irreelles*) inherent" in any one of them (CM, 155). According to Husserl, the "combination" proper is accomplished through repeated representations of an absent original presentation, with each repetition accompanied by the consciousness that the original can be gone back to "with the evidence: 'I can always do so again'". Each repeated representation, therefore, synthetically combines the representation occurring in the present stream of lived-experiences with the relevant separate past representations of "the Same" original presentation. Husserl terms this synthesis "recollection" and maintains that "through the medium of recollective representations, the synthesis extends – within my stream of lived-experiences (which is always already constituted) – from my living present into my currently relevant separate pasts and therewith brings into relief their *combination*" (*ibid.*). Because each of these repeated representations is evident as a separate temporal sequence, each represents the original presentation as an object that is "ideal", that is, as an object that is constituted as "the Same" across a multitude of temporally separate streams of lived-experiences.

Husserl maintains that the combination constituted through a multitude of representations is responsible for "my own lived-experiences" coming to "acquire for me the meaning and validity of something existent, something existing with its identical temporal form and identical temporal content", as well as for "the constitution of objects that are ideal in the precise sense – for example: all logically ideal objects", and, finally, for the "experience of the alien (*Fremderfahrung*)" (CM, 156). In the latter case, a combination comes about between the concrete Ego, together with his primordial sphere, and "the *alien sphere* represented therein". This combination first accomplishes the identifying synthesis of the primordially given lived-body of someone else and the same body, "but *appresented* in other modes of appearance" (*ibid.*). That is, combined into the unity of the consciousness of "the Same" are separate lived-experiences of the other's lived-body, each one linked through a chain of recollections to its initial apperception. From this unity, the experience of the alien accomplishes "identifying synthesis of the same nature, given and verified primordially", which is to say, the nature given "with pure sensuous originality" in "my" uninterrupted, "purely passive original self-appearance" is combined "appresentationally" with the primordial nature constituted by the other Ego's concrete intentional life. Thus, for Husserl, the combination constitutes the "*coexistence of my Ego and the other Ego*", and therewith primordially institutes "a *common time-form*" such that "every primordial temporality automatically acquires the significance of being merely an original mode of appearance of objective temporality to a particular subject" (*ibid.*).

The combination mediated by representations described here is the source of Husserl's confidence that Leibniz was right – although for the wrong reasons – about the impossibilities of both the separate existence of two or more pluralities of monads and of the existence of more than one objective world. Phenomenology, as transcendental idealism, is able to show – on the basis of reflectively uncovered and verifiable evidence – that both the meaning and being of any possible other Ego and any possible world is inseparable from the constitution of each as an ideal unity in "my" transcendental Ego or monad. More exactly, the combination brought about by the multiplicity of recollective representations yields the primordial transcendence of nature that appears in each monad – originally in "my" monad and appresentatively in the other monad – as the one and only source of the meaning and, when this meaning is verified with evidence, the being of the plurality of monads whose community is constitutive of the objectivity of the one spatiotemporal nature and world, as an identical world for everyone.

Criticism of phenomenological cognition: overcoming the naivety of apodicticity

Husserl's account of the constitution of objectivity in the immanent transcendency of the intersubjective community of monads, a community that is itself constituted in the sphere of ownness of each concrete transcendental Ego, occurs by his own admission within "the naïveté of apodicticity" (CM, 178). As mentioned, by this he means that the scope and limits of phenomenologically apodictic evidence are methodically accounted for, but not the mode of its apodicticity, that is, the manner of this evidence's givenness. And, moreover, the criticism of this manner of givenness, owing to the methodically reflexive relation to its own presuppositions that guides phenomenological cognition, is also understood by Husserl to be unaccounted for at this stage (what we are calling the third stage) of phenomenology's development. The fourth and final stage of Husserl's phenomenology represents an *attempt* to *begin* to provide an account of what its third stage calls the mode of its cognition's apodicticity. As mentioned in the Prolegomenon, Husserl's self-interpretation of his last works is that they made "a small beginning". In the fragmentary works that present this beginning he explicitly situates it in relation to what he calls the "'Cartesian way'" (*Crisis*, 157–8/155) to the transcendental *epochē*, which he now characterizes as having "a great shortcoming: while it leads to the transcendental Ego in one leap, as it were, it brings this Ego into view as apparently empty of content". Before we turn to Husserl's "new way" to the transcendental *epochē* via the devotion of "an exclusive, consistently theoretical interest to the 'life-world'", the limits of the Cartesian way need to be articulated, to prevent the misunderstanding, still prevalent today, that in the final stage of his thought Husserl rejects the *results* of his Cartesian way to the transcendental *epochē* and reduction.

The Cartesian way establishes the scope and limits of phenomenology's apodictic evidence in terms of the fundamentality of the concrete transcendental Ego's sphere of ownness as the source of *all* phenomenological cognition, even, as we have just seen, its cognition of the community of monads that compose the foundation of the transcendental intersubjectivity responsible for the objective meaning and being of the natural world. Moreover, this evidence is manifest in manifold subjective streams of multiplicities, which are responsible for constituting the unity and meaning of all possible objects and, at a higher level, are responsible for the constitution of their being and non-being. These multiplicities, in turn, are constituted in the active and passive syntheses intrinsic to the concrete transcendental Ego. The latter, passive syntheses are also responsible for the transcendental Ego's self-constitution as both an immanent temporal unity and as the source of all unity, including the transcendent unity of spatial things. The transcendental Ego's temporal unity is therefore responsible for the temporality that properly characterizes the manifold streams of multiplicities as *its* multiplicities, including its own multiplicity as both a subjective pole and an apperceived unity as one mundane object among the others that compose the multiplicity of worldly objects. Finally, the scope of phenomenology's apodictic evidence includes the transcendental Ego's constitution of the unity of the world as *idea*, the infinitely open horizon that encompasses the manifold of worldly objects without its meaning and being having the status of an object.

The Cartesian way's account of the scope and limits of this evidence is characterized by Husserl as "a matter of '*static analysis*'" (CM, 136) of the objective world's transcendency. By this he means that the objective world is treated as "constantly there before me as already finished, a datum of my livingly continuous objective experience and, even in respect of what is no longer experienced, something I go on accepting habitually" (*ibid.*). Such analysis is neither the defect of a putative "static" method of phenomenology nor an approach to the phenomenological problem of constitution that Husserl abandoned in favour of an equally putative "genetic" method. On the contrary, for Husserl this kind of analysis belongs to what he calls the first stage of phenomenology, which is as necessary as it is incomplete. Its incompleteness concerns the lack of entry into the further and ultimate problems of phenomenology that concern its self-criticism, specifically, those that concern the criticism of the mode of evidence in which its initial analyses establish the scope and limits of its apodictic evidence. As "static", the experience of the objective world, as already there and finished in its constitution, is examined to the end of:

> uncovering intentionally the manner in which it bestows meaning, the manner in which it can occur as experience and become verified as evidence relating to an actual existent with an explicatable essence of *its* own, which is not *my* own essence and has no place as a constituent part thereof, though it nevertheless can acquire meaning and verification only in my essence. (*Ibid.*)

As we have seen, this uncovering discloses both the meaning and verification of the objectivity of the world on the basis of yet another multiplicity of synthetically linked lived-experiences, namely, those of the temporally separate recollective representations that intend the identity of an ideal object as the Same, despite its non-intrinsic (*irreell*) inherence in the multiplicity of recollections that intend it.

Historicity as the mode of givenness proper to the apodicticity of phenomenological cognition

Precisely *this* mode of givenness is subject to criticism by Husserl in the last stage of the development of his phenomenology. On the one hand, the mode of givenness of the ideal structures connected with the constitution of objectivity is subject to criticism. On the other hand, the mode of givenness of the multiplicity of recollections that constitutes the transcendent identity of those structures as the Same is also subject to criticism. The former criticism assumes the guise of a genetic investigation of the sedimented history of the *intrasubjective* intentional genesis of the categorial formations that compose the ideality of ideal meaning structures, which recollectively awakens the "intentional history" of this genesis. The later criticism takes the form of an investigation into the origins of the *intersubjective* intentional establishment of science as both a tradition with an origin in actual history and an essential structure to which belongs the transmission ("handing-down") over time of scientific cognitions. The criticism of these two criticisms, in turn, involves the identification of two presuppositions that, respectively, guide the transcendental-phenomenological enquiry into the intrasubjective constitution of ideality and the intersubjective constitution of a scientific tradition. The former enquiry is guided by the presupposition that the origin of an ideal science is inseparable from the familiarity and handling of things and their material qualities belonging to a pre-scientific life-world. The latter enquiry is guided by the presupposition that the *objectivity* of this origin has as its source an accomplishment of transcendental subjectivity that had to become manifest in actual history as the science's "discovery".

Husserl confronts these two presuppositions in his last texts in a manner that moves towards the recognition of their essential connection. Specifically, he comes to see that there is an essential connection between the multiplicities involved in each of those presuppositions. Hence Husserl came to recognize that (i) the multiplicity of intrasubjective recollections that awakens the history of the intentional genesis of the ideality of ideal meaning structures is inseparable from (ii) the multiplicity of intersubjective recollections that awaken the transcendental conditions of possibility that govern the constitution of the origin of a science and the transmission over time of its cognitions. In other words, Husserl arrived at the conclusion that there is an essential relation and therefore a transcendental connection between the phenomenologically "pure" intentional history that is constitutive of the ideality of ideal meaning and the factically impure "actual" history of agents and events that are, in principle, datable (even if both remain, in fact, unknown).

As we shall see, the "small beginning" made by Husserl in the final stage of the development of his phenomenology is connected with the recognition that phenomenological cognition's very mode of givenness as apodictic involves the essential "historicity" – in the precise sense of the interconnection of accomplishment and sedimentation – that is inseparable from the transcendental constitution of all meaning and being. And we shall see that for Husserl the accomplishments and sedimentations that prove decisive for his diagnosis of the roots of the contemporary crisis of the European sciences have two dates: the Enlightenment and the ancient Greek classical age. In anticipation of the sketchy results of Husserl's historical reflection, we note that they find sedimented in the crowning cognitive achievement of the Enlightenment, mathematical physics, a cognitive method driven by the principled exclusion of both the pre-scientific life-world and the human subject from the proper subject matter of science. And sedimented in the ancient Greek accomplishment of philosophy's beginning, Husserl finds the *telos* of the universal cognition of the totality of what is, a *telos* that the method of transcendental phenomenology, and transcendental phenomenology alone, is capable of working towards.

ELEVEN

The pure phenomenological motivation of Husserl's turn to history

The problem of history in Husserl's last writings

The fourth and final stage of Husserl's development is contained in two fragmentary texts on history and phenomenology written in his last years,[1] texts that unmistakably link the meaning of both the crowning achievement of the Enlightenment (the new science of mathematical physics) and the crowning achievement of his own life's work (the rigorous science of transcendental phenomenology) to the problem of their historical origination. It is striking that in the years following the original publication of these works and their republication in the 1954 *Crisis* volume edited by Walter Biemel, commentary on them has almost universally passed over what Husserl articulated as the specifically *phenomenological* nature of the problem of history.[2] It has been ignored in favour of mostly critical discussions of Husserl's putative attempt to accommodate his earlier "pure" and therefore "idealistic" formulations of transcendental phenomenology to the so-called "problem of history".

The reception of Husserl's last works has therefore been preoccupied with the story of their departure from his own early rejection of historicism and his late attempts to establish what by many has been deemed oxymoronic and therefore impossible: a phenomenology of the *a priori* structure of the historical origination of meaning. As mentioned at the beginning of this work, motivated by the goal of establishing phenomenology as a presuppositionless universal science of *a priori* meanings, Husserl's early thought had identified the "facticity" of history as among those presuppositions standing in the way of a "pure" phenomenology. Husserl's late turn to the problem of history has consequently evoked in many the concern that pure phenomenology and the historical preoccupation of his last texts are intrinsically incompatible.

Husserl's turn to history, however, is characterized by a novel development of the phenomenological method that overcomes the traditional opposition between historical explanation and epistemological investigation. His studies are thus historical without being limited to empirical contingencies and epistemological without being cut off from the historical development of philosophical and scientific knowledge. In other words, Husserl's last works overcome the problem of history that leads to historicism by showing, in effect, that the disclosure of the "historicity" of knowledge does not lead to an opposition between the contingency of history and the universality of knowledge. His work shows this by uncovering the heritage of ideas, meanings and attitudes that underlie the basic concepts of the modern mathematics that makes mathematical physics possible; that is, he uncovers aspects of what he will refer to as the "historical a priori" (OG, 381/373) of modern physics. Husserl therefore presents in his last works the "theory of knowledge ... as a peculiarly historical task" (OG, 379/370), a task he assigns to his final formulation of transcendental phenomenology and its now defining goal of overcoming "[t]he ruling dogma of the separation in principle between epistemological elucidation and historical explanation". Husserl's formulation of the "universal a priori of history" (OG, 380/371) as "nothing other than the vital movement of the coexistence and the interweaving of original formations and sedimentations of meaning" (*ibid.*) serves as the guiding clue for overcoming the "ruling dogma" in question. The methodology that discloses this "vital movement" is to be found in Husserl's sketch of phenomenologically historical reflection. Husserl characterizes such reflection as "*the 'zigzag'* back and forth" from the "'breakdown' situation of our time, with its 'breakdown of science' itself" (*ibid.*), to the historical "*beginnings*" of both the original meaning of science itself (i.e. philosophy) and the development of its meaning leading up to the "breakdown" of modern mathematical physics (cf. *Crisis*, 59/58).

The relation between the problem of origin and history in phenomenology

Husserl's articulation of the phenomenological problem of history in his last writings capitalizes on his lifelong concern with the problems of origin in order to show that there is an essential connection between the approach to the phenomenological origin of things formulated by his earlier writings and the historical reflection on the meaning of philosophy in his last works. This essential connection is found precisely in the concern of Husserl's phenomenology, from beginning to end, with the constitutive problems of origins. Husserl's phenomenological lifelong concern with the "*rizōmata pantōn* [the roots of all things]" (PRS, 340/294) traces a continuous path from his early rejection of historicism as a means of accounting for the origin of logical, mathematical and scientific propositions, to his late formulation of historicity. Thus in his last writings Husserl formulates "historicity" as the historical *a priori* that makes intelligible the original constitution of the ideal, in the precise sense of the objectivity of logically ideal objects.

The key to Husserl's formulation of the role of historicity in the constitution the ideal meaning of logically ideal objects, which is to say, in the constitution of their "ideality", is found in his characterization of the "sedimentation of meaning". As mentioned, Husserl refers in his last writings to meaning formations that have become "sedimented" and are therefore no longer present to consciousness, even though they can nevertheless still be made accessible to it. This status pertains both to the temporal modification of the original experience of meaning formations and the role that passive understanding plays in the apprehension of the meaning of concepts and words. In either case, Husserl holds that it is possible to render the sedimented meanings present to consciousness again in a process called "awakening". In the case of the passive understanding of meaning formations, because it does not reproduce the cognitive activity that originally produced their meaning, the original meaning on Husserl's view becomes diminished and in some sense forgotten. In so far as the original meaning has not completely disappeared, however, it can still be "awakened" in recollections initiated by phenomenological reflection. Husserl's articulation of the phenomenological problem of history focuses on the involvement of both kinds of sedimentation with the problem of constitutive origins and the two distinct yet interrelated aspects of what is sedimented in each case. There is, on the one hand, what can be called the "intentional history" of the essential and objective possibility of each single meaning phenomenon, and, on the other, what can be called the "actual history" connected to the original presentation of the meaning phenomenon within intersubjectively objective temporality. As will become clear, the true character of history is revealed for Husserl when neither of these two "histories" is taken in isolation. Rather, the essential necessity of intentional history's being subjected to a history in the usual sense of the term is disclosed by Husserl in the *Crisis* texts and "The Origin of Geometry", when he confronts in these last works the relation between intentional history and actual history.

The motivation internal to phenomenology for Husserl's seemingly late turn to history

Husserl's account of the phenomenological problem of history grows out of the inability of the constitutive analysis of the internal temporality of each intentional meaning formation to reactivate the original foundations and therefore the roots of modern science and, consequently, the fundamental concepts of both ancient mathematics and philosophy. Husserl's phenomenology is therefore *internally* motivated to widen the scope of its enquiry into the origins of intentional objects beyond the evidence manifest in the analysis of their temporal genesis. Hence this motivation is *not* provided by any new-found interest in history on Husserl's part, but by his recognition that the phenomenology of internal temporality is not up to the task of disclosing these original foundations. Thus, in marked contrast to those who argue that Husserl's turn to history in his last works has its source in his recognition that the most radical and fundamental rationalization of the *factual* is not possible, Husserl's turn to history is motivated by his continued interest in the problem of accounting for evidence that discloses the origin of ideal meaning formations that are *non-factual* and therefore, in precisely this sense, rational. The locus of the problem of history in Husserl's mature phenomenology is therefore inseparable from the problem of the origin of non-factual meaning, that is, from the "ideal" meanings of Galilean geometry and the formalization that make mathematical physics both possible and – so long as the origin of these meanings is restricted to the investigation of their *temporal genesis* – unintelligible.

Hence the phenomenological problem of history as sketched by Husserl does not involve the question of how the facticity of history is compatible with the claim of phenomenology to lead to insights into unconditionally universal essences. It does not involve this question because it is precisely the "unconditioned universality" or the "*a priori*" status of the essences of any meaning formations – beginning with the "exemplary" (OG, 365/353)[3] considerations of the ideal meanings that are constitutive of mathematical physics – which, when traced to their constitutive origins, are revealed to contain within themselves the sedimented history of their origination within actual history. Husserl's articulation of the phenomenological problem of history therefore does not lead to the problem of the opposition between the "facticity" of history and the "apriority" of essences, but rather uncovers their essential connection. Indeed, Husserl not only shows this essential connection, a connection that makes impossible the generally accepted opposition between epistemology and history, between epistemological origin and historical origin, but also discloses its universal and transcendental meaning. This meaning uncovers the real problem of historicity in terms of the combination (*Verbindung*) of transcendental subjectivity, as the constitutive source of all meaning, and its intentional accomplishments, a combination that yields the interweaving of the original production and "sedimentation" of meaning.

Psychologism and the problem of history in phenomenology

Returning now to the problem of history in Husserl's early work, we find that in attacking psychologism, Husserl was, in fact, confronting the problem of history. In criticizing the attitude of historicism in "Philosophy as Rigorous Science", Husserl treats it as structurally continuous with psychologism. Thus he maintains that any "naturalistic" psychological explanation of human knowledge inevitably leads to a history of human development with all its contingencies. In such an account, any ideal meaning is held to originate from earlier experiences that generate it. On this view, the explanation of ideal meaning assumes the guise of a legend. As mentioned, Husserl's radical criticism of psychologism does not imply the simple opposition between unchanging abstract principles and continuously changing empirical things. Husserl's exposure of the inability of the psychologistic and historicistic appeals to the "natural time" of empirically conceived experience to account for the origin of the atemporality of ideal meanings does not rule out all connection of time to the problem of their origin. Rather, Husserl's recognition of the inability of naturalism to account for the origin of ideal meanings in psychologism and historicism is followed by his initial attempt to account for their origin on the basis of phenomenological time.

The fact that the phenomenological descriptions grounding Husserl's account of the internal temporality of phenomenological time have been interpreted as psychological descriptions by many readers of Husserl shows not only that these readers are unable to follow Husserl's thought, but also that psychological and phenomenological research have an affinity. This affinity is based on the commonality of the psychic phenomena with which each is concerned. Thus in the *Cartesian Meditations* Husserl states that "[p]henomenology signifies indeed a fundamental refashioning of psychology", such that "by far the greater part of psychological research belongs in an *a priori and pure intentional psychology*" (CM, 170). Husserl makes it clear that "the word 'pure' means: kept free of everything psychophysical". Hence, "by a means of a change of the natural into the transcendental attitude, it is open to a 'Copernican conversion', wherewith it assumes a new sense of a completely radical transcendental consideration of the world and impresses this sense on all phenomenological-psychological analyses" (CM, 171). Only in this sense, then, does Husserl think, "such a psychology is utilizable for transcendental philosophy and, indeed, gives it a place within a transcendental 'metaphysics'". Indeed, only in the recognition of the latter "lies the ultimate clarification and overcoming of the *transcendental psychologism* that has misled and paralyzed the whole of modern philosophy" (*ibid.*).

As we have seen, the transcendental-phenomenological reduction, which deprives the psyche of its "index of existence", of its being understood as a natural object existing in natural time, considers the psyche as transcendental subjectivity. And thereby transcendental phenomenology, as the universal theory of constitution, is primarily concerned with the problems of origin, the problem of true beginnings. Husserl's characterization of the latter in "Philosophy as Rigorous Science" as the "*rizōmata pantōn* [the roots of all things]" is noteworthy, because in contrast to the traditional term *archē*, which classically signifies the perfect shape of things, the (Empedoclean) term "root" is that out of which things grow until they reach their perfect shape. This signals that for Husserl the radical aspect of phenomenology is more important than its perfection, the evidence for which is found not only in the incomplete state of Husserl's research at his death but also in the continual self-criticism and consequent reformulations of his thought manifest in the clearly discernible stages of its development.

Internal temporality and the problem of the sedimented history of significance

Husserl's liberation of the problem of origin from the naturalistic distortion of psychologism and historicism is, as we have seen, achieved through the phenomenological reduction, which brings about the phenomenologist's fundamentally different attitude over against the empirical psychologist's towards the mind or psyche. The result of this liberation, however, is anything but Husserl's abandonment of the problem of history. On the contrary, his analysis of the roots of the origin of the *eidos*, of the *a priori* form of each meaning formation presupposed both by human knowledge and by the misguided attempts of psychologism and historicism to account for such meaning, results in the phenomenological problem of uncovering its "history of meaning [*Sinnesgeschichte*]".

Husserl's awareness of this problem follows the first step – first in the actual development of his transcendentally phenomenological thought, and first in any transcendental-phenomenological analysis – of finding the invariants within the absolute flow of internal temporality, and therefore determining the essential structures of both the intentional object and the multiplicity that characterizes the lived-experience in which this object becomes constituted. As mentioned, Husserl's critical reflection on this kind of analysis, its implications and significance, led to the realization that, far from being complete in itself, finding and facing an *eidos* requires a further investigation into its genesis. This is the case because the constitution of an *eidos* is not exhausted by the process of the eidetic reduction that initially yields it, namely, the description of its pure possibility on the basis of free fantasy variation. Rather, whatever Husserl describes as having an eidetic structure – an ideal meaning, its essential relations, the co-present "horizon" – also has a "backward reference" (*Rückweisung*) to a more original meaning and the process of its formation. It is precisely this "backward reference" that allows for the uncovering of the history of significance of each meaning formation, which describes its genesis as a constitutive accomplishment of transcendental subjectivity. The historicity at issue in this genesis is, as we shall see, a peculiarity of transcendental subjectivity, whose manner of being is nothing but the constitutive accomplishments tending towards the formation of "units of meaning", accomplishments whose ultimate source is the intentionality that characterizes the transcendental Ego's own most essential mode of being.

TWELVE

The essential connection between intentional history and actual history

The two limits of the investigation of the temporal genesis proper to the intentional object

Husserl's account of how the eidetic possibility of an object's intentional unity contains the sedimented history of its own constitution is guided by two limits that are bound up with and therefore indicated by this possibility. These emerge in his critical analysis of the universal eidetic form of the intentional genesis of each such object's unity, that is, in the analysis of internal temporality. The first limit concerns the general substratum of consciousness that the continuous modification of the retentional consciousness approaches, and beyond which the "prominence [*Abgehobenheit*]" (CM, 80) of the object flows away. The second limit concerns the past history of the original presentation of the object itself. Both limits point to sedimented meanings that can be awakened such that the intentional genesis of the meaning in question is reproduced as the history of its constitution, a history that, of course, does not take place within natural time.

Two "histories", then, are *initially* at issue in Husserl's phenomenological account of the eidetic possibility of an object's intentional unity. The first history concerns the possibility of such an object retaining its unity as an enduring "presence" once it has been presented to consciousness. This history concerns the object's intentional genesis as an objective prominence, its persistence throughout the temporality that is the essential characteristic of its (the object's) experience. The second history concerns the possibility of the object's original presentation to consciousness. This possibility is more fundamental than that of its persistence as a prominence, for what is at issue here is its presentation to consciousness *prior* to any modification in accordance with consciousness's structure of internal temporality. It is important to note, however, that neither of the possibilities or "histories" at issue here concerns the natural existence of objects and their histories.

This has been precluded by the phenomenological reduction's removal of the "index of existence" from the experience of both the object and its history. As a result, what is at issue in the priority of the original presentation of the intentional object to consciousness is decidedly *not* its being experienced "first" in a supposed natural succession of awareness. Rather, the priority involved here is *methodological*, in the sense – to be discussed in detail below – that the evidence uncovered by these analyses discloses an "indication" that points to a more original eidetic possibility belonging to the object than its enduring presence in experience.

Therefore, subsequent to the initial phenomenological access to and analyses of the possibility of an object's intentional unity as the eidetic form of its intentional genesis (which is manifest as its internal temporality), the possibility of its original presentation to consciousness is indicated by Husserl's analysis. As the discussion below will show, it is precisely this enquiry into the original presentation of an object's intentional unity that reveals for Husserl the transcendentally essential necessity of a historical development within natural time.

The phenomenological problem of evidentially uncovering the eidetic possibility of the enduring prominence of an intentional object, an object given originally in the mode of immediate presence, is therefore what is at issue in the awakening of the sedimented meanings to which the first limit points. As we have seen in Husserl's analysis of internal time consciousness, inseparable from this immediate presentation of the object is it being followed, of necessity, by its retention, in which the object appears in the mode of just-having-been-experienced. The continuous retentional modification of the originally given prominence of an object therefore accompanies every living present, such that the initial part of the constitution of an identical object comes about as one that, in the broadest sense, persists. The limit of this continuous modification, the general substratum of consciousness wherein the prominence of the object recedes, points to objects that are at once no longer prominent while yet being capable of being made prominent again. Thus when the sedimented prominences connected with the possibility of the object's givenness in the mode of immediate presence are awakened, what is uncovered by the intentional analyses of the evidence experienced therein is the sedimented history of its intentional genesis, that is, its genesis as an object given to inner experience precisely in the mode of immediate presence. Such evidence is therefore mediated by the retentional modifications that are inseparable from the object's initial givenness to inner experience in the mode of an immediate presence.

The transcendental constitution of an identical object exceeds the sedimented genesis of its temporal form

As mentioned, for Husserl every such retentional modification refers, either immediately or mediately, to its absolute original mode (*Urmodus*), to a consciousness that, to be sure, is modified at once yet is no longer a retentional modification. And it is precisely here, in the "limit" manifest in this reference to the original presentation of the object, that the evidence experienced in the immediate presentation gives rise to the transcendental problem of constitution. It is at this point that the eidetic possibility of the object is revealed out of its categorial formations (*kategorialer Gebilde*), that the intentional genesis leads back to the constitutive origins, that the sedimented history is reactivated into the intentional history. Further, it is here that Husserl shows that the transcendental enquiry into an object reveals the transcendentally essential necessity of its being subject to a history in the usual sense of the term. In other words, the essential necessity of a historical development within natural time proves inseparable from the original presentation that constitutes the ideal meaning constituted by transcendental subjectivity.

Before considering more closely how Husserl attempted to work out the essential necessity of intentional history's subordination to an actual history in his last works, it will be helpful to amplify the distinction, as well as the relation, that he articulates between (i) the sedimented history of the intentional genesis of an object's immediate presentation and (ii) the reactivation of this sedimented history into its intentional history in the investigation of the ideal object's transcendental constitution. This discussion will highlight the basis for what Husserl recognized as an essential connection between intentional history and the historical development that takes place within natural time.

Husserl's analyses of the constitutive origins of the eidetic possibility of the identity of an object find that the evidence experienced in the immediate presentation of that object *cannot* reveal this possibility. The transcendental problem of intentional history, which emerges from the phenomenological investigation into the origins that are constitutive of an object's intrinsic possibility as an identity, involves a mode of access to the object that exceeds its mode of being given as an intentional object that persists as a prominence present to inner experience. The universality of an identical object reveals its peculiarity as the constitution of persisting categorial formations. According to Husserl's analyses, the ideal formation of each identical object appears as the finished accomplishment of a constitution or genesis. Husserl's analysis of the initial appearance of these ideal constituents – as the universality of an identical object – refers to this appearance as the object's immediate presentation to inner experience as a persisting prominence. The transcendental problem of the intentional genesis of the intrinsic possibility of this identity, as it is revealed out of its categorial formations, leads to the investigation of the constitutive origins of these formations. It is precisely the problem of these constitutive origins that leads Husserl's enquiry back to an "intentional history" that exceeds the universal eidetic form of the intentional genesis belonging to the internal temporality of this identity's immediate presentation. Husserl's analysis of the need to investigate the genesis of these constituents makes evident the fact that the constitutive origins of these categorial formations, which compose the intentional meaning of an object's unity, exceed the sedimented history of this meaning as it is reproduced in terms of its internal temporality.

The distinction between the sedimented history of the immediate presence of an intentional object and the sedimented history of its original presentation

The distinction Husserl makes between the history of the meaning belonging to the categorial formations of an object's identity, when this identity is immediately given to consciousness as the finished product of a constitution, and the sedimented history proper to this meaning's original constitution by intentional accomplishments, becomes clear when the two limits identified in Husserl's analysis of any object's intentional genesis are considered. These two limits concern two distinct but nevertheless interrelated dimensions of an object's possibility as an ideal meaning, which is to say, an intentional unity. Our discussion has shown the first limit to involve the reactivation of the sedimented history that is responsible for an intentional object's persisting identity, a reactivation that reveals the intentional history of its immediate presentation to inner experience as a finished product of constitution. The "history" at stake in the persisting identity of an intentional object is therefore very different from the history implicitly appealed to by psychologism and explicitly invoked by historicism. The latter concept of history is empirical, which means that its meaning is inseparable from the contingency and accidental nature of natural reality. Because the identity of a categorial formation is neither contingent nor accidental, empirical history can contribute nothing in the way of an account of the origin of this identity as something that persists as identical throughout internal experience, as an ideal object. The failure of empirical history to address on its own terms the origin of an ideal object does not, however, rule out this origin having a history. As we have seen, Husserl initially sought to account for the source of this history in the retentional flowing away into the general substratum of the consciousness of the intentional object's prominence as one and the same object. Our discussion has also shown that the second limit identified concerns Husserl's recognition that the reactivation of the sedimented history of just these continuous retentional modifications is *unable* to disclose the original presentation – unmodified by retentions – of a categorial object. Husserl thus comes to link (i) the problem of the original presentation of the object with (ii) the investigation of the categorial formations constituting its meaning as an initially given finished product of a constitution, the original presentation of which is investigated through the reactivation of the intentional history of these formations.

Once these two issues have been linked, the evidence experienced in the universal eidetic form of internal temporality – an evidence that reproduces the intentional genesis of an intentional object's enduring presence – can be seen to account for its constitution only in terms of the "possibility" of this enduring prominence for an "inner experience". The constitution of the intrinsic possibility of an object's original presentation to consciousness, prior to the sedimented "history" of its temporal modification, is therefore kept distinct from the constitution of its intrinsic possibility subsequent to its having been given to inner experience and modified in accordance with the internal temporality that essentially characterizes such experience. Husserl's analyses show that the eidetic possibility of an object's original presentation to consciousness and therefore original constitution in consciousness is not itself a modification of its immediate presentation to inner experience as an enduring prominence constituted by internal time. In other words, the constitution of an object in accordance with the form of internal time is derivative, in the sense that the awakening of the intentional history of the sedimented history belonging to *this* constitution points to a more basic constitution, wherein the object's unity is originally fashioned. On the basis of this, for Husserl the derivative constitution of the identity of the object is inseparable from its meaning (*Sinn*) as an identity that already involves the retentional modifications of consciousness manifested by the universal structure of internal temporality. In contrast to this, the problem of the transcendental constitution of the eidetic possibility of the object's meaning points to the temporally unmodified but nevertheless "historical" intentionality that discloses the radical beginnings of the categorial formations that compose its meaning. Such formations, however, do not initially appear according to Husserl's analyses as temporally unmodified. Rather, they are first encountered in accordance with the retentional modification by consciousness of their meaning as unities whose formation has already been accomplished. It is therefore only when the problem of the constitution of the eidetic possibility of the meaning of these categorial formations is investigated with a view to its transcendental origin that every such retentional modification of those formations is encountered as referring to a consciousness that is not itself a retentional modification. In other words, from the retentional modification of the experience of the enduring identity of a categorial formation the transcendental enquiry into the origin of its unity is led to the transcendental-phenomenological problem of its original constitution.

THIRTEEN

The historicity of both the intelligibility of ideal meanings and the possibility of actual history

The historical problem underlying Husserl's concept of intentional history

In the foregoing we have indicated that for Husserl the transcendental enquiry into the problem of the intentional history of the categorial formations of the meaning making up an object's identity reveals the essential necessity of its involvement in a history in the usual sense of the term. That is, the transcendental enquiry into the intentional history of the categorial unity of an object discloses an essential connection between the origin of this unity and its historical development within natural time.

For Husserl the connection between the problem of enquiry that underlies historical reflection and intentional history is established when he – in the works that present the final phase of his thought – once again takes up a task that psychologism cannot solve on its own terms but has addressed in its own way: the investigation of the origin of the unity of the meaning formation of any intentional object. In these works Husserl showed that the enquiry into the constitution of any meaning formation as an invariant that transcends the natural time presupposed by psychologism is itself but a mode of "objective omnitemporality" (CM, 156). As such, its identity is an intentional product of the continual accomplishments of transcendental subjectivity, which bring about the combination (*Verbindung*) constituted through the medium of recollective representations that yields the *objectivity* belonging to the ideal determinations of the unity of meaning. Hence the enquiry into the origin of this unity, as an ideal meaning and therefore as the Same, leads Husserl to the problem of the "mode of apodicticity" in which is given the combination of the meaning brought about by the intentional accomplishments or products (*Leistungsgebilde*) of the constituting subjectivity with the multiplicity of recollections that constitute this meaning as the Same. As mentioned, the problem of the "mode of apodicticity" is a concern of the criticism of transcendental knowledge that Husserl identifies – but does not pursue – in what we are calling the third stage of the development of his phenomenology. Beyond the phenomenological concern with the scope and limits of evidence, this problem addresses this evidence's manner of givenness in its foundational role in phenomenological cognition – and, because of the phenomenological method's reflexive relation to itself, this problem leads to a criticism of this criticism, which Husserl also calls for but likewise does not pursue.

Husserl's pursuit (in his last works) of the criticism of the transcendental knowledge that (in the third stage of his phenomenology) yields the constitution of the objectivity of ideal meaning in the multiplicity of recollections that constitute this meaning as the Same is responsible for historicity – taken in its universal and transcendental meaning – emerging as a phenomenological problem. For the enquiry into the eidetic possibility of ideal meaning, if it is to pursue this possibility in terms of the transcendental origin of its status as an intentional accomplishment or product, must push beyond an articulation of this possibility limited to its intentional genesis as an identity that is immediately present to inner experience. That in the third stage of phenomenology's development this possibility is so limited is evident from the following example, which Husserl provides, of the connection that constitutes the objectivity of a logically ideal object.

> In a living, many-membered thinking action I produce a structure: a theorem or a numerical structure. Subsequently I repeat the producing, while recollecting my earlier producing. At once, and by essential necessity, an identifying synthesis takes place; furthermore a new identifying synthesis occurs with each additional repetition ... It is identically the same proposition, identically the same numerical structure, *but repeatedly produced* or, this being equivalent, repeatedly made evident. (CM, 155)

It is clear that in this example the original production of the ideal structure is *presupposed* as already having occurred, and, therefore, the account Husserl offers of the constitution of its *objectivity* as an ideal object does not establish but rather rests on the presupposition that it has already been generated as an ideal meaning. Establishing the eidetic possibility of the ideal structure or meaning that is presupposed as already present to consciousness must, therefore, enquire into the *manner* of its original givenness to consciousness if its origin as an ideal meaning formation is to be made evident with respect to its original (unmodified by retention) presentation to experience. And it is precisely here that the enquiry into origins reveals that the accomplishing or productive intentionality that constitutes this original presentation implies historicity (as the historical *a priori*), and, moreover, it is here that the enquiry discloses that historicity in this sense makes intelligible not only the omnitemporality of the ideal meaning formations but also the possibility of actual history within natural time as well.

Two distinct senses of historicity and the phenomenological meaning of the historical *a priori*

Husserl's enquiry into the intelligibility of the eidetic possibility of an ideal meaning formation therefore involves "historicity" in two distinct senses. One concerns the intentional history of the eidetic possibility of an invariant intentional object. Historicity in this sense is indicated at the limit of the enquiry into the invariant's sedimented history, an enquiry guided by the eidetic form of its internal temporality. This limit concerns the original presentation of an intentional unity as a meaningful unit that has not yet been modified by retention and, therefore, is not yet structured as an enduring unity within internal time. The other sense of historicity concerns the actual history that is indicated by the limit of the enquiry into the intentional history of precisely this unmodified origination of the invariant's eidetic possibility. It concerns therefore the actual history indicated when the categorial formations that manifest an ideal meaning formation are interrogated with respect to their transcendentally original constitution. Because both senses of "historicity" are inseparable from the phenomenological enquiry into the eidetic possibility of the ideal meaning belonging to the intentional object's identity, the status of the meaning of the history in each of these senses of historicity is different from that of the empirical history of accidents and contingencies that may be associated with the identity of an object. Indeed, it is precisely the inseparable link between each of these senses of historicity and the enquiry into the eidetic possibility of the ideality of an intentional object's meaning that allows Husserl to speak of this historicity in terms of the historical *a priori*. The "apriority" of the "*a priori*" in question here cannot be derived in the manner that it is typically derived, that is, from a supposed opposition between the contingent and the non-contingent. This opposition establishes the *a priori* as something that is somehow *prior* to the contingent. Such an understanding of the *a priori* is "formal" in a sense that is irrelevant in the present context, which is concerned with what is itself "prior" to all formal meaning and therefore also prior to the *a priori* understood formally. As the "*a priori*" of the formal *a priori*, however, the historical *a priori*, in its very "apriority", nevertheless remains inseparable from the eidetic possibility of both formal meaning and the formal *a priori*. It is therefore in this latter sense, and in it alone, that the *a priori* of the phenomenological notion of the "historical *a priori*" is to be understood: that is, as the non-contingent and non-formal condition that makes intelligible both the "omnitemporality" of ideal meaning formations and the possibility of actual history in natural time. Thus we shall see that in Husserl's last works the condition of possibility for this condition, the condition of possibility therefore for the "historical *a priori*", is the transcendental accomplishment of intentionality. That this accomplishment is accessible only via the sedimentations of meanings that are manifest as a given historical tradition is something that we shall also see.

Historicity in phenomenology as distinct from both historicism and the history of the Ego

Thus for Husserl what is indicated at this second limit – the historicity of actual history as implicit in the historicity of "intentional history" – does not mean, as some have argued, that Husserl belatedly recognized the involvement of consciousness in a historical situation that is irreducibly particular. It neither signals a reassessment of his earlier attack on historicism nor accords legitimacy to the historian's standard notion that consciousness is socially and historically conditioned. In addition, the issue here is not a historical meaning derived from the "*universal genesis of the ego*" (CM, 109) in which "[t]he ego constitutes himself for himself in, so to speak, the unity of a 'history'" (*ibid.*).

Regarding the first point, in Husserl's last works he does *not* call into question – in light of the putative social and historical conditioning of all significance maintained by historicism – the ideal status of the meaning formations, such as mathematical and scientific objects, that are the accomplishments of transcendental subjectivity. Rather, what Husserl does in these works is to reveal how the enquiry into the origin of the ideal meaning inseparable from these objects has an essential connection to their original formation in actual history, a connection that does not refer to any known or even knowable historical event. This connection, to be discussed in greater detail below, is established on the basis of the inability of the reactivation of the intentional history of the original presentation of the categorial formations proper to the ideal meaning of mathematical and scientific objects to bring to evidence the origin of this meaning in a manner that is completely intelligible. Husserl's transcendental enquiry into the origin of these meaning formations discloses that their meaning paradoxically appears almost devoid of meaning, unless the connection to the actual history of their origin is investigated. The phenomenological enquiry into the origin of the meaning of these formations discloses not only that this origin is inseparable from their intelligibility, but also that these formations' status *necessarily* remains "emptied of significance [*Sinnentleerung*]" (OG, 377/368), unless the enquiry into the intentional history of their origin is extended to include the enquiry into their actual history. We shall see shortly that Husserl's enquiries show that this paradoxical state of affairs is possible, that is, the state in which mathematical and scientific objects are at once meaningful and yet almost devoid of real meaning, as well as his admirable attempt to restore the integrity of knowledge, which is threatened by this state of affairs. At this point, however, it is important to note that rather than call into question the possibility of the ideality of mathematical and scientific objects, the problem of actual history in Husserl's last works emerges within the context of his response to "the demand, which has spread throughout the modern period and has finally been generally accepted, for a so-called 'epistemological grounding' of the sciences" (*ibid.*).

This account of the emergence of the problem of actual history in Husserl's phenomenology also tells against the attempt to trace the meaning of history at issue here to the historicity of the transcendental Ego's universal genesis (the second point above). This is the case because the status of the transcendental Ego as "the universal *unity-form of the flux*" (CM, 109), whereby in each present moment of its existence the past of the Ego is co-present in the mode of its sedimentation, would clearly have as its analogue the history of the sedimented prominences that make possible an intentional object's givenness in the mode of immediate presence. At issue in the sedimentation of the Ego's past, then, would be the retentions of its universal unity-form, retentions that are inseparable from its constitution as an enduring unity present to inner experience. Therefore the reactivation of the intentional historicity of these sedimented retentions would be disanalogous to the reactivation of the sedimented history of the absolute mode of the unmodified (by retentions) original presentation to consciousness of the categorial constituents of an intentional unity. Husserl's analyses establish the phenomenological problem of actual history in terms of its essential connection with the enquiry into the intentional history of just such unmodified original presentations. Hence the historicity of the transcendental Ego's enduring presence as a universal unity-form is incapable of providing a basis, analogical or otherwise, for the connection between actual history and intentional history that Husserl establishes in his last works.

FOURTEEN

Desedimentation and the link between intentional history and the constitution of a historical tradition

Maintaining the phenomenological integrity of knowledge requires enquiry into its original historical discovery

Husserl's phenomenological enquiry into the transcendental constitution of the origins of the ideal formations proper to mathematical and scientific objects reveals that the evidence of all the meaning formations belonging to a science such as geometry presupposes the link between intentional history and actual history. This link is established by Husserl on the basis of the following considerations. (i) The ideal intentional units at issue in these significant formations are the product (*das Erwirkte*) of an "accomplishment" that arises in their "anticipation" (*Vorhabe*) (OG, 367/356), not in their "retention". (ii) The accomplishment of what is anticipated means evidence to the transcendental subject: herein the product shows itself originally as itself. (iii) Since the product, in the case of geometry, is an ideal product, "anticipation" and the corresponding "accomplishment", as acts of the transcendental subject, are founded on the accomplishments of transcendental subjectivity. The ideal formations of geometry are products of the intentionality that is inseparable from this subjectivity. "Anticipation" and "accomplishment" *translate* into terms of *actuality* what properly takes place within the realm of transcendental subjectivity. (iv) The constitution of these ideal intentional units presupposes, of necessity, the whole complex of experiences leading to the situation in which geometry as a science is capable of being anticipated *and* intended. In other words, "Science, and in particular geometry, with this sense of being, must have had a historical beginning" (OG, 367), that is, a beginning within the course of actual history. At this definite moment the original foundation (*Urstiftung*) of geometry occurred.

The necessity belonging to the presupposition of a definite historical beginning that is inseparable from the constitution of these ideal intentional units brings with it two additional presuppositions. These presuppositions are disclosed by Husserl's transcendental enquiry into the origin of the ideal meaning formations belonging to geometry as an exemplary science. Both presuppositions are inseparable from the "anticipation" and "accomplishment" that yield these formations on the basis of the accomplishments of transcendental subjectivity. They are inseparable in the sense that the transcendental enquiry into the relation between this subjectivity and its intentional products points to the discovery of geometry in an "anticipation" of a "first geometer" whose accomplishment brought about geometry as an omnitemporal product of transcendental subjectivity.

Before addressing Husserl's account of these additional presuppositions, however, it is necessary to consider more closely the enquiry into the origin of the ideal meaning formations that point to the discovery in question. What is at issue here is not a known or knowable historical event. Rather, it is Husserl's realization that an enquiry into the constitutive origins of the meaning of the ideal formations of mathematical and scientific objects guided by exclusively "epistemological" concerns *cannot* fulfil "the presupposition that the foundations of [their] deductive structure have truly been produced and objectified in original evidence, thus have become universally accessible acquisitions" (OG, 375/366). Husserl's phenomenological investigations have, of course, taken it for granted from their earliest beginnings that the meaning of the deductive structure of these ideal formations *necessarily* had to have been produced and objectified in such original evidence. Indeed, Husserl never wavers in holding such an assumption to be inseparable from the integrity of knowledge itself. However, only in his last investigations does one find the realization that "what is lacking [in the epistemologically guided enquiry into this original evidence] is precisely what had given and had to give meaning to all propositions and theories, a meaning arising from the primal sources that can be made evident again and again" (OG, 376–7/367). Moreover, this realization is manifest in the paradoxical situation that these investigations describe, the situation that has increasingly been becoming the state of affairs in recent centuries and is the case now, that the sedimentation of meaning can reach such a degree that a particular science, and science in general, appear almost devoid of meaning. In this case, the primal sources whose evidence is productive of the foundations of scientific propositions and theories are lacking. And it is just this realization that leads Husserl's transcendental enquiry into the intelligibility of the meaning formations of the science of geometry to uncover the reference to the *essential necessity* of their having to have been the product of a discovery. The intelligibility of such formations is therefore inseparable from the original production of the meaning that is now at stake in the transcendental enquiry into their complete intelligibility.

Two presuppositions necessary to account for the historicity of the discovery of the ideal objects of a science such as geometry

The need to enquire into the discovery of the original evidence that is the source for the sought-after intelligibility of a science such as geometry therefore has its basis in the fact that such original evidence is *not* forthcoming so long as the "ruling *dogma* of the separation between epistemological elucidation and historical ... explanation" (OG, 379/370) is maintained. It is precisely Husserl's enquiry into the transcendental problem of the constitutive origins of the original evidence in question here that overcomes this ruling dogma by disclosing that such evidence implies historicity. The two additional presuppositions alluded to above disclose the historicity at issue here, presuppositions that are essentially connected with the constitution of the ideal intentional units of a science such as geometry having of necessity some definite historical beginning. The first presupposition concerns the discovery that geometry is inseparable from a characteristically articulated world and the acquaintance with a definitely shaped and featured material, in short, the experience of things. The second presupposition concerns the first geometer's "anticipation" of what comes into being through his accomplishment, namely, geometry as omnitemporal product of his transcendental subjectivity. The failure to recognize these two presuppositions prevents phenomenological enquiry into the transcendental constitution of the original evidence that yields the ideal meaning formations, such as those that belong to the science of geometry, from disclosing the "true meaning" of these formations, "the meaning that is authentic, true to the origin" (*Crisis*, 53/53).

Sedimentation and the constitution of a geometrical tradition

Husserl's analysis of the essential connection between these two presuppositions and the discovery of geometry is but the first step in his account of the constitution of the historicity of geometry as a science, a constitution whereby geometry's ideal objectivity becomes the property of many individuals. Only when this occurs is geometry and any science dealing with ideal objects thereby capable of assuming the meaning of a tradition with a historical development. It is the first step because the original evidence, experienced during the first actual production, does not transcend the "intrasubjective" sphere of the transcendental subject, the sphere of ownness proper to the transcendental Ego. Thus what is at issue in the discovery of geometry is not the finding of some historical fact – understood as an abiding possession of many subjects – but the transcendental conditions of possibility that give rise to such facts, conditions of possibility that are necessarily inseparable from establishing the intelligibility of geometry as it is *currently* experienced. For the meaning formations whose ideality manifests the intentional objects of the science of geometry as it is "handed down" in the guise of a tradition are inseparable from the original production that *had to* initiate the historicity of its tradition. And it is precisely the latter that is referred to when, in Husserl's transcendental enquiry into the origin of the meaning formations of the science of geometry, it is shown that the full intelligibility of the ideal significance of these formations is not forthcoming so long as exclusively "epistemological" interests guide the enquiry. This state of affairs, which comes to light in Husserl's analysis of the role and status of geometry in the foundations of Galileo's physics, is captured in his term "sedimentation". When used in this context, sedimentation describes the superficial and passive understanding of the significance of a science such as geometry that accrues to its meaning formations as a result of a "'forgetting'" (OG [Fink], 212) of the original evidence that produced those formations.

In order for geometry to reach the stage of an ideal objectivity capable of being handed on, at least three steps are necessary. The first step involves the state of affairs whereby the original evidence, experienced during the first actual production of geometry as an omnitemporal product of transcendental subjectivity, passes over into a retentional consciousness and finally fades away into forgetfulness. This evidence, which presupposes, of necessity, the whole complex of experiences leading to the situation in which geometry as a science is capable of being anticipated *and* intended, that is, presupposes the experience of things and the handling of their shape and measurability according to a more-or-less satisfactory technique, does not disappear completely: it can be reawakened, and the active recollection of the original production of any ideal meaning formation carries with it the evident experience of the sameness of that formation, and carries furthermore the insight into its unlimited reproducibility. A second necessary – and decisive – step is required, however, if such experience is to transcend the intrasubjective sphere of transcendental subjectivity, namely, the embodiment of that experience in words, which makes it communicable to other subjects. Such embodiment enables these others to reproduce the same evident experience beyond the original constitutive accomplishing connected with their discovery. Thus the ideal meaning unit acquires its peculiar manner of existence only through speech and in speech. A last step is required, however, in order to secure the *lasting* existence of the ideal objects, to establish their perfect objectivity. This step involves the embodiment of the spoken word into the written word. At this stage the real history of a science begins.

Husserl's account of the real history of a science characterizes its being, of necessity, not only the history of progress, of the accumulation of knowledge, but also a history of failure. For the means that secure the objectivity of a science at the same time endanger its original integrity. Specifically, no science, in its actual progress, can escape the seduction emanating from the spoken and written word. The signifying function of a word has, by its very nature, the tendency to lose its revealing character. The more we become accustomed to words, the less we perceive their original and precise meaning: a kind of superficial and passive understanding is the necessary result of the increasing familiarity with spoken and written words. The original cognitive activity, the production of meaning embodied in sounds and signs, is not reproduced in the course of actual communication. Yet it is there in every word, somehow forgotten but still at the bottom of our speaking and our understanding, however vague the meaning conveyed by our speech might be. The original evidence has faded away but has not disappeared completely. It need not even be awakened; it actually underlies our mutual understanding in a sedimented form.

The historical *a priori* constitutive of both ideal objects and historical facts

The historical *a priori* at issue in Husserl's last works therefore concerns both the historicity of transcendental subjectivity's original production of the ideal meaning formations that form the basis of a science such as geometry and the transcendental conditions of possibility that constitute such a science with the status of a "historical fact" (OG, 380/371), that is, of something that is "tradition and at the same time a handing-down [*Tradition und zugleich tradierend*]" (OG, 379/370). Each, however – the historical *a priori* and the historical fact – i grasped differently.

On the one hand, the key to grasping the historical *a priori* of the origin of a science such as geometry lies in the historicity of the twin presuppositions necessarily implied by this origin: (i) the origin's necessary "anticipation" by a "first" geometer and (ii) a characteristically articulated world whose shape and measurability are handled with a more or less satisfactory technique. The historicity here emerges from the problem of "'epistemological' grounding or clarification" (OG, 381/373) in so far as the production of the original evidence that "had given and had to give" meaning to geometry's propositions and theories is not made evident so long as these twin presuppositions are not invoked. It is precisely the historicity implicit in these presuppositions that provides the basis for rendering intelligible what according to Husserl would otherwise remain unintelligible, namely, the epistemological presupposition that the deductive structure of the ideal meaning formations of geometry's propositions and theories "have truly been produced and objectified in original evidence" (OG, 381/373). Clearly what is at issue in the enquiry into the historicity thematized here is neither a known nor a knowable historical event, but rather the historical *a priori* that the transcendental enquiry into the intelligibility of the ideal meaning formations discloses as inseparable from their meaning as such.

On the other hand, the key to grasping the historical *a priori* that manifests the transcendental conditions of possibility that enable a science such as geometry to assume the status of a historical fact, of a tradition that is still being handed down, is shown in Husserl's account of the written embodiment of the ideal meaning units making up its propositions and theories. It is therefore the translation of these ideal meaning formations, from their peculiar manner of existence in speech into the written word, that both secures their lasting existence as ideal objects and establishes the possibility of the sedimentation of their original evidence. That is, the possibility of their assuming the guise of a tradition capable of being handed down is coincident with the forgetfulness of the evidence that is inseparable from their original establishment as these very ideal meaning formations. Thus what Husserl calls the "universal *a priori* of history" can be seen to consist in "nothing other" than this interweaving of the original production and the sedimentation of meaning.

The phenomenological historical *a priori* is not a concession to historicism

Hence, rather than representing a radical departure from Husserl's earlier critique of historicism, this critique remains in force in his formulation of these issues in his last works. It does so because the connection they establish between history and both the origination of geometry as a science and the existence of its ideal objects does *not* have its basis in "the relativity of everything historical, of all historically developed apperceptions" (OG, 382/373), as is maintained by historicism, but rather in the following state of affairs:

> All factual history remains unintelligible [*verbleibt in Unverständlichkeit*], always merely drawing its conclusions naïvely and straightforwardly from facts, it never makes thematic the general ground upon which all such conclusions rest, has never investigated

> the immense structural *a priori* that is proper to it. Only the disclosure of the essential general structure lying in our present and then in every past or future historical present as such, and, in its totality, only the disclosure of the concrete, historical time in which we live, in which our total humanity lives in respect to its total, essentially general structure – only this disclosure can make possible historical inquiry [*Historie*] which is truly understanding, insightful, and in the genuine sense scientific. This is the concrete, historical *a priori* that encompasses everything that exists as its historical becoming and having-become or exists in its essential being as tradition and handing-down. (OG, 380/371–2)

Thus the *a priori* in Husserl's concept of a historical *a priori* is *not* rooted in the attempt to overcome the supposed opposition between the *a priori* status of the ideal meaning formations that compose the propositions and theories of a science such as geometry and the contingency of historical facts. Rather, it is rooted in the necessary connection between the very *apriority* of the ideal meaning formations in question and the actual history of both their origination and their historical development. It is precisely the latter state of affairs, or the being in question of the intelligibility of the ideal objectivity of these meaning formations, that motivates the need to extend the transcendental-phenomenological enquiry into the origin of such intelligibility beyond the scope of the question of its epistemological grounding. The being in question of intelligibility, which characterizes the present "crisis" situation of the European sciences, leads to the question and questioning of origin that result in the "exposition of the horizon" of the present. According to Husserl, what is disclosed in this exposition "is not something learned, not knowledge that was at some previous time current and then sank back [into oblivion]", but something whose "horizon-certainty had to be already there in order to be capable of being explicated thematically" as "a past present". Indeed, "[e]very explication and every transition from making explicit to making evident ... is nothing other than historical disclosure" (OG, 379/370). And it is precisely here – and nowhere else – that the necessary connection becomes manifest between the immediate presentation of the meaning formations of a science such as geometry – formations that manifest an ideal *apriority* – and the historical *a priori*. Inseparable from both the origination of their meaning and its present status as a historical fact in a tradition that is still being handed down, the historical *a priori* makes intelligible both the non-contingent meaning of science and its existence as a historical fact.

That for Husserl the possibility of the ideal meaning formations proper to mathematical and scientific objects transcends the individual stream of consciousness is clear from the distinction he draws between "the intrapsychically constituted structure" of such "'ideality'" and its "intersubjective being of its own as an ideal object" (OG, 370/359). The former is characterized by Husserl in terms of the structure of immanent time, in so far as "the original being-itself-there" of ideality, "in the immediacy of its first production", is held by him to turn "into the passivity of the flowing fading consciousness of what-has-just-now-been". On Husserl's view, "this 'retention' disappears, but the 'disappeared' passing and being past has not become nothing for the subject in question: it can be reawakened" (*ibid.*). The reawakening of ideality is likewise understood by him in accordance with the structure of immanent time, that is, as a "recollection" (OG, 370/360) that establishes "the capacity for repetition at will" of "the identity" proper to the structure of ideality. However, for Husserl "even with this, we still have not gone beyond the subject ... we still have no 'objectivity' given". The latter for him requires, as we have seen, first oral and then written communication, whereby "[i]n the unity of the community of communication among several persons the repeatedly produced structure becomes an object of consciousness, not as a likeness, but as the one structure common to all" (*ibid.*).

According to Husserl it is precisely the transcendence – *vis-à-vis* the intrasubjective genesis of ideality – of the objectivity of the meaning formations of mathematical and scientific objects that is responsible for the primal establishment of a science and therewith a scientific tradition. Husserl holds that this primal establishment can be accessed methodically through the historical reflective method of phenomenology, with its provision of a historical reference to "the concrete, historical a priori that encompasses everything that exists as historical becoming and having-become or exists in its essential being as tradition and handing-down" (OG, 381/372). It is Husserl's phenomenological quest for the true beginnings of the ideal meaning formations of mathematics and scientific objects, of the ideal meaning formations proper to the mathematical objects that are inseparable from the possibility of mathematical physics, that renders *necessary* the connection between the sedimented history that belongs to the genesis of these formations' objective prominence in the stream and whole of consciousness and the actual history of their beginnings, which is handed down by the tradition to which these meaning formations belong.

We need look no further than to the phenomenological problem of the genetic origin belonging to ideal meaning formations in order to find the motivation for Husserl's turn to history. This is not to say, however, that Husserl's notion of "concrete history" can be reduced to the epistemological problem of "genetic" origins, but that, instead, Husserl came to recognize that this problem conceals "the deepest and most genuine problems of history" (OG, 379/370). As mentioned, on his view, so long as the "ruling dogma of the separation in principle between epistemological elucidation and historical ... explanation, between epistemological and genetic origin" is maintained, these problems will remain concealed. Because this separation is unwarranted, its overcoming is necessary to uncover the concrete historical *a priori* identified in his last works, an *a priori* both inseparable from the beginnings proper to the development of the ideal meaning formations that make mathematical physics possible and from the very intelligibility of the formations themselves.

Overcoming the separation between epistemology and history is therefore rooted in the fact that the ideal meaning formations that render the science of mathematical physics possible are, for Husserl, at present unintelligible. Their unintelligibility is first manifest in the "feeling of obscurity that asserts itself" (*Crisis*, 55/55) concerning the epistemological grounding of this science. Husserl's "historical deliberation or meditation" in the *Crisis* texts should therefore be understood as his *personal* attempt to unpack this feeling. He says as much when he discusses the historical manner of their investigation: "A historical meditation backwards of the sort under discussion is thus actually the deepest kind of self-meditation aimed at self-understanding in terms of what we are truly seeking as the historical beings we are" (*Crisis*, 73/72). This self-meditation manifests itself in "a constant critique, which always regards the total historical complex as a personal one, [in which] we are attempting ultimately to discern the historical task that we can acknowledge as the only one that is personally our own" (*Crisis*, 72/70).

Husserl's personal self-meditation unpacks this "feeling of obscurity" by tracing it to its roots in the present crisis situation of the sciences. In articulating this crisis, he focuses on two interrelated points. The first concerns the "feeling of hostility among the younger generation" (*Crisis*, 4/6) in their evaluation of what the sciences or science in general can mean for human existence. "Merely fact-minded sciences", we are told, "make merely fact-minded people", the implication being that, having abstracted from everything subjective, neither can possibly have anything meaningful to say about "questions of the meaning or meaninglessness of the whole of this human existence". The second focal point concerns his experience of the unintelligibility of the "completely universal 'formalization'" (*Crisis*, 44/45) to which the instinctive and unreflective praxis of theorizing begun in the Galilean age leads. By "formalization" Husserl understands the theoretical procedure in modern mathematics and logic that empties mathematical and logical concepts of their material meaning and then employs them as the basic units of meaning in mathematical and logical calculation. The result of this is that "until now" "there has been no unambiguous characterization of what in fact, and in a way practically understandable in mathematical work, a coherent mathematical field is" (*ibid.*). This lack of clarity for Husserl then spills over into the self-enclosed modern idea of a *mathesis universalis*, of a universal mathematics, first made possible by this formalization and its development into a formal logic of the "anything whatever" [*Etwas überhaupt*]. The investigation of the materially empty "being" of the latter object presupposed by formal logic is understood by Husserl to be the provenance of a new discipline, "formal ontology".

To be sure, the first focal point for Husserl is grounded in the second, which he identifies as the source of the breakdown of science and the consequent crisis situation of European humanity. The breakdown is not, however, the consequence of formalization *per se*, but of the way it is understood and employed by practitioners of the science of mathematical physics that formalization first made possible. When the latter is not carried out in a "fully conscious" (*Crisis*, 46/47) manner, "dangerous shifts of meaning" occur. Husserl characterizes these shifts as follows. First, what is in truth a method whose goal is to achieve knowledge *about* the natural world is mistaken for the reality of the world itself. Second, the tradition that provided the basis for the invention of this method is mistakenly treated as self-evident, which results in unquestioned assumptions that allow "elements of obscurity to flow into its [the method's] meaning" (*ibid.*). And, third, owing to both of these mistakes, human subjectivity is misunderstood as an epiphenomenon of the formalized natural world and, consequently, it loses its autonomy as a being in the possession of a relation to the world independent of scientific intervention.

For Husserl the unintelligibility of modern science initially shows up in terms of the *referential* obscurity of the formalized meaning structures that make it possible. This obscurity is in turn bidirectional. On the one hand, *what* in the world these structures refer to is not at all clear to Husserl. On the other hand, in so far as these structures, as a function of their expression of a *mathesis universalis*, also refer to themselves as a self-enclosed "mathematical manifold" that seems to exclude – in principle – all relation to the natural world, *how* in the world it is even possible for this manifold to be applied to the natural world is likewise unclear to Husserl. That the formalized meaning structures that characterize physics must refer to the natural world is never in doubt for Husserl. Nor does he ever doubt whether, in order for this reference to occur, the "universal manifolds" that characterize the *mathesis universalis* must lend themselves to being applied to the "definite manifolds" of pure space and time, manifolds that function as the system of axioms that make the predictions of modern physics possible. What is in doubt, however, is the foundation that makes possible both this reference and application. And it is precisely Husserl's experience of the *feeling* of obscurity flowing from the doubtfulness of this foundation that motivates what for him holds the promise of resolving it, that is, motivates the need for a historical reference back to the beginnings of the scientific tradition, a tradition in its present ungrounded state he now *experiences* as its breakdown. To stress Husserl's expression of the felt dimension of his encounter with the obscurity of modern physics is not to suggest that feeling *per se* somehow functions to provide him with a direct link to the historical reference that he maintains is the only thing that "could be of help here" (*Crisis*, 16/17). Rather, it is to suggest that this feeling itself is conditioned by the lack of fulfilment of "the demand, which has spread throughout the modern period and has finally been generally accepted, for a so-called 'epistemological grounding' of the sciences" (OG, 377/368). Thus the claim here is that it is Husserl's endorsement of this demand, combined with the inadequacy of an exclusively epistemological attempt to meet it, that results in his feeling in question and his realization that "in the case of the sciences genuine historical explanation comes together with 'epistemological' grounding or clarification" (OG, 381/373). It is in this sense, then, that we argue that the felt obscurity in question motivates the need for a historical reference back to the beginnings of the scientific tradition in order to provide their sought-after grounding that he endorses and therefore seeks.

That the formalized meaning structures that make modern science possible must refer to the world is rooted in Husserl's conviction that there is a continuity between what philosophy in its "primal establishment" (*Urstiftung*) conceived of as its task and what now needs to be accomplished in order to bring about its "final establishment" (*Endstiftung*). That is, for Husserl a continuity must exist between the "exalted idea of universal knowledge concerning the totality of what is" (*Crisis*, 11/13) of ancient Greek philosophy and the modern attempt "to put metaphysics or universal philosophy on the strenuous road to realization" (*Crisis*, 13/15). Establishing this continuity involves bringing the "reason latent" in the *telos* inseparable from the original establishment of philosophy "to the understanding of its own possibilities … to the insight [of] the possibility of metaphysics as a true possibility" (*ibid.*). Hence the overarching task of Husserl's historical deliberation is to restore faith in "reason itself and its (object) 'that which is'" (*Crisis*, 11/13), a restoration made necessary by the "collapse" of reason in "the actual situation of the present" (*Crisis*, 16/17) and the consequent scepticism about the possibility of reason, its ideas, and the worldly objects to which they relate.

Philosophy in Husserl's sense is therefore, in the last stage of the development of his thought, inseparable from history. And history is in turn inseparable from "science as it is given in its present-day form" (*Crisis*,

59/58). Indeed, it is precisely by following the reference to science's beginnings as a tradition that Husserl hopes to uncover the meaning of its development and, with this, the true meaning of its accomplishment. Tracing this development, as we have already suggested and will now articulate in greater detail, requires a method that proceeds "backward and forward in a zigzag pattern" (*ibid.*). It moves backwards from science's present form to its beginnings and then forwards to its present situation, such that relative clarification of the one brings some clarification of the other, which in turn provides further clarification of the former. What is at issue for Husserl in this clarification is "reactivating" (OG, 372/361) the "original activity" that produced the meaning formations presently experienced in terms of their felt obscurity. Only by proceeding in this way is the "hidden unity of intentional inwardness that alone constitutes the unity of history" (*Crisis*, 74/73) revealed. It is revealed because, when reactivated, the beginnings of the science of the present *themselves* refer to their beginnings, namely to the primal beginnings of science *per se* in Greek philosophy and mathematics. Thus for Husserl the task of revealing the intentional unity of history holds the promise of bringing about the final establishment of the *telos* that belongs to the original establishment of philosophy, that is, the establishment of philosophy as the universal science of what is.

FIFTEEN

Transcendental phenomenology as the only true explanation of objectivity and all meaningful problems in previous philosophy

Scope and limits of Husserl's reactivation of the sedimented origins of the modern spirit

For Husserl, philosophy, as the universal science of what is, has but one goal: intuitive knowledge of what is. As we have seen, both what in the world the formalized meaning formations of mathematical physics refer to, and therefore make intuitable, and how in the world this reference and corresponding intuition is possible, are obscure on Husserl's view. He traces this obscurity to the fact that the formalized meaning in modern mathematics is made possible by the progressive "*emptying of its meaning*" (*Crisis*, 44/44) in relation to the "real" (*Crisis*, 35/37), that is, to the intuitive givenness of the things manifest to everyday sense experience in the surrounding world. Husserl's historical reflection on the beginnings of the development of modern, Galilean science reveals that it is first made possible by this progressive emptying of meaning. The meaning formations of the mathematics that make physics possible are themselves made possible by their "becoming liberated from all intuited actuality" (*Crisis*, 43/44), including the "magnitudes" (*Crisis*, 44/44) that "numbers are supposed to signify" and of course from the intuitively given shapes of actual things. More precisely, the ideal shapes of Euclidean geometry are substituted for the intuited shapes of things, while algebraic calculation with "'symbolic' concepts" (*Crisis*, 48/48) that express numbers in general – as opposed to determinate numbers – excludes the "*original* thinking that genuinely gives meaning to this technical process and truth to the correct results" (*Crisis*, 46/46).

Husserl's investigations in the *Crisis* texts of the emptying of meaning that makes modern physics possible, however, are fragmentary. Their focus is on the origin of geometry and on what he refers to as the "sedimentation" (*Crisis*, 52/52) involved in the Galilean impulse to treat Euclidean geometry in a taken-for-granted, and therefore straightforward, manner. As mentioned in the foregoing, Husserl uses the term sedimentation to designate the "constant presuppositions ... [of the] constructions, concepts, presuppositions, theories" that characterize the significations of the meaning formations of a science – in the case at hand, of Galilean natural science – in so far as they are not "'cashed in' [*einzulösenden*]" (OG, 376/366), that is, reactivated in terms of the original activities that produced their meaning. Cashing in the meaning formations in question requires that we eventually reactivate the "historical beginning" (OG, 367/356) that this science "must have had", which in the case of Galilean natural science means that we eventually have to reactivate the origin of the Euclidean geometry that was taken for granted when its meaning formations were first established.

Husserl's fragmentary analyses of the "*origin of the modern spirit*" (*Crisis*, 58/57), in which he links to Galileo's name "all of our characterizations ... in a certain sense simplifying and idealizing the matter", therefore function in effect to desediment the meaning formations accomplished by this spirit and thereby to reactivate their historical beginnings. Husserl's desedimentation of these meaning formations cashes in both the direct and indirect impulse of the Galilean spirit to mathematize the world by tracing this accomplishment to its origin in "the sphere of immediately experiencing intuitions and the possible experience of the prescientific life-world" (*Crisis*, 42/43). Husserl's access to the latter is mediated by the historical reference to beginnings that issues from the obscure or unintelligible meaning formations of present-day mathematical natural science, the reference he traces in accordance with the backward and forward zigzag pattern that characterizes his epistemological-historical method. Thus it is not as if Husserl, sitting in his study, is somehow able to conjure up the direct experience of the prescientific life-world, the primordial experience of which would then provide the basis for a comparison disclosing the abstract view of the world presumably found in the meaning formations that make up mathematical physics. Rather, it is his experience of the empty meaning formations of the latter that – when combined with his expectation that they must somehow be ultimately founded in a reference to (or, more precisely, an intention towards) the world that is capable being intuitively fulfilled at some level – leads to his discovery (or, more properly, his rediscovery) of the prescientific life-world and its true origins.

Husserl's analyses that led to the rediscovery of the life-world in his *Crisis* texts are, despite their salient results, quite fragmentary in character. Regarding these analyses, Husserl shows that the Galilean impulse rests on both a *direct* mathematization of the appearances of bodies and an *indirect* mathematization of their sensuous modes of givenness as they show up in the intuitively given surrounding world. Husserl's attempt to cash in the ideal meaning formations of the pure shapes of Euclidean geometry, which Galileo took for granted as the "true" shapes of nature, reveals that our direct experience of nature *never* yields geometrical-ideal bodies but "precisely the bodies that we actually experience" (*Crisis*, 22/25). The abstractive directing of our regard to the mere shapes of these bodies cannot yield what the "pure geometry" (*Crisis*, 21/24) pregiven to Galileo understands as "geometrical ideal possibilities", nor can their arbitrary transformation in fantasy. This is because even though the latter yields "'ideal' possibilities" in a certain sense, these possibilities remain tied to sensible shapes, which can only manifest their transformation into other sensible shapes and thus not the "ideal possibilities" in question.

The method of operating with the pure or ideal shapes that characterizes Euclidean geometry therefore does not point directly to the sensible shapes of the bodies we actually experience in the life-world, but rather to "the methodology of determination by surveying and measuring in general, practiced first primitively and then as an art in the prescientific, intuitively given surrounding-world" (*Crisis*, 24/27). It is therefore the praxis of perfecting such measuring, "of freely pressing toward the horizon of *conceivable* perfecting 'again and again'", that yields "*limit shapes* as invariant and never attainable poles" (*Crisis*, 23/26) towards which the sequence of perfecting tends. Euclidean geometry is then born when "we are interested in these ideal shapes and are consistently engaged in determining them and in constructing new ones out of those already determined". This is the geometry that was pregiven to Galileo as a taken-for-granted tradition. Consequently, the original activity in which its ideal meaning formations were accomplished – the original activity that, on Husserl's telling, his historical mediations reactivated in order to cash in and therefore make intuitively evident their reference to the world – remained concealed to Galileo. Thus when Galileo mathematized the intuitive shapes of bodies directly and their sensuous manners of appearing indirectly by substituting for them the "anticipation" (OG, 367/356) of their true being in the ideal shapes of Euclidean geometry, the original intuition of the sensible shapes of bodies, along with their transformation into limit shapes by the praxis of measuring, became sedimented. As a consequence of Galileo's methodical construction of the "true nature" through the substitution of the ideal shapes of Euclidean geometry for the experience of sensible shapes proper to bodies, the original intuition of the latter was lost. It is to this state of affairs that Husserl speaks with his characterization of Galileo as "at once a *discovering* and a *concealing genius*" (*Crisis*, 53/52).

Husserl's analyses of the mathematization that makes possible the "'method of the true knowledge of nature'" (*Crisis*, 43/43) takes cognizance of the fact that "one thing more is important for our clarification". This "one thing more" is the "'arithmetization of geometry'" (*Crisis*, 44/44). Aided by "the algebraic terms and ways of thinking that have been widespread in the modern period since Vieta", this arithmetization transforms the ideal shapes of Galileo's Euclidean approach to the world into algebraic structures whose symbolic formula-meaning displaces – "unnoticed" (*Crisis*, 44/45) – the signification of magnitudes. Husserl considers this the "*decisive accomplishment*" (*Crisis*, 42/43) of the natural scientific method, which in accordance with its "complete meaning" makes possible the anticipation of systematically ordered, determinate predictions about the practical life-world. Accomplished through the hypothetical substruction of undetermined generality by the mathematical idealities that make up the formula-meaning, the determinate prediction arises through the projection of empirical regularities in advance of the immediately experienced intuitions that ground the possibility of knowledge of the prescientific life-world. Consequently, "[t]his arithmetization of geometry leads almost automatically, in a certain way, to the *emptying of its meaning*" (*Crisis*, 44/44). Husserl points out that this unnoticed emptying of meaning eventually "becomes a fully conscious methodical displacement, a methodical transition from geometry, for instance, to pure *analysis*, treated as a science in its own right" (*Crisis*, 44/45). Thus this process of methodical transformation leads beyond arithmetization to "a completely universal 'formalization'", which, in the guise of a *mathesis universalis*, transcends both the pure theory of numbers in algebra and that of magnitudes in analytic geometry. Thought of in "empty, formal generality", manifolds are "conceived of as defined by determinate modalities of the anything whatever" (*ibid.*). As mentioned, the theory of the "formal-logical idea of a 'world-in-general'" at issue in a "systematic development" of the *mathesis universalis* is what he refers to as the task of the discipline of "formal ontology". In contrast to his analyses of the Galilean geometrization of nature, however, Husserl's clarification of the meaning formations that make up the *mathesis universalis* and formal ontology does not attempt to reactivate the historical beginnings of the original accomplishment that makes them possible. Thus, for instance, he makes no attempt to cash in the sedimentation of meaning that is inseparable from the displacement of the immediate intuitive experience of the life-world that takes place in the arithmetization of geometry, a displacement accomplished in Descartes' formulation of the *mathesis universalis*.

The *epochē* of objective science and the task of a science of the life-world

Rather than pursue such a specific line of desedimentation, Husserl instead traces in broad outline the general effect of the mathematization of nature on modern philosophy. The systematic occlusion of the life-world that composes the methodological point of departure for mathematical physics leads to a corresponding "naturalization" of cognition, to the very great extent that mathematical physics, in light of its great achievements, comes to assume the status of the paradigm for all rigorous knowledge – and not, more appropriately, exclusively the paradigm for rigorous knowledge about nature. Thus, on the one hand, the philosophy of nature now takes as its "natural" subject matter mathematized nature, the nature that is discovered subsequent to its investigation in accordance with the Galilean methodical hypothesis of the fundamentally mathematical mode of its being. Nature in this sense, which is understood as the true and therefore "objective" nature, is then opposed to the "subjective" being of the psyche and mind, whose non-objective mode of being comes to assume both a cognitive and ontological liability. Thus, on the other hand, the specifically human dimension of being is dismissed as a "merely" subjective being even as it is investigated according to the methodology of the natural sciences and therefore "objectified", that is, implicitly or explicitly treated as a being whose true being is akin if not continuous with the "objective" nature investigated by modern natural science.

On Husserl's view, the mathematization of nature therefore leads irrevocably to "physicalistic naturalism", by which he understands the supposition that the true being of nature is accessible only to mathematical physics and the supposition that is implicit in this supposition, namely, that the *sine qua non* for "objective" knowledge is an abstraction from subjectivity *per se*. Both modern mathematical physics and modern natural philosophy explicitly embrace the first supposition, while the latter is made implicitly by modern rationalism, which Husserl characterizes as "unclearly imitating … the dubious character of the mathematization of the world" (*Crisis*, 68/67). As such, the paradigm of modern natural science (today, of course, simply called "physics"), together with modern philosophical rationalism, rests on the unexamined *presupposition* of the pregivenness of the life-world. For Husserl, the latter is composed of the original evidences given both in what is experienced in perception as "'the thing in itself'" (*Crisis*, 128) and in the experiencing of the scientific activities in which originate the logical formations and theoretical structures that compose "the knowledge of the objective scientific world" (*Crisis*, 133/130). This knowledge is therefore "'grounded' in the evidence of the life-world", such that "[i]f we cease being immersed in our scientific thinking, we become aware that we scientists are, after all, human beings and as such are among the components of the life-world which always exists for us, ever pre-given". The objective world yielded by the theoretical constructs of scientific thinking therefore has its basis in a hypothesis that "is but *one* among the many practical hypotheses and projects which make up the life of human beings in this life-world" (*Crisis*, 133–4/131).

Subsequent to the critical–historical reflection that uncovers the presupposition of the life-world as "merely a problem of the fundamental basis of the objective sciences or a partial problem within the universal problem of objective sciences", the problem of the relation between objective scientific thinking and intuition founded in the life-world proves to be "the genuine and most universal problem" (*Crisis*, 137/134). It does so "as soon as the empty and vague notion of intuition – instead of being something negligible and insignificant compared to the supremely significant logical sphere in which one supposedly already has genuine truth – has become the problem of the life-world". Husserl describes this problem in no uncertain terms as that of "the ineradicable illusion of a pure thinking which, unconcerned in its purity about intuition, already has its self-evident truth, even truth about the world – the illusion which makes the sense and the possibility, the 'scope', of objective science questionable" (*ibid.*).

Husserl's response to the results of this critical–historical reflection is "an explicit, universal formulation" of the first methodical step necessary in order to address them in a philosophically responsible manner. This formulation is presented as "the *epochē* in respect to all objective sciences" (*Crisis*, 138/135), whereby what is meant is the suspension "of all participation in the cognitions of the objective sciences", the suspension "of any critical position-taking which is interested in their truth or falsity, even any position on their guiding idea of an objective knowledge of the world" (*ibid.*). Subsequent to the *epochē* of objective sciences, not just a science but also an *a priori* science of the life-world is made possible. For whenever this *epochē* is in effect, the life-world's pregivenness, to not only the objective sciences and scientists, but also to all pre- and non-scientific interests and concerns, is made manifest. Most generally and formally, the life-world is manifest in terms of an *a priori* correlation between thing and world on one side and thing and world consciousness on the other. Two possibilities are then possible for its investigation. The first is an *a priori* ontology of this structure carried out within the straightforward natural attitude. The other is a consistently reflective attitude towards the "how" of its manner of givenness to consciousness. To pursue the former mode of investigation the *epochē* of objective sciences alone suffices. The pursuit of the latter mode, however, requires a universal *epochē* that "puts out of action, with one blow, the total performance running through the whole of natural world-life and through the whole network (whether concealed or open) of validities – precisely that performance which, as the coherent 'natural attitude', makes up 'simple' 'straightforward' ongoing life" (*Crisis*, 153/150). The attitude that results from this, the transcendental-phenomenological attitude, is characterized by Husserl as being:

> *above* the pregivenness of the validity of the world, *above* the infinite complex whereby, in concealment, the world's validities are always founded on other validities, *above* the whole manifold but synthetically unified flow in which the world has and forever attains anew its content of meaning and its ontic validity. (*Ibid.*)

Moreover, all of this is "put out of action in advance by the *epochē*", and, with this, "the whole ongoing life which is directed toward the actualities of 'the' world" (*ibid.*).

The paradox of subjectivity and its resolution through a reduction to the absolute Ego

Subsequent to the universal *epochē*, "everything objective is transformed into something subjective" (*Crisis*, 182/178), yielding "the 'Heraclitean flux' of constituting life" (*Crisis*, 181/177), which gives rise to the problem of how such life "can be treated descriptively in its individual facticity". Husserl's answer to this question in the fourth and final stage of the development of his phenomenology is the same as in its previous stages: such life cannot be treated descriptively on an individual basis, "in the sense of establishing *individual* transcendental correlations as they factually occur and disappear" (*ibid.*). As already mentioned, it is misleading – if not an outright falsification of Husserl's presentation of phenomenology – to claim that it is distinguished by a "first-person" perspective, if by this is meant that:

> the single philosopher by himself, within the *epochē*, can hold fast to anything in this elusively flowing life, repeat it with always the same content, and become so certain of its this-ness and its being-such that he could describe it, document it, so to speak (even for his own person alone), in definitive statements. (*Ibid.*)

Thus, for Husserl, "the full concrete facticity of universal transcendental subjectivity" can only be "scientifically grasped … through an eidetic method", which undertakes the "great task" of "investigating the essential form of the transcendental accomplishments in all their types of individual and intersubjective accomplishments, that is, the total essential form of transcendentally accomplishing subjectivity in all its social forms". And he could not be clearer that "[t]he fact is here, as belonging to its essence; there is no way of documenting it empirically in a sense analogous to what is done in the objective sphere through inductive experience" (*ibid.*).

The eidetic investigation of functioning transcendental subjectivity, however, encounters what Husserl calls the "paradox of human subjectivity" if it is guided by what he characterizes as the naivety of his own developmental approach to the world constituting functioning of subjectivity. Husserl characterizes this approach as, first, failing to recognize the problem of the constitution of intersubjectivity, and, then, of attempting to correct this shortcoming by embracing transcendental intersubjectivity in a methodically incorrect manner. Specifically, the initial aspect of this naivety involves the exclusive nature of the focus on "the correlation belonging to the first level of reflection: i.e., the object pole *vs.* manner of givenness (manner of appearance in the broadest sense)" (*Crisis*, 186/182), which limits the status of the Ego to that of the enduring subject pole underlying all manners of givenness. The attempt to correct this, via "the change of signification of [the form] 'Ego' – just as I am saying 'Ego' right now – into 'other Egos', into 'all of us', we who are many Egos, and among whom I am but *one* 'Ego'", is, according to Husserl, "wrong, methodically" (*Crisis*, 188–9/185). What is wrong with this approach to the problem is that it attempts "to jump immediately into transcendental subjectivity" and thus "to leap over the primal 'Ego', the Ego of my *epochē*, which can never lose its uniqueness and personal indeclinability" (*Crisis*, 189/195). By stressing the latter, Husserl here highlights the distinction, introduced in the third stage of his phenomenology's development, between the unity that characterizes the transcendental Ego's constituting functioning and the unity characteristic of it as a constituted object. The incomparable unity of the transcendental Ego that functions as the constitutive source of all worldly objects is both unique and irreducible to the "personal" Ego that, as its constitutive accomplishment, is *apperceived by it as one worldly object among a multiplicity of worldly objects, including other egos*.

When the uniqueness of the primal Ego is lost sight of or remains unrecognized, the "universal concept of the subjective" (*Crisis*, 183/179), which, subsequent to the universal transcendental *epochē*, "encompasses everything: Ego-pole and universe of Ego-poles, multiplicities of appearance or object poles and the universe of object-poles", is unavoidably and mistakenly grasped as having a worldly meaning. It is therefore assumed that "[u]niversal intersubjectivity, into which all objectivity, everything that exists at all, is resolved, can obviously be nothing other than mankind; and the latter is undeniably a component part of the world" (*ibid.*). Hence the paradox of human subjectivity, as being both a subject for the world, and, as such, its constitutive source, while, at the same time, being an object in the world, a worldly object among other such objects. According to Husserl, crucial to the resolution of the paradox is the recognition that:

> The "Ego" that I attain in the *epochē* ... is actually called "I" only by equivocation – though it is an essential equivocation since, when I name it in reflection, I can say nothing other than: it is I who practice the *epochē*, I who interrogate, as phenomenon, the world which is now valid for me according to its being and being-such, with all its human beings ...; it is I who stand above all natural existence that has meaning for me, who am the Ego-pole of this transcendental life, in which, at first, the world has meaning for me purely as world; it is I who, taken in full concreteness, encompass all that. (*Crisis*, 188/184)

It is therefore "only an apparent contradiction" that the Ego attained in the *epochē* "makes itself [personally] declinable, for itself, transcendentally; that, starting from itself and in itself, it constitutes transcendental intersubjectivity, to which it then adds itself as a merely privileged member, namely, as 'Ego' among the transcendental others" (*Crisis*, 189/185). Rather than articulating a contradictory state of affairs, Husserl invokes the results of the third stage of his phenomenology's account of the constitution of intersubjectivity, maintaining that "[t]his is what philosophical self-explication in the *epochē* actually teaches us" (*ibid.*). Thus this self-explication shows how "the original constituting life" proceeding within the transcendental Ego:

> constitutes a first sphere of objects, the "primordial" sphere; how it then, starting from this, in a motivated fashion, performs a constitutive accomplishment through which an intentional modification of itself and its primordiality achieves ontic validity under the title of "alien-perception", perception of others, of another "Ego" who is for himself an "Ego" as I am. (*Ibid.*)

Husserl's resolution of what the fourth and final stage of the development of phenomenology articulates as the paradox of human subjectivity is therefore brought about by the "conscious reshaping of the *epochē* through a reduction to the absolute Ego as the ultimately unique center of function in all constitution" (*Crisis*, 190/186). In other words, the methodical reduction to the sphere of ownness of "the always singular 'Ego'" (*Crisis*, 189/185) developed in the third stage of the development of Husserl's thought also characterizes a key element of its fourth stage. Thus Husserl writes that "[t]his determines henceforth the whole method of transcendental phenomenology" (*Crisis*, 190/186).

The direction and scope of the development of transcendental phenomenology adumbrated by the "small beginning" of Husserl's last works

Taken in isolation from Husserl's final and fragmentary investigations of the historicity inseparable from both the origin of ideality and the essence of a scientific tradition, including the handing down of such a tradition's objective knowledge, Husserl's account of the methodical reduction requisite for the resolution of the paradox of human subjectivity would seem to lend credence to Gadamer's claim, mentioned in the Prolegomenon, about Husserl's new way in the *Crisis* leading, in the end, to the same old transcendental phenomenology. However, the distortion contained in this seeming is dispelled once and for all with the realization that prior to the *Crisis* texts the investigation of objective nature was a matter of *static* analysis. As we have seen, such analysis treats the world's objectivity, and hence its transcendency, as something that has already been accomplished and, as such, as something "finished". According to this analysis, the transcendental legitimization of this objectivity and transcendency is accomplished when the constitution of the intersubjective availability of the objective world, which is inseparable from its very meaning as objective, is accounted for. In contradistinction to this, in the *Crisis* texts Husserl clearly recognizes that the objective world's intersubjective availability has a deeper source than that of its genesis as an intentional modification of the concrete transcendental Ego, namely, its source in historicity. That is, its source in a historical tradition, the essence of which is composed of the interweaving of two inseparable moments: an original transcendental constitution of ideal meaning formations that becomes manifest in *actual* history, and the evitable *forgetfulness* and consequent sedimentation of this original accomplishment, as a necessary epiphenomenon of its embodiment in spoken and, especially, written language.

Husserl's recognition of the *phenomenon* of historicity and the "practical" task that it leads to, the desedimentation of the mathematization of the life-world that is an essential phenomenological condition of possibility for the meaning of the *objectivity* proper to modern physics, represents therefore the "small beginning" that he claimed, on his deathbed, was the significance of his last works. Despite, therefore, the state of incompleteness of the articulation and realization of this task in the final stage of the development of Husserl's phenomenology, its adumbration of the further development of phenomenological philosophy in the direction of the historicity belonging to the mode of givenness proper to its apodicitic evidence remains undeniable. The intention behind Husserl's last work leaves no doubt that this development is *consistent* with the retention of the methodological purity – in the sense of an *a priori* science and, therefore, an *a priori* mode of cognition – that drives both phenomenology's origin and development. And this intention likewise leaves no doubt that this development is up to the task of taking up "the problems of genesis, of transcendental historicity" (*Crisis*, 192/188), and of doing so in a manner "that proceeds back to their transcendental and thus absolute signification".

Equally beyond doubt is Husserl's final conviction that "there is no conceivable problem in previous philosophy, and no conceivable problem of being at all, that could not be arrived at by transcendental phenomenology along its way" (*ibid.*). Transcendental phenomenology, after all, then, proves to have the status of not so much the realization of the secret longing of modern philosophy – with its subjectively limited understanding of objectivity – but of the realization of the ancient Greek *telos* of a universal *epistemē*, of a method capable of investigating the truth of the whole of what is. To this conviction, Husserl's last work adds the observation that "[o]ne must finally achieve the insight that no objective science, no matter how exact, explains or can ever explain anything in a serious sense" (*Crisis*, 193/189). That "[a]ll natural evidences, those of all objective sciences (not excluding those of formal logic and mathematics), belong to realm of what is 'obvious', what in truth has a background of incomprehensibility", and that "the knowledge [attained through] the constitutive 'internal' method, through which all objective-scientific method acquires its meaning and possibility, cannot be without significance for the scientist of nature or any other objective scientist", is thus of one piece with this observation. What is at stake in Husserl's final conviction is nothing less than the idea of the "profound self-reflection of accomplishing subjectivity" being of service "in protecting the naïve, ordinary accomplishment [of subjectivity] from misunderstandings such as are observed in abundance, for example, in the influence of naturalistic epistemology and in the idolization of a logic that does not understand itself" (*ibid.*).

The criticisms of Husserl's phenomenology by his most prominent critics, Heidegger and Derrida, not only call the legitimacy of Husserl's understanding of the philosophical significance of all of this into doubt, but they do so on the common ground of their claim to be able to expose hidden presuppositions in Husserl's thought under the guidance of its relation to the history of philosophy. In the Epilogue we shall test the most salient claims of these critics by likewise relating Husserl's thought to a key moment in philosophy's history, namely, to controversy between Plato and Aristotle over the proper mode of being of the *eidē*, a controversy that, given the centrality of the *eidē* in Husserl's phenomenology, is strangely absent in both Heidegger's and Derrida's critiques of Husserl's phenomenological philosophy.

SIXTEEN

The methodological presupposition of the ontico-ontological critique of intentionality: Plato's Socratic seeing of the *eidē*

Heidegger's critique of Husserl's formulation of phenomenology takes its bearings from both the last phase of the first stage of its development and from the entirety of its second stage. Heidegger presents his critique as stemming from phenomenology's most basic principle, the "return to the things themselves", and thus as a "phenomenological" critique. As such, his critique purports to be an immanent critique, in the precise sense that it claims to show that when taken on its own terms as a phenomenology guided by the principle of philosophical radicalism, Husserl's formulation of phenomenology falls short of its stated intention. Heidegger's critique has interrelated ontological and methodological foci. The former challenges Husserl's claim that intentionality is the most basic phenomenon of phenomenology; the latter challenges the capacity of not just Husserl's but of any reflective and eidetic method to encounter the *source* of the meaning of Being that is *presupposed* by the mode of access to phenomena made possible by this method.

Heidegger's ontological critique has in turn two interrelated moments. The first claims that the "being characters" (*Seinscharactere*) of the entity that exhibits intentionality as an essential structure are not originally secured by Husserl. The second claims that the "meaning of Being" that guides Husserl's formulation of intentionality in terms of the "immanent" being of the *intentio* and the "transcendent" being of the *intentum* is attained by going back not to the matters themselves proper to the entity that has the structure of intentionality but to a traditional idea of philosophy. According to Heidegger this idea is the modern one inaugurated by Descartes' theory of reason, which equates "Being" with "being known" by consciousness, and, thus, with "objectivity" in the precise sense of an entity's becoming an object for consciousness. On Heidegger's view, then, Husserl's "four determinations of the phenomenological region: immanent being, absolute being in the sense of absolute givenness, absolute being in the sense of the a priori in constitution, and pure being, are in no way drawn from the entity itself"

(Heidegger 1985: 106/146).[1] By the "entity itself" Heidegger means "consciousness", in the sense of the intentionality inseparable from "the singular field of my own stream of lived-experience" (*ibid.*: 100/136). Rather than consider "the intentional in its very being", Heidegger's critique of Husserl's phenomenology claims that it determines the being of intentionality only in so far as "it is placed under scrutiny as *apprehended, given, constituting* and grasped in *ideation* as an essence" (*ibid.*: 106/146).

Thus Heidegger claims that Husserl's phenomenology determines the Being of intentionality on the basis of that region of being, namely consciousness, in which intentionality can become the object of an absolute science. On Heidegger's view, this understanding of the "determination of the Being" (*Seinsbestimmungen*) of intentionality is ontologically deficient, because it does not take its bearings from the manner of being belonging to the entity that has intentionality as an essential structure but from the determination of the Being of this structure itself. Hence his conclusion, that the "question of the *Being of this region*, of the *Being of Consciousness*" (*ibid.*: 102/140), together with the "*question of the meaning of Being*" that guides Husserl's elaboration of the correlation between the absolute being of consciousness and the transcendent being of the world, remain unasked in Husserl's phenomenology.

Husserl's erroneous "objectivizing" and "subjectivizing" of intentionality

Heidegger's ontological critique hinges on its capacity to show both that Husserl's account of intentionality as phenomenology's most original phenomenon is wrong and that the reason it is wrong is that it attributes to the Being of the entity structured by intentionality a meaning that is inappropriate to the most proper meaning of its Being. Heidegger endeavours to show the derivative nature of intentionality by first disclosing its natural meaning as the discovering in perception of what is there to be discovered in entities, and then by distinguishing an entity's intentional "discoveredness" from the disclosure of its Being. By showing that this is the natural meaning of intentionality, Heidegger believes he is able to overcome Husserl's account of the intentional relation as most originally the relation obtaining between a psychic subject and a perceived physical object. On Heidegger's view, Husserl's account is based in an erroneous "objectivizing" and "subjectivizing" of intentionality. Heidegger identifies the objectivizing error in Husserl's characterization of the intentional relation as something that falls to the subject with and through an object – the "*intentum*" – being present to it. And he locates Husserl's subjectivizing error in Husserl's account of the subjective origin and therefore its status as a subjective property of the "directing-one-self-towards" – the "*intentio*" – that is an essential characteristic of intentionality.

Heidegger thinks that his phenomenological exhibition of the natural meaning of intentionality as something that manifests not just the "directedness towards" of the *intentio* and the *intentum* as the "object" of this directedness, but with similar originality, a "mode of discoveredness" of the *intentum* that is discovered in the *intentio*, overcomes both of Husserl's errors. The mode of discoveredness of the *intentum*, however, is limited according to Heidegger to that of the "showing itself from itself" of a perceived entity, which means for him that intentionality is intrinsically incapable of manifesting the "disclosedness" of the perceived entity's Being. The latter, characterized by Heidegger as the "showing itself from itself" of the Being of an entity, is therefore inaccessible to Husserl's phenomenology precisely because it (i) understands intentionality to be the fundamental phenomenon of phenomenology and (ii) understands the meaning of the Being of this phenomenon in a derivative manner. Husserl's derivative formulation of the proper meaning of the Being of intentionality, that is, his account of it as the relation between the immanent being of the *intentio* and the transcendent being of the *intentum*, is not an accident according to Heidegger's critique, but rather a necessary manifestation of the *ontological* limits of Husserl's phenomenological method. Specifically, it is a manifestation of Husserl's method's reflective mode of access to phenomena, eidetic articulation of their structure, and, most of all, of the phenomenological *epochē* and bracketing within which his phenomenological method operates.

The necessary inability of Husserl's reflective method to determine the mode and meaning of the being of intentionality

Reflection, as the self-directness towards the stream of lived-experiences, is characterized by Heidegger as an act performed by the Ego that grasps something objective, namely, the intentional act as having the character of "directing-itself-towards" (the *intentio*) and the "towards which" of this directedness (the *intentum*). Because both the grasping reflection and grasped reflected object are lived-experiences, they belong to one and the same sphere of being. On Heidegger's view, it is precisely the "intrinsic" (*reell*) interpenetration of the grasped and grasping characteristic of reflection that Husserl understands as the immanent being of intentionality. In contrast, the transcendent world is not an intrinsic content of lived-experiences, although by virtue of their intentionality it, too, is "there" in lived-experiences, although not intrinsically. Moreover, again in contrast to the "grasped and grasping" relation characteristic of intentionality's immanent being, the world may be there in lived-experience, as the "towards which" of the *intentio*, without being there in the specific sense of its being grasped as an object of reflection. Intentional grasping and intentional directing-itself-towards are therefore not identical, and this non-identity is crucial for Heidegger's account of the necessary limits of reflection when it comes to determining both the being characters and the meaning of the Being of the entity that manifests intentionality as *a* – but decidedly not *the* – structure of its being.

The ontological limits that Heidegger's critique of Husserl's phenomenology maintains are inseparable from its reflective method are brought to the fore in his account of the reflectively executed transcendental and eidetic reductions. Heidegger's position on this is unequivocal: not only is the question of the being character belonging to the intentional not raised by Husserl's methodical reductions, but "it *gets lost precisely through them*" (1985: 151–2/110). This is the case because the transcendental reduction "has but the sole function of making the entity present in regard to its Being" (*ibid.*: 136/99), such that its categorial structure as a "what", which is to say "its pure appearance (*eidos*)" (1962: 88/61),[2] is encountered in the cognitive viewpoint characteristic of phenomenological reflection. Ruled out by this reflection is what Heidegger characterizes as the "way to be" of lived-experiences, which Husserl's phenomenological reflection "does not thematize" (1985: 151/109). This "way to be", according to Heidegger, is not categorial but "existential", in the precise sense that its "*what is precisely to be and nothing but to be*" (*ibid.*: 152/110). Heidegger calls the entity whose "what" exhibits this way to be "Dasein", and recasts phenomenology in a manner that permits it to serve, first, a fundamental ontology of Dasein, and then a universal ontology of the meaning of Being as such. Before turning, however, to the critical relation of Heidegger's reformulation of phenomenology to Husserl's formulation of it, the precise limits that Heidegger locates in the methodical reflection that drives Husserl's phenomenology need to be identified.

Heidegger's account of the limits of reflection finds them in what he presents as its structural relation to intentionality. Because not all intentional lived-experiences are "grasping", it is possible for reflection to make a theme of an act's directedness, in which case its "towards which" is not grasped as a reflected theme. This possibility of reflection is how Heidegger characterizes the phenomenological *epochē*. It is also possible that this "towards which" be co-apprehended with the theme of the act's directedness, such that the grasping reflection does not live directly in the act but rather "lives thematically" (*ibid.*: 135/98–9) in the grasping of it. This is Heidegger's characterization of "bracketing". Together, these reflective possibilities result in the "reduction" of the absorption of the natural direction of acts in the transcendent thesis of the world to "the acts themselves in their full structure" (*ibid.*: 137/100). By thematically positing the act and its object as it is there in the act, the object is now "thematized in terms of the how of its being meant in the corresponding intention". For Heidegger this thematization comes at a high price, namely, the disregarding of the "thematic meaning" of the act's object, because in "not going along with the concrete intention", this "not going along" lives rather "in the attitude of immanent reflective grasping" (*ibid.*: 135/98). Thus, on the one hand, phenomenology's reflective method, in accordance with its very structure, is cut off from an investigation of the lived thematic meaning of the intentional object. On the other hand, as a function of its "methodical meaning of a disregarding" (*ibid.*: 150/109) of the lived direction of concrete life, "the reduction is in principle inappropriate for determining the being of consciousness positively". Hence Heidegger's conclusion that "[t]he meaning of the reduction involves precisely giving up the ground upon which alone the question of the Being of the intentional could be raised" (*ibid.*).

In addition to the transcendental reduction's exclusion of the ground on which alone the question of the Being of the intentional is capable of being raised, Heidegger claims that the eidetic reduction explicitly disregards the existential individuation of the entity that possesses intentionality as an essential structure of its existence. The meaning of the "that it is" of the Ego is therefore incapable of being investigated by Husserl's phenomenology, precisely because the ideation through which it grasps the *a priori* of intentional phenomena is determined by "seeing the what as grasped, given, constituted" (*ibid.*: 152/110). This "seeing" is therefore intrinsically blind to ways or modes of being other than the categorial "what" that is seen in its exemplary and phenomenologically "pure" intuition.

Pure phenomenology's intrinsic inability to interrogate the *a priori* understanding of being included in the *intentio*

The full force of the intended immanence of Heidegger's critique rests on his own "phenomenological" interpretation of the "natural" meaning of intentionality, which, as mentioned, maintains that it is most properly characterized as the discovering in perception of what is there to be discovered in an entity that is "extant" (*Vorhanden*). By the latter, Heidegger means an object that is *present* in the perceptual field, but "concealed" (*verdeckt*). The consequent "self-showing" of the present entity in its perception, which Heidegger characterizes as its "discoveredness", therefore belongs not to its being as an extant entity but to intentionality as a natural mode of what he calls the "comportment" of the entity – Dasein – that exhibits intentionality as an "existential possibility" of its being. Heidegger holds that "the mode of the possible discoveredness of the extant entity in perception must already be traced out (*vorgezeichnet*) in the perceiving itself" (1982: 99/70),[3] such that "the *intentio* itself includes an understanding of an extant entity's presence, even if it is only pre-conceptual" (*ibid.*: 100/71). This understanding is characterized by Heidegger as an "a priori understanding of Being [*Seinsverständnis*]" inseparable from Dasein as existing, which, as such, already understands the "Being present of the extant entity [*Vorhandensein*]" to which it comports itself; and does so, "regardless of how far this present entity is discovered and whether or not it is or is not adequately and suitably discovered". It is precisely in this *a priori* understanding of Being that Heidegger speaks of the "disclosedness [*Erschlossenheit*] given in the understanding of the Being present of the extant entity". Hence, from his own phenomenological analysis of the natural meaning of intentionality, Heidegger draws the conclusion that the possibility of perceivedness is grounded in an *a priori* understanding of Being, namely the "presence of the extant entity [*Vorhandenheit*]" (*ibid.*).

The conclusion Heidegger draws about the intrinsic understanding of Being characteristic of the natural meaning of intentionality is crucial to his immanent critique of Husserl's pure phenomenology in two vital respects. First, it claims to establish that despite Husserl's transcendental reduction of the transcendent being of the world, "the meaning of Being" remains an issue for phenomenology. Second, it establishes the basis for his claim that Husserl's pure phenomenological account of the "being" characteristic of the "immanent being" of absolute consciousness, and the "meaning of the Being" that guides his characterization of the intentional correlation between the *intentio* and *intentum* given in the immanent being of consciousness, are *phenomenologically* deficient. Because the deficiency Heidegger identifies in Husserl's account of the immanent being of absolute consciousness concerns the status of consciousness as an "entity", Heidegger characterizes it as an "ontical" deficiency, as it pertains to "*onta*" (beings or entities). And because, in contrast, the deficiency identified in Husserl's account of the intentional correlation between the *intentio* and *intentum* concerns the "meaning of the Being" of the structure itself of intentionality, for Heidegger the deficiency in question here is "ontological", as it pertains to the "Being" ("*on*") of an entity. Heidegger's critique of Husserl's phenomenology is therefore aptly characterized as an "ontico-ontological" critique, as it is directed to Husserl's accounts of both the character of the intentional entity and the meaning of the Being of this entity's Being.

As we have seen, the common denominator for Heidegger's "ontico-ontological" critique is the understanding of Being that he claims belongs to the meaning of intentionality. Indeed, this common denominator is responsible for the seeming inconsistency of this critique, in so far as it claims, on the one hand, that Husserl's phenomenology does *not* ask the question of the Being of the intentional and is therefore incapable of interrogating the meaning of Being that guides its formulation of intentionality, while, on the other hand, it claims that the sole function of Husserl's reduction is to make an entity present with regard to its Being. The seeming of this inconsistency is dispelled, however, with the consideration that for Heidegger *the manifestation of an entity with regard to its Being and the interrogation of the meaning of this Being are not the same*. And, as we have seen, his claim is that Husserl's pure phenomenology does not question the meaning of the Being that guides its account of the originality of the phenomenon of intentionality because it cannot. It cannot interrogate the meaning of Being because, on Heidegger's view, its reflective and eidetic method is structurally incapable of "seeing" and therefore encountering as a problem the showing itself from itself of that which is responsible for making an entity present with respect to its Being. In other words, Husserl's method is guided by the presupposition – which it, in principle, is unable to question – that the proper meaning of Being is the "presence" that is responsible for the showing itself from itself of a perceived entity.

The ultimate historical origin of pure phenomenology's neglect of the Being question: the Greek understanding of the meaning of Being as presence

The *phenomenologically* unexamined meaning of Being as "presence" therefore guides both Husserl's formulation of the immanent being of intentionality, as the "being present" to one another of the grasped reflected object and the grasping reflection, and his formulation of the intentional relation that structures the Being of intentionality, as the "presence" to one another of two entities, the immanent *intentio* and the transcendent *intentum*. Heidegger's critique of the ontological deficiencies of Husserl's phenomenology appears to be devastating, for not only does it point to a fundamental neglect on the part of a form of research whose most basic principle is "to the things themselves", but also it provides an account of why this form of research is constitutionally barred from ever redressing this neglect. Indeed, Heidegger connects the fundamental ontological limitation of Husserl's pure phenomenology to an original precedent in Greek ontology, adding historical depth to the already mentioned historical connection drawn by him between "the field that Descartes glimpsed under the heading of *res cogitans*" (1985: 139/101) and Husserl's formulation of the immanent being of intentionality. Heidegger's appeal to the Greek origin of ontology adds a dimension of historical inevitability to the shortcomings he identifies in Husserl's formulation of phenomenological research. Thus, once he works out the basics of the "analytic of Dasein" in connection with his reformulation of phenomenology as fundamental ontology, Heidegger says that "pure intuition, which corresponds noetically to the traditional ontological priority of the extant [*Vorhanden*], has been deprived of its priority" (1962: 147/187).

But has it really? Does Heidegger really show, first, that the pure intuition that guides phenomenology corresponds to traditional Greek ontology, and, second, that this ontology is constrained by its theoretical orientation to entities in their Being present, an orientation that is incapable of interrogating – because it presupposes as true – the meaning of Being as "presence"? Despite the undeniable and enduring philosophical significance of Heidegger's interpretation of ancient Greek ontology, the answer to this question has to be no. Heidegger's interpretation of what he very often simply refers to as "*Greek ontology*" (1982: 150/106) is itself determined by two fundamental constraints. The first is Husserl's "discovery of categorial intuition" (1985: 64/48), which Heidegger characterizes as "the demonstration ... that there is a simple apprehension of the *categorial*", and which Heidegger himself uses as a guide for his interpretation of the "constituents in entities which in traditional fashion are identified as *categories* and were seen in crude form quite early in Greek philosophy, especially by Plato and Aristotle". The second is Heidegger's failure to clarify the general distinction between the manner of being of the *eidē* in Plato's and Aristotle's philosophies, and, more precisely, to address, let alone to clarify, the distinction between the Socratic and arithmological accounts of the *eidē* in Plato's thought. As we have seen, this last distinction is crucial not only for understanding the Platonic account of the *eidē* but also in Aristotle's dispute with Plato over their true manner of being.

Heidegger's reliance on Husserl's discovery of categorial intuition as the guide for his interpretation of Greek ontology

These constraints are not unrelated. It is precisely Heidegger's reliance on Husserl's discovery of categorial intuition to interpret the status of the *eidē* in Plato and Aristotle that is behind Heidegger's inattentiveness to the radically different accounts of their manners of being in Plato's and Aristotle's philosophies. This inattentiveness, in turn, elides the distinction between Plato's Socratic and arithmological accounts of the *eidē* that are the targets of Aristotle's criticism of his teacher, and it also renders questionable Heidegger's claim that the same understanding of the meaning of Being is operative in the "ontology" of both Greek philosophers.

Heidegger credits Husserl's phenomenological discovery of categorial intuition with breaking through to what is truly objective in entities in a manner that "arrives at the form of research sought by ancient ontology" (Heidegger 1985: 98/72). Thus, for Heidegger, "[t]here is no ontology *alongside* a phenomenology. Rather, *scientific ontology is nothing but phenomenology*" (*ibid.*). Moreover, Heidegger credits Husserl's account of "pure" categorial intuition, "ideation", with discovering the original meaning of the *a priori*, a discovery that "stands in connection with or is actually identical to the discovery of the concept of Being in Parmenides or Plato" (*ibid.*: 102/75). Very significant in this regard is Heidegger's claim that:

> [Husserl's] thesis that everything categorial ultimately rests upon sense intuition is but a restatement of the Aristotelian proposition: *oudepote noei aneu phantasmatos ē psuchē*: "the soul can intend nothing, grasp nothing objective in its objectivity, if beforehand something as such has not been shown to it" [*De an.* 431a16f[4]].
> (*Ibid.*: 94/69)

Equally significant is Heidegger's also crediting Husserl, with "his concept of intentionality" (1997: 598/413–14),[5] as being the first to rediscover Plato's "fundamental insight into *logos* ... that *logos* is *logos tinos* [speech about something]" (*ibid.*).

Finally, and most significantly, there is Heidegger's claim that Plato "does not yet possess a real understanding of the structure and concept of the *genos*" (*ibid.*: 362/524), while Aristotle does. Thus "Plato uses *genos* and *eidos* promiscuously" and thereby does not achieve Aristotle's level and clarity of understanding of *genos* as something that "refers to an entity in its Being, thus that which an entity, as this entity, always already was". Plato's "term for entities in their Being is *eidos*", which, according to Heidegger, "in its structural sense is not oriented toward the provenance of entities, toward the structure lying in them themselves, but instead concerns the way the Being of entities may be grasped" (*ibid.*). Hence Heidegger maintains that "[t]he *eidos* is relative to pure perceiving, *noein*; it is what is sighted in pure perceiving". As such, Heidegger concludes that:

> *Eidos*, as a concept pertaining to the givenness of entities, basically says nothing about the Being of these entities, beyond expressing the one directive that entities are to be grasped primarily in their outward look, i.e., in their presence, and specifically in their presence to a straightforward looking upon them.(*Ibid.*: 363/524)

Heidegger's interpretation of the act of ideation in Husserl's phenomenology characterizes what is at stake therein as categorial acts that give their object, understood as the "*species*", the latter merely being the Latin translation of "*eidos, the outward appearance of something*" (1985: 91/66). Heidegger's interpretation captures both Husserl's account of the "founded" character of ideation, its necessary givenness on the basis of a "manifold" (*ibid.*: 91/67) of individual perceptual acts, and its abstractive character, in the precise sense that "the founding objectivity is *not* taken up into the content of what is intended in ideation" (*ibid.*). Thus, as can be seen from our own account of ideation in Husserl, Heidegger is absolutely right that for Husserl ideating abstraction involves "comparative considerations", such that "[t]hat toward which I see in comparing, with respect to the comparable, can in its own right be isolated in its pure state of affairs, and therewith I acquire the idea" (*ibid.*: 92/67).

But can Heidegger's claims about the relation of Husserl's discovery of categorial intuition to the ontology of Aristotle and Plato, together with his critique of both the general limits of this ontology and those specifically tied to Plato's account of the *eidos*, withstand critical scrutiny? Is it really the case that Husserl's "thesis" about categorial intuition "is but a restatement" of a statement of Aristotle's about the impossibility of the soul thinking without the showing to it beforehand of something? When they are compared, two very obvious inconsistencies emerge in Husserl's account of categorial intuition and Aristotle's account of *noēsis*.

The impossibility of harmonizing Husserl's and Aristotle's accounts of *eidē*

First, we have seen that for Aristotle the *eidos* cognized by *nous* is emphatically *not* a "one over many", nothing apart from the things that share in them, but a common thing. Thus, despite its being "shared in" (*metexein*) by many individuals, the conclusion Aristotle draws from this is that the soul knows the *eidos* by becoming the "same" as it, in the precise sense that *nous*'s potency to become the *eidos* of *eidē* is "actualized", and *nous*, literally, becomes "one" with the "being-at-work" of the *eidos* acting on it. This "unity" of the *eidos* and *nous* in *epistēme* composes the "common thing" proper to the manner of being of the *eidos* for Aristotle. Thus, in the most radical contrast possible to Husserl's account of categorial ideation, for Aristotle apprehension of the unity of the *eidos* excludes – in principle – that unity's relation to a multiplicity.

Second, for Aristotle, abstraction has nothing to do with the soul's knowledge of an *eidos*, again in marked contrast to Husserl's account of ideating abstraction. And while it could be argued that Husserl's account of ideating abstraction is akin to the one place where Aristotle talks of abstraction, mathematical abstraction, we have seen that Aristotle presents his account of the abstracted manner of being of mathematical objects as a pointed critique of the Platonic account of their "one over many" manner of being. This makes it impossible to harmonize Husserl's account of precisely this mode of being proper to the *eidos* and Aristotle's account of the abstracted manner of being of mathematical objects. Moreover, Husserl's account of the "pure" categorial intuition involved in the grasping of the *eidos* characterizes the intuiting "regard" as a mode of "*seeing*" and the grasped *eidos* as something that *appears* to this regard and is therefore something "*seen*". For Aristotle, however, strictly speaking the cognized *eidos* is *not* even an appearance. What appear are *phantasmata*, and it is through their appearances that *nous* – although Aristotle's texts are none too clear on how – cognizes the indivisible and uncombined intelligible things, the *eidē*. Once cognized, as mentioned, the unity of *nous* and *eidos* can hardly be said to "appear", as the "seeing" and "seen" – *noēseōs noēsis* – are *one and the same*.

Heidegger's claim about the nature of the relation between Husserl's categorial intuition and Aristotle's ontology is therefore problematic. What about his claim that situates Husserl's concept of intentionality with the rediscovery of Plato's insight into the *logos tinos*? As we have seen, Husserl's concept of intentionality emerges from his initial psychological investigations of symbolic presentations in the *Philosophy of Arithmetic*, that is, of cognitive presentations in mathematics that do not intuitively present their object but only indirectly, if at all, refer to it. Precisely Husserl's attempt to come to terms with the descriptive psychological status of the "symbolic" character of (what he then called) a symbolic presentation (later calling it a "symbolic representation") is behind his formulation of the concept of an "empty intention", which is arguably the most important aspect of his phenomenological account of intentionality.

Heidegger's interpretation of these matters quite accurately characterizes the concept of intentionality that grows out of Husserl's concerns mentioned here as involving "the interrelation of the modes of presentation manifested in a distinct sequence of levels ranging from mere empty intending (signitive acts) to originally giving perception (intuitive acts in the narrowest sense)" (1985: 65/48). Heidegger's account is again on target when he characterizes empty intending as "being unfilled in its meaning; what is presumed in it is there in the how of its non-fulfillment" (*ibid.*). And his sure grasp of Husserl's phenomenological account of intentionality is especially evident in his articulation of the functional interrelation between the modes of intentional presentation, when he stresses that the intentional relation between the unfulfilled intention and the fulfilling intention "is always predelineated in their intentionality", and that "the fulfillment itself is of an intentional character" (*ibid.*: 66/49).

Granting, then, that Heidegger's interpretation of Husserl's concept of intentionality along these lines is in keeping with Husserl's understanding, the question before us is whether Heidegger's claim that it amounts to a rediscovery of Plato's insight into the *logos tinos* is a claim that can withstand critical scrutiny. As we have seen, both Plato's Socrates and the Eleatic Stranger characterize *logos* as an image with an *archē* (beginning) and *telos* (end) that are inseparable from intelligible beings (*noēta*), from *eidē*. And the Stranger's account of *logos* makes it patent that the *eidos* proper to the being of *logos* is such that it is *impossible* for it to *be* and *not* to *be* about something. Hence Heidegger claims the *logos tinos* as Plato's great insight. For Husserl's concept of intentionality to amount to a rediscovery of Plato's insight, the relation between the image and original characteristic of both the Socratic and arithmological accounts of *logos* and *eidē* would have to exhibit intentionality's main structural features summarized by Heidegger. Not only, then, would *logos* have to exhibit the "direction towards an object" that is the most intrinsic aspect of Husserl's concept of intentionality, but the character of this relation would also have to exhibit the functional interrelation between empty and fulfilled meaning intentions.

Husserl's concept of intentionality cannot be viewed (per Heidegger) as the rediscovery of Plato's insight into *logos tinos* (speech about something)

To be sure, if by "intentionality" all that is meant is the intentional relation in the sense of its "being about something", then Husserl's concept and Plato's *logos tinos* are in accord. However, if something more than this is meant, if the signitive character of Husserl's empty intention, its predelineation in the how of the emptiness of its meaning of the conditions for its fulfilment, is meant, then such an accord becomes very problematic.

To begin with, as we have seen, both Plato's Socrates as well as his Stranger understand *logos*'s manner of being as a kind of image, in the sense of the "looks" (*eidolon*) of things that reflect the *eidē* that are inseparable from their (the things') appearances as what they are. As we have also seen, because their reflections in *logoi* are likewise inseparable from the appearances of the *eidē*, Socrates distinguishes the image–original relation characteristic of *logos*'s function to "reflect" *eidē* from the natural image–original relation characteristic of perception. Whereas the relation between image and original in perception makes it possible to bypass the original's reflected image and apprehend it directly in a perceptual apprehension, in the case of *logos* the original – the *eidos* – cannot be apprehended in any other manner than through its image mediated through *logos*.

Moreover, the Stranger's account of the *logos* as image presupposes the Socratic account, adding to it the distinction between images whose "looks" function as "likenesses" (*eikones*) and those whose "looks" only seem like something and are therefore "apparitions" (*phantasmata*). In addition, and this is decisive for assessing Heidegger's claim about the relation between *logos* in Plato and Husserl's concept of intentionality, the Stranger's account maintains that once falsehood has been shown to mix with *logos*, the very distinction between "likeness" and "apparition" cannot be established at the level of the *logos*. That is, the criterion for distinguishing true and false *logoi* cannot be established on the basis of an exclusive appeal to the way things look to the *logos*, to how they appear in its images. But, rather, the criterion for this distinction must be sought dialectically, "through" the *logos* and therefore beyond its images in a way that confronts the manner of being of the originals of these images: the *eidē* in community with themselves, and, especially, the manner of being of the greatest *genē* responsible for any community of beings – sensible or eidetic – whatsoever.

The question, then, is whether Plato's *logos*, in the sense of its function as an image to refer to something more original, is appropriately characterized along the lines of Husserl's "empty" intention, that is, as a signitive representation of a meaning that predelineates the conditions for its "fulfilment" in the thing or object signified or otherwise "meant" (*vermeint*) and therefore "intended" by its empty meaning intention. The answer would certainly have to be no, if Husserl's phenomenological characterization of an image is attributed to Plato's account of its "being". The reason for this is simple: Husserl's account of the phenomenon of image leaves no doubt that its essence is intuitive, not signitive.

For Husserl, then, the phenomenon of image is characterized by the structural distinction between the imaged object and the image, a distinction that he maintains is immediately and therefore intuitively evident. This structural distinction, in turn, is established by the essential distinction Husserl draws between the image proper and the sensible basis required for an image to appear at all as such. Thus the sensible basis for the appearance of the image is structurally distinct from the image itself, as the image is what appears when the sensible basis is looked at. This, in turn, guarantees that the subject of the image, that which appears through the image's sensible basis, is structurally distinguishable from the image itself. For Husserl, therefore, the image is directly presented in what he calls "image-consciousness", and the imaged object is represented mediately, and therefore indirectly, through the medium of its perceptual basis. The image for Husserl is therefore not a sign that signifies or otherwise refers to the imaged object, but the intuitively given – albeit indirect – appearance of this very object.

As mentioned, for Plato, in contrast, the "being" of an image is characterized by its manner of *not being* what it *appears* to be, not by the structural distinction between image and its original (i.e. the subject in Husserl's idiom). Of the two possible modes of an image's not-being, likeness and apparition, only likeness, properly speaking, can be characterized as being structurally distinct from its original. This is the case because the not-being of an apparition is characterized precisely by the inability of the soul to which it appears to distinguish between image and original. This distinction, therefore, is manifestly not something that is given with the appearance *per se* of an image, but, rather, it is something that can be made only subsequent to the dialectical enquiry into the truth of the "looks" of that which appears. Moreover, Plato's characterization of *logos* as a kind of image is no more signitive than the image is in Husserl's phenomenological account. We have seen that, as the "community" of verbs and names and therefore as the whole that is irreducible to the functioning of the latter as "vocal marks" (*sēmeion*), *logos* is in "community" with Being – and it is so in a manner that is responsible for the manifestation of Being's very *appearance* as Being.

Plato's arithmological account of the *eidē* is guided by neither *logos* nor the meaning of being as presence

Even though we have shown that this last point cannot be legitimately tied to Husserl's concept of empty intention, it nevertheless might seem to confirm the basis of Heidegger's criticism of Plato and indeed Aristotle and therefore Greek ontology in general, namely, that for Plato as for Aristotle, the questioning of entities with regard to their Being is guided by *logos*.

This means for:

> the explication of a given theme – even if only the sheer something in general [*Etwas überhaupt*] – speech is the guiding thread. This irruption of *logos*, of the logical in this rigorously Greek sense, in the question of *on*, is motivated by the fact that *on*, the Being of entities, is primarily interpreted as presence, and *logos* is the primary way in which one makes something present, namely that which is under discussion. (Heidegger 1997: 155/225)

As we have seen, precisely this understanding of Being is what Heidegger maintains is intrinsic to the *intentio* of the natural meaning of the phenomenon of intentionality. And we have also seen that its basis for a criticism of both Greek ontology and Husserl's phenomenology presupposes Heidegger's ability to establish that such an understanding of Being is intrinsically deficient, because so long as it is unquestionably assumed to present the true meaning of Being, both the meaning of Being that it presumes, as well as the meaning of Being as such, will remain unquestioned. But before addressing this last point, the question has to be asked and answered whether Heidegger's claim that the *eidos* for Plato is relative to pure perceiving (*noein*), that it is what is seen when the multiplicity of entities are reduced to one look in common, is Plato's last word on the *eidos*.

We need look no further than our discussion of the Stranger and Theaetetus' arithmological account of the community of *eidē* to see that the account of the *eidos* that Heidegger attributes to Plato is the Socratic account, which we have shown must be distinguished from the arithmological one. The two most salient distinctions of the latter account are sufficient to render untenable Heidegger's claims about both the role of the *logos* as the guiding clue for the explication of any given theme in Plato and the meaning of Being operative in Plato's ontology originating in what is sighted by *noein* as present in the *eidos*.

Regarding the first, we have seen that it is precisely *logos*'s character of being about something, and, therefore, being about *one* thing, that is responsible for it being an unsuitable guide for the arithmological account of the manner of being of the *eidē* in their "community" with one another. Specifically, the "one" presupposed by *logos*, being a homogeneous unit (the kind used in counting), is unsuitable for accounting for the "unity" of the five greatest *eidē* in their community, as the latter is characterized, above all, by the necessary opposition of the "units" of *eidē* composing it. The appearances of the latter in philosophical dialogue therefore in no way represent the fulfilment of meaning intentions, signitive or otherwise, predelineated in the *logos*. On the contrary, it is only with the dialectical abandonment of *logos*'s most basic presupposition – about the *kind* of unity necessary for speech to be meaningful – that the most original *eidē* appear. And their paradoxical appearance, as being mixed with their opposites, explodes once and for all what can now be recognized as the *myth* not only of Plato's philosophy being limited by an *a priori* understanding of the meaning of Being as presence but, also, of it being fundamentally driven by an "ontology".

For if by "ontology" is understood an investigation that supposes that the most fundamental philosophical question or problem is knowledge of the Being of entities, our discussion of both of Plato's accounts of the *eidē* (the Socratic and arithmological) shows that they are guided by the supposition of a more fundamental philosophical problem than that of the question of Being. Rather than concern or be guided by the presupposition that the meaning of Being is the "presence" responsible for entities being present, this problem concerns the origin of the unity that is inseparable from the appearance of all multiplicity and motion. That this problem can be reduced to neither the question of Being nor to that of its basic meaning as presence is apparent from both the Socratic images of the idea of the Good and the arithmological account of the *genos* Being and its *archai*. The multiplicity of Socratic images rules out both their determination in terms of any one of them or all of them being present as well as the presence of that to which they ultimately point out to the seeing that guides *noēsis*. And the *genos* of Being, as the unstable whole that encompasses the *genē* of Motion and Rest, is no more capable of being present than the *genē* responsible for the "mixing" of these opposites, the even more encompassing opposite of the Same and the Other, can be present or otherwise determined in terms of their presence.

Heidegger's critique of Plato therefore presupposes that Plato's Socratic account of the seeing of the *eidē* is Plato's last word on the subject. And this means that the extent to which Heidegger's ontico-ontological critique of Husserl's concept of intentionality appeals to its historical precedence in the limits of Greek ontology is methodically limited by its presupposition that Plato's Socratic mythological account of seeing *eidē* is Plato's definitive account of their manner of being.

SEVENTEEN

The mereological presupposition of fundamental ontology: that Being as a whole has a meaning overall

We have shown that Heidegger's critical interpretation of Greek ontology, especially Plato's, is limited by his employment of Husserl's discovery of categorial intuition as his guide. Because Heidegger's critique engages the early stages of Husserl's development, before history became a positive thematic concern of Husserl's phenomenology, we shall defer discussion of the implications of the limits exposed here of Husserl's early thought *vis-à-vis* the Greek origins of philosophy until our discussion of the transcendental criticism of the criticism of phenomenological cognition. What needs to be discussed now is the other side of Heidegger's critique: that Husserl's reflective and eidetic method is incapable of overcoming its ontological limitations. This is especially the case because, by having shown the limits of Husserl's phenomenology (his early phenomenology, at any rate) as a guide to Plato's and Aristotle's accounts of the *eidē*, it may seem that we have indirectly confirmed Heidegger's criticisms of its ontological limits.

As mentioned, the ontological limitations that Heidegger claims are inseparable from Husserl's reflective and eidetic method concern the structural limitations that condition their exclusive focus on discovering what is there to be discovered in entities with their perception. What is excluded by this focus is supposed to be the way to be of entities when they are not being perceptually apprehended and the interrogation of the meaning of their Being that is presupposed by this exclusive mode of their apprehension. Heidegger's shorthand for this exclusive mode of apprehension is '"discovery" and his shorthand for that which it excludes is "disclosure". For Heidegger, then, entities are "discovered" and their Being and its meaning is "disclosed". Husserl's reflective and eidetic method (and not just his but any such method) is, on Heidegger's telling, limited to the pure seeing of what can be discovered in entities: to what, Heidegger assures us, the Greeks (and presumably both Plato and Aristotle) understood as pure appearance, *eidos* in the sense of their "outward look". Because of this, the method is therefore supposed to be cut off from the disclosure of the Being of entities and the interrogation of both the meaning of their Being and that of Being overall (*überhaupt*).

Rather than try to show that a reflective and eidetic phenomenological method can, indeed, disclose the Being of entities and interrogate the meaning of their Being, however, we shall examine the phenomenological method Heidegger proposes is necessary in order to advance phenomenology beyond the limits posed by Husserl's method. This will allow us to examine Heidegger's critical methodical claims without necessarily presupposing the suppositions that guide them, namely, that the Being of entities is the most fundamental philosophical theme and that the question of the meaning of Being overall is philosophy's most basic question. This manner of approaching Heidegger's critique will also allow us to examine the presupposition that is implicit in his claim that ontology is possible only as phenomenology, which is that only as ontology is philosophy possible.

The phenomenological distinction between fundamental and universal ontology

Heidegger formulates the method of what he characterizes as the "preliminary concept" of phenomenology in terms of a "hermeneutic" of Dasein, wherein what is meant by "hermeneutic" is the "interpretation" (*Auslegung*) of the phenomenological self-showing of Dasein as an entity together with the meaning of Being that properly belongs to this entity. What makes this concept of phenomenology "preliminary" is its function to establish the horizon for what Heidegger characterizes as the "idea of phenomenology", in which he projected (but never developed) the working out of an "*existential concept of science*" (1962: 357/408) by clarifying "the meaning of Being and the 'connection' between Being and truth" (*ibid.*). Heidegger calls the ontology executed under phenomenology's preliminary concept "fundamental ontology", to indicate its thematic focus on "making known" (*kundgebegen*) to "the understanding of Being that belongs to Dasein itself" the "proper meaning of its Being" together with its "basic structures" (*ibid.*: 37/62). Opposed to fundamental ontology is the universal ontology projected, in the guise of the idea of phenomenology, by Heidegger to investigate entities other than Dasein and the meaning of Being overall. Heidegger envisaged the universal ontological interrogation of the Being of entities to issue from within the "horizon for all further ontological research" (*ibid.*) exhibited by the results of fundamental ontology.

Heidegger positions the explicitly interpretative meaning of the method guiding the preliminary concept of phenomenology in explicit opposition to Husserl's method when he states "that the methodological meaning of phenomenological description is interpretation" (*ibid.*: 36/61). By interpretation he means the business of "wresting" from the objects of phenomenology their encounter in the mode of phenomenon, which is to say, making these objects manifest in their "self-showing". Thus, in contradistinction to Husserl's reflective and eidetic phenomenological method, the very structure of which assumes (according to Heidegger) that the objects of phenomenology are either already present and available for phenomenological cognition or, if presently unavailable, that they can, in principle, always be made available, on Heidegger's view the proper objects of phenomenology are "proximally and for the most part" unavailable in terms of their self-showing.

By the "objects" of phenomenology Heidegger means the Being of entities generally, and the Being of the entity Dasein in particular. What phenomenology "has taken into its 'grasp' thematically as its object" (*ibid.*: 35/59) is something that "demands to become a phenomenon in a distinctive sense, in terms of its own most proper content [*Sachgehalt*]" (*ibid.*). And this can only mean that, at the outset, the "object" of phenomenology in Heidegger's sense is not yet properly a phenomenon but, rather, precisely something that requires hermeneutic phenomenology's methodical intervention in order to be brought to its self-showing. Strictly speaking, then, for Heidegger, phenomenology's methodical concern is not with the Being of entities but with the *phenomenon* of the Being of entities. Heidegger situates this concern within the context of two basic claims: first, the question of Being and its urgency for philosophy as *the* fundamental question is something that needs to be reawakened; second, the "primary meaning" (*ibid.*: 37/62) of the hermeneutical character of phenomenology, as the method proper to fundamental ontology, is "an analysis of the existentiality of existence" (*ibid.*).

The basis of Heidegger's first claim is his view that despite sustaining "the avid research of Plato and Aristotle" (*ibid.*: 2/21), the question of Being has "from then on ceased to be heard *as a thematic question of actual investigation*" (*ibid.*: 2/2). His second claim grows out of his "formulation" of the question of the meaning of Being on the basis of the "structural moments" belonging to a question in general. According to Heidegger, questioning, as a seeking, is guided by what is sought, which is "an entity with regard to the that and how of its Being" (*ibid.*: 5/24). The seeking inseparable from questioning has three moments: that which is asked about, that which is interrogated and that which is to be found out by asking the question. After articulating the "formal structure" of the question of the meaning of Being in terms of these three structural moments, Heidegger then establishes both the ontic and ontological priority of the analysis of the structure of the being of the questioner as the point of departure for the investigation of the meaning of Being overall. He does so by making "transparent" "all the constitutive characters of the question itself" (*ibid.*: 5/25) in a manner that, he claims, establishes this priority.

The circular structure of the questioning and question about the meaning of Being

In the question of the meaning of Being, what is asked about is that which determines entities, Being; what is interrogated are these entities themselves in regard to their Being; and what is to be found out by asking the question is the meaning of Being. Heidegger maintains that despite the ignorance of the meaning of Being that is inseparable from the formal structure of asking the question about this meaning, three things can be established about Being by attending to this structure: first, that the very asking of the question presupposes the "average and vague" understanding of Being by the questioner; second, that what is "asked about", the Being of entities, "is" not itself an entity; and third, that the entity that asks the question has a priority over all other entities.

The "average and vague" understanding of Being by the questioner means that this entity is already determined in its Being without the availability of the explicit concept of this Being. Heidegger characterizes this determination as "existence", in the precise sense that the questioner's "way to be" is something that is always in question for it, and, as such, "an issue". Thus the relation between this entity's questioning of Being and the question of Being is a "concrete" circle, in so far as what is asked about in its questioning is something that it already – in a *pre-conceptual* manner – understands. Heidegger insists that this way of working out the connection between questioning and the question in the case of the meaning of Being is *not* a "circular proof", and he also maintains that the questioner's pre-conceptual understanding is what is behind both its ontic and ontological priority for answering the question about this meaning. The questioner is ontically prior because its Being, as an entity, is defined by existence. It is ontologically prior because the pre-conceptual understanding of Being definitive of its existence "includes an understanding of the Being of all entities unlike itself" (*ibid.*: 13/34).

Now it is precisely this ontico-ontological priority of the questioner that Heidegger maintains deprives of its priority Husserl's understanding of phenomenological cognition. Because what is asked about in the question of the meaning of Being is not an entity, Husserl's reflective and eidetic method – which is limited in its very structure (according to Heidegger) to describing that which can be *discovered* in entities on the basis of consciousness's intentional (and therefore perceptual) comportment towards them – is incapable of interrogating the understanding of Being characteristic of the existence of the entity whose very existence makes possible the *disclosure* of the Being of entities that makes possible their discovery. In direct opposition to Husserl's articulation of the basic structures of entities in terms of their categorial or (equivalently for Heidegger) *eidetic* structure, Heidegger's hermeneutic of Dasein articulates the structure of its existence, or, more precisely, the structure of the self-showing (phenomenon) of its existence, in terms of what he calls "existentials" – structures of existence. Thus, not only does it have to be said that for Heidegger the proper object of phenomenology is not the Being of entities but the self-showing of this Being, but it also has to be said that it is *not* the self-showing *per se* that is of concern for him, but its *structure*. As mentioned, because this self-showing is proximally and for the most part unavailable – at least initially – phenomenological description assumes the guise of interpretation, according to Heidegger. For our purposes, the consideration of one such interpretation, namely, of the "existentials" that structure what Heidegger terms the "wherein of intelligibility", "meaning", will be considered with a view to answering the following questions: what is the understanding of "structure" that guides Heidegger's existential analytic disclosure of the basic structures of the "there" wherein the Being of entities is disclosed? And what is the source of the "sight" that thematizes and presumably grasps or otherwise makes known these basic structures?

Heidegger's indefinite postponement of the discussion of the connection between categories and existential structures

We have seen that Heidegger initially establishes the structure of the question about the meaning of Being and the ontico-ontological priority of the being of the questioner on the basis of appeals to the *formal* structural moments of, first, any question, and second, the question of the meaning of Being. Curiously, especially given their importance for Heidegger's ontological refashioning of phenomenology, the status of the formality of these formal structures is not addressed by him. But Heidegger does address, if only to postpone indefinitely, an account of the connection between the self-showing of the "existence structure [*Existenzstruktur*]" (1962: 45/71) of Dasein, which as a "whole" is composed of "being characters" determined by "the existentiality of its existence" (*ibid.*: 43/69), and that of the categories of the tradition, which refer to the "what", the presence, of an extant (*Vorhanden*) entity whose being character is other than existence. Not "until the horizon for the question of Being has been clarified" (*ibid*.: 45/71) can "the connection between these modes of being characters be dealt with", and, as mentioned, Heidegger never realized the project of a universal ontology that was to take its departure from this horizon. Hence he never addressed this connection.

This is significant on two related counts. First, the relation of the ontologically restricted categorial structures of the "what", which, according to Heidegger, both define Husserl's method and determine its phenomenological limits, to "the existential structures in which the Being of the 'there' holds itself" (*ibid*.: 142/182), remains obscure in Heidegger's reformulation of phenomenology. Thus, precisely how, in its self-showing, the structural moment of a category is to be distinguished from the self-showing of the structural moment of an existential is not addressed in Heidegger's account of the existential structures that guide the hermeneutic clarification of the horizon for the question of Being. And, second, related to this structural issue, precisely how Heidegger's hermeneutic method achieves access to existential structures remains a mystery. For Husserl, as we have seen, the reflective thematization of a multiplicity is clearly requisite for the "seeing" and apprehension of the categorial structure of an entity. What about the "seeing" guiding Heidegger's hermeneutic method? As mentioned, he clearly understands "reflection" as a derivative manner of securing access to the structure of phenomena. But does he also reject the requirement of a multiplicity, which for Husserl provides a basis for the comparisons from out of which the structure of a phenomenon is uncovered? As we shall see from our consideration of Heidegger's account of the existential structures within which the "there" holds itself, he remains silent about the methodical role of multiplicity in "the *logos* of the phenomenology of Dasein", which, as we have seen, "has the character of *hermēneuein*" (*ibid*.: 36/61).

The structural whole of Dasein's most basic phenomenon is a phenomenal multiplicity

But that "the structural whole" (1962: 180/225) of the most basic phenomenon proper to Dasein is composed of a "phenomenal multiplicity [*Vielfältigkeit*]" is something to which Heidegger calls explicit attention. This phenomenon, "being-in-the-world", characterizes the "way" that Dasein, *qua* existing, is its "there": as the "clearing" that makes possible the encounter with entities, both like and unlike the entity Dasein. Heidegger writes that being-in-the-world "is a structure which is originally and constantly *whole*" (*ibid.*), even if "the *unified* phenomenological view of the whole as such" is easily distorted because of this very multiplicity. One crucial component of the phenomenal multiplicity is the existential structure of "understanding" (*Verstehen*). "Understanding", for Heidegger, is manifestly not a mode of knowing that arises "first from immanent self-perception" (*ibid.*: 144/184), but rather it pertains to the most basic composition of being-in-the-world, which is tied to the "understanding of Being" that is inseparable from Dasein's existential character of being. As an existential structure of this character of being, "understanding" is "versed" (*Gekonnte*) not in a "what" but in the disclosure of Dasein's relation to itself and to inner-worldly entities with which it deals "for the sake of itself". This relation is most originally manifest in terms of definite possibilities from which Dasein cannot escape and on which it, as existing, "has itself always already projected" (*ibid.*: 145/185) the "surge" (*dringt*) of its understanding *qua* its being-in-the-world. "Projection" is therefore "the existential structure which the understanding has in itself" (*ibid.*: 145/184–5).

The projective character of "understanding", in turn, makes up what Heidegger characterizes existentially as "sight" (*ibid.*: 146/186). This "sight" is coextensive with the "there" of Dasein's disclosedness, and thus shows itself in both Dasein's dealings with inner-world entities and in the orientation "towards Being over all, for the sake of which Dasein is as it is" (*ibid.*). Heidegger sharply distinguishes the existential structure of understanding's "projective sight" from the traditional "seeing" that orients philosophy as the way of its access to the Being of entities. Traditional "seeing" occurs when understanding's projective sight is "formalized" to yield "access in general to entities and to Being" (*ibid.*: 147/187); this formalization, as we have already mentioned, is what is behind Heidegger's claim that "[i]ntuition and 'thinking' are both already remote derivatives of understanding", including, of course, Husserl's "pure intuition, which corresponds noetically to the traditional ontological priority of the extant" (*ibid.*).

Understanding's development as interpretation: meaning as the "wherein" of intelligibility

The whole composed of understanding's projective sight "has its own possibility of development" (Heidegger 1962: 148/188), which Heidegger calls "*interpretation*". Through "the recoil" (*Rückschlag*) of the possibilities disclosed by the understanding, understanding "becomes itself". Based existentially in understanding, "[i]nterpretation is not the acknowledgement of what has been understood, but rather the development of possibilities projected in understanding" (*ibid.*). This development culminates for Heidegger in "meaning" (*Sinn*), characterized as "the formal, existential framework of the disclosedness belonging to understanding" (*ibid.*: 151/192). This framework is manifest as the "existential *fore-structure* of Dasein itself" (*ibid.*: 153/195), whereby interpretation "is never the presuppositionless grasping of something previously given" (*ibid.*: 150/191), but rather it is always "grounded" in an "existential" *a priori*, structured as a "fore-having", "foresight" and "fore-conception". "Fore-having" characterizes the situation whereby interpretation is always grounded in the understanding of "entities, or Being" (*ibid.*: 151/193). "Fore-sight" characterizes interpretation's always being guided by a "perspective that fixes that with regard to which what has been understood is to be interpreted" (*ibid.*). And, finally, "fore-conception" characterizes interpretation's either drawing the conceptuality belonging to what is to be interpreted from the entities themselves or Being itself, or else forcing them into concepts "opposed in their kind of Being".

Heidegger's account of meaning makes it clear that it "is an existential of Dasein, not a property that is attached to beings". Therefore "*only Dasein can be meaningful or meaningless*", and this means that it "'has' meaning in that the disclosedness of being-in-the-world can be 'fulfilled' through the entities discoverable in it" (*ibid.*). His account also makes it clear that "when we ask about the meaning of Being, our enquiry does not become profound and does not brood on anything that stands behind Being, but questions Being itself in so far as it stands within the intelligibility of Dasein" (*ibid.*: 152/193). And Heidegger is consistent in the conclusion he draws from this: "strictly speaking, what is understood is not the meaning, but entities, or Being" (*ibid.*: 151/193), from which it also follows: that "[t]he meaning of Being can never be contrasted with entities or with Being as the supporting 'ground' of entities because 'ground' is only accessible as meaning, even if that meaning itself is an abyss of meaninglessness" (*ibid.*: 152/193). That is, because both Being's "meaning" and the "ground" of entities have their locus within Dasein's intelligibility, neither can be contrasted with entities or Being *per se*, because this intelligibility has its source in the interpretive "recoil" of the understanding upon itself, the formal meaning structure of which Heidegger distinguishes from the entities and Being disclosed by the understanding's original projective surge. Finally, Heidegger could not be clearer that his pursuit of the analysis of the "phenomenon of interpretation" in *Being in Time*, which is the *locus classicus* for not only his but the "hermeneutic" development of phenomenology generally, is limited to "interpretation in the understanding of the world" (*ibid.*: 148/189). Such interpretive understanding deals exclusively with inner-worldly entities that are on hand (*zuhanden*) and have already been understood and interpreted with regard to the mode of Being belonging to entities that are used "in-order-to" do something.

What is not at all clear in Heidegger's account of the phenomenon of interpretation, however, are two related issues. On the one hand, there is the issue of the character of the method that is responsible for making manifest the phenomenal structure of interpretation itself articulated in his analysis. On the other hand, there is the issue of the precise status of the structural distinctions that emerge in the analysis. To be sure, ready responses to both these issues are available and, indeed, have been appealed to for more than eighty years. The character of Heidegger's method is hermeneutical, not reflective, and the structural distinctions are existential, not categorial. But these responses do not address satisfactorily the following issues: (i) the source of the "sight" that presumably guides the *phenomenological* interpretation that makes manifest the phenomenal structure of interpretation; (ii) precisely how this "sight" brings about the "thematization" of the existential structures Heidegger credits it with thematizing; and (iii) the structural character of the most fundamental distinction governing his account of interpretation, namely, that between understanding and meaning.

Because Heidegger restricts his analysis to interpretation in understanding the world, his account of the understanding's "recoil" on Dasein, such that this understanding comes to itself interpretatively, deals *exclusively* with how an inner-worldly entity "comes *explicitly* into the sight of understanding" (*ibid.*: 149/189). His account of the way it does so, according to "the structure belonging to *something as something*", is taken by him to characterize "the original 'as' of an interpretation (*hermēneia*)", the so-called "existential-hermeneutical 'as'" (*ibid.*: 158/210). The hermeneutical "as", as the structure of interpretation, is contrasted with the "as" operative in the determining statement that manifests its explicitness, what Heidegger calls the "*apophantical* 'as'" (*ibid.*). Any "pre-predicative seeing" (*ibid.*: 149/189), therefore, is "in itself already understanding and interpretative", and its "'as' therefore does not first show up in the statement, but is only first stated, which is possible only because it is there as something to be stated" (*ibid.*).

The incompleteness of Heidegger's analysis of the interpretive character of phenomenological "description"

This account of the hermeneutical "as" is clearly not presented by Heidegger as a general theory of interpretation, in the sense of advancing the claim that not just the interpretation of entities on hand in the world, but *any* interpretation, whether it be of entities or the Being of entities, is manifest according to the structure of something *as* something. He is quite clear that his analysis pertains to the interpretation of entities that are on hand in the world, as does the structure of the "as". Unaddressed, then, by Heidegger in this analysis is the *interpretation* – in the sense of interpretation having the methodological meaning of phenomenological description – that functions both to make *explicit* and to articulate conceptually the fore-structures of interpretation and its development into meaning *in the case of understanding the world*. That is, Heidegger articulates these structures and their development with respect to entities on hand in the world, but not with regard to the phenomenological interpretation that is carrying out the analysis of the existentials that structure the interpretive manifestation of innerworldly entities. Unaddressed, then, is precisely *how* these structures of the interpretive understanding of the world show themselves *interpretively* to the "interpretation" characteristic of the phenomenological method that manifests them. Do they appear according to the structure "something as something"? Perhaps "as" existential structures, seen within the "perspective" of existential structures? Moreover, what is the source of the "sight" guiding the phenomenological interpretation? This "sight" cannot be the same "sight" as the "sight" that structures the seeing of something as something, because the structure of this latter "sight" is something that is *being seen* by phenomenological interpretation, while the former "sight" is the "sight" doing the "seeing" of the phenomenological structure being seen. And, finally, what about Being? Is the structure of the interpretation of Being also governed by the structure "something as something"? But would this not be *analytically* impossible on the basis of Heidegger's own distinction between the mode of self-showing of entities and their Being, because the former are discovered while the latter are disclosed?

Given the incompleteness of Heidegger's analysis of interpretation, these questions are as necessary as they are unanswerable on its basis. Heidegger, in fact, is himself aware of this, as he describes ontological investigation as a "possible mode of interpretation" (1962: 231/275), namely, "an interpretation [*Auslegung*], as Interpretation [*Interpretation*]" (*ibid.*: 232/275), which "becomes an explicit task for research". His account of ontological Interpretation, which adumbrates rather than fully carries out such an Interpretation, is very instructive for our purposes. His account stipulates that the ontological Interpretation of the Being of an entity must:

> first bring into the fore-having the phenomenal characterization of the thematic entity, to which the following steps of the analysis must conform. These steps require, however, at the same

> time guidance through the possible fore-sight towards the mode of Being belonging to the entity. And this fore-having and fore-sight then trace out the conceptuality that will bring into relief the structures of Being. (*Ibid.*)

In the case of the entity Dasein, the ontological projection operative in its existential Interpretation takes as its clue "the 'presupposed' idea of existence as such" (*ibid.*: 313/361), which has the character of an understanding projection in which:

> such understanding allows the developing Interpretation of that which is to be interpreted *to come itself into words for the very first time, so that it may decide of its own accord whether it, as this entity, yields the composition of being upon which it has been disclosed in projection in a formal indicative manner.*
> (*Ibid.*: 314–15/362)

Heidegger's account here, with its reference to the fore-structures of meaning, suggests that the analysis of the interpretation of inner-worldly entities is, in a sense, exemplary, such that even though the theme of the analysis is interpretation in understanding the world, the structure of interpretation made manifest by the analysis would not be limited to this thematic content. The absence of any reference to the "as" in Heidegger's account of ontological Interpretation, however, makes it difficult to conclude one way or the other whether the structure of "something as something" is limited to inner-world entities or extends to the phenomenological interpretation of any existential structure whatever. In the latter case, presumably the interpretation of "Being" itself would be made explicit by the "as structure", which, as already mentioned, would mean that the meaning of Being is structured existentially in the same way as the meaning of an entity.

Heidegger's unwitting exchange of "seeing" with "being seen" in the existential structure of "sight"

For our purposes, however, settling these issues is not crucial. Even granting that the fore-structures of meaning manifest the formal existential structure of any interpretive understanding whatever of any entity and of the Being of any entity whatever, Heidegger's account of ontological interpretation, as the capital "I" Interpretation that becomes an explicit task for research, does not address the issue we have raised about the absence of an account of the methodical interpretation presupposed by the existential analytic. Rather, his account of ontological Interpretation, as taking its own methodical point of departure from the bringing into its own fore-having the phenomenal characterization of the thematic entity whose structures of Being are to be traced out in its Interpretation, proceeds as if the methodical basis of the interpretation that makes manifest this phenomenal characterization has already been secured. That it has not been secured is patent in Heidegger's account of ontological Interpretation as already operating within what he calls "the *hermeneutical situation*" (1962: 232/275), namely, the "'presuppositions'" that belong to every interpretation: fore-having, fore-sight and fore-conception. Thus, rather than provide an account of the methodically interpretive *sight* that is presupposed in the *being seen* of the structures that compose the hermeneutical situation, Heidegger's account of ontological Interpretation is exclusively concerned with having "a fore-sight of Being", which "must see it with respect to the *unity* of the possible structural factors belonging to it". The methodical "sight" guiding the interpretative method of either entities or the Being of entities is therefore not only not secured, but Heidegger's account of ontological Interpretation proceeds as if the "fore-sight" presupposed by the hermeneutical situation is also the source of the "sight" that makes this presupposition explicit. In other words, that which, in his own account of this situation, is characterized as an existential structure of the "there" of Dasein and therefore a structure that is "being seen", is also treated by him as being responsible for the "seeing" of the methodical sight that makes explicit this structure in its '"being seen".

What is at issue in Heidegger's failure to distinguish "sight" as an existential structure that is "being seen" and "sight" as the methodical "seeing" that is the source of this "being seen" is manifestly *not* the circular nature of interpretation as the development of understanding. Getting into the "hermeneutical circle" in the proper way prescribed by Heidegger, such that understanding is projected on the fore-structures of meaning as the wherein of the intelligibility of anything, does not remedy the failure to distinguish the "seeing" and "being seen" of an existential structure that is presupposed by his account of the methodical interpretation that makes explicit the circularity of the hermeneutical situation. The problem here is not that interpretation and understanding *are* related as a circle, but rather the unwitting exchange of what is the *same* and what is *other* in Heidegger's account of the *circularity* of this circle. What is "other", the "being seen" of the existential structure of fore-sight, is taken to be something the "same" as the "seeing" that is responsible precisely for *this* "being seen". Not only is this a *mistake*, but it is also a mistake that is *not* made by the phenomenological method that the hermeneutical method of phenomenology is designed to supersede. As we have seen, transcendental-phenomenological reflection clearly distinguishes the "being seen" of the object made thematic by the reflecting regard of phenomenology's methodical reflection, the *reflected* object, from the *reflective* "seeing" that is the source of the thematization accomplished by this methodical regard. The latter is initiated by a *reflection* whose lived-experience is structurally distinct from the lived-experience that is reflected on. This distinction is confirmed by a "higher"-level methodical reflection that encompasses both, the *reflected* and the *reflecting*, and thematizes their structural difference.

The fundamental presupposition of Heidegger's hermeneutical reformulation of phenomenology

Directly related to the methodical obscurity at the heart of Heidegger's hermeneutical reformulation of phenomenology is the presupposition responsible for the most fundamental distinction governing its account of interpretation. This is the distinction between what is understood in understanding – an entity or entities, or Being – and meaning, which, as mentioned, is not a property attached to entities but the "wherein" of their intelligibility. By the presupposition responsible for the distinction we do not have in mind the supposition that, as objects of the *understanding*, entities and Being *are* distinct from their *meaning* as entities and Being made explicit in interpretation. Rather, the presupposition that concerns us is that there is a kind of "seeing" that is capable of "seeing" the difference between entities and Being and the meaning of entities and Being. As we have seen, Heidegger's account of the fore-having characteristic of understanding cannot see this difference, because the objects of its understanding are entities, or Being, not their meaning. And his account of the formal existential structure of interpretation as meaning rules out the fore-sight of understanding's development as interpretation as a candidate for the "sight" responsible for "seeing" the difference in question. This is the case because this "sight" is a moment of the structural whole of "meaning", while what is at stake in the presupposition we are calling attention to is a "sight" capable of "seeing" not just meaning, but also entities and Being, such that their *difference* is *seen* and thus made explicit as something *being seen*. Once the fore-sight of interpretation is ruled out as the source of the "sight" that sees the difference in question here, the conclusion becomes unavoidable that Heidegger's account of interpretation *presupposes* something *other* than what can be seen in the fore-sight proper to interpretation, when it posits as fundamental the difference between that which is understood in understanding and that which is made intelligible in meaning.

The "other" that is presupposed in the hermeneutical positing of a fundamental difference between entities and Being and the meaning of entities and Being therefore has the status of a whole that encompasses the distinction between entities, Being and their meaning. Because the "sight" of interpretation cannot surpass the "whereupon" of its projection, namely meaning, it not only must *presuppose* that when entities and Being are understood in understanding's fore-having that this understanding is unmediated by meaning, but, also, it must presuppose that entities and Being are such as to have a meaning. In the case of the hermeneutical investigation of the question of the meaning of Being, then, these considerations lead to the unavoidable conclusion that Heidegger's formulation of fundamental ontology is guided by the *mereological* presupposition that to the Being of entities there belongs a meaning of Being overall.

The mistaking of what is *other* for the *same* in fundamental ontology's account of the seeing and being seen of the fore-sight proper to the hermeneutical situation, and the presupposition of something "other" than what can be seen by interpretation in its account of the relation between understanding entities and Being and the meaning of entities and Being, is no doubt what is behind Heidegger's abandonment of the *explicitly* phenomenological phase of his philosophy in 1928. In his own words, "the question of the extent to which one might conceive the interpretation of Dasein ... in a universal-ontological way ... is a question which I myself am not able to decide, one which is still completely unclear to me" (Heidegger 1984: 210/271).[1] For the mistaking of the "being seen" of an existential for the "seeing" that is responsible for its "being seen" makes it impossible for the interpretation of Dasein to become explicitly ontological, that is, to thematize and eventually conceptualize the existential structures that are projected as the basis of ontological Interpretation. And the mereological presupposition operative in hermeneutic phenomenology, that to the Being of entities there belongs a meaning of Being overall, prevents fundamental ontology, in principle, from preparing the horizon for an interrogation of the meaning of Being overall.

EIGHTEEN

The presupposition behind the proto-deconstructive critique of intentional historicity: the conflation of *intra*subjective and *inter*subjective idealities

Derrida's pre- or proto-deconstructive work focuses above all on opposing Husserl's concept of intentional history to empirical history, to the history that falls under Husserl's transcendental *epochē* and is therewith "bracketed" and "put out of play". Indeed, in order to highlight this opposition, Derrida speaks of intentional history as "transcendental historicity" (Derrida [1978] 1989: 121). Derrida characterizes this opposition by drawing attention to the role Husserl assigns to language generally and written language pre-eminently in the constitution of the historicity of the objective meanings at stake in "transcendental historicity". For Derrida, the phenomenological condition of possibility belonging to Husserl's early static investigations of objective meanings involves the exclusion of both empirical history (and therewith seemingly history *per se*) and the empirical significance of words (and therewith seemingly language *per se*), an exclusion that Derrida takes to be what Husserl thinks ensures the "purity" necessary for the phenomenological cognition of objective meanings.

In contrast, Derrida takes note of the fact that, as we have seen, in Husserl's late essay "The Origin of Geometry" language and history are *not* excluded from Husserl's account of the origin of the objectivity of the ideal meanings that, as a mathematical science, belong to geometry. On the contrary, it is language, in the guise of the graphic embodiment of words, which is to say, "writing", that Husserl maintains is responsible for the objectivity – in the sense of the enduring intersubjective accessibility that constitutes the phenomenological meaning of a tradition – of the ideal meanings constituted by the first geometer. Derrida maintains that as a result of this graphic embodiment, the first or proto-geometer's original insight into his ideal creation becomes "virtual" and, with this, *not* subject to, but rather the very *medium* of, history. This is the case because inseparable from the virtual embodiment of the original insight in the written word is the possibility of its becoming forgotten: forgotten in the sense that those who subsequently read it may do so without the illumination of the original insight that it was supposed to make virtual. Such forgetting is therewith coincident with the origin of the "sedimentation" of the original meaning, a sedimentation that Derrida, following Husserl, endorses as one of the two essential aspects of the *a priori* constitutive of historicity, with the other aspect of this *a priori*, again for Derrida as for Husserl, being the original production of the ideal meaning by the proto-geometer. Because of this, language is now understood by Derrida to function for Husserl as an indispensable *transcendental* condition for the very constitution of the objectivity belonging to ideal meanings, the "ideality" of which he now characterizes, for this very reason, as being both constituted by and subject to the *a priori* structure of historicity.

Derrida's opposition of ideality and the empiricality of language yields his concept of "transcendental language"

Derrida characterizes this account of the historicity belonging to the ideality of ideal meaning, an account that he understands to be respectful of Husserl's "intention" in "The Origin of Geometry", as nevertheless being in a certain opposition to Husserl's account of the meaning of historicity and therewith of the relation between ideality and history. The opposition, however, is one that Derrida thinks cannot be avoided and therefore one that he makes no effort to censure. On the contrary, he is intent on exploring its significance for the phenomenological method's disclosure of both the meaning of historicity and historicity *as* meaning, since on his view "phenomenology alone can make [the] infinite historicity [at issue here] appear" (Derrida [1978] 1989: 152). The opposition concerns, quite literally, the fact that for Derrida the "empirically bound" ideality of language is called on by Husserl, in "The Origin of Geometry", to constitute an ideality that, at its origin, cannot be so bound if the geometrical ideality in question is to come into being. It is for this reason that Derrida characterizes as "transcendental language" the net effect of this intersection of the proto-geometer's transcendental constitution of geometric ideality and the empirically bound ideality of the language whose medium renders it "virtual". Hence, for Derrida, inseparable from the origin of geometrical ideality is also its *telos*, in the guise of this ideality's inevitable sedimented "passage" through the written word. For this reason, Derrida maintains that the "desedimentation" of this passage is at once the awakening of the historicity of meaning and the meaning of its very historicity. Desedimentation is historicity's awakening because the recognition of the need to recover the ideality of the original insight by an enquiry into its origin is inseparable from the recognition that it has not been preserved by the written word. And the meaning of this very historicity is likewise this desedimentation, because historicity's appearance is coincident with the attempt to recover the lost original insight.

Derrida's account of the deferral of ideality as manifest in its infinite *telos*

It is important to note here that Derrida is not in any way contesting the original emergence and perdurance of the being of ideality. Ideality for him not only is something that *is*, but also something whose very manner of being as ideal *is* precisely what is in question. This manner of being for Derrida is such that its origination, by virtue of the historicity inseparable from its very manner of being, is always already beyond the ambit of the only method that he thinks is capable of disclosing its true manner of being, namely Husserl's transcendental-phenomenological method. Hence the opposition in question between the empirical bondage of ideality made virtual through the written word and the absence of such bondage necessary for the transcendental constitution of ideality itself is not determined according to Derrida by an "either or", but by a "both and". Ideality is *both* the empirically inaccessible unbound origin *and* the infinite *telos* announced by this origin's linguistically empirical embodiment. That is, because the transcendental constitution of ideality is inseparable from its embodiment in something that is intrinsically not ideal, its pure appearance, which is to say, its empirically unmediated "presence" as ideal, is not only not coincident with its origin but it is also unrealizable as its *telos*. Ideality's manner of being *is* therefore the meaning of historicity, in the precise sense of its non-coincidence with either its origin or its *telos*. At the same time, this historicity itself is the meaning of its being, in the precise sense that it is the manifestation of this very non-coincidence. Ideality is therefore constituted by this insuperable interplay between the empirically conditioned "delay" of its origin and the absoluteness – in the sense of the intrinsic unrealizability – of its "passage" through empirically bound language to its *telos*. This delay and passage mean that ideality can only appear in terms of the alterity of its absolute origin, an alterity in which is announced the infinitely deferred *telos* of its absolute presence. Ideality is therefore constituted by the phenomenological apprehension of the infinitude of the "difference" between its equally inaccessible origin (or origins) and its *telos*.

Derrida's account of the impossibility of ideality apprehending the "alterity" of its origin

The transcendental historicity of ideality as both the meaning of historicity and the historicity of meaning does not rule out the question of what Derrida calls *de facto* history but, on the contrary, it prepares the way for asking the question that only Husserl's phenomenology can ask, without, however, being able to provide an answer, namely, "*What is the primordial unity of meaning and fact, a unity which, by themselves alone, neither can account*" (Derrida [1978] 1989: 151)? That only Husserl's phenomenology can ask this question is rooted for Derrida in the pure certainty of its "thought". That it cannot provide an answer to it is rooted in the "interminable disquietude of [its] thought striving to 'reduce' difference" (*ibid.*), to overcome the historicity of ideality and the ideality of history in a manner that would at once chart the infinitude announced by the delay in its origins and the deferral of its *telos* and embrace the singularity of the "Fact" – not the right – of history.

Ideality and "Fact", transcendental historicity and "actual" history, are thus separated according to a necessity whose overcoming for Derrida would be rooted in an impossibility, namely, the impossibility of ideality appropriating the alterity of its origin. That such an appropriation is not necessarily impossible it shall be the burden of the rest of my discussion to call attention to by making two points. The first will concern the phenomenological constitution of ideality, the second the role of crisis in Husserl's formulation of the method of historical reflection generally and specifically the place of the essay "The Origin of Geometry" within the context of the execution of this reflection.

Derrida misses Husserl's twofold account of the problem of the origin of ideality

The phenomenon of ideality, or "irreality",[1] as Husserl also and indeed preferably comes to refer to it, has, as we have seen, two interrelated and interdependent moments: one is the constitution of an object as "*numerically identical*" (Derrida [1978] 1989: 154) across numerically distinct acts of consciousness, the other the constitution of the identical object's "ontic meaning" (*Seinssinn*). At issue in the former is the representation of certain subjective processes wherein the "same" object can – at will – be made evident. In the latter, the intentional explication of the mode of being of the objective identity that is constituted in the subjective representation is at issue. The reason why the term "irreality" is preferable to "ideality" for designating this phenomenon can be easily illustrated. Both a singular physical thing, for instance Husserl's writing desk, and a geometrical object, for instance an equilateral triangle, can be constituted at will as numerically identical objects by my initiating the appropriate acts of representation. However, only one of these identities is "ideal" according to the traditional meaning of that word, namely, in the sense of a non-particular object that does not exist in space and time.[2] They are both, however, "irreal", that is, constituted in acts of representation. It is important to note that Husserl's account in his late work of the essential involvement of language in the constitution of this first moment of irreality mentioned above does not entail its involvement in irreality's second moment. On the contrary, the modes of being of different "irreal" objects, for instance, ideal and formalized mathematical objects, point to the very opposite conclusion. The ideal mode of being of pre-modern mathematical objects and the formalized mode of being of the modern ones is not, in any way, contaminated or otherwise infected by their putative bondage to an empirical *logos*. The ideal being of the number used to count two chickens is "two", no matter what empirical language its being two is expressed in. And the formalized being of the formula $y = mx + b$, in virtue of the very mode of being of its irreality, bypasses completely the empiricity of the symbolic conventions of the "language" – or, more precisely, letter signs – in which it is expressed.

As we have seen, Husserl's articulation of the methodical necessity of a historical reflection back to the origin of modern science (mathematical physics) is inseparable from the account of his personal feeling regarding the unintelligibility of the formalized meaning structures that make modern mathematics possible. Specifically, the symbolic calculational technique inseparable from mathematical formalization is conceptually blind, which is to say "empty" of the kind of meaning that refers to objects in the world and that itself arises from mental concepts. Its epistemic foundation and ontological meaning are therefore incomprehensible to a human existence that still wants to take its cosmic bearings from the intuition of worldly objects and the concepts that are somehow related to these objects. It is thus the crisis precipitated by this double unintelligibility of the meaning formations of modern science that turns Husserl's methodical reflection to the history of the foundational mathematical innovations that make modern natural science possible. Specifically, to the history of the mathematization of nature referred to by the collective noun Galileo, to the historical investigation and reactivation of the intentional constitution of the meaning of nature that the concealing and revealing genius of Galileo accomplished by taking for granted the ideal objects of Euclidean geometry handed down to him by "tradition". And then, finally, it is this crisis that leads to Husserl's fragmentary intentional–historical reflection on the intentional constitution of these ideal objects themselves in the meaning accomplishments of the forever unknown but transcendentally necessary proto-geometer.

Attentiveness to the second moment of "irreality" mentioned above, to its mode of being and therefore to the phenomenological necessity of an intentional investigation of its ontic meaning, is at the basis of Husserl's claim in the *Crisis* texts that, in the case of the ideal objects of science, the intentional history of their constitution is inseparable from the actual history of their origin. That is, accounting for the capacity of acts of representation, mediated by the written word, to constitute the first mentioned moment of irreality, namely, its numerical identity as the same across a multiplicity of temporally individuated acts, does *not* account for its second moment, the specific ontic meaning of the content of its ideal irreality. Hence, to cite a relevant example, a line in Euclidean geometry and the algebraic formula $y = mx + b$ are both irreal meanings. Their irreal modes of being, however, are not only radically different, but this very difference is something that can only be fully accounted for by a historically oriented intentional investigation of the genesis belonging to the meaning structures in question that links up with an actual historical investigation of their origins. Husserl's *Crisis* texts, to be sure, provide only fragments of the intentional–historical investigation necessary to account for the genesis of these radically different meaning structures. But the "small beginning" evident in these texts points the way to a recovery of the origins of ideal meaning structures that Derrida's proto-deconstructive meditation on historicity rejects as being – in principle – impossible.

Derrida's collapse of the problem of the origin of ideality into that of the origin of the objectivity of an intersubjective tradition

The principle behind Derrida's rejection of the possibility of a recovery of the origins of the ideal meanings belonging to science stems from his collapsing all talk of ideality into its first moment mentioned above, that is, into the acts of representation that constitute the irreality of an intentional unity as a numerically identical intentional object. This moment of the constitution of irreality is, as we have just seen, radically different from the all-important moment of the ontic meaning that composes the mode of being of a given irreality's intentional unity. We have seen that Husserl's account of the meaning of historicity and the historicity of meaning not only does not elide this difference, but that the "small beginning" of his last works adumbrates a transcendental-historical method whose goal is to recover the origin of a given moment or moments of the ontic meaning composing ideal irreality.

This adumbration is not visible to Derrida. Consequently, he is unable to see that what he calls the "alterity" of the origin of ideality is not something that necessarily has to remain inaccessible to thought. Indeed, Derrida's very notion of the "alterity" of the origin is suspect precisely because his very claim regarding its inaccessibility presupposes that *his* thought has sufficient access to ideality's origin to be able to rule out certain things about it. Moreover, this notion of Derrida's is suspect because it arises on the basis of his conflation of Husserl's account of the role of language in the constitution of the objectivity belonging to an intersubjective tradition with Husserl's account of the constitution of the ideality proper to the ontic meaning of the ideal irreality that is transmitted by a tradition, such as geometrical science, via its intersubjective objectivity.

Thus, as we have seen, Husserl's claim that the necessity – in order to account for the transcendental constitution of the ideal meaning structures belonging to a science such as geometry – of positing a proto-geometer whose initial anticipations of ideal geometrical meaning structures are fulfilled in geometrical evidence and subsequently available at will in his *intra*subjective representations is different from his claims regarding the necessity of linguistic embodiment for the constitution of a scientific tradition. While these latter claims are indeed concerned with the constitution of the ideality of the objectivity presupposed by the intersubjectivity of a tradition, they presuppose rather than establish the initial *intra*subjective constitution of ideal meaning. And it is the ideality of the latter, which, according to Husserl, has already been constituted before its embodiment in both spoken language and written language, that forms the ontic content that is taken up in an intersubjective ideality and therewith the *original* basis of a tradition that is handed down over the ages.

Derrida's claim that the necessity of linguistic embodiment for the constitution of ideality introduces a "difference" into its being that is as inseparable from this being as it is ineradicable from it is therefore based on the unwitting exchange of what is other than ideality in the sense of *intra*subjective ideality with what is the same as this ideality. That is, Husserl's account of the constitution of the ideality that composes an *inter*subjective tradition is mistaken by Derrida for an account of the *intra*subjective ideality wherein originates the specific ideal content of a given tradition. This exchange is what makes it impossible for Derrida to see that the true *difference* operative in Husserl's late account of ideality is that between precisely these two idealities and their origins. We shall reserve discussion of the extent to which Husserl's adumbrations of this difference in his last writings are sufficient to establish it both phenomenologically and philosophically for our discussion of the transcendental criticism of the criticism of phenomenological cognition.

NINETEEN

The presupposition behind the deconstruction of phenomenology: the subordination of being to speech

As we have seen, Derrida's pre- or proto-deconstructive critique of phenomenology credits Husserl's phenomenology with posing a question about the relation between meaning and fact that it alone (presumably alone among philosophies) can pose, even though it is incapable of providing the answer. The question concerns their "primordial" unity, and Derrida maintains that neither an account limited to meaning nor one limited to facts can by itself answer this question. Neither, however, can both types of an account answer it together, because to answer the question of the unity of meaning and fact would be tantamount to eliminating their difference. The unity at issue here for Derrida is therefore not one of the identity of meaning and fact but of their primordial belonging together despite the opposition that defines their difference. We have also seen that the specifically critical moment of Derrida's proto-deconstructive critique of Husserl is contained in his claim that Husserl's phenomenology nevertheless attempts to eliminate this difference by reducing the infinitude wherein appears the alterity of both the origin and *telos* proper to ideality's historicity to the singularity of an origin in actual historical fact.

Derrida's deconstruction of Husserl's phenomenology also takes issue with its ability to deal with the inseparable alterity belonging to difference. However, at stake in the deconstruction of phenomenology is something far more monumental than identifying the putative dynamic of an unlimited "disquietude" at work in Husserl's late attempt to come to terms with historicity. At issue in its deconstruction is Derrida's attempt to show that the ultimate, and therefore most original, condition of possibility of any phenomenological appearance is itself inseparable from a phenomenon that cannot appear within the conceptuality of Husserl's transcendental phenomenology. The recognition of this, which is to say, the encounter with this phenomenon, like the "gesture" or "strategy" that generates it, is most decidedly not "paradoxical" but, rather, in as precise a sense as what sense it has will admit, "deconstructive". Phenomenology's deconstruction is not paradoxical because what deconstruction desconstructs is precisely the ground that heretofore has made any paradox as such possible, namely, the unity of Being and therewith the identity of its meaning presupposed by "*doxa*" from its ancient Greek inception to Derrida's present. And, according to Derrida, because Husserl's phenomenology brings this unity and identity to consummate clarity, phenomenology's deconstruction coincides with the deconstruction of the tradition it brings to completion. Neither "beside" nor "beyond" the phenomenon it brings to appearance in phenomenology, and not just despite the putative limits of its conceptuality but on the basis of what deconstruction's inventor presents as its rigorous contestation, deconstruction signifies nothing while exposing phenomenology's, and with it, the metaphysics of presence's, significative limit. Deconstruction signifies nothing because any signification whatever has already been determined by what it, deconstruction, purports to contest definitively and thus bring to a closure, namely, the singular limit of the signification *determinative* of metaphysics since its Greek beginning, the interpretation of the infinitive "to be" of Being in "the third person singular of the present indicative" (Derrida 1973: 74).

The focal point of the deconstruction of phenomenology: the absence of a phenomenological account of the sign's power to signify

Whereas Derrida's proto-deconstructive critique of phenomenology presented itself as working within Husserl's intentions, even if, in the end, he gave himself permission to draw conclusions at variance with Husserl's, what is at stake in its deconstruction is so significant that it warrants, on Derrida's view, bypassing its author's intentions. For at stake is the origin of something both infinitely more chthonic than historicity and more singularly irreducible than the ideality of the smallest unit of meaning. In a word, at issue in Derrida's deconstruction of phenomenology is the origin of the sign's power to signify. That this issue is not – as we have seen – a problem for Husserl's phenomenology is not only not beside the point but precisely Derrida's point. The "difference" that plagues phenomenology, Derrida comes to realize, is not exhausted by the difference between the ineluctable empiricity of written language and the demand of the ideality embodied therein for empirical purity, but, rather, it is something originally manifest in the "phenomenological voice" that, by keeping silent, divides its self-presence according to what it supposes is a *pure* difference.

As "pure", this difference is supposed to ensure the immediacy and therefore transparency of that which it divides: the phenomenological self-relation that has methodical priority over the appearance of any object, the appearance of the Being of any object, or the appearance of any meaning whatever. As "voice", this priority is "signitive", which is to say, with Derrida, it "*gives itself*" (*ibid.*: 76) as "the phenomenological and the ideal face of" the signifier. As silent, it is free of empirical signs and the empirical reality signified by them, having instead the status of the "absolute" appearance of the pure possibility of the sign's power, as a "signifier", to signify, together with that of the appearance of the ideality proper to the signified that is inseparable from this power's innermost condition of possibility.

The "purity" of this *pure* difference, however, is anything but, and therein lies the crux of phenomenology's deconstruction. For as the origin of any signification whatever, which, with Derrida, is to say any idealization whatever,[1] the manifest *impurity* of what the phenomenological voice takes to be the *pure* difference of its divided self-presence in "auto-affection", in "hearing oneself speak", *deconstructs* the voice's apparent signification of the pure presence inseparable from its idealizing potency. With this, the *telos* of this potency, which from its ancient Greek inception until its completion in Husserl's transcendental phenomenology had heretofore baptized every notion, thought and concept of the sign with the indelible mark of its origin in "the metaphysics of presence" (*ibid.*: 51), is henceforth "disrupted".

Given what is at stake in these claims, it is not unreasonable to ask exactly how deconstruction makes manifest both the supposition of pure difference and its untenabilty, which is the basis on which the truth of Derrida's claims about Husserl's phenomenology ultimately rest. Heeding deconstruction's fundamental premise that something more original is at stake in Husserl's phenomenology than the intention of its author, we will look not to the letter of Husserl's text for our answer but to what Derrida doubtless thinks such texts, indeed, above all, one such text, adumbrates. The first adumbration, right at the beginning of Husserl's breakthrough phenomenological text, the *Logical Investigations*, is that Husserl's distinction between two meanings of the word "sign", as "expression" and "indication", amounts to the "reduction of indication", in so far as Husserl makes this distinction in order to limit his logical investigations to expressions. Derrida finds this reduction as significant as it is problematical. It is significant because the "possibility of all the reductions to come, be they eidetic or transcendental", and, therefore, the "future problematic of the reduction" together with "all the conceptual differences through which it is pronounced (fact/essence, transcendentality/mundaneity ...) would deploy themselves in a separation between two types of signs" (*ibid.*: 30).

It is problematical, because the reduction of "indication" from linguistic (expressive and therefore discursive) signs is illegitimate, as "we know ... already that, in fact, the discursive sign ... is always ... held in an indicative system; held, that is to say, contaminated" (*ibid.*: 20).

Before looking more closely at the status of the distinction between expression and indication behind the first adumbration, the second adumbration Derrida finds in Husserl's same text bears noting. Husserl's claim that a merely imagined expressive sign in a soliloquy does not communicate but functions solely to facilitate the logical presentations requisite for conceptual thought adumbrates, for Derrida, "against Husserl's express intention", that "the *Vorstellung* [presentation] itself" depends "on the possibility of repetition, and the most simple *Vorstellung*, presentation (*Gegenwärtigen*)", depends "on re-presentation (*Vergegenwärtigung*)" (*ibid.*: 52). For in Husserl's claim that in soliloquy the expressive sign communicates nothing while nevertheless assisting the work of logical presentation, Derrida finds the opening to the reversal of the roles Husserl assigns to presentation and re-presentation, because the expressive sign, albeit as a merely imaginary sign, appears to be recognized by Husserl in soliloquy as functioning to generate presentations. Moreover, this function, being tied to the representative function of the expressive sign – even if imagined – provides still another opening, this time for the *priority* – over the presentation of that which is signified – of this potency proper to the sign to generate, via its "repetition", the signified. Thus, for Derrida, the "sign is never an event", which means that its appearance is not singular but always "implies representation" (*ibid.*: 50).

Derrida's adumbration of the primordial unity of "expression" and "indication" in the texts of phenomenology

Returning now to what is behind Husserl's distinction between expressive and indicative signs, it is beyond dispute that the *ispsissima verba* of the text deconstructed by Derrida do not present this distinction as an answer to the question what is a sign in general. Expression and indication for Husserl are therefore not two kinds of signs unified by the general concept of sign. Rather, it is patent for him that, despite both being called "signs", they *neither* have common features *nor* are conceptually grounded on, or in relation to, one another. An expression, or, more precisely, its *essence* for Husserl, is a whole with two non-independent parts: articulated sounds and an intentional act that instantiates an ideal species. An indication, on the contrary, is, again in *essence*, a motivational relation in which belief in one existent, for example smoke, leads to belief in another, for example fire. Thus, not only do they not have common features, such as "representing something else" or "transcending themselves", but, rather, as Derrida himself recognizes, an expression is a sign that for Husserl has been *purified* of all indication.

Husserl's conclusion, then, that the term "sign" is equivocal, as it is a name to which pertains a "double meaning [*Doppelsinn*]" (LI, 30/269), therefore cannot possibly be accurately construed to presuppose, as Derrida maintains, an unexplored metaphysical assumption of the essence of the sign (cf. 1973: 25–7). And this is the case for the simple reason that for Husserl the essences of expressions and indications are different.

Of course, it is precisely the stability of this essential difference that Derrida not only contests, but also that he maintains breaks down in Husserl's own text. For, on the one hand, the identity of an indicative signifier, no less than an expressive one, "must be formally recognizable", because a sign "can function as a sign, and in general, as language, only if a formal identity enables it to be issued again and to be recognized". Inseparable, then, from this recognition is the realization that a "signifer (in general)" must possess ideality, "the possibility of reproductive repetition in general" (1973: 50). On the other hand, if, in its imagined, non-communicative employment, the expression's representative function deviates from Husserl's standard account of the essence of representation, as the reproductive modification of an ultimately *original* presentation whose mark of originality is manifest precisely in its *non*-reproductive character, then, even in its purest form as an expression, the sign will be implicated in the *difference* between sign and signified characteristic of the indicative sign.

The instability that Derrida thinks he shows here "in" the essential distinctions drawn by Husserl's texts, although not, to be sure, by the conceptuality that draws them, is what is behind his claim that Husserl's account of the sign's "double meaning" presupposes an "unexplored metaphysical assumption of the essence of sign". Among other things, this means that were it possible to show that the indication's empiricity, its signitive embeddedness in factual relations, and the expression's ideality, its signitive instantiation of ideal meaning, were somehow encompassed by a unity responsible for their inseparable signitive belonging together despite their essential differences, then Derrida's claim that Husserl's account of the "double meaning" of sign is undergirded by a metaphysical presupposition would be within hailing distance of being borne out. For all that would be required to show this would be to establish that the metaphysical status of a "signifer in general" is defined precisely by the primordial unity of ideal meaning and Fact, a unity in which is implicated the infinite reiterability inseparable from the phenomenon of ideality and the irreducible singularity determinative of its signitive embodiment.

The "auto-affection" of the phenomenological voice implicates phenomenology in the "metaphysics of presence"

We have seen that Derrida's pre- or proto-deconstructive critique of Husserl credited his phenomenology alone with the capacity to raise the question of this primordial unity and attributed its inability to answer it to the irreducibility of the difference between the terms in opposition. We have seen, too, that Derrida had critically defined Husserl's late phenomenology by its attempt nevertheless to "reduce" this difference to the singularity of a factual origin. Now, with his deconstruction of phenomenology, we see that, for Derrida, Husserl is not alone in the attempt to reduce the difference in question, and that not only does his thought have this in common with metaphysics, but also we see that the *telos* of Husserl's attempt is driven by metaphysics in a manner that transcends his authorial intentions. Metaphysics, then, or, more precisely, the "metaphysics of presence", is what composes this primordial unity of – to use Husserl's terminology – expression and indication. Owing to their irreducibility, this unity is not only unstable, but it is also as impossible to realize in terms of its metaphysical origin as it is in terms of its phenomenological closure.

Derrida returns to Husserl's discussion of soliloquy in order to find the final adumbration in Husserl's text that establishes both the supposition of *pure* difference at the heart of Husserl's phenomenology and, by extension, the metaphysics that determines this phenomenology, together with its untenability in both. By doing so, metaphysics' commitment to presence as the supreme criterion of the Being of anything that is, as well as the impossibility of maintaining the *purity* of the difference that must be presupposed by both metaphysics and phenomenology in the service of this criterion, is exposed with Derrida's deconstruction of the *signitive* conditions of the possibilities of each. Thus in Husserl's allusion to the non-communicative status of soliloquy Derrida finds adumbrated a pure and ideal *semblance* of "speech" (*parole*), in which not just both the signifers, the *phonemes* (meaningful units of sound), but also the signs themselves, signifiers and signifieds, are disconnected from any source in empirical language, in either its conventional signs or real sounds. Rather, as the *pure* appearance of speech, of discourse, and, therefore, of expression, hearing oneself speak "has already suspended the natural attitude and the thesis of the existence of the world" (1973: 78). It is this suspension operative in auto-affection that is responsible for both the appearance that phenomenological propinquity is ensured by the voice as well as that this appearance itself manifests the sign's pure possibility as *self-presence*. That the supposition that the voice's auto-affection "would" suppose, in order to ensure this self-presence, namely, that the difference between its speaking and hearing itself speak is *pure*, is a supposition that is untenable, is made manifest by what Derrida calls "the movement of *différance*" (*ibid.*: 82). Specifically, what is made manifest is that the *pure* difference supposed by the voice cannot be seized "in its identity, nor its purity, nor its origin", because "[it] has none of these" (*ibid.*).

The impurity of the difference supposed to be pure by the phenomenological voice has its source in "*différance*"

Within the context of Derrida's deconstruction of Husserl's phenomenology, "*différance*" signals the impossibility of the "the possibility of all one believes able to exclude from auto-affection", that is, "space, outside, world, body ..." ([1978] 1989: 82). And this impossibility, for Derrida, is not rooted in anything extrinsic to Husserl's phenomenology but precisely in the *phenomenological* voice's pure appearance, which, as the pure signitive condition of possibility for all transcendentally reduced appearances, is also the condition of possibility for the impossibility of maintaining these appearances in their purity. For its (the voice's) supposition that the *difference* between its pure speaking and pure hearing of itself speak is marked by the pellucidity of the *phenomenon* of its auto-affection breaks down as soon as that which it has excluded in order to "affect-itself" reappears with its *talk* about all objects, including its talk about itself as absolute consciousness. The conclusion is therefore inevitable: "no pure transcendental reduction is possible" (*ibid.*).

Independent of the answer to the question of the fidelity of Derrida's interpretation of phenomenology to its original, which, as we have seen, is a red herring, given deconstruction's fundamental premise that something more original is at stake in Husserl's phenomenology than the intention of its author, two problems nevertheless render null and void phenomenology's putative deconstruction. The first, and more serious, is that the metaphysics of presence as a Greek phenomenon is an invention of Heidegger, the source of which, we have seen, is his projection of Husserl's discovery of categorial intuition back into the Greeks. The second, and related, problem – which is less serious only because, absent the legitimacy of the historical context within which to frame the self-importance of its "auto-affection", the deconstruction of phenomenology, perhaps not in the hands of Derrida but certainly in the hands of others, is continually in danger of becoming a joke – is the following: the notion that the functioning of the voice, "lived as absolutely pure auto-affection" (1973: 79), manifests not speech but its *semblance*, cannot withstand critical scrutiny if it is attributed to the Greek metaphysics that Derrida, following Heidegger, apparently thought could be exhausted in its essence without taking into account Aristotle's dispute with Plato over the true manner of being of the *eidē*.

These two problems, of course, are not unrelated. Derrida not only follows Heidegger, as mentioned, in maintaining that the fundamental limit of Husserl's phenomenology is predetermined by the historical precedent of the Greek understanding of the meaning of Being as presence, but he further situates this limit in terms of its interrelated sources in "logocentrism" and "phonocentrism". By the former, Derrida understands the interpretation of language that privileges speech, that is, the capacity to say something about something and thereby provide what, we have of course already seen, its Greek innovators called a "*logos*", an "account". By the latter, he understands the privileging of the *phone* (sound, voice) as the medium of signification over all others, a privileging that, because of its privileging of speech, is inseparable from "logocentrism". Derrida's deconstruction of the phenomenological voice purports to show both of these "centrisms" at work in determining the limit of Husserl's phenomenology. And, by tying them to the historical predetermination of Western metaphysics, Derrida is committed to the presupposition of their role in determining the limit of Greek metaphysics as well.

The absence of the phenomenological voice in Plato's portrayal of *logos*

We need look no further than Plato's portrayal in *logos* of the Stranger and Theaetetus' *logos* about the relation between thinking and speech in the *Sophist*, mentioned above, to see that an adumbration here of something along the order of the "pure phenomenological" voice Derrida claims to find in Husserl is out of the question. As we have seen, "thinking" (*dianoia*) and "speech" (*logos*) are the same for Plato, in the sense that they have the same *genos*, but for one exception: thinking occurs without voice, as the soul's inner conversation (*dialogos*) with itself, while speech flows through the mouth in a vocal stream. Speech, for Plato, therefore, can no more be the expression of thinking than thinking can privilege speech, *because* their *genos*, their origin together with their looks (*eidos*) is the same, in virtue of each belonging to the same *genos*. Of course, they are not the same in the sense of being identical and therefore indistinguishable, but, rather, they are the same in the sense that they share a structural commonality, and do so, moreover, in spite of the recognition of the one difference between them: thinking is speech without voice while speech is thinking made vocal.

Even *if* this account of thinking and speech could be construed as privileging voiceless speech over its embodiment in sounds – and there is absolutely no evidence in Plato's texts to support such an interpretation – the status of voiceless speech in Plato simply cannot be understood, as Derrida understands the phenomenological voice in Husserl, as the *pure* appearance, and, therefore, the *semblance* of expression. For, as we have seen, *both* voiceless and uttered speech are engaged for Plato in assertion and denial, and, moreover, when both kinds of speech share the *genos* of opinion (*doxa*), their assertions and denials, their expressions, as it were, are called by that name. This means, among other things, as we have seen, that for Plato both voiceless and uttered speech can appear as a semblance, that is, can appear to be what they, in truth, are *not*. The one *logos*, the voiceless, is therefore decidedly not the *appearance* of the other, the uttered *logos*; both, rather, are emphatically "*logos*", speech, for Plato. Thus, contrary to Derrida's interpretation of the *pure* phenomenological voice – whose appearance as well as purity is calibrated in relation to the positing of the impurity of an empirical voice, that is, a voice embedded in language's empiricity, its conventional words and *phonetic* manifestation – Plato's voiceless speech is neither more pure nor less empirical than uttered speech. The category of "the empirical" posited in these terms neither exists nor can possibly make any sense within the context of Plato's thought.

Deconstruction's most basic, and unwarranted, presupposition: the subordination of being to speech in Greek philosophy

Only by recognizing what we have already shown in this connection, that the fundamental meaning of *logos* for Greek philosophy is speech, and that for speech to be speech it need not be uttered, can Plato's discussion of voiceless and uttered speech make sense. Derrida's claim that Greek philosophy privileges speech in its interpretation of language therefore amounts to the claim that Greek philosophy privileges speech in its interpretation of speech. Such a claim, then, can be based only in the unwitting exchange of what Plato's arithmological account of the *eidē* identifies as the Other and the Same, the two *genē* that manifest the *archai* of the *genos* Being. For the very notion of a logocentric interpretation of speech in Greek philosophy takes, as we have just shown, what is the same, namely speech, and treats it as something other, namely its logocentric interpretation. And we have shown that for the Plato that emerges when the controversy over the proper manner of being of *eidē* is taken into account, this exchange is at the root of all tautologies.

It is also worth mentioning in this connection that Plato's Socrates' privileging of spoken *logos* over written *logos* makes sense only in connection with the account of *logos* in the *Sophist*. For just as uttered speech cannot be understood to have in Plato the status of the expression of voiceless speech, since voiceless speech, as speech, is already inseparable from expression, so, too, written *logos* cannot be understood as the expression of spoken *logos*, because, as written, it is no longer fundamentally *speech*, but its *imitation*. The hierarchy here is one of image and original, and, indeed, of a second-order image, because, as we have seen, speech itself for Plato already has the *eidos* of an image.

The unwitting exchange of the two most fundamental *genē* of Plato's arithmological account of the *eidē* that we have found embedded in Derrida's expressions about the being of *logos* in Greek metaphysics points to the fundamental presupposition that we can now identify as underlying deconstruction: the subordination of Being to speech. As we have seen for Plato, the arithmological account of the *eidē* rules out precisely the priority of speech over Being, for the simple but profound reason that the kind of unity that functions as the most fundamental presupposition of speech itself is recognized by Plato, at so-called metaphysics' inception, as forever falling short of the unity responsible for the belonging together, the community, of the five greatest *genē*. And it is so recognized precisely because of the role that one *genos*, the Other, plays not only as one of the two original sources of Being, but, also, in the Not-Being and falsehood that is inseparable from the very manner of being, from the *eidos*, which is to say, from the invisible looks that are responsible for *logos*, speech, appearing as it *is* in the *dialectical* investigation of its being (*on*).

EPILOGUE

Transcendental-phenomenological criticism of the criticism of phenomenological cognition

As we have seen, Husserl's call for a phenomenological criticism of the criticism of phenomenological cognition occurs within the context of the third stage of the development of his phenomenology, and it refers to the critical reflection on the presuppositions that inform the "naïveté of apodicticity" belonging to the "Cartesian" character of this stage of his phenomenology. This naivety, characterized by Husserl as the methodically necessary limit of the "first" phase of phenomenological cognition to determine the scope and limits of phenomenological evidence at the expense of attending to its mode of givenness, is, as we have also seen, addressed by the fragmentary investigation of the historicity of the givenness of phenomenological cognition that composes the last stage of Husserl's thought.

As the interrelated moments of primal accomplishment and eventual sedimentation of the meaning that makes possible the handing down, over generations, of a science such as geometry, Husserl's adumbration of historicity reveals its essential structure to consist in precisely the intentionality that connects these two moments. These moments, in turn, are accessible to phenomenological cognition only in a historically motivated phenomenological reflection whose intentionality enquires *backwards* from its reflected object to the original acts of transcendental subjectivity responsible for its constitution. The movement of the intentionality belonging to this "backwards reflection" thus charts a course from its reflected object's *irreal* meaning, which is given in the living present of the experience belonging to the transcendental Ego as a "numerically identical" unit of meaning across the multiplicity of its temporally individuated lived-experiences, to the "reactivation" of the evidence-giving acts belonging to the experience of a possible transcendental Ego that are presupposed by this meaning. The explicitly *historical* character of this reflection emerges with the critical recognition that the evidence necessary to justify the cognitive foundation proper to the *irreality* of a given unity of meaning constituted in the manifold of discrete lived-experiences is unavailable to the epistemically motivated and informed reflection charged with the task of providing just such a justification. It is precisely the unavailability of the evidence requisite to secure the foundation of meaning in the case of a science that Husserl characterizes as this evidence's being "sedimented" in this very meaning. And it is likewise precisely the "desedimenting" enquiry in search of this evidence that manifests for Husserl the *historicity* proper to the mode of givenness of phenomenological cognition.

By way of a conclusion to this introduction to Husserl's thought, I shall point out that the incompleteness of Husserl's concrete investigations directed to the desedimentation of Galilean physics and the origin of Euclidean geometry nevertheless leaves intact the phenomenological and philosophical legitimacy of the "small beginning" Husserl credited them with on his deathbed. As mentioned, these investigations involve the methodical extension of the epistemological quest for foundations to desedimentation of the historicity connected with the primal establishment of the foundations responsible for a given science. And, in concert with this, I shall identify the philosophical superiority of Husserl's phenomenology over Heidegger's conception of ontology as phenomenology and Derrida's deconstruction of phenomenology on the following crucial point: that Husserl's method alone is able to identify presuppositions in both its cognitive claims and the principles behind these claims and to adjust both accordingly in a manner consistent with its overriding commitment to the principle of philosophy as rigorous science. Neither Heidegger's hermeneutical method nor Derrida's deconstructive interventions can overcome their presuppositions, and this for the simple but profound reason that they are inseparable from what we have shown is an interpretation of ancient Greek ontology that elides the controversy between Plato and Aristotle over the proper mode of being of the *eidē*. As we have seen, the failure to appreciate the fundamental difference between the status of *eidē* in Plato and Aristotle, as well as the related restriction of *eidē* in Plato to Plato's Socratic account of them, limits the cognitive status of both Heidegger's and Derrida's accounts of the ancient Greek ontology supposedly determining Husserl's phenomenology to little more than a superficial and facile myth.

Of course, from the fact that Heidegger's and Derrida's criticisms of phenomenological cognition in Husserl attribute to it a historically determined limit and construe this limit in a historically implausible way, it neither follows that phenomenological cognition as Husserl conceived it is not historically determined nor that its method is in a better position than these critiques to construe its own historical preconditions – should these be somehow established as in some way relevant to its cognition. The superiority of Husserl's method, rather, has its basis in its commitment to the principle of presuppositionlessness, its pursuit of this principle in pure reflection, and the directedness of its cognitive intention to evidence that is intuitive and essential. While much maligned, once liberated from their spurious source in the equally spurious ontology of presence and logocentricism of ancient Greek metaphysics, and as operative in the final stage of Husserl's development of phenomenology, these principles are capable of both disclosing its most basic presuppositions and pointing phenomenological research in the direction of their overcoming.

In the final stage of its phenomenological development, the principle of presuppositionlessness is manifest in the transcendental-historical project of desedimentation, pure reflection assumes the guise of the historical reflection that drives this project, and essential intuition is charged with the task of delineating the *a priori* proper to both the historicity of the intentionality belonging to the desedimented meaning and to the reactivated acts originally responsible for its constitution. While in Husserl's own development of phenomenology the transcendental-historical project of desedimentation was not directed to phenomenology itself, there is not only nothing in principle to preclude this, but also such a self-critique is a consistent and therefore legitimate extension of the phenomenological principle of transcendental criticism of phenomenological cognition. Indeed, on the capacity to execute just such a critique hinges the answer to the question of whether Husserl's phenomenology warrants not only the mantle of rigorous science, but also that of rigorous philosophical science.

As we have seen, Husserl's own account of phenomenologically historical reflection is connected to his encounter with the limits of phenomenologically foundational epistemological reflection to account for the constitution of certain meaning fundaments of modern science. We have also seen that his initial recognition of these limits was not a matter of methodical exactitude but rather, in Husserl's own words, "a feeling of obscurity that asserts itself" concerning the epistemological grounding of mathematical physics. Precisely this feeling is what initiated the zigzag course of phenomenologically historical reflection, from the presently ungrounded meaning fundaments of modern science, backwards to the historically datable discoveries that yielded these fundaments, and then forwards again to these fundaments, then back again, and so on, in order to clarify their meaning by explicating the conditions of possibility of its historically original constitution.

The necessity of desedimenting multiplicity and unity as the meaning fundaments of phenomenological cognition

Thanks to Husserl's adumbration of the method of historical reflection and desedimentation, we do not have to rely on our feelings to detect the obscurity of the meaning fundaments of his phenomenology, as we are in a position to manifest this obscurity by using Husserl's own method as a guide. The meaning fundaments we have in mind are those that are presupposed by each of the four stages of Husserl's phenomenology, namely, multiplicity (*Mannigfaltigkeit*) and unity as they function in his account of the constitution of the appearance and appearances of what appears. As we have seen, from the initial to the final stage of the development of his thought, Husserl describes the phenomena of meaning and being, which is to say, their respective appearances, as unities that are constituted through multiplicities. Moreover, he also characterizes as a unity the concrete transcendental Ego in its function as the constitutive source of all the multiplicities through which the unities of the appearances of meaning and being appear. Finally, according to Husserl, the essential structure, the *eidos*, of the unity proper to what appears, as well as of the unity responsible for generating the multiplicities wherein appears the appearance of what appears, is itself as a unity that appears through a multiplicity.[1]

The obscurity of multiplicity and unity as the meaning fundaments of phenomenological cognition manifests itself when Husserl's most developed account of the evidence in which the unity of the *irreal* object is constituted is considered. As we have seen, he characterizes it as "numerical", in the precise sense of its constitution as a *numerically identical* meaning that is immanent to a multiplicity of temporally individuated lived-experiences. As numerically identical, the *irreal* object *appears* as one and the same in more than one discrete lived-experience, which is to say, the evidence for its *unity* is its *being seen* as such by a *seeing* that is dispersed in a *multiplicity* while nevertheless remaining *unitary*. Thus, for Husserl, both the *being seen* of the *irreal* object and its *seeing* are given in evidences that he characterizes as *numerical*, in the precise sense of each, albeit in different modes, *appearing* as the unity of a multiplicity.

The obscurity in this account that we wish to call attention to does *not* concern Husserl's description of numerical identity as a unity that encompasses a multiplicity but rather his attribution of this *kind* of unity to the *constitution* of the objective *being seen* of the *irreal* object as well as to the subjective *seeing* in which it is constituted. According to Husserl's own account of the matter, what he calls the "ontic meaning" (*Seinssinn*) of the *irreal* object, that is, the formations of meaning that are inseparable from its phenomenological mode of being, is not necessarily numerical. This means, minimally, that the evidence in which the non-numerical meanings that compose the ontic meaning of the *irreal* object cannot be exhausted by and therefore must exceed any numerical character that it may exhibit. Hence "*irreality*" has for Husserl two interrelated and interdependent moments: one is an object's constitution as numerically identical across numerically distinct acts of consciousness, the other the constitution of the object's characteristic ontic meaning. At issue in the former aspect of *irreality* is the representation of certain subjective processes wherein the "same" object can – at will – be made evident. In the latter aspect of *irreality*, the intentional explication of the phenomenological mode of being of the objective identity that is given in the subjective representation is at issue. And unless the objective identity of an *irreal* object is itself numerical, its phenomenological mode of being, which is to say, its "ontic meaning", is manifestly *not* numerical. In connection with this, it is extremely important to recall that Husserl's account of the ontic meaning of the *irreal* object in the final stage of phenomenology's development explicitly links its constitution to an "origin in an accomplishment" that "must have had a historical beginning". Thus Husserl can say, "Science, and in particular, geometry, with this sense of being, must have had a historical beginning; this meaning itself must have an origin in an accomplishment" (OG, 367/358).

That this obscurity in the meaning fundaments of phenomenology as Husserl formulated it contains sedimented evidences in need of desedimentation can be seen by recalling the main point of focus in Aristotle's dispute with Plato over the proper manner of being of the *eidē*. The point in contention concerns precisely the issue we have just called attention to in these meaning fundaments, namely, the proper relation of mathematical, or, better, arithmetical, unity to the unity belonging to *irreal* objects, which is to say with these ancient Greeks no less than with Husserl, to *eidē*.

That Husserl's thought has the resources neither of his prominent critics has to address its most fundamental presuppositions while still maintaining its integrity can be seen by attending to the fact that the project of their desedimentation remains phenomenological notwithstanding its necessary departure from Husserl's own self-understanding of phenomenology. Neither Heidegger's ontological reformation of phenomenology nor Derrida's deconstruction of it are capable of something similar with respect to their most basic presuppositions. As we have seen, Heidegger himself recognized the failure of his attempt to establish phenomenologically his most fundamental philosophical presupposition: that only as ontology is philosophy possible, on the basis of a hermeneutical reformulation of ontology as phenomenology. For once he encountered the mereological presupposition of the hermeneutics of Dasein, that entities and Being are something *other* than the meaning wherein Dasein interprets the intelligibility of entities and the meaning of Being, Heidegger realized he had to abandon the project of grounding universal ontology within the horizon of the fundamental ontology of Dasein. And while Derrida himself, as we have seen, apparently remained convinced that his deconstruction of Husserl's phenomenology rests solely on the presuppositions proper to it (Husserl's phenomenology), once the presuppositions guiding Derrida's reading of ancient Greek philosophy are exposed as unsupportable, the deconstruction of the historical determination of Husserl's phenomenology by the supposed *metaphysics of presence* is arrested.

The resources that maintain the integrity of Husserl's phenomenology despite the critique of the most basic meaning fundaments pertaining to phenomenological cognition are precisely those that bring about the recognition of unwarranted presuppositions within the context of its philosophical commitment to presuppositionlessness. Crucial in this respect are both phenomenologically *pure* reflection, that is, reflection driven by the epistemic goal of providing *evidence* for all cognitive claims, including the claims made by phenomenological cognition, and the commitment to articulating this evidence in a principled manner, that is, in an intuition that is eidetic. The recognition that Husserl's articulation – in terms of numerical identity – of eidetic intuition, of the seeing and being seen of an *eidos*, harbours sedimented evidence requires, in addition to awareness of the mentioned obscurity in his account of the relation between numerical and eidetic units of meaning, significant knowledge of the foundational texts in the philosophical tradition to which Husserl belongs that contain the origin of eidetic cognition. Because, as we have shown, these texts document a controversy over the proper manner of being of *eidē* that is more or less coincident with the primal establishment of eidetic cognition in the Western philosophical tradition, desedimenting the sedimentation of this controversy in Husserl's account of eidetic cognition will necessarily involve phenomenology in the controversy. Indeed, phenomenology has quite a lot at stake in resolving this controversy, if possible, because of the fundamentality and priority that Husserl, in his role as the founder of phenomenology, assigned to eidetic cognition for phenomenology's status not only as a new science, but as a philosophy with the cognitive aspiration of rigorous science.

It is, of course, beyond the scope of any introduction to Husserl's thought to undertake the truly foundational and most originary task of desedimenting, to the end of resolving, the evidence of the ancient controversy over the true being of the *eidē* that we have shown is sedimented in this thought's most basic phenomenological presuppositions. Instead, it will be sufficient for our purposes to call attention to two salient features connected with the necessity of this task. The first is that the original appearance that composes unity as well as the original appearances that compose multiplicity are, in the most rigorous phenomenological sense, inseparable from their *historicity*, when the latter is understood as Husserl understood it, namely as the desedimentation of the meanings sedimented in the meaning fundaments of a science. Second, the possibility of resolving the controversy over the true being of these original appearances, which is to say, the possibility of mediating the historicity of this controversy to the end of eliminating its mediation through historicity, hinges on the appearance of a criterion for distinguishing the truth and falsehood of appearances that would resolve a second matter that we have seen was in dispute between Plato and Aristotle, namely, that of the role of the *phantasma* in the *appearance* of the truth of that which *is*.

Historicity's inseparability from the appearance of unity and multiplicity is manifest to phenomenological reflection the moment it *combines* its present awareness of the obscurity of the relation between mathematical unity and multiplicity and eidetic unity and multiplicity in the meaning fundaments of Husserl's formulation of phenomenology with its attempt to *reactivate* the different and conflicting accounts of their true manner of being in Plato and Aristotle. The *recollective* combination (*Verbindung*) that results from this yields the *appearance* of the obscurity of the meaning fundaments in question within the horizon of the *appearance* – to the extent that it is currently reactivated – of the controversy between Plato and Aristotle. And, with this *appearance*, the zigzag movement of historical phenomenological reflection is initiated, whereby the evidence sedimented in the meaning fundaments in question is gradually desedimented and thereby brought to evidence in a manner that clarifies their present obscurity on the basis of the reactivated *original* evidences in Plato and Aristotle.

On the basis of our provisional discussion of the different and conflicting accounts in Plato and Aristotle of these matters, the initial historicity of the appearance of the relation between mathematical and eidetic unity and multiplicity will appear within the horizon of Plato's account of the arithmological (but not, strictly speaking, mathematical) character of eidetic unity and Aristotle's account of its ultimate basis in sense perception. Depending on whether precedence is given to one or the other of these accounts, eidetic unity will *appear* to originate in either a thinking from which all connection to sensible *appearances* (*phantasmata*) has been eliminated (as it does in Plato) or it will *appear* to originate in a thinking illuminated by *appearances* (*phantasmata*) that are most intimately connected with sense perception (as it does in Aristotle). Because Husserl's account of the *origin* of eidetic unity clearly involves appeals to both an abstractive origin that is based in sense perception as well as an ideative origin that prescinds from and imaginatively varies sense perception, his account of its origin doubtless involves an obscurity whose focus is not unrelated to Plato's and Aristotle's historically original and conflicting accounts of the truth of the matter. When faced with this relation, the conclusion becomes unavoidable that the mode of givenness of the meaning fundament "appearance" in Husserl's formulation of phenomenology is itself likewise inseparable from its historicity. And, to the extent that Husserl's perceptual and non-perceptual accounts of the origin of eidetic unity point to an obscurity in his formulation of the meaning of "appearance", sedimented evidences in this formulation in need of desedimentation will be signalled by phenomenology's guiding principle of presuppositionlessness.

Truth and falsehood as appearances and the appearance of truth and falsehood: beyond metaphysics?

Finally, to the extent that truth and falsehood are inseparable from both the *appearances* of meaning and being and *their* – truth's and falsehood's – appearance in Husserl's formulation of phenomenology, Plato's and Aristotle's controversy over the *corrigibility* of the *phantasm*, whether sedimented or not in Husserl's formulation of phenomenological truth, cannot but be recognized as fundamentally crucial to Husserl's formulation of the phenomenological theory of reason. For, on the one hand, the original incorrigibility of the *phantasm*, in the sense of its *appearance* rendering faithfully the truth or falsity of what *is* through the sense perception in which it originates, guarantees that *phantasmata* having their origin in true sense perceptions will themselves present true appearances of that which *is*. While, on the other hand, the *phantasm*'s original corrigibility, in the sense that the restriction of the *appearance* of that which *is* to its appearance in sense perception (that is, to the *phantasm*), will definitively rule out the *phantasm* from ever presenting true appearances of that which *is*.

We have seen that Husserl's formulation of the phenomenological *epochē* presupposes this first, Aristotelian, account of the *phantasm* and therefore that the most fundamental status of the *appearance* in his formulation of phenomenology follows Aristotle. Whether, however, Husserl's Aristotelian account of the fundamental status of *appearance* in phenomenology would be able to hold up to the Platonic critique of the *phantasm*'s intrinsic corrigibility – whether, in other words, the putative truth of Husserl's *phenomenological* account of the *phantasm* is immune from a *metaphysical* critique rooted in Plato – would seem to hinge on the following: whether phenomenology, post Husserl, is able to resolve the controversy between Plato and Aristotle over the true manner of being of *eidē*, and, if it is able to do so, precisely how it would resolve it. For, on the one hand, a Platonic resolution of the controversy would not only mean that eidetic unity has been established to have its origin in something *other* than sense perception, but, also, that this unity is, likewise, *other* than arithmetical unity, notwithstanding its inseparability from multiplicity. From this, among other things, it would follow that the Aristotelian character of the incorrigibility of the original *appearance* in Husserl's formulation of phenomenology as *phantasm* would need to be abandoned in favour of the Platonic character of the corrigibility of the original *appearance*, its corrigibility stemming from its always, in principle, *questionable* manifestation by *logos*. On the other hand, an Aristotelian resolution would leave intact Husserl's formulation of the originality of appearance as *phantasm* but mean, among other things, that his account of the fundamental connection between multiplicity and the appearance of eidetic unity would have to be abandoned.

However post-Husserl Husserlian phenomenology works out these issues, one thing should be apodictically apparent by now: that even though Husserl's formulation of phenomenology is neither driven by an ontologically deficient metaphysics nor somehow representative of the completion of metaphysics *per se*, the philosophical vitality of phenomenology as rigorous science remains in no way *beyond* the original controversy that defines metaphysics' origin in the Western tradition of philosophy.

CODA
Phenomenological self-responsibility and the singularity of transcendental philosophy

Husserl's methodical reliance on *reflection* for philosophical purposes is clearly out of fashion. Apart from the enduring negative influences of the hermeneutical critique of consciousness and phenomenology's deconstruction, the main reason for this is rooted in the assumption that reflection *per se*, and therefore phenomenological reflection, is somehow a pejoratively modern, specifically Cartesian, phenomenon. Thus Husserl's careful description of the difference between modern inner perception as *introspection* and phenomenological reflection as an *immanent* but in no way *inner* – in contradistinction to *outer* – perception remains unreflected today. And it does so in direct proportion to the prevalence of the unwarranted supposition that phenomenological reflection is unable to escape the bounds of consciousness and engage the world, because of its putative world-transcendence-defying *turn inwards* as *inner perception*.

As we have seen, not only is phenomenological reflection capable of accounting for the *evidence* in which the transcendence of the world is given, but, also, in the final stage of its development, it effectively transcends – in the guise of historical recollection – the scope and limits that Husserl himself assigned to it in what we have called the third stage of phenomenology's development. In the latter stage of development, reflection, as recollection, is "Cartesian" in the precise sense that the recollective *reawakening* of passive contents currently beyond the reach of consciousness is described by Husserl as something that recollective reflection is capable of generating *at will*. In phenomenology's final stage, the limit of the wilful reactivating of contents once present to consciousness and now beyond its grasp is not only reached, but also actively embraced by Husserl as a specifically historical recollection.

Husserl's connection of sedimentation with *forgetfulness* – "sedimentation is always somehow forgetfulness" is how he puts it – means that phenomenology's historical reflection is driven by the intention of reflecting something *other* than what is reflected in the sedimented evidence that the reflective critique of its own cognition has made manifest. This intention, like the critique that generates it, is *cognitive*, and so, too, therefore, is the intentional relation it seeks to establish by reactivating the sedimented origin that it confronts – in its forgetfulness – in front of its very regard. Overcoming this forgetfulness is not only necessarily beyond the direct power of the will, but also beyond the scope of exact methodical intervention. For all that, however, the intention directed towards the sedimented origin remains not only cognitive, but also *transcendentally* cognitive, in so far as it and *it alone* is capable of responding to the sedimented *telos* of philosophy in the Western tradition at stake in this origin: the commitment, before all decisions, to the singularity of truth and therefore to the unity of the *one* philosophy that serves it. Husserl, perhaps more than any other twentieth-century philosopher, realized that absent this singularity and unity, philosophy is consigned not only to multiplicity but also to the oblivion that necessarily follows the absence of its (multiplicity's) limit.

Notes

Prolegomenon

1. Edmund Husserl in a conversation reported by Adelgundis Jaegerschmid, OSB, in 1936. See A. Jaegerschmid, "Conversations with Edmund Husserl, 1931–1938", Marcus Brainard (trans.) [hereafter *Conversations*], *New Yearbook for Phenomenology and Phenomenological Philosophy* **1** (2001), 331–50, esp. 340.
2. Husserl's 1913 book *Ideas I* includes the subtitle "A General Introduction to Pure Phenomenology". The 1931 French translation of his Paris lecture likewise includes "introduction" in its subtitle: "Introduction to Phenomenology", as does the *Cartesian Meditations* ("An Introduction to Phenomenology") and the *Crisis* ("An Introduction to Phenomenological Philosophy").
3. Husserl's "The Vienna Lecture" is published in English translation in the *Crisis*, Appendix A, 269–99.
4. Edmund Husserl to Arnold Metzger, 4 September 1919, in Schuhmann (1994), 407–14, esp. 413–14.
5. David Carr, "Translator's Introduction", in *Crisis*, xxxvii.
6. "*Energeia*" is derived from the Greek neuter adjective "*energon*", meaning "at work right now". Its traditional Latinized translation as "actuality", as the state or condition of acting or doing, obscures both the immediacy as well as "concreteness" of an *eidos*'s manner of "being-at-work", which is always working on some "material" (*hulē*), the "product" of which is always something single.

Chapter 1: Plato's Socratic theory of eidē: the first pillar of the ancient precedent to pure phenomenology

1. Both "*noēsis*" and "*nous*" will be left untranslated here and throughout the text because of the inherent difficulty in translating their general and more specific meanings for Plato and Aristotle and because Husserl will adopt "*noēsis*" as a technical term in his phenomenology.
2. Number (*arithmos*) in the ancient Greek context is a multitude of perceptible or intelligible "ones". Two is therefore the first number and "one", which (when originally combined in counting) composes the parts of each number, is not a number (because it is not a multitude) but the *archē* (source) of number. Because each single number is

composed of an exact amount of "ones", it appears to the soul as both one and many, and thus as a mixture of opposites.

3. Socrates' distinction here between numbers with "visible or tangible bodies" and the sort that "only admit of being thought" illustrates a peculiarity of the ancient Greek concept of number most probably introduced by Plato, namely, that the nature of the things that compose a number's multitude can be things perceived through the senses or things that cannot be sensibly perceived but only apprehended in thought. Hence the numbers that number sensible things are understood in the passage here to be composed of visible and tangible beings, while those that can only be thought are understood to be composed of intelligible beings.

Chapter 2: Plato's arithmological theory of eidē: the second pillar of the ancient precedent to pure phenomenology

1. "*Genē*" is the plural of "*genos*", which is derived from "*gignesthai*", meaning coming to be and being born. "*Genos*" means both a group whose members share a kinship through birth (family) or generation (tribe) and the "common look" (*eidos*) characteristic of their members. "*Genos*" is therefore often employed by Plato in a way that is interchangeable with "*eidos*", although in his dialogue titled *Sophist* the "greatest *genē*" are more often referred to as "*genē*" than "*eidē*". While this dialogue lays the philosophical foundation for the technical distinction between their Latin translations "genus" and "species", this distinction is not at work in the dialogue.
2. Being is "many" in the sense that the *genē* other than Being *are* by virtue of their community with the *genos* Being. Being is "one" by virtue of it *not* being either these *genē* or sensible things, both multitudes of which nevertheless *are* in virtue of their "partaking" in Being, albeit in different ways.
3. When the soul forms an opinion about something that fails to keep distinct two things that, respectively, have the looks of the Same and the Other, its opinion is "contradictory". Contradiction, therefore, is an error based on the identification of the Same and the Other.
4. When the soul forms an opinion that aims to keep distinct things that have the look of the Same and those that have the look of the Other, but, nevertheless, unwittingly takes what has the look of the Other for what has the look of the Same, its opinion is "mistaken". A mistake, therefore, is an error based on the confusion that takes the Other for the Same.
5. When the soul forms an opinion that again aims to keep distinct things that have the look of the Same and those the look of the Other, but, notwithstanding this, unwittingly takes what has the look of the Same to have the look of the Other, its opinion is "tautologous". Tautology, therefore, is an error based on the confusion that takes the Same for the Other.
6. The Socratic "dialogue" that first shows that sensing is not knowledge is not, strictly speaking, a philosophical dialogue, because the very fact that Socrates' interlocutor in such a dialogue is in need of being shown the necessity of making this presupposition is a sign that his interlocutor's dialogue is not philosophical.
7. The purpose at hand is "catching" the sophist by establishing that it is possible to say and opine what *is not*, and therefore to speak falsely, in order to refute the sophist's claim that Not-Being cannot be in community with speech.
8. It is significant to note that the names and verbs – "with whom I am now conversing" – that make this speech longer when measured by the standard of speech's most basic unit speak about and therefore manifest precisely that aspect of speech characterized by

Plato as its most basic necessity. That is, they manifest speech's being "about something" and they do so by making patent that this speech is about Theaetetus.

Chapter 3: Aristotle's criticism of Plato's theory of eidē: the third (and final) pillar of the ancient precedent to pure phenomenology

1. See Chapter 1, note 2.
2. The standard translation of "*ousia*" as "substance", which is derived from the Latin "*substantia*", meaning "standing under", not only fails to capture in English Aristotle's meaning, but actually distorts it, in so far as it invites understanding "*ousia*" exclusively and therefore incompletely in terms its "material" (*hulē*) component.
3. See Chapter 1, note 3.
4. Aristotle's references to a "heap" in connection with the question of the being of number are embedded in discussions that do not explicitly claim that number is like a heap. Rather, in each case number being "like a heap" is presented as the conclusion that follows if number is "not one" (*Metaph.* H 3, 1044a5), or not "a whole that is something over and above the parts" (1044a10), or "not some one thing [*hen ti*]" (M 8, 1084b21). Aristotle, however, is clearly intent on establishing that the manner of being of numbers, as a mathematical thing, is "derivative" (M 2, 1077a19–20) in the sense that its being does not "take precedence over sensible things" (1077a17–18), and, therefore, that "they are not capable of being somewhere as separate" (1077b14–15). That from numbers' incapacity to have being in this regard it follows for Aristotle that "each is not one but is like a heap" (H 3, 1044a4) can be seen as the positive result of his polemic against those people who speak of numbers as being one in the sense that thinghood (*ousia*) is one. Thinghood is not one "in the way they say it is, as though it were a unit or point, but each independent thing [*ousia*] is a complete being-at-work-staying-itself [*entelecheia*], and a particular nature [*phusis*]" (1044a7–9); and number for Aristotle is manifestly not one in this sense of an independent thing. Thus, when Aristotle asserts that "it is necessary to a number that there be something by means of which it is one" (1044a2–3), he immediately qualifies this assertion (following Ross's and not Jaeger's text of the *Metaphysics*) by adding, "that is, if it is one" (1044a4); and he goes on to claim that those who make the claim that number is one are unable to say by what means it is so. Aristotle's point, then, is that those (i.e. Plato and other members of the Academy) who claim that number is one are (i) wrong, because their claim is based on the mistaken supposition that number is one as thinghood is one and that therefore the unity of number is capable of being separate from sensible things, (ii) deserve criticism because they cannot say by what means number is one, and then (iii), because of (i) and (ii), number is not some one thing but rather is like a heap.

   A syllable is the opposite of a heap according to Aristotle, in that a syllable is something else than the letters (elements) out of which it is composed, the implication clearly being that the heap is not something else than the elements that compose it. In the case of both a heap and a syllable, Aristotle maintains that "the whole is one" (Z 17, 1041b11–12), although the something else than the elements in the instance of a syllable is likened to "the thinghood [*ousia*] of each thing (for that is what is primarily responsible for the being of it)" (1041a27–8), which is "not an element but a source [*archē*]" (1041a31) of its being an independent thing. In the case of the heap, Aristotle's point is that the whole is not one in this sense. Thus he argues that "if number is separate" (M 8, 1084b2–3), and, therefore, "in so far as a number is composite" (1084b4), "the one is prior", but "in so far as the universal and form are prior, the number is; for each of the units is part of the number as its material, but number is the manner of *eidos*". Because the *eidos* is indivisible, the Platonists say that it is also one, so that both the units, as the parts that compose the material (*hulē*), and the *eidos* and thinghood (*ousia*) of number are one, and, as such, are sources (*archai*). Aristotle holds, however, that "this is impossible" (1084b19): "for if the number is some one thing and not like a heap", then its *eidos* and material are not only one in different senses, but "in truth each unit has being as a potency [*dunamis*]" (1084b21) and "not as fully at-work [*entelechia*]" (1084b22–3). Number, then, cannot be separate as the Platonists say, that is, in accord with the two sources of its being one thing that they identify: the indivisibility of the *eidos* and the units proper to the material. Not being separate, it follows that number is not some one thing, but like a heap, that is, like a whole whose being one and therefore thinghood is derived, in this case, from the multitude of units as such that compose the whole's elements, in the precise sense of the "how many" indicated by this non-independent whole (see below).

Chapter 4: Origin of the task of pure phenomenology

1. Brentano writes in a footnote to his discussion of intentionality: "Aristotle himself spoke of this mental in-existence. In his books on the soul he says that the sensed object, as such, is in the sensing subject; that the sense contains the sensed object without its matter; that the object which is thought is in the thinking intellect" (*Psychology from an Empirical Standpoint*, A. C. Rancurello, D. B. Terrell & L. McAlister [trans.] [London: Routledge, (1924) 1973; 2nd edn, 1995], 88n.).
2. In the same text, Husserl accepts Paul Natorp's characterization of the *Logical Investigations*' presentation of pure logic as "'the ideal in this truly Platonic sense'" (ILI, 113). And Husserl goes on to credit his study of Hermann Lotze's reconstruction of Platonic Ideas in Lotze's *Logik* as a major influence on his formulation of pure logic: "With regard to the logic that before I had interpreted psychologistically and which had perplexed me as a mathematical logician, I, thanks to a fortunate circumstance [i.e. his study of Lotze], no longer needed lengthy and detailed deliberations regarding its separation from that which is psychological" (*ibid.*: 119).
3. In the second edition of the *Logical Investigations* Husserl made it clear that he had changed his mind about even "rational" psychology being capable of clarifying the formation of the objectivity of the ideal concepts belonging to pure logic and, indeed, the objectivity of any kind of ideal object. This change was signalled by his eliminating all reference to psychology in his revised characterization (in the second edition) of that work's method, which he now characterized as "pure phenomenology".
4. Husserl's early writings used the adjective "*reell*" as a technical term to indicate aspects of the phenomenal structure of conscious acts that belong to them as a proper part, in contrast to that aspect of their phenomenal structure that characterized what he termed the "intentional object", which does not so belong. The presentation of red sensations that accompany the perception of an apple would be an example of the perceptual act's "*reell*" contents, while the presentation of the apple in the perception exemplifies the act's "intentional content". Husserl's criterion for making this distinction is discussed below.

Chapter 8: Limits of the transcendental-phenomenological investigation of pure consciousness

1. The term "pre-reflective" originates with Jean-Paul Sartre, who used it to characterize what he called the "pre-reflective cogito", which he argued is "the condition of the

Cartesian cogito" (1956: liii). As we shall see from the discussion below, the reciprocal foundational relation between reflectively and unreflectively modified lived-experiences in Husserl's pure phenomenology rules out the latter being *the* condition for the former.

2. Husserl's "Appendix XII" to his lectures on internal time consciousness do, in fact, maintain that "[w]e must distinguish: the pre-phenomenal being of lived-experiences, their being before we have turned towards them in reflection, and their being as phenomena" (PITC, 129/178). However, he goes on to make the point made here in response to the unwarranted speculation about the being of "pre-reflective" acts, namely, that "the setting-in-relation of the object of our turning-towards and our turning towards it, together with the original taking cognizance of this relation, is a new phenomenon" (*ibid.*).

Chapter 10: The intersubjective foundation of transcendental idealism: the immanent transcendency of the world's objectivity

1. Husserl's discussion of the "eidos Ego" reinforces the importance of "eidetic intuition" (and, presumably, the "eidetic reduction") for his conception of phenomenology. He writes in this connection: "'In itself', then, the science of pure possibilities precedes the science of actualities and alone makes it possible, as a science. With this we attain the methodological insight that, *along with phenomenological reduction, eidetic intuition is the fundamental form of all particular transcendental methods* (that both of them determine, through and through, the legitimate sense of a transcendental phenomenology)" (CM,106).
2. Gottfried Wilhelm Leibniz's "The Principles of Philosophy, or, the Monadology" (1714), in *Philosophical Essays*, R. Ariew & D. Garber (eds & trans.), 213–25 (Indianapolis, IN: Hackett, 1989) consists of ninety numbered statements of principle, to which the references in the citations that follow correspond.

Chapter 11: The pure phenomenological motivation of Husserl's turn to history

1. The two texts are Husserl's "Die Krisis der europäischen Wissenschaften und die transzendentale Phänomenologie: Eine Einleitung in die phänomenologische Philosophie", published in English as *The Crisis of European Sciences and Transcendental Phenomenology* (1970) [*Crisis*], and "Die Frage nach dem Ursprung der Geometrie als intentional-historisches Problem", originally published in a substantially edited form by Eugen Fink (1939), and published in English as "The Origin of Geometry", in *The Crisis of European Sciences and Transcendental Phenomenology* (1970) [OG]. Fink's typescript of Husserl's original, and significantly different, 1936 text of "Die Frage nach dem Ursprung der Geometrie" (which is the text translated by Carr in *The Crisis of European Sciences and Transcendental Phenomenology*) was published as Beilage III in *Die Krisis der europäischen Wissenschaften und die transzendentale Phänomenologie: Eine Einleitung in die phänomenologische Philosophie*, W. Biemel (ed.), Husserliana VI (The Hague: Martinus Nijhoff, 1954; 2nd edn 1976). The text of "Die Krisis der europäischen Wissenschaften" is reprinted as §§1–27 of this volume in the Husserliana.
2. The one significant exception to this is a little known and even less cited essay by Jacob Klein, "Phenomenology and the History of Science" (1940). For a discussion of Klein and Husserl, see my *The Origin of the Logic of Symbolic Mathematics*: *Edmund Husserl and Jacob Klein* (forthcoming).

3. Husserl understands his considerations to have "exemplary significance" for the "problems of science and the history of science in general, and indeed in the end for the problems of a universal history in general" (OG, 365/353).

Chapter 16: The methodological presupposition of the ontico-ontological critique of intentionality: Plato's Socratic seeing of the eidē

1. References to Heidegger's *History of the Concept of Time: Prolegomena* (1985) give the page number therein, followed by the page number in the German text *Prologomena zur Geschichte des Zeitbegriffs* (1979).
2. References to Heidegger's *Being and Time* (1962) give the page number therein, followed by the page number in the German text *Sein und Zeit* ([1927] 1979).
3. References to Heidegger's *The Basic Problems of Phenomenology* (1982) give the page number therein, followed by the page number in the German text *Die Grundprobleme der Phänomenologie* (1997).
4. A translation in line with our interpretation of Aristotle would run: "the soul never thinks without an appearance of things".
5. References to Heidegger's *Plato's Sophist* (1997) give the page number therein, followed by the page number in the German text *Platon: Sophistes* (1992).

Chapter 17: The mereological presupposition of fundamental ontology: that Being as a whole has a meaning overall

1. References to Heidegger's *The Metaphysical Foundations of Logic* (1984) give the page number therein, followed by the page number in the German text *Metaphysiche Anfangsgründe der Logik* (1978).

Chapter 18: The presupposition behind the proto-deconstructive critique of intentional historicity: the conflation of intrasubjective and intersubjective idealities

1. Thus Husserl writes: "the *transcendence of the real, as such, is a particular form of "ideality"* or, better, of *psychic irreality*" (FTL, 166).
2. "Physical objects too make their appearance 'in the field of consciousness'; and, in respect of what is most general, no differently than ideal objects – that is to say: as intentional unities" (FTL, 163).

Chapter 19: The presupposition behind the deconstruction of phenomenology: the subordination of being to speech

1. Derrida writes, "between idealization and the voice, the complicity is indefeasible" (1973: 75).

Epilogue: Transcendental-phenomenological criticism of the criticism of phenomenological cognition

1. In the final stage of Husserl's thought, the following multiplicities and unities can be identified: the multiplicity of the lived-experience in which the unity of the object of perception is given; the multiplicity of the lived-experience in which the unity of the non-objective world horizon is given; the multiplicity of the lived-experience in which the unity of primordial nature is given, including the concrete Ego's lived-body; the multiplicity of the lived-experience in which the unity of the alter Ego is given, and the related multiplicities of lived-experiences in which the unity of the intersubjective community of transcendental Egos is given; the multiplicity of lived-experiences in which the unity of a given *irreal* object is given as the *same*, including the multiplicity of lived-experiences belonging to the community of transcendental Egos in which the all-encompassing *idea* of the world is given; the multiplicity of lived-experiences in which the multiplicity of culturally relative life-worlds are given as unities founded in the multiplicity of the lived-experience in which the unity of primordial nature is given; the unity of the multiplicity of all the preceding lived-experiences as a multiplicity that belongs to *my* constitutionally primal monad; the desedimented multiplicities of lived-experiences in which the intentional histories of the meaning fundaments of modern science and Euclidean geometry are given; the multiplicities of the reactivated lived-experiences in which these historically dated meaning fundaments are originally given as unities; and finally, the multiplicities in which the unities of the *eidē* proper to the phenomenological cognition of the preceding multiplicities and unities are given.

Bibliography

Husserl bibliography

Spileers, Steven (ed.) 1999. *The Husserl Bibliography*. Dordrecht: Kluwer.

Lapointe, François 1980. *Edmund Husserl and his Critics: An International Bibliography* (1894–1979). Bowling Green, OH: Philosophy Documentation Center.

Primary sources

Philosophie der Arithmetik. Halle a.d. Saale: C. E. M. Pfeffer, 1891. Published in English as *Philosophy of Arithmetic*, Dallas Willard (trans.). Dordrecht: Kluwer, 2003.

Logische Untersuchungen. Erster Teil: Prolegomena zur reine Logik. Halle a.d. Saale: M. Niemeyer, 1900. *Logische Untersuchungen. Zweiter Teil: Untersuchungen zur Phänomenologie und Theorie der Erkenntnis*. Halle a.d. Saale: M. Niemeyer, 1901. Published in English as *Logical Investigations*, 2 vols, J. N. Findlay (trans.). London: Routledge, 2001.

Ideen zu einer reinen Phänomenologie und phänomenologischen Philosophie, I Buch: Allgemeine Einführung in die reine Phänomenologie. Halle a.d. Saale: M. Niemeyer, 1913. Published in English as *Ideas Pertaining to a Pure Phenomenology and to a Phenomenological Philosophy. First Book. A General Introduction to Pure Phenomenology*, Fred Kersten (trans.). The Hague: Martinus Nijhoff, 1982.

"Entwurf einer 'Vorrede' zu den *Logischen Untersuchungen*" [1913], Eugen Fink (ed.). *Tijdschrift voor Philosophie* 1 (1939): 106–33. Published in English as *Introduction to the Logical Investigations*, P. J. Bossert & C. H. Peters (trans.). The Hague: Martinus Nijhoff, 1975.

Vorlesungen zur Phänomenologie des innern Zeitbewussteins, Martin Heidegger (ed.). Halle a.d. Saale: M. Niemeyer, 1928. Published in English as *The Phenomenology of Internal Time Consciousness*, J. S. Churchill (trans.). Bloomington, IN: Indiana University Press, 1964.

Formale und Transcendentale Logik. Versuch einer Kritik der logischen Vernunft. Halle a.d. Saale: M. Niemeyer, 1929. Published in English as *Formal and Transcendental Logic*, D. Cairns (trans.). The Hague: Martinus Nijhoff, 1969.

Méditations cartésiennes: Introduction à la phénoménologie, G. Peiffer & E. Levinas (trans.). Paris: A. Colin, 1931.

Erfahrung und Urteil, L. Landgrebe (rev. & ed.). Hamburg: Felix Meiner, [1939] 1985. Published in English as *Experience and Judgment*, J. S. Churchill and K. Ameriks (trans.). Evanston, IL: Northwestern University Press, 1973.

Cartesianische Meditationen und Pariser Vorträge. The Hague: Martinus Nijhoff, 1950. Pub-

lished in English as *Cartesian Meditations: An Introduction to Phenomenology*, D. Carins (trans.). The Hague: Martinus Nijhoff, 1960.
Phänomenologische Psychologie. Vorlesungen Sommersemester 1925. The Hague: Martinus Nijhoff, 1968. Published in English as *Phenomenological Psychology: Lectures, Summer Semester 1925*, J. Scanlon (trans.). The Hague: Martinus Nijhoff, 1977.

Significant articles

"Philosophie als strenge Wissenschaft", *Logos* **1**(3) (1910–11): 289–341. Published in English as "Philosophy as Rigorous Science", Marcus Brainard (trans.), *The New Yearbook for Phenomenology and Phenomenological Philosophy* **2** (2002): 249–95.
"Die Krisis der europäischen Wissenschaften und die tranzendentale Phänomenologie: Eine Einleitung in die Phänomenologische Philosophy", *Philosophia (Beograd)* **1** (1936): 77–176. Reprinted as Beilage III in *Die Krisis der europäischen Wissenschaften und die transzendentale Phänomenologie. Eine Einleitung in die phänomenologische Philosophie*, W. Biemel (ed.), Husserliana VI (The Hague: Martinus Nijhoff, 1954; 2nd edn 1976). Published in English as *The Crisis of European Sciences and Transcendental Phenomenology: An Introduction to Phenomenological Philosophy*, David Carr (trans.). Evanston, IL: Northwestern University Press, 1970.
"Die Frage nach dem Ursprung der Geometrie als intentionalhistorisches Problem", *Révue internationale de philosophie* **1**(2) (1939): 203–25 [published after Husserl's death by his assistant and collaborator Eugen Fink]. Published in English as "The Origin of Geometry", David Carr (trans.), in *The Crisis of European Philosophy and Transcendental Phenomenology*, 353–78.

Other Husserl publications

Husserl, E. 2005. "Lecture on the Concept of Number (WS 1889/90)". *New Yearbook for Phenomenology and Phenomenological Philosophy* **5**: 278–309.
Jaegerschmid, A. 2001. "Conversations with Edmund Husserl, 1931–1938", Marcus Brainard (trans.). *New Yearbook for Phenomenology and Phenomenological Philosophy* **1**: 331–50.
Schuhmann, Karl (ed.) 1994. *Edmund Husserl Briefwechsel*, vol. IV. Dordrecht: Kluwer.

Secondary literature and works by other authors

Bell, D. 1991. *Husserl*. London: Routledge.
Bernet, R., I. Kern & E. Marbach 1993. *An Introduction to Husserlian Phenomenology*. Evanston, IL: Northwestern University Press.
Brainard, M. 2002. *Belief and its Neutralization: Husserl's System of Phenomenology in* Ideas I. Albany, NY: SUNY Press.
Brentano, F. [1924] 1973. *Psychology from an Empirical Standpoint*, A. C. Rancurello, D. B. Terrell & L. McAlister (trans.). London: Routledge. 2nd edn 1995.
Brough, J. 1972. "The Emergence of an Absolute Consciousness in Husserl's Early Writings on Time-Consciousness". *Man and World* **5**: 298–326.

Bruzina, R. 2004. *Edmund Husserl and Eugen Fink: Beginning and Ends in Phenomenology: 1928–1938*. New Haven, CT: Yale University Press.

Crowell, S. G. 2001. *Husserl, Heidegger, and the Space of Meaning: Paths Toward Transcendental Phenomenology*. Evanston, IL: Northwestern University Press.

Crowell, S. G. 2002. "Does the Husserl/Heidegger Feud Rest on a Mistake? An Essay on Psychological and Transcendental Phenomenology". *Husserl Studies* **18**: 123–40.

Derrida, J. 1973. *Speech and Phenomena*, D. B. Allison (trans.). Evanston, IL: Northwestern University Press. Published in French as *La Voix et la Phénomène*. Paris: Presses Universitaires de France, 1967.

Derrida, J. [1978] 1989. *Edmund Husserl's Origin of Geometry: An Introduction*, J. P. Leavey (trans.), D. B. Allison (ed.). Lincoln, NE: University of Nebraska Press. Published in French as *L'Origine de la géométrie*, Jacques Derrida (trans.). Paris: Presses Universitaires de France [1962], 1972.

Drummond, J. 1990. *Husserlian Phenomenology and Non-Foundational Realism: Noema and Object*. Dordrecht: Kluwer.

Drummond, J. 2008. *Historical Dictionary of Husserl's Philosophy*. Lanham, MD: Scarecrow Press.

Elveton, R. O. (ed.) 1970. *The Phenomenology of Edmund Husserl: Selected Critical Readings*. Chicago, IL: Quadrangle.

Elveton, R. O. (ed.) 2000. *The Phenomenology of Edmund Husserl: Selected Critical Readings*, 2nd edn. Seattle, WA: Noesis Press.

Fink, E. 2000. "The Phenomenological Philosophy of Edmund Husserl and Contemporary Criticism". In *The Phenomenology of Edmund Husserl: Selected Critical Readings*, R. O. Elveton (ed.), 70–139. Seattle, WA: Noesis Press.

Gadamer, H.-G. 1972. "The Science of the Life-World". *Analecta Husserliana, Vol. II: The Later Husserl and the Idea of Phenomenology*: 173–85. Published in German as "Die Wissenschaft von der Lebenswelt", in *Gesammelte Werke*, vol. 3, 147–59. Tübingen: J. C. B. Mohr [Paul Siebeck], 1987.

Heidegger, M. 1962. *Being and Time*, J. Macquarrie & E. Robinson (trans.). New York: Harper & Row. Published in German as *Sein und Zeit*. Tübingen: Max Niemeyer Verlag, [1927] 1979.

Heidegger, M. 1982. *The Basic Problems of Phenomenology*, A. Hofstadter (trans.). Bloomington, IN: Indiana University Press. Published in German as *Die Grundprobleme der Phänomenologie*. Frankfurt: Vittorio Klostermann, 1975.

Heidegger, M. 1984. *The Metaphysical Foundations of Logic*, Michael Heim (trans.). Bloomington, IN: Indiana University Press. Published in German as *Metaphysiche Anfangsgründe der Logik*. Frankfurt: Vittorio Klostermann, 1978.

Heidegger, M. 1985. *History of the Concept of Time: Prolegomena*, T. Kisiel (trans.). Bloomington, IN: Indiana University Press. Published in German as *Prologomena zur Geschichte des Zeitbegriffs*. Frankfurt: Vittorio Klostermann, 1979.

Heidegger, M. 1997. *Plato's Sophist*, R. Rojcewicz & A. Schuwer (trans.). Bloomington, IN: Indiana University Press. Published in German as *Platon: Sophistes*. Frankfurt: Vittorio Klostermann, 1992.

Hopkins, B. 1993. *Intentionality in Husserl and Heidegger: The Problem of the Original Method and Phenomenon of Phenomenology*. Dordrecht: Kluwer.

Hopkins, B. (ed.) 1997. *Husserl in Contemporary Context: Prospects and Projects for Phenomenology*. Dordrecht: Kluwer.

Hopkins, B. 2006. "Husserl's Psychologism, and Critique of Psychologism, Revisited". *Husserl Studies* **22**: 91–119.

Hopkins, B. forthcoming. *The Origin of the Logic of Symbolic Mathematics: Edmund Husserl and Jacob Klein*. Bloomington, IN: Indiana University Press.

Klein, J. 1940. "Phenomenology and the History of Science". In *Philosophical Essays in Memory of Edmund Husserl*, M. Farber (ed.), 143–63. Cambridge, MA: Harvard University Press. Reprinted in his *Lectures and Essays*, R. B. Williamson & E. Zuckerman (eds), 65–84. Annapolis, MD: St John's Press, 1985.

Landgrebe, L. 1981. *The Phenomenology of Edmund Husserl: Six Essays*, D. Welton (ed.). Ithaca: NY: Cornell University Press.

Leibniz, G. W. [1684] 1989. "Meditations of Knowledge, Truth, and Ideas". In *Philosophical Essays*, R. Ariew & D. Garber (eds & trans.), 23–7. Indianapolis, IN: Hackett.

Leibniz, G. W. [1714] 1989. "The Principles of Philosophy, or, the Monadology"). In *Philosophical Essays*, R. Ariew & D. Garber (eds & trans.), 213–25. Indianapolis, IN: Hackett.

Majolino, C. 2008. "Husserl and Vicissitudes of the Improper". *The New Yearbook for Phenomenology and Phenomenological Philosophy* 8: 17–54.

McKenna, W. R. 1982. *Husserl's "Introductions to Phenomenology": Interpretation and Critique*. The Hague: Martinus Nijhoff.

Mickunas, A. 2001. "Self-Identity and its Disruptions". *The New Yearbook for Phenomenology and Phenomenological Philosophy* 1: 161–79.

Mickunas, A. & D. Stewart [1974] 1990. *Exploring Phenomenology*. Athens, OH: Ohio University Press.

Mohanty, J. N. 1974. "Husserl and Frege: A New Look at their Relationship". *Research in Phenomenology* 4: 51–62.

Mohanty, J. N. 1985. *The Possibility of Transcendental Philosophy*. The Hague: Martinus Nijhoff.

Mohanty, J. N. 2008. *The Philosophy of Edmund Husserl*. New Haven, CT: Yale University Press.

Mohanty, J. N. & W. R. McKenna (eds) 1989. *Husserl's Phenomenology: A Textbook*. Lanham, MD: University Press of America.

Moran, D. 2005. *Edmund Husserl: Founder of Phenomenology*. Cambridge: Polity.

Natanson, M. 1973. *Edmund Husserl: Philosopher of Infinite Tasks*. Evanston, IL: Northwestern University Press.

Sartre, J.-P. 1956. *Being and Nothingness*, H. E. Barnes (trans.). New York: Philosophical Library. Published in French as *L'Être et le néant*. Paris: Gallimard, 1943.

Seebohm, T. 1973. "Reflexion and Totality in the Phenomenology of Edmund Husserl". *Journal of the British Society for Phenomenology* 4: 20–30.

Sokolowski, R. 1967–68. "The Logic of Parts and Wholes in Husserl's 'Investigations'". *Philosophy and Phenomenological Research* 28: 537–53.

Willard, D. 1980. "Husserl on a Logic that Failed". *Philosophical Review* 89: 46–64.

Willard, D. 1984. *Logic and the Objectivity of Knowledge: A Study in Husserl's Early Phenomenology*. Athens, OH: Ohio University Press.

Zahavi, D. 2003. *Husserl's Phenomenology*. Stanford, CA: Stanford University Press.

Index